The Mexican Press and Civil Society, 1940–1976

BENJAMIN T. SMITH

The Mexican Press and Civil Society, 1940–1976

Stories from the Newsroom, Stories from the Street

The University of North Carolina Press *Chapel Hill*

© 2018 The University of North Carolina Press
All rights reserved
Set in Arno Pro by Westchester Publishing Services
Manufactured in the United States of America

The University of North Carolina Press has been a member of the
Green Press Initiative since 2003.

Library of Congress Cataloging-in-Publication Data

Names: Smith, Benjamin T., author.
Title: The Mexican press and civil society, 1940–1976 : stories from the newsroom,
  stories from the street / Benjamin T. Smith.
Description: Chapel Hill : University of North Carolina Press, [2018] |
  Includes bibliographical references and index.
Identifiers: LCCN 2017049080 | ISBN 9781469637099 (cloth : alk. paper) |
  ISBN 9781469638089 (pbk : alk. paper) | ISBN 9781469638119 (ebook)
Subjects: LCSH: Journalism—Social aspects—Mexico—History—20th century. |
  Journalism—Political aspects—Mexico—History—20th century. |
  Mexican newspapers—History—20th century.
Classification: LCC PN4974.S6 S65 2018 | DDC 302.230972—dc23
LC record available at https://lccn.loc.gov/2017049080

Cover illustration: *Hombre lee periódico recargado en un automóvil estacionado*
[Man reads a newspaper while leaning against a parked car] (used by permission of
Mexico's Fototeca Nacional del Instituto Nacional de Antropología e Historia).

To Eleanor

Contents

Illustrations

Acknowledgments

The idea for writing something on the Mexican press emerged from my earlier work on the twentieth-century history of Oaxaca, was inspired by a close reading of the satirical local newspaper *El Momento/El Chapulín*, and was confirmed by a couple of chance meetings with two of Oaxaca's most important publishers, Claudio Sánchez and Gabriel Quintas. I am extremely grateful to both of them for setting me off on this journey. I am also very grateful to Claudio's father, the famous Oaxaca journalist Néstor Sánchez, whose collection forms the basis of the wonderful Hemeroteca Pública de la Ciudad de Oaxaca. It was also inspired by my mentor at Michigan State University, David Bailey—whom I miss deeply—and my doctoral supervisor, David Brading, who always thought I should look at civil society rather than the infrapolitics of Oaxaca's *caciques*, which he termed "just one damn fight after another."

In terms of institutional support, I should flag up three organizations that have helped me put together this manuscript. The first is the British Academy, which awarded me a Small Research Grant for a project on the history of the Mexican press in 2014. The second is the Center for U.S.-Mexican Studies at the University of California, San Diego. Here, Michael Lettieri and the center's postdoctoral students, academics, and administrators helped put together a wonderful two-day conference on the history and reality of Mexico's press, also in 2014. Many of the opinions heard and contacts made over those few days formed the basis of much of my thinking on the country's newspaper industry. Clearly things have improved since Raúl Salinas was made a visiting scholar. Finally, I would like to thank the University of Warwick History Department, which has proved a welcoming space for my research and that of my colleagues.

This book has also generated many personal debts and I could not have completed it without the help of a group of leading historians of Mexico, research assistants (who will or have gone on to be leading Mexicanists), and UK-based Latin Americanists. In particular I would like to thank Pablo Piccato, whose genuinely paradigm-shifting ideas have deeply influenced this book and should in the next few decades influence many more; Paul Gillingham, whose increasingly strange Facetime conversations—now accompanied by a loud and obstreperous parrot—have shaped a lot of my thinking about the Mexican press, Mexican politics, and life in general; Wil Pansters, whose copious knowledge, clear thinking, and kindness have been invaluable to the completion of this manuscript; *mi tocayo*, Ben Fallaw, who has never failed to offer his insights and support for every project I have unwisely gotten involved in; Rebecca Earle, Trevor Stack, Guy Thomson, Camillia Cowling, Peter Watt, Bill Booth, Rosie Doyle, Alan Knight, and Thom Rath, whose presence in the UK has made the transition back to my home country so enjoyable, intellectually stimulating, and interesting; the journalists Javier Garza and Jacinto Rodríguez Munguía, whose time, support, and knowledge were much appreciated; and José Luis Ortiz Garza, whose generosity and expertise in the Mexican media was vital in putting together this book, especially the chapter on José García Valseca. Finally, I must also thank the two anonymous readers of the manuscript who clearly spent significant time reading the text and whose comments markedly improved the work.

Furthermore, I would also like to thank a host of other colleagues and friends who have helped, directly or indirectly, to shape this text. They include Aaron Van Oosterhout, John Milstead, Elizabeth O'Brien, David Tamayo, Elizabeth Henson, Roger Fagge, Tim Lockley, Charles Walton, Claudia Stein, David Lambert, Aditya Sarkar, Laura Schwartz, Adela Cedillo (whose knowledge of the Mexican Cold War is so extensive and insights so sharp that I presumed she had finished her PhD about a decade ago), Rupert Knox (ditto but replace Cold War with human rights), Andrew Paxman, Nat Morris, Matthew Butler, Renata Keller, Vanessa Freije (whose book on the Mexican press will soon supersede my own), Jorge Felix-Baez, Ioan Grillo, José Brambila Ramírez, Paulo Drinot, Alex Aviña, Isaac Campos, Carlos Pérez Ricart, Rogelio Hernández, Lydia Cacho, Anabel Hernández, Ev Meade, and Paul Eiss.

I would also like to thank the usual friends and relations, who get a shout out in most of my books and are now unimpressed by the novelty. They include John, Abi, Ed, Susanna, Ted, Fanny, Andy, Mary, Mum, Dad, grannies and grandfather, Claire, Nick, Sue, Paul, Sue, Laura, Amy, Alex, Laura, Don Eloy, Doña Cata, Eloy, Jeff, Avi, Patricia, Catalina, Isabella, Efrain, Edith, Troy, Elvia, Michael, Ceilmor, and Melissa. A really special mention must go to Eiji, whose friendship has made my time in Mexico City so enjoyable. Finally, I thank my immediate family—Noemi, Emilia, and Eleanor—who have put up with my poor humor and dull conversation and still look quizzical when anyone asks what I actually do. Just for the record I do have a job; but I am not "a useless doctor," "a silly doctor," a "history-mystery writer," or a "boring spy." I wish I were.

Abbreviations Used in the Text

AC	Asociación Cívica
ACM	Acción Católica Mexicana
ACNR	Asociación Cívica Nacional Revolucionaria
AEE	Asociación de Editores de los Estados
AMP	Asociación Mexicana de Periodistas
CCI	Central Campesina Independiente
CCO	Comité Cívica Oaxaqueña
CCPRI	Comisión Calificadora de Publicaciones y Revistas Ilustradas
CDDC	Coalición Defensora de los Derechos Ciudadanos
CDEM	Comité de Defensa de Expendedores de los Mercados
CLR	Comité de Lucha Revolucionaria
CNH	Consejo Nacional de Huelga
CNOP	Confederación Nacional de Organizaciones Populares
CNP	Consejo Nacional de Publicidad
CPJDC	Comité Pro-Justicia y los Derechos de Ciudadanos
CTM	Confederación de Trabajadores de México
DAAC	Departamento de Asuntos Agrarios y Colonización
DAPP	Departamento Autónomo de Prensa y Publicidad
DFS	Dirección Federal de Seguridad
DGI	Dirección General de Información
DGIPS	Dirección General de Investigaciones Políticas y Sociales
EIM	Ejército Insurgente Mexicano
ELN	Ejército de Liberación Nacional
EZLN	Ejército Zapatista de Liberación Nacional
FEP	Frente Electoral del Pueblo
FLN	Fuerzas de Liberación Nacional

FUFO	Frente Unido de la Fuente Obrera
FUL	Frente Unico de Lambiscones
IPN	Instituto Politécnico Nacional
LRUAO	Liga de Resistencia de los Usuarios de Agua de Oaxaca
MLN	Movimiento de Liberación Nacional
NF	Nacional Financiera
OEM	Organización Editorial Mexicana
OIPP	Oficina de Información Periodística Popular
PAN	Partido Acción Nacional
PCM	Partido Comunista Mexicana
PIPSA	Productora e Importadora de Papel
PP	Partido Popular
PRI	Partido Revolucionario Institucional
PRM	Partido de la Revolución Mexicana
PT	Partido del Trabajo
SCOP	Secretaría de Comunicaciones y Obras Públicas
SEP	Secretaría de Educación Pública
SIP	Sociedad Interamericana de Prensa
SNRP	Sindicato Nacional de la Prensa
SOMEX	Sociedad Mexicana de Credito Industrial
UEM	Unión de Expendedores de Mercados
UGOCM	Unión General de Obreros y Campesinos de México
UNAM	Universidad Nacional Autónoma de México
UPI	United Press International
USIS	U.S. Information Service

The Mexican Press and Civil Society, 1940–1976

Introduction

From 1958 to 1962, middle-aged Mexico City shopkeeper Andrés Prado Rivera wrote a string of letters to the Mexican president, Adolfo López Mateos (1958–1964). The letters voiced the concerns of his civil association, the Coalition in Defense of Citizens' Rights (Coalición Defensora de los Derechos Ciudadanos, CDDC). Like many of the capital's residents, CDDC members were alarmed over police corruption and sought reform of the city's forces. But Prado's dispatches did not take the form of most complaints. They were not telegrams, handwritten memos, or typed letters. Instead they comprised dozens of clippings from the capital's tabloid newspapers, scrawled over with Prado's comments. On some, the shopkeeper simply generalized the article's thesis. "Beware the monstrosities that the secret service commits," he wrote under a piece on the secret police planting evidence. On others, he engaged in reading between the lines and ironic commentary. He scribbled "This shows that to rob in Mexico, you don't need a gun, you only need to utter the words 'Police Secret Service'" beside a story about thieves dressed as policemen holding up a cinema. Together, the letters not only reveal residents' deep distrust of the police but also highlight an important shift in the relations between members of Mexican civil society and the state. By the middle of the twentieth century, most urban Mexicans read the press. Between 1940 and 1976, newspapers, rather than individual experience, interpersonal gossip, radio, or TV, became the key mediators between citizens and the state. Most city dwellers now viewed politics—from the corruption of the police to the infrapolitics of the president's inner circle—through the prism of the press. Officials now viewed the press as the best way to influence the country's citizens. In a 1968 interview, the former Institutional Revolutionary Party (Partido Revolucionario Institucional, PRI) head, Carlos Madrazo, summarized the shift in concerns. "Do you know what one minister told me the other day? He said that the people don't count. What does count is the impression we create with our newspapers."[1] The rise of this mass reading public generated profound changes in Mexico's newspaper industry and reshaped relations among press barons, journalists, politicians, bureaucrats, and readers. These changes, in turn, transformed the practice of everyday politics.

The story of how this happened and the effects it had form the basis of this book. Over the next eight chapters, I assess the extent of this expansion of the reading public, evaluate the government's attempts to control press content, gauge how businessmen sought to take advantage of the new print economy, look at the writings and culture of Mexican journalists, and examine how members of civil society interacted with this swell of newspapers, fly-sheets, and magazines. In doing so, I make three main arguments. First, between 1940 and 1976 readership of the press—particularly of tabloid and local newspapers—rose markedly. By the early 1960s Mexican town and city dwell-ers from all the social classes read the press. Second, during the same period the state invented increasingly sophisticated means to control what these newspapers printed. By the end of the 1960s, both state and federal govern-ments employed well-manned press departments and invested large quanti-ties of money in ensuring newspapers and other publications toed the official line. But state control of the press was never inescapable. It increased in influ-ence over time; it was concentrated in Mexico City, where the major national newspapers were based; and even here it was never fully institutionalized but instead relied on the uncoordinated efforts of multiple government offices. Third, geography delineated the nature of the press. In the capital, print pub-lications were relatively *oficialistas*. But in the provinces, civil society played an important role in shaping what newspapers printed. Here, functioning (if geographically curtailed) public spheres existed and newspapers provided forums for citizens to discuss and critique local politics.

Tilting at Windmills

"Writing the truth," one Mexican journalist remarked, is like the "endeavors of Don Quixote," a hopeless, thankless, and lonely task.[2] Until recently, writing a history of the relationship between journalism and politics in Mexico seemed similarly futile. Appreciations of the mid-century Mexican news-paper industry were almost wholly negative. According to these assessments, the country's press was "submissive and unconditional"; newspapers were "fac-tual deserts," "timid, oversensational, overinfluenced by official optimism and possibly more concerned over profits than honest and objective presentation of the news."[3] Although commentators held that institutional and coercive forms of censorship were rare, they argued that official control of newspapers was pervasive. From 1929 to 2000, one admittedly shape-shifting party, the PRI, ran the country. The press was "one of the sectors of the country where subor-dination to power was most obvious." Empty eulogy and the flattery of officials were commonplace, while the "core features of the political system—presidential authority, official corruption, state violence and electoral fraud etc.—were decidedly off limits."[4] At best, the press was free but never "made use of its freedom"; at worst freedom of expression was a "great lie," which was "subject to so many limits, it does [did] not exist."[5]

As a result, the political influence of newspapers was marginal. "The mass media were in essence ineffective, they persuaded those already persuaded and could inhibit those still on the fence, but they did nothing more."[6] It was, according to Daniel Cosío Villegas, not the fourth but the "fifteenth" estate.[7] Illiteracy, state control, high prices, unpopular subject matter, and obscurantist, overelaborate language alienated potential readers. Public opinion was "the patrimony of the initiated"; the public sphere was small, exclusive, and limited to a thin section of the privileged class.[8] If nonelites did read the newspapers, they either imbibed an array of "unified messages and symbols reinforcing regime legitimacy" or they did so with cynicism.[9] Writing in the 1970s, Cosío Villegas argued that the "incredulity of the immense majority of readers" had arrived at such a level that they "didn't simply judge journalists as liars but took it as a rule to believe exactly the opposite of what they wrote." If nonelites did exchange political opinions, they did so through gossip "in the confines of the family or the café."[10] If they sought to challenge state authority, they did so not through the printed press but through demonstrations and rituals.[11] The press and the practice of everyday politics were, in short, antithetical.

Such opinions have considerable weight. During the early postrevolutionary period, the state attempted to assert control over the country's diverse populations. As most Mexicans were illiterate, they predominantly employed nonwritten forms. These included public celebrations, hero cults, theatre performances, murals, dance, music, comic books, radio, film, and education. Some relied on a new breed of cultural entrepreneurs, like the rural teachers, who fanned out into the country's provinces during the 1920s and 1930s. Others relied on new technologies, like the cheap, compact home radio, the color printing press, or the portable projector. Despite the state's efforts, audience reactions were far from uniform. Instead communities drew on local cultural traditions and political dynamics to impose their own meanings on these new rituals and practices. By the middle of the century, such negotiations had produced an agreed upon, if regionally varied, national revolutionary culture.[12] Newspapers played a minimal role in these early stages of state formation. Low literacy rates and poor communications militated against the expansion of the reading public into the country's rural villages and hamlets. Even when literacy and roads improved, many newspapers remained elitist, supine, and state-controlled. Many were also, as a result, roundly ignored, especially after particularly obvious examples of press corruption. In the immediate wake of the cover-up over the 1968 student massacre, a U.S. survey on media habits concluded that nearly 50 percent of readers judged newspapers the least truthful news medium.[13]

But such condemnations only tell part of the story. On the one hand, they rest on an imaginary yardstick of the U.S. and European press. As a generation of media scholars has argued, such comparisons grossly overestimate the relative freedom and openness of the developed world's media. During the Cold War, shared ideologies, common financial interests, and, if needed, dirty tricks kept newspapers in check. Even after the fall of the Berlin wall, similar pressures narrowed debate and restricted popular input.[14] Furthermore, other print cultures may have lacked the grandstanding self-confidence of the U.S. and European media, but they were not simply stale replicas of these modes of communication. They developed their own intellectual traditions and languages, their own sui generis relations to the state, and their own distinct connections to reading publics.[15]

On the other hand, such opinions are also based on a distinct model of media liberalization. From the late 1980s onward, journalists and scholars started to connect economic reforms, the perceived growth in civic organizations, and the opening up of Mexico's media to the declining power of the PRI. Such opinions united commentators across the political spectrum. On the left, they praised the efforts of Julio Scherer and the other journalists expelled from *Excélsior* who went on to found radical, civic-minded publications like *Unomásuno, La Jornada,* and *Proceso.*[16] On the right, they lauded the rise of financially independent newspapers with well-trained journalists like *Reforma* and *El Economista.*[17] In doing so, they not only overestimated the liberating effects of commercial and political competition, but also overstated the break with the past. As Robert Darnton wrote of the eighteenth-century French revolutionaries, they saw "nothing but newslessness" in the old regime.[18]

Toward a New History of Communication in Mexico

In fact, as scholars are increasingly discovering, mid-century Mexico was anything but newsless.[19] Even under the soft authoritarian rule of the PRI, journalism flourished and literate, urban, citizens read, engaged with, discussed, wrote into, and only occasionally dismissed the thousands of dailies, weeklies, and monthlies that were being produced. The shopkeeper Prado's epistolary approach may have been unusual but his appreciation of the press was not.

Getting at the mechanics and effects of changes within the world of the press, however, is another matter. Over the past fifty years, scholars have imagined an array of approaches to understanding the shifting relations among the state, capital, civil society, and the print media or what Darnton has termed the "communications circuit."[20] They have included focuses on technological innovation, discourse analysis, quantitative examination of state-business links, and qualitative studies of the connections between the private and the public spheres. Especially in the United States and Europe, such methods have generated a series of normative models, which through the expansion of the discipline of media studies, have been imposed on other countries with differing degrees of success.[21] Rather than pursue any of these fixed schema, this book relies on a more open-ended approach to appreciating the varied ways in which politicians, businessmen, and readers managed and transformed the newspaper industry. Despite this flexible—some might say loose—methodology, three broad frameworks structure this work.

The first is empirical. Over the past decades, most appreciations of the mid-century Mexican press have relied on the writings of a small group of Mexico City–based journalists. These texts remain invaluable. They provide ample insights into the associations among media owners, journalists, and the state; and have been joined by a flurry of recent publications by less high-profile reporters. But they also warp our understanding of the mid-century newspaper industry by focusing on the big nationals, overstating the power of the state, overselling the link between democratization and press liberalization, and dismissing both nonbroadsheet publications and the reactions of civil society.[22] Fortunately over the past decade, new archival sources have allowed the historian to move beyond such a heavy reliance on hindsight and memory. They include documents from the state's spy organizations, the State Office of Political and Social Investigations (Dirección General de Investigaciones Políticas y Sociales, DGIPS) and the Federal Office of Security (Dirección Federal de Seguridad, DFS), which not only provide evidence for the mechanics and limits of press control but also reveal street-level responses to national and regional newspapers. They also include reports from the U.S. Cold War information bureau (the U.S. Information Service, USIS). From the 1950s, U.S. policy makers took an obsessive interest in the penetration of both capitalist and communist propaganda in the developing world. At the same time, they inadvertently provided the first large-scale reviews of newspaper circulations and reading habits. Finally, they comprise the increasingly well-kept compendia of newspapers collected by the national newspaper archive, state newspaper archives, and various private collections. These have permitted the historian to peer beyond the carefully choreographed writings of the big nationals and examine the approaches of less regimented publications like the satirical magazine *Presente*, the student weekly *Por Qué?*, and the confrontational Oaxaca City flysheet *El Chapulín*.[23]

The second is geographical. Until recently, most studies of the Mexican press "privileged the center" or the world of national broadsheets like *Excélsior*, *El Universal*, and *Novedades*.[24] Provincial newspapers, Carlos Monsiváis wrote, were devoted to "banality, adulation, local credulity and parochial anticommunism."[25] For Cosío Villegas, they showed "neither novelty nor imagination in their make up," contained "little national news," and "their editorials [were] unimportant."[26] Over the past two decades, scholars have started to disaggregate and decenter the Mexican press, particularly in the nineteenth and early twentieth centuries.[27] This book builds on such research and posits that, despite the growth of the capital's industrial newspapers, we should look for the relationships between politics and printed publications outside these broadsheets, particularly in regional and local newspapers. Investigations of these print media—from the large-scale García Valseca chain to the Chihuahua peasant weekly, *Acción*—form much of this book. These publications were subject to both state censorship and market forces, but to a much lesser extent than the capital's broadsheets. Here, political controls were impromptu and diffuse; press owners could afford to break alliances with the state; and contrary to what Cosío Villegas argued, thematically, temporally, and geographically bound arenas for debate did emerge.

The third is theoretical. In general, scholars of the media have viewed print journalism as shaped by three extraneous powers—the state, commercial interests, and civil society. Together they interact to construct the "field of force" in which journalism is formed.[28] In Mexico, most analysts have focused on the first two forces to the exclusion of the latter. They have argued that financial alliances between politicians and economic elites structured the country's press.[29] There is something to this. In chapters 2, 5, and 6, we shall examine the way in which both politicians and businessmen shaped the newspaper industry in the immediate postwar era. But such approaches are also based on questionable assumptions. They presume a coherent, powerful, pyramidal structure of state control, stretching down from the president, through the cabinet, to the state governors and the local party branches. In fact, power under the PRI was thinly spread. The power of individual presidents ebbed and flowed. And, throughout the period, they had to contend with divided political elites, recalcitrant governors, strong *caciques*, and an understaffed and underfunded party system. At the local level especially, formal vertical hierarchies continually intersected with informal horizontal relations.[30] In the arena of the mass media, this often translated into the flouting of top-down dictates, especially at the edges of the newspaper world in the regions or in the so-called marginal press. Here, competing factions often took the risk of sponsoring more critical journalists and publications.

Such opinions also reproduce a rather static vision of Mexican business-men, which stress their stable and reciprocal relations with the state. Again, there is something to this. In chapter 2, we shall observe how ideas of mutual self-interest extended throughout the capital's press during the 1950s and 1960s. In chapter 6 we shall see how regional press baron, José García Valseca, made a similar deal with the federal government. But again such notions sim-plify what were often dynamic, multivalent connections. Outside the capital business leaders often fell out with both federal and regional authorities over the introduction of economic and cultural policies and the shape of local power.[31] In regions where the revolution had left provincial elites relatively united and unscathed, they funded and backed combative right-wing news-papers like Monterrey's *El Norte* or Merida's *El Diario de Yucatán*.[32] In other states smaller-scale factory owners and merchants floated more radical, con-trarian publications often linked to democratic civil movements.[33] Even in Mexico City, by the 1960s alternative sources of funding, including the Cu-ban, Chinese, and Soviet governments, had started to undermine the press's exclusive reliance on the federal state, and homegrown capitalists.[34]

Finally, such appreciations underestimate the extent to which civil society shaped Mexico's mid-century newspapers. For over half a century scholars have played down the scope and force of the country's civil society.[35] For these writers interpersonal distrust, the expansion of the corporatist party, and inequality militated against the formation of a strong civil society at least until the mid-1980s.[36] Yet such assumptions are overstated. They rely on sim-plified cultural reifications, are often based on limited observation of Mexico City, and miscalculate the cooptive power of the state. As we shall see in chapters 3 and 4, in the capital the federal government did employ substantial political and economic power to buy off autonomous networks, dissolve cross-class alliances, and limit discussion. In 1948, economic concessions, propaganda, and violence put an end to the postrevolutionary tradition of popular, antisystemic satire. During the 1960s similar policies hemmed in the influence of left-wing magazines like *Política*, *Sucesos Para Todos*, and *Por Qué?* But even these strategies were not entirely successful. Together *Política* and *Por Qué?* provided space for Mexico's new left for a total of thirteen years.

Furthermore, in the country's provincial cities, such policies were not only unsuccessful, but also counterproductive. Here, state authorities were underpowered and independent networks between citizens remained influential, at least until the expansion of the party's popular sector during the 1960s. As a result symbiotic relationships between civil society and the press often emerged. Individuals and associations expected local newspapers to voice their demands or to engage in what media scholars now term "civic journalism."[37] In exchange these local newspapers relied on sales and the small-scale disbursements of local capitalists to stay afloat. In contrast members of civil society shunned, lampooned, or even physically attacked newspapers, which they held to be ignoring their demands or being paid to serve unpopular authorities. As we shall see in chapters 7 and 8, such close relations generated powerful social movements, which could shape local politics and even remove governors from power. And as we shall see in chapter 6, even large-scale local newspaper chains could risk official opprobrium by linking up with strong local civic organizations. Taken together these case studies reveal that even during the heyday of the PRI, the press and grassroots politics were not antithetical but instead closely interwoven.

Such conclusions, in particular the importance of civil society in shaping the press, in turn suggest the cautious employment of some of Jürgen Habermas's ideas about the public sphere. Wholesale application of his emancipatory ideal of an open, rational arena of public debate is obviously impossible.[38] If Mexico ever incorporated such an ideal, it was probably during the 1860s and 1870s, when journalists argued over the possible shape of the new liberal state. Even in this period, the public sphere was founded upon the exclusion of working-class and female writers.[39] Furthermore in the following decades increasing state control (first by the Porfirian and then by the revolutionary state) and the growing influence of private capital further eroded the public sphere's emancipatory potential. Yet, as my case studies of Oaxaca and Chihuahua make clear, even in the mid-twentieth century there were still spaces for open debate especially in the country's provinces. Here public spheres were geographically limited (the vast majority of news in these papers focused on local events), often (but not always) rested on the exclusion of women, were squeezed by financial demands, were vulnerable to sporadic acts of government censorship, and were patrolled as much by violent crowds as by rational debate. But, they did exist. Though inserting prefixes before "public sphere" has become somewhat of a cottage industry, I would argue that even under the rule of the PRI Mexico was alive with multiple, decentered, if limited public spheres.[40]

Investigating the press can seem a never-ending task. There are multiple possible methodologies and vast quantities of sources. (In the late 1930s over "six tons" of broadsheets, tabloids, and magazines were delivered to Mexican readers every day.)[41] Decisions over what to include and exclude must be made. In general I have chosen my case studies by weighing up the availability of documentary evidence, evaluating the relative importance and representativeness of particular stories, and assessing the narrative possibilities of these subjects. As a result, stories of the media's treatment of certain historical conjunctures mix with general analyses of reading habits and censorship and individual case studies of particular journalists. To order the work, I have split the book into three sections. In the first section, I examine the rise of Mexico's newspaper-reading public, analyzing the causes of this development and assessing its influence on various genres of the printed press. In the second section, I look at the Mexico City press. Here, I examine the state's shifting attempts to control the capital's newspapers as well as publications, which attempted to undermine this blend of ideological confluence, government publicity, and financial reliance. In the last section, I assess the regional press. Again I examine the means by which state authorities sought to control the press. I also look at how Mexico's most infamous press baron, José García Valseca, built up and then lost a countrywide chain of local newspapers and how smaller-scale artisan newspapers, like Oaxaca's *El Chapulín* and Chihuahua's *Acción*, survived and thrived in the postwar era by sustaining close connections to local reading publics.

Part I

The Reading Public

CHAPTER ONE

Who Read What?

The Rise of Newspaper Readership in Mexico, 1940–1976

In 1958 Carlos Fuentes published *Where the Air Is Clear*, his sprawling novel of mid-century Mexico City. The book described a nation divided, where new political elites ruled over the urban poor. Wealth, not lineage, now defined social status. ("Give me cash, and I'll give you class.") But so did everyday pursuits, including parties, leisure activities, and relations to the written word. At the top was a group of self-obsessed elites; the men entangled in a ruthless parlor game with "cheating capitalists and lying newspapers"; the women "bewitched by the compliments they read about [themselves] in the press." At the bottom were the poor, the ignorant, and the illiterate. For these, newspapers were "wadded derelict dailies," part of the "cornucopia of refuse," the "soggy garbage" that was scattered in the streets, comprised the beds of the poor, and filled the cracks in their hastily erected homes.[1] Outside a small elite, Fuentes claimed, few read the press. In fact, for most Mexicans newspapers were construction material, not reading matter. In this chapter I argue that this was not the case. In the years following the Mexican Revolution, both socioeconomic shifts and transformations in the newspaper industry pushed press readership beyond the elites and to the masses. By the 1960s literate Mexicans read the news.

For over half a century most commentators agreed with Fuentes. Illiteracy, state control, high prices, elitist subject matter, and impenetrable language alienated the majority of potential readers. The press was an elite talking shop, "read by politicians for its hidden messages, used by the government to float controversial ideas and exploited as a forum for infighting between different political mafias."[2] Such opinions carried baggage. For social scientists, low levels of newspaper reading generated political ignorance, what Pablo González Casanova termed "the kind of alienation and political ignorance characteristic of a close, traditional and peasant—even archaic—society."[3] For media scholars and journalists, low numbers of readers deformed the news, forcing editors to rely on government advertising and loans rather than profits from sales and advertising.[4] Some assertions hinged on statistical analysis, most commonly comparisons of aggregated print runs with national population figures. These concluded that by 1970 Mexico produced around 11 dailies per 100 inhabitants or just over the UNESCO estimate for basic readership of newspapers.[5] But many claims rested on inferences drawn from the enormous cultural gulf between the Mexico City elite and the poor and the provincial masses. (The U.S. State Department, no stranger to withering unconcern for the marginalized, concluded that Fuentes's writings "reveal[ed] indifference, almost contempt for the social and economic plight of the average Mexican."[6]) For intellectuals, most Mexicans did not read the right *type* of newspapers, which they defined as the ones they wrote in—the Mexico City broadsheets, or the so-called *gran prensa*.

To an extent they were right. Most Mexicans did not read the big nationals like *Excélsior, Novedades,* or *El Universal.* But as this chapter demonstrates, they did read the press, in the form of tabloids and provincial newspapers. During the late nineteenth century the audience for newspapers had gradually extended beyond Mexico's elite. Mass-produced newspapers, like *El Imparcial,* drew in a cross-class public and the satirical penny press attracted working-class readers.[7] But during the middle decades of the twentieth century, the growth in audience numbers really gathered pace. Social shifts, such as rises in literacy, urbanization, and communications, produced a mass reading public. Changes in the newspaper industry, including the availability of cheap paper, the increase in advertising, and falling start-up costs complemented these shifts. By the late 1950s, Mexico produced thousands of both large and small publications. Many Mexicans read them. Careful analysis of print run statistics, U.S. government surveys, and a handful of internal newspaper reports indicate that by the late 1950s literate urban Mexicans read the papers on a regular basis.

Social Changes

From 1920 to 1976, literacy in Mexico rose dramatically. During the Porfiriato, only around 14 percent of the population could read. By 1940 this had risen to 42 percent, and by 1970 more than 76 percent of Mexicans were literate. In cities, the figures were even higher. As early as 1960, around 79 percent of urban men and 76 percent of urban women were literate.[8] Examinations of particular communities bore this out. In the 1950s, Oscar Lewis discovered that 92 percent of the inhabitants of the poor Mexico City neighborhood of Casa Grande were literate.[9] A decade later, in the rambling squatter community of Ciudad Nezahualcóyotl, 83 percent of inhabitants could read.[10] The expansion of state education was the primary cause of these rising literacy rates. During the 1930s and early 1940s, the government spent between 10 and 14 percent of its budget on schooling. Although the amounts declined under President Miguel Alemán (1946–1952), they rose again under his successors, peaking at 14 percent of public expenditure in 1963. Per capita spending on education also rose, from 11 pesos per citizen in 1952 to over 30 pesos in 1963.[11] Increasing investment drove up the number of schools and teachers. Between 1946 and 1970 they both increased fourfold.[12]

Focused government literacy campaigns complemented sustained funding. At first, these failed. José Vasconcelos, the revolution's first minister of education, printed thousands of cheap copies of the great works of foreign and Mexican literature. But even at a peso a book, these rarely sold, leading one Mexico City bookshop owner to conclude that the project was "a disaster." But other programs were more successful. Under President Lázaro Cárdenas (1934–1940), education was conceived as a means to liberate workers and peasants from exploitation. Teachers and cultural missions founded hundreds of literacy centers throughout the country. Night schools for adults were established. In markets, factories, and other centers of work, private citizens were encouraged to teach their illiterate comrades how to read. The government buttressed the campaign with the publication of practical guides, including nearly 2 million copies of a guide for reading directed at urban primary schools and over 3 million copies of a rural textbook.[13] During the 1940s and 1950s, literacy campaigns endured. Government propaganda encouraged literate Mexicans to teach coworkers and family members, and the publication of easy-reading guides and popular, educational texts continued. Officials also started to use radio programs to teach literacy to the masses. By 1947 the state network, Radio México, ran twelve hours of educational programs each week. Six years later, the station put out three hours of shows directly aimed at teaching Mexicans how to read, with nationalist titles like "The Roots of Mexico" and "The Soul of Mexico."[14]

If top-down programs increased literacy, so did the shifting necessities of everyday life. Between 1940 and 1976, written rather than oral communication became the predominant means of transmitting information, especially in the country's cities. The public display of the written word grew, as signs, posters, flysheets, printed songs, and hand-scrawled messages increasingly directed, enticed, and entertained the urban Mexican. Like nineteenth-century New York, mid-century Mexico's public spaces became "strikingly inclusive arenas for impersonal communication."[15] Public advertising was widespread. In 1963, advertising companies spent 13 percent of their budgets on "outside advertising" and produced 250 million posters, hand sheets, and flyers per year.[16] In fact, by the 1970s, public advertising had become so omnipresent that officials threatened to ban billboards around the Mexico City ring road because they affected drivers' concentration.[17] As early as the 1950s photographs of the capital show streets ablaze with neon advertisements ("Every House Mortgage: Rapid Processing"), buildings inscribed with political propaganda ("A. Ruiz Cortines: National Unity"), and side streets bedecked with cheap, paper adverts for cinemas and theaters ("Cinema Palatino"; "Ay Jalisco No Te Rajes").[18] If literacy became essential for commerce, politics, and culture, it also fed more mundane pursuits. By the middle of the century jokers wrote gags as well as told them. Buses and trucks were scrawled with "taunts, puns, gibes, repressed desires and unrepressed desires, all splattered with grammatical mistakes and such poor writing that the best calligrapher cannot decipher them."[19] Such changes made literacy necessary. Even in poorer communities with few schools, urban inhabitants were forced to learn to read. In Ciudad Nezahualcóyotl in the late 1960s, over half of literate adults had no formal education.[20]

If more Mexicans could read, more Mexicans also had access to newspapers. Most newspapers were produced and sold in cities, and between 1940 and 1976 the number of Mexicans living in urban centers increased dramatically. By 1960 more than half of Mexicans lived in towns or cities with populations greater than 2,500. By 1970, the proportion had increased to 58.65 percent. As rural-urban migration increased, Mexico's cities swelled. Between 1940 and 1970, the number of cities with populations over 15,000 grew from 55 to 173. Three cities (Mexico City, Monterrey, and Guadalajara) had populations of over a million.[21] Outside the cities, growing communication networks also increased the market of the Mexican press. During the 1920s, revolutionary governments had built roads to extend commerce and state power. During the following decades, state funding for road building increased, and by 1960 Mexico boasted 45,089 miles of public highways and toll roads.[22] These roads compressed space and time, drawing rural dwellers into the urban world. In 1941, a taxi full of peasant merchants made the round trip between the remote village of San José de Gracia and the market town of Sahuayo every day. By the end of the decade, buses took prospective sellers the three-hour journey to the bustling city of Guadalajara five times a day.[23]

Expanding road networks also increased the penetration of the postal service and by extension the printed word. In a bid to increase rural reading in 1937 President Cárdenas decreed that the postal service was to deliver newspapers and magazines free of charge.[24] Three decades later there were 4,500 post offices throughout Mexico.[25] These now delivered newspapers to the small towns and villages opened up by the new roads. In the Morelos town of

Tepoztlán, these changes increased contact with the outside world. Between 1936 and 1944, the number of postal items arriving in the town grew from eighty-four to two hundred per week. These now included numerous flysheets, printed songs, and newspapers.[26] A tourist who visited the central Mexican mining town of Taxco in the early 1960s witnessed how these new communications affected provincial reading. "Unless the night bus from Mexico City is delayed, you can buy the morning papers in Taxco as early as half past seven. They are neatly displayed on the narrow pavement at the side of the cathedral, next to a gigantic choice of comics and tales of robbery and murder in glaring covers."[27]

Finally, at least in the cities, wages also rose. The hourly wage of a factory worker in Mexico City increased from 0.57 pesos in 1940 to 1.50 pesos in 1950 to 4 pesos in 1960 to 7.50 pesos in 1970. Even the lowest-paid urban worker, the construction laborer, saw his salary rise from 21 pesos a week in 1940 to 281 pesos thirty years later. These wage rises were often wiped out by inflation. Real wages (i.e., wages adjusted for inflation) did not actually recover their 1940 level until the mid-1960s. But for reasons I shall explain in the next section, newspaper prices consistently undercut inflation. As a result, the price of newspapers as a proportion of the hourly wage declined; the press became more affordable. A Mexico City tabloid cost around twenty minutes' work in 1940, fifteen minutes' work in 1950, and six minutes' work in 1960.[28]

The Newspaper Industry

Between 1940 and 1976, the newspaper industry also changed, expanding to meet the demands of Mexican readers. The federal government took the lead, establishing a paper monopoly, the Producer and Importer of Paper (Productora e Importadora de Papel, PIPSA), which made newsprint both available and cheap. Changes in the private sector also played an important role. As the market for consumer goods increased, companies invested more on advertising in the press. And as the bigger presses bought up new technologies to speed up printing, they sold off their old equipment, creating an accessible market for aspirant newspaper owners in the provinces. Together, these changes kept costs relatively low, encouraging the spread of newspaper reading among the middle and lower classes. Finally, competition from other media was relatively slight. Most city homes contained radios, but they rarely interfered with press advertising revenue or the purchase or reading of newspapers. Television would prove a greater threat, but was too expensive for most households until the 1970s.

Few works have explored the Mexican paper monopoly in depth. Most scholars have simply viewed PIPSA as a means to regiment wayward newspapers.[29] *Política* head Manuel Marcué Pardiñas described it as the "sword of Damocles" hanging over independent editors.[30] As we shall see in chapter 2, this was often the case. But PIPSA was also much more than this. Postwar newspapers throughout the world struggled to maintain secure paper supplies over the succeeding decades. In Mexico, PIPSA managed to do just this, sustaining the expansion of the Mexican press. During the 1930s the organization put a private paper monopoly out of business; during the 1940s it smoothed over the fluctuations of the international paper market; and during the following decades it made newsprint both affordable and available. The director of PIPSA in the 1970s was not entirely disingenuous when he argued that the monopoly kept many smaller papers afloat. "Some of them publish only 10 pages a day with almost no advertising. There are small papers that exist on street sales alone and actually make a small profit without a significant amount of advertising."[31] Low paper prices allowed such newspapers to survive.

The Mexican government did not establish PIPSA to control newspapers' editorial policy. In fact, President Cárdenas originally created the company to lower paper prices and support Mexico's print culture. Until the 1930s, one private company ran the paper industry in Mexico. In 1892 two Spaniards bought the San Rafael ranch in Chalco, Mexico State. Within a decade, they had gained permission to log the surrounding mountains, imported machinery to turn the lumber into paper, and bought further properties in Puebla. By 1910, the company was one of the largest in Mexico with a capital of 7 million pesos and contracts to provide paper to all the major nationals. During the revolution, the San Rafael firm cemented control of the trade. According to a whistleblower who spoke to *Excélsior* in 1938, the company took advantage of declining U.S. paper imports to charge newspapers 15¢ a kilo for paper that only cost 8¢ a kilo to produce. Such dominance of the market had other secondary effects, pushing less successful companies out of business. By the 1920s San Rafael was the only paper firm in Mexico, selling newsprint to the big nationals at the price it dictated.[32]

During the early 1930s, Mexico's big national newspapers were approaching financial ruin. The depression cut into the purchasing power of Mexico City's middle classes and newspaper sales declined. According to Guillermo Enríquez Simoní, who was editor of *Excélsior* at the time, *El Universal's* sales dipped to 25,000 a day and *Excélsior's* to a miserly 18,000. In 1932, the San Rafael company raised paper prices to 22.5¢ a kilo, threatening national newspapers with extinction. By June 1932, the combined debts of *Excélsior*, *El*

Universal, and *La Prensa* to the company totaled nearly a million pesos. At this point, *Excélsior* and *El Universal*'s tactics diverged. *Excélsior* halved its price, attempting to ride out its financial problems by increasing sales. According to Enríquez, the plan was successful; *Excélsior*'s sales doubled to 40,000 per day.[33] In contrast, Miguel Lanz Duret, the director of *El Universal*, attempted to confront the San Rafael monopoly.

In July 1932, *El Universal* started the campaign, publishing an article that claimed that high paper prices not only threatened Mexico's newspapers but also the nation's print culture. They compared San Rafael's prices to those in Europe and the United States and concluded that the company was running an exploitative and illegal monopoly.[34] Newsvendors, print workers, and journalists soon joined the movement. They accused the San Rafael factory of overpricing paper, throttling the production of books and newspapers, and putting them out of work. They also dredged up the company's past, asserting that the firm had put pro-German newspapers out of business during World War I. They asked the government to either bury the monopoly or free up the market by getting rid of taxes on U.S. paper imports.[35] By late August, the complaints had reached both Congress and the Treasury, which agreed to investigate the claims. Over the next six months, *El Universal* kept up pressure on both institutions, hinting that the San Rafael company was trying to bribe officials to back the firm. Eventually Congress and the Treasury effectively fudged the matter, arguing that they were unable to cut taxes on U.S. paper imports and passing the question of the monopoly up to the president.[36] By March 1933, President Abelardo Rodríguez (1932–1934) had forced the company to lower paper prices 2¢ to 20.5¢ a kilo.[37]

For two years, the paper company and the national newspapers maintained stable relations. But in 1935, cooperation declined again. First, the San Rafael director raised the price of paper to 23¢ per kilo. Then, an independent union of San Rafael paper workers threatened to strike.[38] This time, all the Mexican national newspapers united against the private monopoly. In early August, *El Universal*, *Excélsior*, and the official newspaper *El Nacional* ran editorials that supported the proposed strike, accused the San Rafael company of refusing to sell them paper, and demanded an end to the "abusive and illegal practices that have made the paper monopoly a tyrant."[39] Instead they requested that the government cut duties on imported paper and force the San Rafael company to keep to strict price regulations. Backed by the leftist president Lázaro Cárdenas, government officials publicly supported the campaign. The secretary of education claimed that the "price charged for paper . . . [was] a strong barrier to the diffusion of culture, since it is the one factor that makes textbooks and all Mexican publications in general too expensive for the working class."[40]

Finally, on August 21, 1935, Cárdenas ordered the creation of a government paper company. His decree laid out his reasons for the move. Many echoed the more general complaints of the national newspapers and print workers. The price of paper influenced "the development of educational work fiercely promoted by the Revolutionary government and also . . . the normal life of the newspapers of the country, which . . . help the cultural and economic progress of the people." But the solution offered was not that proposed by *El Universal* or *Excélsior*. Rather than simply reducing import tariffs, Cárdenas established a nonprofit company that would engage in the import, transportation, and sale of paper at an affordable price. By selling paper cheaply, the new government company would either force San Rafael to lower its prices or put it out of the paper industry entirely. The plan was classic Cardenista economic policy, benevolent state intervention in an unfair market. Similar institutions were established to aid the producers of agricultural products like henequen and sugar and to undercut private monopolies in the case of food and, perhaps more surprisingly, narcotics.[41]

In September 1935, the government paper company established its offices in Mexico City's version of Fleet Street: Bucareli Avenue. At first, the firm simply competed with the San Rafael company, subsidizing the import of paper from abroad, and selling it cheaply to newspapers and book producers. Gradually the pressure on the San Rafael company started to tell. In 1936, the factory's workers went on strike, claiming that the firm was manipulating the paper market, ignoring new forest conservation laws, and supporting ex-president Plutarco Elías Calles in his conflict with the current president, Cárdenas.[42] Finally, in February 1938 the Mexican senate met to discuss the status of the firm. The union of newspaper workers presented their complaints, arguing that the San Rafael company was a ruthless foreign monopoly. Since the establishment of PIPSA, they claimed, the firm had run small-scale paper merchants out of business and refused credit to newspapers, which declined to sign exclusive contracts with San Rafael.[43] The big national newspapers backed the assertions and the senate ordered the factory to stop producing and selling newsprint.[44] The end of San Rafael's newsprint production made PIPSA an effective monopoly. From 1938 onward the public company would become a controversial tool of state power. As we shall see, the government would increasingly use the monopoly to manipulate the contents of the big nationals and put pressure on smaller independent newspapers. But PIPSA, as its defenders argued, also supported the boom in Mexican newspaper production by making paper in Mexico available even when the international market floundered, by heavily subsidizing the price of newsprint, and by allowing newspapers to rack up extensive debts.

During the 1940s and 1950s, the international availability of paper declined initially due to wartime transport problems and then due to expanding newspaper markets in postwar Europe. Mexican newspapers often suffered a scarcity of newsprint.[45] In November 1943, for example, the big nationals were forced to reduce their number of pages.[46] Despite these shortfalls, the Mexican government repeatedly used PIPSA to meet newspapers' demands for paper. For example, after the 1943 cuts, newspapers started to complain about the newsprint shortages. President Manuel Avila Camacho (1940–1946) ordered the national railways to give priority to the transportation of paper and provided PIPSA with another twenty cars to carry the loads.[47] Two years later, shortages occurred again. The director of the National Railways of Mexico (Ferrocarriles Nacionales de México) tried to persuade the president to order another cut in newspaper production. "The use of paper in the capital is exorbitant," he argued, reminding Avila Camacho that the U.S. and U.K. governments had recently forced newspapers to reduce their size. But in August 1945 the president yet again used the government company to solve the problem, giving priority to the transport of paper on the railways, increasing imports to Mexico City from 500 to 1,200 metric tons per week, and bargaining with the Canadian government for the purchase of another 20,000 metric tons.[48] In 1951 the Mexican press faced another newsprint crisis. By July the PIPSA warehouses were running low. Prompted by the editors of the big newspapers, the government again refused to enforce cuts. Instead President Alemán doubled PIPSA's credit, authorizing the firm to make bigger purchases and maintain its reserves. In August he sent the secretary of the economy and two representatives of PIPSA to bargain with U.S. and Canadian suppliers. The discussions were successful. By August 15, the negotiators returned to Mexico, announcing that they had managed to up Mexican paper imports from 45,000 to 60,000 metric tons a year.[49]

By the mid-1950s, the Mexican government tried to move beyond these informal solutions to shortages. PIPSA changed from a company that bought, transported, and sold paper to a large industrial organization that stored paper on a massive scale and produced its own newsprint. On June 7, 1954, President Adolfo Ruiz Cortines (1952–1958) inaugurated the company's new paper warehouses. These could store nearly 28,000 metric tons of newsprint—triple their former capacity and nearly half Mexico's annual supply. The new buildings were located in the Colonia Industrial Vallejo in north Mexico City, just yards from the Pantaco railway terminal.[50] Six months later, Ruiz Cortines announced the construction of PIPSA's first newsprint factory near the Papaloapan Hydroelectric dam in the tropical lowlands of Tuxtepec, Oaxaca. George Wise, a U.S. entrepreneur and close friend of former president Alemán, headed the project, using money from the Bank of America, a U.S. paper company, and the Mexican government.[51] By 1957, the plant was completed at the cost of 180 million pesos. Local loggers cut down surrounding trees and the plant was hooked up to the power supply from the dam. The Mexican government also managed to buy back a controlling share in the factory from the U.S. investors.[52] Finally, in September 1959 the plant started to produce newsprint. For the next two decades, production made up for shortfalls on the international market. In 1959, the factory produced 10 percent of Mexican demand; by 1968, the mill produced 22 percent or 35,000 metric tons of newsprint.[53]

PIPSA not only ensured the availability of newsprint, the organization also saved newspaper companies millions. Despite fluctuations in the international paper market and two peso devaluations, PIPSA maintained paper at artificially low prices. In 1944, prices in the United States doubled, but in Mexico the PIPSA price stayed the same. Between 1957 and 1961 the company even dropped the price by around 5 percent.[54] Purchasing PIPSA paper avoided taxes, which outside PIPSA added 80 percent to the purchase price. PIPSA also saved newspapers money on the storage and transport of newsprint through its Mexico City warehouses, its fleet of transport trucks, and its network of branch warehouses.[55] Finally, PIPSA also let newspapers build up enormous debts. By the end of 1968, 252 newspaper companies had debts totaling over 71 million pesos with the organization.[56]

Throughout the period, other government initiatives also undergirded the finances of the Mexican press. They included low-interest loans, government advertising, paid news stories, or *gacetillas*, direct subsidies, and regular payments for journalists. Like PIPSA, they helped keep papers relatively cheap. At least indirectly, they enlarged the Mexican newspaper industry and increased the reading public. But more so than PIPSA, they were tied up with another story, the government's control of the press. As such, I shall leave discussion of these disbursements to chapters 2 and 5.

The expansion of the newspaper industry relied on both public and private money. The growth in advertising also fed the press boom. Mexico's modern publicity industry had its roots in the Porfiriato, when large merchants, and alcohol and cigarette companies moved to popularize their products.[57] During the revolution, investment in advertising dropped, and in 1922 there were only twenty-five advertising agencies in Mexico.[58] Two decades later the number had risen to seventy, but observers still complained that companies spent little on publicity, that newspapers often refused to set up ads according to companies' specifications, and that editors often declined to give out readership data and surveys.[59] But attitudes to publicity gradually changed. During the 1940s, large U.S. advertising agencies moved into the Mexican market. Companies like J. Walter Thompson and Grant Advertising hired leading Mexican publicists and offered national and international firms not only advertisements but also marketing strategies and media plans.[60] Mexican companies like that of Eulalio Ferrer also moved into the trade. Within a decade his company was competing with the large U.S. firms. By 1970, it was the fourth-biggest advertising agency in Mexico, channeling over 80 million pesos of publicity to the mass media per year.[61]

Together, U.S. capital and Mexican know-how created a flourishing advertising industry. Between 1948 and 1960, the number of advertising agencies in Mexico doubled from 70 to 140; six years later there were 160. These funneled increasing amounts of money to the mass media. Between 1960 and 1970, spending on advertising increased from 1,200 million to 3,935 million pesos per year. Six years later authorities assessed that firms spent an estimated 6,000 million pesos on publicity. During the 1960s Ferrer claimed that up to 15,000 Mexicans made their living from the advertising industry, and by 1973 this had jumped to 35,000.[62] Compared to the U.S. or Western European economies, the Mexican publicity industry was still relatively small. In the United States 2.6 percent of per capita income was spent on advertising; in Mexico it only reached just over 1 percent. But Mexican expenditure still dwarfed other developing nations and accounted for around the same proportion as Japan, Spain, and Portugal.[63]

Furthermore, a considerable part of advertising spending was on newspapers and magazines. In 1941, the U.S. State Department estimated that firms spent around 18 million pesos on publicity in the Mexican press annually.[64] By the 1960s, the figure had increased by a factor of over thirty. In 1963, print media earned 34 percent of total advertising expenditure or 547 million pesos.[65] Four years later, newspapers and magazines received 30 percent of publicity spending or 610 million pesos. Over the next decade, expenditure on television advertising really took off, increasing by 231 percent between 1965 and 1971. But spending on printed media still rose gradually. In the same period, spending on newspaper advertising grew by 133 percent and magazine advertising by 162 percent.[66]

Studies of advertising in the big nationals testify to this growing reliance on publicity. In 1948, observers claimed that the Mexico City press averaged around 30 percent advertising per issue. Seven years later, *Excélsior* contained around 50 percent advertising, *El Universal* 41 percent, and *Novedades* 38 percent. By 1972, the proportions had risen even further. *Excélsior* now comprised 54 percent advertising and *Novedades* 46 percent.[67] Outside Mexico City, the effects of the growing advertising industry on printed media were even more marked. During the 1940s commentators regularly denigrated regional newspapers for running "horse and cart" publicity operations.[68] In 1941, the U.S. State Department estimated that companies only spent around 313,000 pesos per month on advertising in the regional press. Even large newspapers based in industrial cities struggled. In Monterrey, *El Porvenir* brought in 26,000 pesos per month; its competitor, *El Norte*, earned an estimated 20,000.[69] By 1965 advertising earnings had grown dramatically. *El Norte* now contained 56 percent advertising and earned around 1.68 million pesos per month. *El Porvenir* was not far behind, comprising 51 percent publicity, which brought in around 1.3 million pesos.[70]

The rapid increase in advertising expenditure clearly played a role in upping regional publicity revenues. But so did new strategies. The editor of *El Norte*, Rodolfo Junco de la Vega, boasted that the paper's advertising department now comprised an advertising manager, solicitors, draftsmen, and production experts. They also brought in a monthly matrix service from the United States, which offered different layouts for different types of business. After ads were completed the department sent the drafts back to the advertisers to check the quality.[71] Tapping into publicity revenues in Mexico City also helped. In the 1940s, a group of large regionals, including Guadalajara's *El Informador* and Merida's *El Diario de Yucatán*, teamed up, formed the Association of Editors of the States (Asociación de Editores de los Estados, AEE), and established a publicity office in Mexico City, which channeled ads to the provincial newspapers.[72] Regional newspapers in the northern states also went directly to U.S. companies to acquire publicity revenue. *El Norte*'s editor sent advertising agents to Texas to gain additional income; Tijuana's *El Mexicano* sent agents as far north as Los Angeles to tap into the U.S. advertising market.[73]

Cheap paper and increasing advertising revenue provided the basis for the expansion of the Mexican newspaper industry. Together they reduced costs and increased revenues. But other changes within the industry also expanded the ambit of the Mexican press. During the period, entry costs for starting a newspaper or magazine dropped. Technological shifts triggered the change. From the 1920s, big nationals moved from linotype presses to much faster and clearer rotogravure presses. In the 1960s, they switched again, upgrading to even faster rotary offset machines.[74] Upgrading to faster presses had two important, if indirect, effects. First, it allowed major nationals to provide an extended range of printing services for smaller firms. In 1944, *La Prensa* earned 205,000 pesos from commercial printing, around a tenth of its total earnings.[75] This obviously profited the nationals, but it also allowed the owners of small concerns to save capital by printing their weeklies on the big firms' faster machines. Such savings cut the start-up costs of the print media. When journalist Roberto Blanco Moheno suggested establishing a cheap, popular, progovernment magazine in 1948, he claimed he needed only 10,000 pesos to begin the project.[76] Second, upgrading to these faster machines generated a market in out-of-date presses. By the late 1940s, prospective newspaper owners could purchase thirty-year-old linotype presses in Mexico City for around 4,000 to 5,000 pesos. According to one U.S. observer, there was a "surfeit of old used presses on the market." He estimated that for 50,000 pesos one could establish a small daily.[77] Of course, this was a vast sum. But it was not completely out of reach for middle-class Mexicans with access to an inheritance, loans, or a few well-off friends.

Finally, as a news medium, the press faced scant competition. Obviously the use of radios grew exponentially during the period. By the late 1950s, Lewis estimated that 79 percent of the houses in the Casa Grande neighborhood had them. In fact, radios "ha[d] become so common [that] they [were] no longer diagnostics of wealth."[78] Such widespread use had huge effects. As early as 1938, Salvador Novo speculated that it had changed domestic communication patterns as families listened to the radio rather than conversing.[79] But radio was primarily an entertainment rather than an information medium. So despite this growth, papers still held their own as sources of news. In a 1958 U.S. survey, 69 percent of urban Mexicans judged newspapers important sources of information, compared to only 60 percent for radios.[80] Furthermore, as mass media, radios and newspapers coexisted relatively stably. Papers often provided the format and content for radio programs, and both media shared advertising revenue equally between them.[81]

In the long run, television was more of a threat. By the late 1970s TV trumped both radio and newspapers in terms of advertising revenue and as a source of information. Mexicans watched more hours of TV than any other nation.[82] But TV watching took off relatively slowly. During the 1940s and 1950s, TVs were expensive luxury items; barely a handful of wealthy households could afford one.[83] At the same time, owners saw TV as an entertainment rather than a news medium. According to TV producer Gabino Carrandi Ortiz, up to

1969 "television news programs barely occupied a corner in the screen and in the studio."[84] And big national newspapers like *Excélsior* and *Novedades* actually provided the scripts for the nightly news. In fact, in a 1967 U.S. survey, only 24 percent of respondents claimed that they received their news from watching TV.[85]

The Mass Reading Public

Social changes and shifts in the Mexican newspaper industry generated a boom in newspaper production. But readership did not increase evenly throughout the newspaper industry. Print runs of the capital's broadsheets and political magazines rose gradually; even during the 1960s they rarely penetrated beyond upper-middle-class Mexico City consumers. In contrast, print runs of popular printed media grew rapidly. Tabloids and magazines devoted to sport, crime, and romance became the everyday reading material of Mexico City's masses. In the provinces, regional and local newspapers also flourished, spreading their reach over smaller towns and penetrating existing markets more deeply. By the 1960s urban literate Mexicans read the news. In the countryside, press readership increased, but only slowly. Small newspapers penetrated market towns and surrounding villages. But low incomes, a limited advertising market, and poor communications still vaccinated against large-scale rural readership.

Before examining the penetration of the press, it is worth commenting on the confusion over print run statistics and circulations. Observers often denigrated the official print run numbers produced by Mexican newspapers. They argued that companies inflated the figures to persuade advertising companies of mass readership and to make overstated purchases of PIPSA newsprint and sell the remainder on the black market. Scholarly approximations of newspaper penetration frequently reduce official figures by between one- and two-thirds to even out these exaggerations.[86] Such criticisms have validity. No doubt, many newspapers did overstate circulations.

But I have decided to take most if not all numbers at face value, partly because the degree of these reductions seems arbitrary, and partly because other evidence suggests that these figures were not radical exaggerations. First, government print run numbers, based on the number of newspapers handed over to wholesalers, are relatively close to the official claims. The morning edition of *Ovaciones*, the Mexico City sports and crime tabloid, claimed to sell 87,000 copies in 1960 and 158,250 in 1967. In 1966, the wholesalers figure (excluding subscriptions and editions sold outside Mexico City) was 104,394. Second, Mexican newspapers increasingly used outside companies to prove print runs.

In 1960, only seven newspapers audited their circulations through the international Audit Bureau of Circulation or the accountancy firm Casas Alatriste. Four years later, twenty-six newspapers and magazines audited their numbers, including small papers like the Piedras Negras daily *El Diario*, which only sold 7,000 copies. Again, these correlate relatively closely to preaudit figures and their nonaudited competitors.[87] Third, more than one person read individual newspapers. As early as the 1920s, newspapers posted their publications on billboards outside their offices "so that the impecunious may learn about the events of the day free of charge." Sharing texts among family members, neighbors, or friends was frequent. In 1950, a detailed U.S. report on the Guadalajara daily *El Informador* claimed that "the Mexican custom is to share a single newspaper among all the members of the family or among the office staff or among the club members"; the owner asserted that around twenty readers perused each issue. Surveys backed this up. In 1962 U.S. advertisers estimated that most newspapers averaged 3.2 readers; a 1967 survey claimed that each copy of García Valseca's *El Sol de México* newspaper had 3.4 readers. Magazines had even more. Surveys of political weekly *Impacto* indicated an average of over ten readers per issue and *Life en español* over seven.[88]

During this period, Mexico witnessed a dramatic increase in the sheer number of newspapers and magazines. Between 1931 and 1958, the total number of printed publications circulating the country increased sevenfold from 491 to 3,415. Though numbers dropped dramatically after President López Mateos's 1958 election, there were still 2,462 in 1974.[89] The total number of current affairs and news publications also increased from 244 in 1940 to 1,249 thirty years later. Dailies grew from 44 in 1931 to 256 in 1974. These increases far outstripped the standard rise in population. Between 1940 and 1970, Mexico's population grew by around 165 percent. In the same period, the total number of publications had increased by 250 percent; the number of current affairs publications by 400 percent; and the number of dailies by 250 percent.[90] Another useful indicator of this increased production is importation of newsprint. In 1950, PIPSA imported 39,900 metric tons; five years later, it imported 60,000. Even though the Tuxtepec paper factory had started to operate, paper imports nearly doubled between 1960 and 1969, rising from 87,000 to 160,000 metric tons.[91]

Media production grew, but new readers were not spread evenly over society. The capital's broadsheets and political magazines actually experienced rather scant gains. The most popular, *Excélsior*, increased from a print run of 66,557 in 1931 to 93,945 in 1948 to 120,753 in 1963 and to 149,572 in 1970. *Novedades*'s improvements were broadly similar, running from 104,000 in 1948 to

140,773 in 1970. *El Universal* actually experienced severe problems with labor unions and sales during the period, rising from a circulation of 74,582 in 1948 to only 76,292 in 1963. Other broadsheets were minimally read. During the 1940s, the left-leaning *El Popular* sold around 12,000 copies per issue. In 1963, its effective replacement, *El Día*, barely registered 7,000 sales. During the entire period, *El Nacional*'s sales were always low; most copies were handed out free to the country's functionaries.[92] The capital's political weeklies also experienced low sales growth. Increasingly *oficialista* magazines like *Hoy*, *Mañana*, and *El Tiempo* barely registered 20,000 sales even during the 1960s. Even the more balanced *Siempre!* rarely sold over 25,000 copies.[93]

Together, such sales figures were relatively low. They were proportionally less than national population increases let alone the fourfold increase in Mexico City's inhabitants. They suggested that neither broadsheets nor political weeklies ever penetrated beyond the capital's upper middle class. Sales in the provinces were also low, rarely rising above 20 to 25 percent of total transactions. In 1954, *Excélsior* sold 21,375 copies beyond Mexico City. Only seven states had more than 1,000 readers. In the northern state of Durango, *Excélsior* sold only 149 copies; in the eastern state of Quintana Roo, only 12.[94] U.S. reviews of reading habits support these paltry figures. In 1967, even in the Mexico State capital of Toluca, only 7 percent of respondents read the capital's press.[95] The big nationals were really just a Mexico City press. In a lament, which would strike a chord with any academic, reporter Carlos Moncada wrote, "the Mexico City journalist apparently writes for the most numerous public in the world. But he rarely knows if his articles have been read beyond his circle of family members and friends."[96]

Furthermore, even in the capital, class limited the readership of the major broadsheets. The rich were the principal readers of the *gran prensa*. As early as 1941, the U.S. State Department claimed that 65 percent of *Excélsior* readers and 70 percent of *El Universal* readers came from the upper and upper middle classes.[97] Thirteen years later, U.S. observers again argued that readers of both newspapers came from the "high and middle economic classes."[98] By 1970 little had changed. According to an internal survey, *Excélsior* was predominantly read by "people of the upper middle-class, merchants, professionals, and industrialists."[99] Even the more colorful, photo-heavy broadsheets founded in the 1960s failed to penetrate beyond this section of society. A 1967 survey of *El Sol de México* discovered that only 12 percent of readers earned less than 1,000 pesos per month. In comparison, around three-quarters of Mexicans earned less.[100] Political magazines also rarely penetrated beyond the upper middle class. In 1954, U.S. diplomats claimed the readers of *Siempre!*,

Hoy, Mañana, and *Todo* comprised "politicians and businessmen." They were not intended for the whole family and predominantly circulated in offices and a handful of high-class barbershops.[101] In short, broadsheets and magazines remained what Marxists would term a bourgeois press.

The question remains, why? Why did Mexico City's broadsheets and political magazines fail to access broader social and geographical markets? High prices played an important role. Glossy magazines were particularly expensive. During the 1940s they cost a peso. As Blanco Moheno argued, "the common man is not disposed to pay this."[102] Herón Proal, a left-wing activist, agreed, claiming he did not read *Hoy* because "its tendency and the price made it exclusive to the bourgeoisie."[103] By 1952, most magazines had increased to 1.50 pesos a copy, and by the following decade they cost three. Throughout the period, they cost around a worker's hourly wage. Broadsheets were not so expensive. But sales remained extremely vulnerable to price rises, which would exclude members of the lower middle and working classes. In 1966, for example, broadsheet prices rose from 60¢ to 80¢. Sales immediately dropped between 10 and 15 percent.[104]

The *gran prensa's* subject matter was also defiantly elitist. When *Excélsior* launched in 1917, it announced that it was not "any old newspaper" but the "daily of the gente culta [cultured people]."[105] Thirty years later, Blanco Moheno described political magazines as "antipopular": "from their excessive formality to their format, they misunderstand what interests people."[106] On the one hand, international news dominated. A 1960 study found that *Excélsior* and *Novedades* contained more international news than the seven largest South American newspapers combined. In fact, they published more international news than the *New York Times.*[107] On the other hand, when journalists covered national politics, they used a language and style that made it extremely difficult to understand. Political columns, in particular, were only for the "initiated," those who understood their particular "brand of witchcraft." As journalist Carlos Ortega explained, politicians were described in a semi-ironic political argot that only top officials could decipher. "Discreto y eficiente" (literally, discreet and efficient) meant a politician was happy to remain within the shadow of his patron and would never "roba cámara" (literally, rob the camera or hog publicity) or make wayward declarations. "Talentoso y capaz" (literally, talented and capable) actually denoted a politician "with few lights on," or thick. Columnists often described the director of the Department of Agrarian Affairs and Colonization (Departamento de Asuntos Agrarios y Colonización, DAAC), Norberto Aguirre Palancares, in this way although in official circles he was known as "the volcano" (because he was white on top and stone underneath).[108]

Even outside the columns, political news was hard to read. In 1972, novelist Jorge Ibargüengoitia, a keen observer of press language, explained his own confusion at reading the rather anodyne news that Sánchez Pérez had been removed from the cabinet in order to eliminate "old-fashioned pessimism." He, like "most average Mexicans," concluded that Sánchez Pérez was an "old-fashioned pessimist." But the next day he read that Sánchez Pérez had actually been moved to head of another department. Was this a promotion or a demotion? Did this indicate that pessimism was in or out? Most Mexicans, he concluded, "cannot work out the problem, ... turn over the page and simply pass to the sports section." Two years later, he pondered the incomprehensible nature of political news once again. Reading that an unnamed politician had performed a "madruguete" (a sucker punch) by starting his presidential campaign, he considered what "madruguete" actually signified. Was it the *tapado* (the chosen PRI presidential candidate), who was confident in his position and was wasting no time in putting together a workable coalition? Was it someone who believed he might be the *tapado* and was trying to discover what the party might think of his nomination? Or was it somebody who was definitely not the *tapado*, who had been told to run an early campaign so he could be "burnt" (or shot down) and make way for the actual candidate? Ibargüengoitia speculated that the term was so hard to define "in the year 2000, a professor of Political Science from the University of Iowa" would make his career "by discovering the real meaning" of the word.[109]

Ibargüengoitia's examples were deliberately amusing. But they were not far from the truth. In the early 1980s Ilya Adler studied the reading habits of bureaucrats working for the Ministry of Health (Secretaría de Salud). She found that they spent forty minutes a day poring over broadsheets and political magazines. All the officials stressed that one had to "read between the lines" and could not take the information at face value. "As the years pass, you learn to decode the press. ... It's hard to know how one learns, but after a while you become more comfortable with this. You know, you learn to understand how struggles and alliances are often reflected in the press, but of course, it is not obvious to the general public." Despite this experience, health administrators rarely agreed on an article's meaning. When she showed them an advertisement paid by the health workers union, which demanded better salaries, some thought it was an indirect attack on the ministry, others thought it was a piece of empty propaganda designed to demonstrate that lazy union leaders were actually doing something, and others thought that it was probably dreamed up "by the ministry and the union together" as a ploy to get more funds.[110]

Nonpolitical sections were also directed toward exclusive interests. The society news pages were defiantly snobbish, full of the baptisms, marriages, and parties of the elites. Under the stewardship of baseball impresario Jorge Pasquel, *Novedades* even ran a column on the rarefied social world of African safaris.[111] Even society sections, which reached beyond the wealthy, displayed a marked distaste for those who were not well-to-do. In the late 1940s, the weekly magazine *Hoy* ran a regular feature called "King for a Day," in which working-class Mexicans were photographed eating with politicians and actresses in sumptuous hotels.[112] In fact, broadsheet society pages were so exclusive that even the government worried that they might heighten class conflict (if anyone beyond the elite ever read them). In September 1968, high-up official Mario Moya Palencia wrote to the secretary of the interior, Luis Echeverría, that *El Sol de México* and *El Heraldo de México* were "underlining and amplifying bourgeois fiestas and celebrations" to such an extent that he suggested asking them to "lower the tone." Three months later, Moya was still concerned. "Every day they acclaim exaggeratedly bourgeois attitudes and treat certain sectors of Mexican and foreign society like nobility." He worried that such sections "damaged the real image of Mexican society, magnifying the dazzling leisure activities of a minority, which thinks of itself anachronistically as a plutocracy. . . . If they published the communist manifesto . . . it would do less damage."[113]

If Mexico's broadsheets experienced only slow growth in circulation, tabloids and popular crime magazines witnessed rapid increases. During the 1930s, Mexico's leading tabloid, *La Prensa*, battled to increase its readership. In 1941, observers estimated that it only sold 32,500 copies. But over the next three decades, sales grew rapidly. By 1952 it sold 90,000 copies and by 1954 117,000. By 1967 it was the highest-selling paper in Mexico, shifting 185,361 copies per day.[114] *Excélsior*'s tabloid stablemate, *Ultimas Noticias*, also struggled initially. When young journalist Luis Spota took over the paper in 1947, he claimed it only sold 32,000 copies a day. Within two years, editorial changes and new sales strategies pushed sales to 94,000 copies. By 1960, audited circulation figures claimed sales of 168,565 a day.[115] Other tabloids used low prices to move into the Mexico City market. In 1958, Alfredo Kawage Ramia started to sell the anticommunist *El Tabloide* at 20¢ per copy, half *La Prensa*'s cost. Within two years it claimed a circulation of 150,000 copies. Sports tabloids also took off. By 1969, *Esto*, García Valseca's flagship sports and entertainment daily, sold 246,800 copies per day. In the same year, its main competitor, *Ovaciones*, sold a total of 280,850 copies of its two daily issues.[116] Readership of popular magazines also grew. Crime magazines had always outsold their more po-faced political competitors. As early as 1932, *Detectives* claimed to sell 42,720 copies a week.

But in the 1960s they really expanded. *Alarma*, Regino Hernández Llergo's bloody weekly, claimed to sell a staggering 567,550 copies in June 1967; its competitors, *Alerta* and *Policia*, declared circulations of 228,000 and 120,000.[117]

Outside the capital, the tabloids, like the broadsheets, struggled to compete with local papers. But unlike the broadsheets, tabloids and popular magazines did attract nonelite Mexico City readers. Anecdotes and surveys bore this out. During the late 1930s, labor leader Vicente Lombardo Toledano worried about *La Prensa*'s antiunion policy as it "reached the home of the worker and peasant."[118] The 1941 U.S. survey on reading habits concluded that *La Prensa* and *Novedades* (at this point a tabloid) were the most popular newspapers among lower-middle- and working-class consumers. Of the interviewees, 33 percent read *Novedades* and 26 percent *La Prensa*. Only 20 percent read *Excélsior*, *Universal*, and *El Nacional* combined.[119] In 1954, U.S. observers rather snottily asserted that although *La Prensa* had the second-highest circulation, it was "not listed among the most influential publications, because the great majority of its readers [were] not representative of influential groups."[120] In short, they were too poor. The dozens of clippings, which the middle-aged Mexico City shopkeeper Prado sent to the president, were almost all from the capital's tabloids. Of the ninety-seven news stories he commented on, 30 percent were from *Ultimas Noticias*, 21 percent from *Atisbos*, 18 percent from *La Prensa*, 7 percent from *El Diario de la Tarde*, and 6 percent from *Ovaciones*.[121]

Anthropologists' observations backed this up. In Oscar Lewis's *Five Families*, most members of the less well-off families read the tabloid press. Alberto Gómez, a bus driver, read the later edition of *Ultimas Noticias* although his mother disapproved of the paper's emphasis on crime. His fourteen-year-old sister and her friends laughed as they read ads from the paper out loud. Jesús Sánchez pored over *Ultimas Noticias* every day. For Jesús, a newsvendor, albeit a relatively wealthy one, reading the news was a rare moment of calm. After work he read and "no one spoke because they knew he wanted them to be silent." In the night he snatched a few minutes of reading by the light of a kerosene lamp.[122] During the 1970s, anthropologists also observed how the residents of squatter communities on the city's periphery read "comics, photo-romances, and sports sheets" or "the morbid magazine of the day."[123] Visual representations of the mid-century city also stand testament to the growth in popular tabloid reading. In *Nosotros los Pobres* the carpenter and hero, Pepe, reads *La Prensa* together with the other prisoners. Even the jail thug peruses the paper, before putting it down to shove a corrupt official.[124] In one of Nacho López's photographs he captures a parking valet breaking up the night shift by reading a tabloid while cars rush by in a blur of artificial light. In another, entitled "The Street Reads," a worker wearing a sombrero rests his hand on his chin and ponders a scrap of tabloid. In his series of photographs on pulquerias, two women quaff the drink while a copy of *La Prensa* lies on the table.[125]

How did tabloids and popular magazines secure Mexico City's growing audience for the printed word? Subject matter was important. Tabloids contained large sections devoted to the *nota roja,* or crime news—and crime news sold. Novelist and editor Martín Luis Guzmán called crime "the key to circulation."[126] U.S. observers agreed. In 1958, they asked readers what type of news articles interested them the most; 37 percent replied the *nota roja.*[127] As Pablo Piccato argues, the *nota roja* not only exposed the crimes of society's top tiers (like a kind of bloody inverse of the society pages), it also provided a forum for public discussion of political elites and judicial inequality. In fact, crime news "was the terrain on which civil society addressed the separation between truth and justice, the disjuncture between people's knowledge about the reality of criminal acts and the state response to these acts."[128] In the crime news, nonelite voices of victims, criminals, and bystanders were common. Polls of readers were frequent and readers could even write in, give their opinions on the most recent cases, and speculate more broadly on corruption among the elites. Veteran reporter César Vallejo claimed that the crime page had "the most contact with the people, with reality. . . . I believe that is the most human, the nearest to the problems of the people."[129]

The simple language of the tabloids was also central to their popularity. The editor of the 1950s tabloid *Zócalo* insisted that his journalists employed a style that "was colloquial, anecdotal, seasoned with jokes and wordplay" and "used the greatest amount of popular terms but without losing grammatical form." (Philologist Modesto Sanchez even took *Zócalo* to his classes to show his students how to write good idiomatic prose.)[130] Manuel Buendía, editor of *La Prensa,* was similarly exacting. "*Grandes notas, si, notas grandes, no*" (big stories, yes, long stories, no), he wrote to his reporters in 1963. "Even if there is space I ask you never to cram the paper with outsized articles and I will resolve never to substitute quantity for quality. . . . Whoever lacks the power of synthesis should not be called a journalist."[131]

Outside Mexico City, regional papers also experienced a dramatic rise in readership. In 1940, there were around 192 publications in Mexico's provinces. But by 1974, there were 931 publications, including 191 dailies. They were distributed throughout Mexico's growing towns and cities. By the 1970s, there were newspapers in 134 of Mexico's 173 towns or cities with populations of more than 15,000. Readers in major cities like Monterrey and Guadalajara maintained a variety of industrial broadsheets and tabloids. But even smaller communities like the rural market towns of Atotonilco el Alto, Jalisco, or Acayucán, Veracruz, supported low-selling, locally focused concerns. In fact, newspapers were spread so widely that in one 1970 study U.S. observers concluded that Mexico possessed the second-lowest geographical concentration of newspapers out of thirty-two countries.[132] By this decade, Mexico's urban dwellers even in small towns could easily pick up a paper that contained local news.

Newspapers were not, however, spread evenly over the republic. Some states possessed greater concentrations of publications than others. Rates of literacy and urbanization played important roles. According to one mid-1970s study, in the northern, heavily urbanized states of Coahuila, Nuevo León, and Tamaulipas newspaper production was extremely high, with about two inhabitants per newspaper produced. Other states, with strong journalistic traditions like Yucatán where the right-wing *El Diario de Yucatán* and the progovernment *Diario del Sureste* had competed since the 1930s, also supported strong readerships. In these locations there were about three inhabitants per newspaper. But newspapers in more rural states like Morelos and Oaxaca struggled to penetrate the hundreds of geographically diffuse towns and villages.[133]

Mexico's regional newspapers were also extremely varied, in terms of ownership structure, technology, and subject matter. There were two large regional chains, one owned by anticommunist impresario José García Valseca and another by the opportunist Argentine businessman Mauricio Bercún. Throughout the period, García Valseca founded forty-six regional dailies, although when he lost control of the chain in 1976 only thirty-seven remained. Bercún's enterprise was smaller; he owned dailies throughout the center and northeast of the country in Tampico, Torreón, San Luis Potosí, León, Irapuato, and Aguascalientes.[134] There was also a group of well-established, often family owned, regional dailies. These included the members of the AEE (Merida's *El Diario de Yucatán*, Monterrey's *El Porvenir*, Guadalajara's *El Informador*, Torreón's *El Siglo*, and Veracruz's *El Dictamen*) as well as other large concerns like Monterrey's *El Norte* and Tijuana's *El Mexicano*. By the 1970s the national broadsheet, *Novedades*, had also established small, regional offices in Campeche, Puebla, Quintana Roo, and Yucatán. These were all industrial newspapers.[135] They used modern technology, produced thousands of copies, and employed a diversified staff of journalists, copyeditors, advertising agents, salesmen, and print workers. They also gradually expanded into broader geographical markets (by the 1970s *El Mexicano* ran separate editions in Mexicali and Ensenada) and into diverse formats. By the 1960s, most ran cheap, crime-heavy, tabloid editions of their newspapers.[136] The editor of the sensationalist García Valseca tabloid, *La Voz de Puebla*, explained that "*El Sol de Puebla* is for the home, *La Voz* is for the bus and the office."[137]

Beyond these industrial businesses, there were also hundreds of smaller, often fleeting, newspaper enterprises. These printed on printing companies' machines or used outdated, secondhand presses, employed few staff, and produced only a few thousand copies. Some were news dailies. During the early 1960s Tijuana's combative daily *Las Noticias* was maintained by a local lawyer, employed four journalists, possessed only seven typewriters, and the "composing room" resembled "a junk heap."[138] Others were more irregular, but they both echoed and shaped the specific concerns of their readers. In the north, editors ran crime newspapers and magazines, which focused on exposing the links between local authorities and the vice industry. In Tijuana, anti-narcotics crusader, private detective, and occasional police official Joaquín Aguilar Robles ran the *nota roja* monthly *Detective Internacional*. In the heavily Catholic center-west, religious papers predominated. In 1953, 135 of the country's 178 religious publications were printed in the region.[139] And throughout the country small, narrowly focused satirical newspapers also emerged. They were often extremely disparaging of local authorities and included Oaxaca City's *El Chapulín*, Ciudad Juárez's *El Alacrán*, and Tepic's *La Escoba*.

Whatever their quality, these regional newspapers were widely read. A quick comparison of circulations and the number of households bears this out. In 1967, Monterrey's five dailies produced around 241,000 copies for 114,000 households. In Torreón four dailies generated 81,500 copies for just 30,000 households. Down south, where literacy rates were lower, local newspapers still managed to make substantial gains. In Merida notarized estimations of *El Diario del Sureste*, *El Diario de Yucatán*, and *Novedades de Yucatán's* circulations were 101,900. Households totaled just 28,000. Even in Oaxaca City, newspaper circulation was around double the number of households.[140]

Large-scale U.S. surveys also indicated high levels of provincial newspaper reading. In 1958, the U.S. government employed a marketing company to assess the penetration of its weekly supplement, imaginatively titled *Semanal*, in the city of Aguascalientes. The survey was based on 991 personal interviews conducted among citizens from across the social spectrum. The supplement, they discovered, was a complete disaster. It was inserted in a low-selling publication, rarely read, and focused on a population broadly unconcerned with international news. But the results on readership habits were revealing. The survey found that 77 percent of Aguascalientes citizens read newspapers regularly. Almost all read the García Valseca newspaper *El Sol del Centro*, while

28 percent read its competitor *El Heraldo*. Class shaped reading conventions: 98 percent of upper-class respondents and 88 percent of middle-class interviewees read the news. But it did not define habits completely: 64 percent of lower-class and poor respondents read the local news. Provincial broadsheets were less class-bound than the capital's counterparts. Gender, interestingly, was even less important. The same proportion of men and women read the press.[141]

Nine years later, the United States again tried to assess the readership of *Semanal*. This time the survey was countrywide. The company interviewed 9,000 citizens in 30 provincial cities. This was a huge undertaking, involved substantial fieldwork, and encompassed a broad range of Mexican townspeople. Unlike contemporary academic surveys, which relied on telephone interviews and as a result included a high proportion of wealthy interviewees, these were conducted face to face. In fact, over 92 percent of respondents were from what they defined as the lower middle, lower, or poor classes. Once more, they found the supplement was an abject failure, but again the survey was revealing. By 1967, they found that 79 percent of urban Mexicans read local newspapers regularly. Class again stratified reading habits: Higher ratios of upper- and middle-class city dwellers read the papers (95 percent and 89 percent, respectively), but nevertheless 72 percent of the workers, artisans, and housewives read the news. So did education: Around 98 percent of those who finished high school read the press, 94 percent of those who finished primary school, and only 69 of those who only completed a few years of primary education. Furthermore, some cities had more enthusiastic reading publics than others. In eighteen mostly northern cities, over 70 percent of citizens got their news primarily through the written press. But in towns with weaker journalistic traditions, like Zitácuaro, Tepic, and Jiquilpan, fewer than 50 percent of interviewees received their news through the written word, preferring either radio or word of mouth.[142]

Internal marketing surveys, practiced by large provincial papers, also indicated broad readerships in the provincial cities. In 1959, one such assessment discovered that 84 percent of Torreón families took a daily newspaper. Most (68 percent) read the popular *El Siglo*, while around a third read the Bercún chain's *La Opinión*. Again, class structured reading habits. Two years later, another survey found that 98 percent of upper-class Torreón inhabitants read the press, 90 percent of the middle class, and around 50 percent of the lower-middle and poor classes.[143] A few years later, in Monterrey, another private market research firm conducted a similar survey. They found that 74 percent of inhabitants read newspapers regularly. Another 10 percent read a paper occasionally. Most read the conservative, probusiness *El Norte*. But among the lower classes, readers favored the cheaper tabloid, *El Tiempo*.[144]

How did regional newspapers gain readers throughout Mexico's growing cities? First, most were cheap. During the 1950s, most local dailies cost around 20¢ to 25¢, half the price of a Mexico City newspaper. The following decade most cost around 40¢, two-thirds the price of a capital paper; smaller tabloids still cost 20¢.[145] Second, they concentrated on news which interested provincial readers. International news was sparse. In 1950, only 7 percent of Guadalajara's *El Sol* and *El Occidental*'s coverage dealt with events outside Mexico. Instead they capitalized on "local interest in local affairs."[146] Nearby elections, celebrations, and disasters got top billing, irrespective of international or even national events. As one U.S. observer remarked, "Rarely does a single news story usurp top page one position in [all the] Mexican provincial dailies on any given day. . . . Intense interest in local affairs usually precludes any national uniformity of story emphasis."[147] Close contact between local writers and readers was key. As Sonora journalist Abelardo Casanova explained, national newspapers "lacked local flavor. The provincial reader wants to know who is telling him things."[148] Third, they were often written in simple, colloquial prose. Apolinar Ochoa Andrade's "Tric Trac" column in Ciudad Juárez's *El Mexicano* was designed to give his readers a lesson in "speedy and elegant reading." His style "created a school" within the Ciudad Juárez press. "Short paragraphs. Simple terms. Digestible concepts. . . . A combination of the funny and the serious."[149] Together, as the second part of this book describes, such approaches generated communities of readers that shaped and were shaped by the concerns and language of the regional press.

If Mexico's urban inhabitants embraced the new vogue for newspaper reading, its rural peasants did not. Literacy rates were much lower in rural areas. Despite the opening up of roads, bus routes, and mail services to the country's smaller villages, few papers arrived. Newspaper owners rarely pushed their products in the countryside. Advertisers didn't mind; they targeted the growing purchasing power of the urban classes, not the falling incomes of *ejidatarios* and laborers. Of 800 residents of the Morelos village studied by Erich Fromm and Michael Maccoby, no more than ten regularly read newspapers.[150] In San Miguel Coatlinchán, Mexico State, in the early 1960s, there were "no sales of newspapers, no newsvendor," and "little interest in the national news from the capital." Only four inhabitants read the newspapers regularly and another four from time to time.[151]

But the growth in newspapers still affected rural regions. Although newspaper production was centered in Mexico's cities, some rural inhabitants produced their own, small-scale papers by whatever means. In 1952, over fifty newspapers were still produced on mimeograph and five were still written on typewriters. In Chihuahua, Arturo Orpinal printed a "travelling newspaper" called *El Pyllaca* in the town of Guadalupe y Calvo before selling it 300 kilometers away in the small village of Guachochi. In the same state, journalists whispered of a newspaper that only produced one copy and was passed hand to hand and read out at community meetings until it finally disintegrated.[152] Perhaps these were apocryphal tales, journalists' versions of fishermen's yarns. But small, rural newspapers did exist. During the 1940s, in the Tlaxcala town of Apizaco (population 9,000), Aristarco Montiel started *Don Roque*, a four-page weekly, in his small printing business. The paper was designed to publicize his campaign to raise 30,000 pesos to build a local gymnasium. At first the newspaper contained rather anodyne local news—school timetables, fiestas, and sports results. But gradually Montiel started to receive letters of complaint from his readers. They complained about everything—corrupt health officials, monopolizing merchants, high electricity prices, taxi drivers' catcalls, and the kidnapping of local girls.[153] As we shall see, Montiel's shift from small-town organizer to spokesman of the oppressed provoked considerable repression. But his mouthpiece of local grievances was not a one-off. In the small market town of Huajuapan (population 10,000) the opposition party ran a newspaper throughout the 1950s and 1960s that decried federal teachers, peasant land invaders, and other "communists."[154] To the south, in Tehuantepec (population 12,500), two political groups within the local PRI ran opposing weeklies that condemned local corruption and police incompetence.[155]

If rural inhabitants sometimes produced low-cost weeklies, they also read newspapers produced in the cities. The printed word had power. Both *caciques* and cultural intermediaries employed their ability to read the press to influence fellow villagers. As early as the 1940s, in Tepoztlán, Morelos, the rural elite read Mexico City broadsheets like *El Universal* and *Excélsior* as well as right-wing tabloids like *El Sinarquista*, *Hombre Libre*, and *Omega*. These readers "played an important role in determining public opinion."[156] Luis Rodríguez, the strongman of Oaxaca's Región Mixe, had two-week-old editions of *Excélsior* delivered to his house in the remote, mountainous village of Zacatepec every day.[157] By reading the paper, he could come up with ways to solidify local control by claiming to implement current government policy. Furthermore, not all rural readers were so cynical. Historian Frank Tannenbaum described the following: "One of the most interesting things I have seen in Mexico is men and women, sitting under a gasoline lamp or the light of homemade candles, listening to a story read from the Sunday newspaper (some very old

Sunday newspaper) by the teacher (of the village school) and I have seen this in the remotest sections of Mexico, in the tropical forests of Yucatán and Tabasco, in the mountains of Nayarit. Everything about the Sunday paper becomes useful. The stories, the news, the pictures, the funny sheet, the games, the designs for dresses, the cooking recipes. In fact, I have seen the teacher cut out the separate sections and sew them together as a sort of book for future reference."[158]

A Popular Press

Contrary to Fuentes's vision, mid-century Mexicans read the press. Rising literacy rates, urbanization, expanding communications, and growing wages (at least in comparison to newspaper prices) generated a potential reading public. Shifts in the newspaper industry, including the cheap price of paper, the rise in advertising, and the dip in printing costs, allowed newspapers and magazines to take advantage of these broader social changes. By the late 1950s, Mexico was awash with the printed word. But mass reading did not affect the newspaper industry in a uniform manner. Mexico City broadsheets struggled to extend their market beyond the capital's upper middle class. In contrast, tabloids, crime magazines, and provincial newspapers took off, acquiring wide readerships in Mexico City's poorer barrios and in provincial cities and towns. As we shall see in the following chapters, both federal and state authorities used cash, favors, and violence to control what these newspapers printed. But such censorship was extremely haphazard, particularly outside Mexico City. Civil society and local journalists often formed important political alliances.

Part II
The Mexico City Press

CHAPTER TWO

How to Control the Press

Rules of the Game, the Government Publicity Machine,
and Financial Incentives

Freedom of the press was a key part of the postrevolutionary state's public transcript.[1] It was enshrined in articles 6 and 7 of the 1917 Mexican Constitution, which guarded "the liberty to write and publish writings on any subject."[2] From 1952 onward, presidents and editors testified to its existence and vowed to maintain it at sumptuous public celebrations on the Day of Press Freedom.[3] As the Cold War ramped up, the principle became a cornerstone of the country's international policy. Mexican editors sat on the board of the U.S.-backed Inter American Press Association (Sociedad Interamericana de Prensa, SIP), lauded their own track record on press freedom, and condemned that of communist countries like Cuba.[4] Despite these public affirmations, more critical observers of the capital's media repeatedly condemned the state's control of the Mexico City papers. As early as the 1950s, Cosío Villegas described the city's papers as "a free press, which does not make use of its freedom."[5] In 1964, a visiting Brazilian journalist described newspapers like *Excélsior* and *El Universal* as "tepid and bland" with "an exaggerated exaltation of the figure of the president through daily publications of his photographs, the reproduction of his phrases and speeches, information on his administrative activities, and their supposed global repercussions."[6] Most of the capital's residents held similar sentiments. In 1968, students passed the offices of the big nationals on Bucareli Avenue shouting "prensa vendida" (sold-out press).[7] And two years later, over 82 percent of surveyed Mexico City inhabitants thought that the newspapers lied about politics and elections.[8]

The question remains: How did the state manage to assert control over the capital's major newspapers? As Darnton argues, censorship is a culturally specific phenomenon, which not only reveals the mechanics of the state but also a multitude of unwritten understandings among bureaucrats, writers, and members of civil society. In Mexico City, unlike in many authoritarian regimes, coercive or regulatory censorship was extremely rare. National politicians took the veneer of press liberty very seriously. There was only one dedicated censorship agency, the Assessment Commission of Publications and Illustrated Magazines (Comisión Calificadora de Publicaciones y Revistas

Ilustradas, CCPRI). This was set up to deal with the moral threat of comic books but subsequently expanded to include sports, crime, and glamour magazines. Yet regulations regarding public morality were rarely applied and the CCPRI's campaigns were seldom effective.[9] There were laws limiting press freedom, in particular the rather restrictive 1917 Law of the Press. But in Mexico City (if not in the provinces), the law was infrequently enacted. In fact, authorities only brought the regulations to bear once during the entire period.[10] Furthermore, at least until the mid-1960s, more ad hoc forms of violence toward journalists were very sporadic. As we shall see in chapters 3 and 4, at moments of extreme political tension state-backed thugs smashed presses and beat up journalists. But attacks focused on the marginal press. Workers for the large nationals went completely untouched. Only two of the capital's journalists were murdered during the entire period.

Instead, most censorship in Mexico City was self-censorship—similar to what Darnton terms the "scissors in the head" of East German writers.[11] In the capital's newsrooms, "censorship extended and implanted itself as something natural."[12] All journalists knew "the limits of what they could write."[13] The reasons for this self-censorship were threefold. First, by the 1940s most owners, editors, and journalists shared the government's policy aims. What cultural theorists term "constitutive" or "structural" censorship—that is, the filtering out or framing of stories according to dominant convictions or discourses—was commonplace.[14] Like the political elite, most editors and journalists came from the postrevolutionary middle class. Relatively hegemonic ideologies of anticommunism, industrial growth, and political stability structured their works. If some left-wing press workers failed to share these beliefs, regular social interaction, common ideas over what constituted proper journalism, and the threat of sacking kept them in line or excluded them. Second, the state backed this ideological confluence with an increasingly sophisticated publicity machine. By the 1950s, government publicists not only handed out cash bribes, but also produced thousands of news bulletins designed to regiment coverage of particular events. These narrowed what Pierre Bourdieu termed the "structure of the linguistic market" and limited the parameters of debate.[15] Like modern spin doctors, they also increasingly phoned, bullied, and threatened editors and journalists. They even successfully implemented elaborate plans to manipulate newspaper reporting of controversial or unpopular policies. Third, officials complemented this orientation with increasing amounts of economic support. From the 1940s, cheap paper, low-interest loans, government advertisements, and paid news stories subsidized Mexico

City's newspapers. Together they sustained both investment in technology and increasing overheads. They also offered editors substantial sources of private cash. The occasional removal of these inducements not only weakened more independent publications, but also reminded big nationals of their principal basis of support. In the newsrooms monthly payments, one-off bribes, and offers of houses, lucrative jobs, and expensive presents also persuaded many journalists to follow official pronouncements.

If this chapter lays out the methods of state press control, it also tries to historicize them. Historians sometimes read back the constrictive controls of the 1960s and 1970s onto the earlier era of state-press relations. Throughout the period, certain assumptions about national progress, anticommunism, and journalistic practice remained fairly constant. But government intervention increased in frequency and sophistication over time. By the 1960s, left-leaning writers became increasingly common and the prominence of right-wing journalists started to wane.[16] But at the same time, state censorship in the form of government bulletins, press offices, press monitoring, and spin doctors tried to complement and enforce dying traditions. Financial support for newspapers and journalists also increased markedly.

Everyday Forms of Press Domination

Even without publicity campaigns or financial rewards, most owners, editors, and journalists shared the more conservative policies of the post-1940 Mexican governments. For upper-class press barons and cooperative directors, these policies protected their other business interests and chimed with their own worldviews. For most middle-class, university-educated, male journalists, they did the same. If not, the social world of the *gran prensa* worked to regiment recalcitrant journalists independent of direct government pressure. Shared expectations over what constituted proper journalism persuaded many to moderate their published opinions. Interaction in the bars, restaurants, and cabarets of Mexico City reinforced social ties. And, as a last resort, editors sacked journalists who repeatedly refused to adopt the required editorial line.

From 1940 onward, Mexican government policies changed. Successive presidents retreated from the social redistribution implemented by President Cárdenas. Coherent support for land reform, increasing workers' wages, and socialist education declined. Cold War anticommunism now shaped government attitudes to peasants, workers, and other radical organizations. The Mexican Communist Party (Partido Comunista Mexicana, PCM) was banned, and although concessions never disappeared, officials increasingly used force to repress left-wing groups like teachers, miners, railway workers, students, and peasant land invaders. Instead postwar governments, starting with Alemán, embraced the twin policies of industrial growth and political stability. Infrastructure investment, favorable tax breaks, and protectionist trade policies benefited financial entrepreneurs, factory owners, and large-scale merchants. Increasingly restrictive voting controls and electoral fraud minimized disruption and kept the system in place.[17]

The government's move to the right intertwined with the interests of Mexico City's press barons. Most of the owners of the *gran prensa* emerged from the postrevolutionary elite. They shared upbringings, links to the political elites, and substantial interests in nonmedia businesses. Rómulo O'Farrill Sr., the owner of *Novedades* from 1948 onward, was the son of a Puebla-based Irish immigrant and physician. During the revolution, he used his father's cash to open up his first auto-repair shop. Within a decade he had moved into selling cars and opened Ford and Dodge franchises throughout central Mexico. In late 1939 he founded an assembly plant for Packard and Mack trucks in Puebla. During the 1940s, he also got involved in the television industry, establishing XHTV and broadcasting the country's first television transmission: President Alemán's state of the union address.[18] His son, Rómulo O'Farrill Jr., formed part of the second generation of postrevolutionary elites, whom critics disparagingly termed "juniors." Born in 1917, educated at an exclusive U.S. Catholic college and married to President Avila Camacho's niece, he took over the running of the automobile and media empire in 1955. During his tenure, he was a stalwart member of the business elite, branching out into air transport, sitting on the boards of U.S. banks, and helping to found the Mexican Council of Businessmen (Consejo Mexicano de Hombres de Negocios). By the late 1950s, he ran *Novedades* out of the television company's offices. The United States concluded that "his interests were so diverse that newspapers were only marginal."[19]

The Lanz Duret family, which owned the rival *El Universal*, also emerged from the postrevolutionary elite. Miguel Lanz Duret was born into an upper-class Mexico City family, was educated as a lawyer, and married into the family of Porfirian intellectual Justo Sierra. Although he moved into journalism, he kept up his law practice and was also elected a congress deputy.[20] On his death, his son, also called Miguel Lanz Duret, took over the newspaper. Like many "juniors," he possessed none of his father's easygoing charm. He was involved in Mexico's World War II conscription drive and would dress up in military uniform to impress his official standing on guests. The results were underwhelming. Gonzalo Santos called him a "pendejo" [jerk] and told him that he "insulted the army by playing games with conscripts." Journalist Jorge Piño Sandoval complained, "That bastard behaves like a general to journalists and like a journalist to generals."[21] As well as managing the newspaper, he presided over (and took private loans from) the Bank of Graphic Arts (Banco de Artes Gráficas). On his death in 1959, his widow, Francisca Dolores Valdés Delius, took control, presiding over a period of near financial ruin. In the late 1960s, she effectively ceded control to another well-connected member of the elite: her son-in-law, Juan Francisco Ealy Ortiz.[22]

Other major nationals like *Excélsior* and *La Prensa* were not privately owned. They were cooperatives; in theory they were managed by their employees. But during the postwar period, powerful directors controlled both companies with limited interference. These directors were less connected to the new business elite than the press barons. Rodrigo de Llano, editor of *Excélsior*, came from a middle-class Monterrey family, only finished secondary school, and started work as a journalist for the mass market *El Imparcial* at the age of seventeen.[23] Luis Novaro, the editor of *La Prensa* from 1940 to 1950, was a publicist from a middle-class Mexico City family; his successor, Mario Santaella, started his career as an office boy. But over the years, all acquired substantial business interests beyond their actual newspapers. De Llano branched out into the advertising industry and founded a New York–based publicity firm, which funneled U.S. ads toward the Mexican press.[24] Novaro established a private printing company, which gained exclusive rights to print Disney and other U.S. comics.[25] And Santaella used his position as general manager of *La Prensa* to acquire a vast fortune in cash and land.[26]

Such interests generated substantial progovernment support. Press barons and cooperative directors backed policies that buttressed their own business interests. In the words of one journalist, they aimed "to maintain the status quo . . . which has produced a substantial amount of income, a very comfortable lifestyle and a privileged place among the elites."[27] Public statements of ideological preference back this up. All spoke out against the threat of communism in the pages of their own newspapers or in front of assembled journalists at the annual Day of Press Freedom.[28] Most also expressed some degree of government support. Rómulo O'Farrill Jr. argued that the most important aspect of any political solution was that "it was structured within the PRI" and the vice president of another Mexico City paper, *Avance*, said that his paper's job was to "help the president."[29] In private letters, owners offered their backing more explicitly. In the midst of the 1968 student movement, Francisco Lanz Duret, the director of *El Universal*, confessed to the secretary of the interior that he too believed that "professional agitators" had taken over the student movement, declared that he was "in complete agreement with the authorities" and hoped that "peace and order" would be reestablished as soon as possible.[30]

Editors and journalists encompassed a slightly broader social and ideological spectrum than press owners. But most were middle-class and university educated. Guillermo Enríquez Simoní, editor of *Excélsior*, was from a wealthy, conservative Guadalajara family; *Excélsior* columnist Carlos Denegri was the son of a Mexican ambassador and secretary of finance; even the famous *nota roja* reporter Eduardo Téllez was from a wealthy lawyer's family.[31] Of the seventeen editors and writers profiled in the collection on postrevolutionary journalists, *La Vieja Guardia* [The Old Guard], fourteen were of clear middle-class heritage.[32] By the 1950s most journalists were also university graduates. *Excélsior* reporters Scherer, Manuel Mejido, and Jorge Velasco went to the National Autonomous University of Mexico (Universidad Nacional Autónoma de México, UNAM); *El Universal* correspondent José Pérez Moreno studied medicine.[33] Growing university courses in journalism cemented this trend. By 1964 UNAM produced 121 graduates in journalism per year; six years later, it produced 336.[34] In fact, by the 1970s, one U.S. observer discovered that three-quarters of journalists now had degrees.[35]

If most political journalists were middle class, they were also male. The press pack was not called the "chicos de la prensa" or "boys of the press" for nothing. During the immediate postrevolutionary period, a handful of female journalists moved into the newsrooms of Mexico City. Crop-haired, cigarette-smoking Cube Bonifant was the enfant terrible of the 1920s press and wrote a series of columns that challenged gender stereotypes and political norms.[36] But during the following decades, female political journalists were few.[37] Most female journalists, including dozens who graduated from the journalism degree at the Women's University of Mexico (Universidad Feminina de México), could only find work in what men disparaged as "the kitchen of journalism"—the society pages.[38] In fact, during the 1940s and 1950s women came to dominate the departments. By 1957, five of *El Universal's* six society correspondents were women. None were allowed in the journalists' union. Here, they covered marriages, baptisms, and births and carried out in cozy interviews with the rich and famous. Even the interviews with PRI politicians were boring. As one society correspondent remarked, "They were always the same; they simply got older."[39]

Finally, most editors and journalists of the big nationals were differing shades of right-wing. Most cut their teeth critiquing the social reforms of the Cárdenas era. Many, like *Hoy* head José Pagés Llergo, *Ultimas Noticias* editor Manuel Ordorica, *El Universal* columnist Alfonso Junco, and *Excélsior* editorialist Alfonso Pérez Vizcaíno, sympathized not only with Spanish Falangists but also with fascist dictators in Germany and Italy.[40] Salvador Borrego, *El Sol de México* editor and author of the first widely used journalism textbook, also wrote a tome in praise of the Third Reich.[41] Other writers like *Excélsior*'s Bernardo Ponce and Carlos Denegri were less extreme, but were still Catholic Hispanophiles. Denegri gave favorable interviews to Franco and wrote his "Miscelánea" column with an image of the Virgin of Guadalupe above his desk.[42] Others still, like *Tiempo* owner Martín Luis Guzmán, were liberal conservatives, who shared the early revolution's anticlericalism but not its commitment to social reform.[43] During the 1940s and 1950s, these right-wing writers dominated the editorials and columns of the big nationals. As late as 1964 the government classified four of *Novedades*'s editorialists as center-right, one as a "defender of the regime," and only one as "moderate."[44] Six years later, they put together a list of suspected "communists" working for the big nationals. They could find eight; only five were Mexican.[45] For these middle-class, right-wing journalists, supporting the PRI regime came easy; with the onset of the Cold War in the late 1940s, it tied in with their own interests and beliefs. Questioned about the *gran prensa*'s motives, an *El Universal* editor claimed that it "wasn't even an issue of corruption, it was an issue of ideological conviction." Most reporters "considered themselves part of a valid system."[46]

Of course, not all journalists were middle-class and right-wing. Some came from relatively poor backgrounds and some were also left-wing. They included writers for the low-selling Popular Party (Partido Popular, PP) organ, *El Popular,* and its successor, the marginally more successful *El Día*. And they comprised a handful of journalists for the deliberately pluralist weekly magazine *Siempre!* (Rius described the publication's varied correspondents as "of the right, of the left and of the extreme center, progovernment buffoons and defenders of the system. The corrupt and the incorruptible."[47]) This growing ideological diversity brought editors and journalists into sporadic conflict with the government throughout the period. But in general the culture of the *gran prensa* militated against open confrontation. Most journalists, even on the left, accepted the parameters of what constituted proper or good journalism.

These rules of the game were reiterated annually by officials and editors at the Day of Press Freedom, repeated in newspaper editorials, flagged up in discussions of papers that refused to follow these rules, and embedded in Mexico's handful of journalism textbooks. They also imbricated the everyday life of journalists, providing a set of cultural understandings that persuaded many writers to modify or tone down their critiques.

First, journalists accepted that they had certain responsibilities. Presidents regularly repeated this dictum in public announcements. President Ruiz Cortines claimed that the press "had a transcendental mission that brought with it serious responsibilities."[48] President Eustavo Díaz Ordaz (1964–1970) argued that freedom of the press "should be used with a deep sense of responsibility, in such a way that it is not used against the social body which maintains it and makes it possible."[49] Editors and journalists internalized this idea and reiterated it in public statements and editorials. For Santaella, journalism should only be practiced "with an awareness of the deep responsibility" the job entailed.[50] For Federico Barrera Fuentes, the director of *ABC*, good journalism "necessitated an understanding of the responsibility of the journalist to the nation."[51] Second, journalists believed that the public sphere, the area in which journalists worked and public opinion was formed, was a predominantly male space. This belief structured the division of labor. Men produced the political news, the *nota roja*, the editorials, and the columns; women were relegated to the society pages. Such assumptions also influenced the everyday language of the press. *Excélsior* editor Rodrigo de Llano was fond of saying that "the journalist should never sign anything that a gentleman cannot sign."[52] Good journalists were repeatedly described as virile or manly. Strong columns, powerful editorials, and news scoops demonstrated "virility."[53] But gendered language also configured what was unacceptable. For many journalists, personal attacks on politicians' private lives were nothing more than "chisme" or gossip, at best the subject of the female-run society pages, and at worst the preserve of illiterate women.[54]

These common understandings undergirded the aims of acceptable journalism. Responsible journalism, for example, was overtly nationalist. A speaker at a 1959 editors' meeting said that every journalist should be "a gentleman and a patriot."[55] In 1950, Miguel Alemán praised the Mexican press, whose mission, he stated, was to "let people know of the high cultural values and constructive efforts of the nation."[56] Three years later, Santaella told his fellow journalists that they should learn to "better serve the nation."[57] After the Day of Press Freedom in 1966, *El Universal* claimed the event proved that politicians and journalists had the "common idea of working incessantly in the construction of a strong and progressive father-land."[58]

Responsible journalism was also what Mexicans termed "transcendental"; that is, it concerned itself with the wider social consequences of the news. In Borrego's textbook he wrote that the job of a journalist was to make sense of various, apparently random events, and "perceive the future that the majority cannot see." This attitude shaped the way Mexican news articles were written. Borrego explained that journalists should write up relatively minor government achievements, like new roads or schools, by emphasizing what he called "significance of the work." A new road, for example, would "invigorate certain regions," "provide an impulse for certain economic activities," and "allow agricultural and industrial products to appear on the market." It also affected subeditors' roles. A new antinarcotics policy should not be headlined "Agreements against Drug Trafficking," but rather "Mexico Will Crush Drug Trafficking." Finally, it also structured the hierarchy of news stories. Thus Borrego advised editors to favor international over national stories and reports that highlighted the state's solutions to problems over those that dwelled on the problems themselves.[59] As the examples demonstrate, the implications of such an approach were profoundly conservative. It not only downplayed news that reflected negatively on the government, but also bathed everyday stories in a strange, optimistic, forward-looking glow or what one commentator called the "unmeasured and routine exaltations of national successes."[60]

Cultural assumptions of journalists' roles also marked the boundaries of what was deemed unacceptable or irresponsible. Irresponsible journalism attacked the private lives of public figures or indulged in what ministers and writers termed *libertinaje* or debauchery. The term had gendered connotations and was often used to describe female or homosexual licentiousness. The rule against attacking private lives was embedded in Article 6 of the Constitution and the 1917 Press Law.[61] In the capital, officials rarely invoked the law, but when they did, journalists used the opportunity to share their own understanding. For example in 1944, the Mexican government used the law to put the editor of *El Sinarquista* on trial for "attacks on . . . the rights of third parties." In an editorial during the trial, *El Universal* explained that in "well-organized societies," there were not "absolute liberties. . . . The rights of individuals have as a limit the rights of others." Journalists should be held to the same rules. Where they are not, "this is not liberty of the press, it is libertinaje."[62] Legal cases of *libertinaje* faded away, but officials and press workers repeatedly invoked the ideal. At a meeting of editors in 1959, the head reminded journalists that "liberty must be exercised with dignity and patriotism without arriving at degeneration and libertinaje."[63]

Irresponsible journalism also practiced "demagoguery," the deliberate whipping up of the masses for political ends. After the Cuban Revolution, officials and journalists increasingly warned against this style of writing, arguing that it could lead to disorder. At the Day of Press Freedom in 1961, López Mateos accused "some hidden and some visible forces ... with their insistence on using freedom of expression" of "trying to confuse free and independent peoples by promoting among them undue antagonisms and unfounded alarm."[64] Throughout the 1960s, editorials repeated this refrain. *El Sol de México* attacked publications that "made attacks on public peace through spreading distortions and lies about the life and realities of the country." *La Prensa* warned that journalism "should not be an instrument of permanent struggle, but motivated by the liberty to search for the good."[65]

Finally, irresponsible journalism wallowed in negativity and scandal. Again, officials warned against this. Ruiz Cortines told journalists not to "encourage skepticism or amplify ... negative events ... and, in so doing, sow versions that ... drive our compatriots to think that they live in inferior situations to that which they really do."[66] Press owners echoed these sentiments. O'Farrill Jr. refuted the idea that "we should engage in yellow journalism or sensationalism, since in doing so, we would distort information and misguide our readers."[67] Again, journalists reiterated these assumptions. In 1967, Scherer claimed that it was not the role of journalists to "foment illegitimate scandal or the morbid exploitation of the lowest feelings." Linking scandal-mongering back to *libertinaje* and demagoguery, he argued that such acts "damaged public order and the interests of third parties."[68]

If common ideas of what constituted acceptable journalism disciplined journalists, the boozy world of the *gran prensa* solidified the ties among politicians, press owners, and writers and normalized these ideas. This world comprised shared social spaces like the high-class Ambassadeurs restaurant, located next to the offices of *Excélsior*. Here Rodrigo de Llano entertained politicians, celebrities, and other journalists, who paid 50 pesos (a worker's daily wage) for lunch or 15 pesos for a small scotch.[69] Other journalists' haunts included more bohemian spaces like the bullfighter journalists' favorite, the Café Campoamor on Bolivar, or Café Kiko on the corner of Juárez and Bucareli, where the tables were covered with "notebooks and sheets of paper" and journalists "dictated, wrote, and noted" nursing one coffee or soda for an entire afternoon.[70] They included down-at-heel cantinas like El Morro, next to the National Lottery where journalist Renato Leduc, porn entrepreneur Vicente Ortega Colunga, and six-times-married Antonio Arias Bernal chatted up Sinaloa waitresses.[71] They include private houses like Carlos Denegri's home in south Mexico City where *Excélsior's* managers and journalists mixed with artists, politicians, and gangsters' molls.[72] And inevitably, they also included cabarets and brothels like the infamous Casa de la Bandida.[73]

This world also included shared leisure activities. Most involved drinking. Leduc depicted Pagés Llergo as "one of the worst drunks, not so hammered that you would know it, but he always had a bottle of vodka there. . . . He drunk two or three bottles and did it every day."[74] Scherer described De Llano aka el Skipper as drunk twice a day, "once at 3 p.m. and once again at night." He "drank until the limit of drunkenness."[75] Fellow *Excélsior* writer Bernardo Ponce often missed deadlines because he was "in a state of drunkenness from Friday to Wednesday." Though he claimed a chronic illness, his editor confirmed that his only sickness "was from drunkenness."[76] Drinking exploits added to journalists' reputations. Julio Manuel Morales Ferrón would arrive half-cut at a vaudeville performance every Friday night and give a five-minute condensed version of a contemporary book in front of a jeering, beery audience.[77] Journalists' memoirs are replete with references to the daily meetings at the cantina where they would share stories and notes.[78] Drinking even overran the newsroom itself. Confronted with a poor article, Ordorica gave the offending journalist 5 pesos, ordered him to swig three drinks and write down the information again. The journalist obeyed. "You write much better when you're drunk," Ordorica complimented him.[79]

This world also comprised a shared language. As we saw in chapter 1, columnists developed a lexicon of terms to describe the murky world of electoral politics and shifting ambitions. They also developed an array of nicknames, shorthand phrases, and slurs to describe individual politicians. As we shall see they all shared terms for the small acts of corruption that constituted their everyday relations with government officials. In their exchanges they mixed this private patois with a littering of friendly insults and sly digs. Spanish émigré Luis Suárez admitted that the journalists on the congressional beat even came up with a word for refusing to share stories—*chacalear* [a slang term that usually meant "to rob"].[80] Although it was not their intention, during the 1960s secret service agents often picked up these rich, funny conversations when they tapped editors' phones. Take this conversation between *Siempre!* editor Pagés Llergo and muckraking journalist Blanco Moheno in July 1962:

Blanco: *No estas jugando ningún chingado jueguito.*

Blanco: You're not playing some fucking game.

Pagés: *No que chingados le importa a usted eso . . . a ver.*

Pagés: What the fuck do you care . . . come on.

Blanco: *Cómo que chingados me importa, tenemos que consultarle a usted una cosa.*

Blanco: What do you mean what the fuck do I care; I need to ask you about something.

Pagés: *Me importa madre, alguna pendejada tiene que ser.*

Pagés: I don't give a fuck; it has to be some stupid shit.

Blanco: *Vaya usted mucho a la chingada. . . . mira, es absolutamente cierto que existen los dos cacicazgos, una en Puebla, y otro en Michoacán de los dos hermanitos.*

Blanco: Go fuck yourself . . . look, it's absolutely certain that there are two *cacicazgos*, one in Puebla and another in Michoacán of the two little brothers.

Pagés: *Uno es de AC, el otro es de otra naturaleza.*

Pagés: One is of AC [Avila Camacho] and the other is of another sort.

Blanco: *Es de Don Lázaro.*

Blanco: It's of Don Lázaro [Cárdenas].

Pagés: *No, no, no.*

Pagés: No, no, no.

Blanco: *Ah, hay esta, ya no me suponia yo, es absolutamente cierto, Pagés, incluso cuando este cabrón Damaso agarró el gobierno, Don Lázaro no le habló más de un año, Pagés . . . deveras . . . José*

Blanco: That's how it is, I'm not making it up, it's absolutely certain, Pagés, including when that bastard Damaso [Lázaro's brother] got the governorship, Don Lázaro didn't speak to him for more than a year, Pagés . . . it's true . . . José.

Pagés: *Pero esas cosas no se pueden decir.*

Pagés: But these kind of things you can't say.

Blanco: *Y tu?*

Blanco: And you?

Pagés: *No es que no . . . no es que no . . . no se deben de decir fundamentalmente . . . no.*

Pagés: It's not no . . . it's not no, . . . I don't know, these things should not be said fundamentally . . . no.

Blanco: *Es una cosa en beneficio de Don Lázaro.*

Blanco: It'll benefit Don Lázaro.

Pagés: *No, no es en beneficio de nadie ... no ... no ... al contrario, no para destruir el prestigio de una persona que es un cabrón. Es una ... es un ahorro que uno tiene al banco.*

Blanco: *Puedo chingar a López Arias, piensa que es Al Capone y mandó a 100 soldados a invadir un pueblo cómo si fuera una guerra. ... Esta enfermo este cabrón ... Lombardo dice que lo único que desea es que se le de en la madre a López Arias ... ver la forma de joder a López Arias, no?*

Pagés: *Pues si.*

Pagés: No, it'll benefit no one ... no ... no ... on the contrary not to destroy the prestige of a big man. It's a ... it's a saving in the bank.

Blanco: Can I fuck up [Fernando] López Arias instead? He thinks he's Al Capone and sent 100 soldiers in to invade a village like it was a war. ... he's sick that bastard. ... Lombardo [Toledano] says that all he wants is that I fuck up López Arias ... find a way to fuck up López Arias no?

Pagés: Ok, yes.[81]

The exchange reveals the ways in which editors and journalists negotiated over sensitive subjects (in 1962, Lázaro Cárdenas was balancing support for the left-wing Movement of National Liberation [Movimiento de Liberación Nacional, MLN] with occasional pronouncements on behalf of the government), the sensitivity of any discussion of politicians' private lives, the coded ways in which they talked about not publicizing stories (not putting out the Cárdenas article is referred to as a "saving in the bank," presumably to be withdrawn, when necessary, later on), but perhaps, above all, the way that insults and profanities formed the lingua franca of the Mexico City press.

This world not only offered space to unwind, it also solidified close friendships. Just as in the political world, friendship proved the key currency in securing jobs and favors.[82] By the 1970s, one U.S. survey found that over 70 percent of journalists claimed their friends were fellow writers.[83] Blanco Moheno described journalism as the "camaraderie of drink and the distributing of centavos."[84] Berta Hidalgo nostalgically remembered "the press room in which we got to know each other and shared experiences, chats, anecdotes, advice, and cups of tea." Here, she concluded, "there was camaraderie and comradeship."[85] These friendships spanned internal newspaper hierarchies and ideological differences. When De Llano laughed, "everyone laughed with him."[86] Mejido and Scherer were both left-wing sympathizers, but they both liked and admired the conservative Denegri. In fact, most of the leftists who took over the newspaper in the mid-1960s were Denegri's protégés.[87] Such friendships spread rumors and gossip but also general understandings of the unwritten rules, which guided news writing in the immediate postwar era. Old hands like Pagés Llergo, De Llano, Denegri, and Ordorica mentored their enthusiastic younger colleagues, reinforcing the bounds of acceptable and unacceptable journalism. Blanco Moheno remembered them berating young journalists: "What class of disgusting betrayal to publish what is not in the bulletin, or what the minister doesn't want, or what is going to irritate the ambassador."[88]

Finally, if implicit codes of conduct and peer pressure didn't work, owners and editors had other methods to discipline troublesome journalists. Foremost among them was sacking. In 1952, for example, the political magazine *Tiempo* published a photograph of workers angrily beating a government secret service agent at the annual May Day demonstrations. The subeditor adulterated the photograph in order to avoid the authorities identifying the assailants. The editor, Martín Luis Guzmán, immediately fired him and sacked or forced the resignation of the left-wing journalists who supported him, claiming that they were "agents or linkmen to international communism."[89] Nine years later, Ramón Beteta, the editor of *Novedades*, sacked the editor of the cultural supplement, Fernando Benítez, for communist sympathies.[90] In fact, during the increasingly divided Cold War atmosphere of the late 1950s and 1960s, some individual journalists were regularly sacked for expressing left-wing views. Cartoonist Rius found it hard to hold down a job. In 1959, Beteta sacked him for going to Cuba in the immediate wake of the revolution. In the following years *Ovaciones* sacked him (because his cartoons "didn't agree with the editor's desires"); *El Universal* sacked him twice (once for including "red propaganda" and once for describing the American Revolution as left-wing); and the *El Diario de México* sacked him for joining a union.[91]

The Government Publicity Machine

Broadly hegemonic ideologies and internalized beliefs on journalistic practices, enforced by close friendships and the threat of dismissal, persuaded many *gran prensa* writers to cover stories about the state and the ruling party in a relatively favorable manner. But during the period, the government's spin machine also played an increasingly important role. The first efforts were underfunded and poorly organized. Officials viewed controlling newspaper output as very much a secondary concern. During the 1940s newspaper control was still impromptu and sporadic. It also often involved rather cack-handed direct intervention. During the 1950s, things changed. Under President Ruiz Cortines, the government imposed press offices on all government departments and started the mass production of bulletins, intended to guide journalists' copy. At the same time savvy publicity agents concocted subtle press campaigns designed to soften or misdirect coverage of controversial policies. During the next decade, Cold War political divisions and the emergence of a mass readership combined to harden and professionalize government attitudes to the press. Public relations ideas penetrated the government and the Ministry of the Interior (Secretaría de Gobernación) expanded its role. The president's press officer bullied and intimidated editors and journalists. The ministry expanded and refined its bulletin-writing, creating fake news agencies and forcing newspapers to accept prewritten columns.

Mexico's postrevolutionary governments had always used publicity strategies. But in 1937 the government institutionalized the state's propaganda role, creating a central office within the Ministry of the Interior, the Autonomous Department of Press and Publicity (Departamento Autónomo de Prensa y Publicidad, DAPP). The new department had an extremely broad remit. Officials were instructed to direct the government's entire propaganda effort. To do so they needed to coordinate between different ministries, provide information to national and international media outlets, issue letters, circulars, and bulletins, and run all the stand-alone government publications, state radio stations, *El Diario Oficial*, the national archive, and the state printing company.[92] At the same time, the DAPP comprised a fairly small staff. The head, Agustín Arroyo Ch., was a journalist and politician, a former governor of Guanajuato, and the subsecretary of the Ministry of the Interior. He was popular and self-effacing. Novo described him as "chubby, talkative, cordial, and open."[93] But he only had eighteen employees, and most were inexperienced. In fact, Arroyo himself used to mock his department's limited capabilities. In a 1937 *Hoy* article, he admitted that the department couldn't "produce enough information to fill the needs of the dailies" and joked that journalists thought DAPP stood for "Dame Algo Para Publicar" or "Give me something to publish." He even confessed that writers played on the meaning of his surname, *arroyo*, or stream, to complain about the new department's poor service. "Nos dijeron que iba a ser un mar de informaciones, pero resulta un arroyo" [They told us that there would be a sea of information, but there is only a stream].[94]

Glancing through the jumbled documents of the DAPP archive, one quickly gets the impression that the department was chaotic and overworked. Individual staff members do not seem to have specialized in any one project or media, and replies to inquiries took months rather than weeks. At the same time, in these early years the department concentrated on broad visual and audio campaigns, designed to appeal to an illiterate audience. In 1937, it promoted the Six-Year Plan with an exhibition at the Bellas Artes and short radio spots. Next, it ran a visual campaign to promote both internal and foreign tourism called Pro México. The two state radio stations took up much of the staff's time. Here, they recorded official speeches but also wrote educational programs on national geography, history, sports, music, and literacy.[95]

In 1939, the DAPP changed its name to the State Office of Information (Dirección General de Información, DGI). During the early 1940s, the office focused on producing propaganda for the war effort, writing circulars, radio broadcasts, and posters. The department was still fairly chaotic. In 1942, the department head, former *El Nacional* journalist José Altamirano, complained that propaganda was still not centralized. Rather, there was an "anarchy of systems" and publicity was often produced by "unprepared persons."[96] Furthermore, dealing with the press came second to producing comprehensible visual and audio propaganda for a mass audience. In Altamirano's 1942 proposals for improving the publicity effort, he never mentioned the Mexico City press, instead advising that the government invest in cinema ads, trucks with loudhailers, street drama, and conferences. The aim was national coverage, not targeted manipulation. Peasants were the intended audience. The only printed texts that he mentioned were "pamphlets, posters, cartoons, and corridos," designed for the illiterate and semiliterate.[97] Other propaganda plans demonstrated a similar indifference toward the printed press. As late as 1949, a Ministry of the Interior program to "establish a complete system of information" and "orient the people with respects to the big national problems" failed to even mention newspapers.[98]

Rather than use the new publicity department to deal with Mexico City's newspapers, state officials instead took a personal, informal approach.[99] Such interventions could be both public and uncomfortable. On May 10, 1941, *Hoy* published a small article entitled "National Politics," which described President Avila Camacho's cabinet attending the birthday party of former president Cárdenas's young son. Written in a light manner, the piece claimed that some of the children were "100 years old" (a reference to the balding minister Eduardo Hay). But the piece ended with a sharp rebuke, clearly designed to embarrass the president. "It is easy to understand that the first of May was not a day that favored high politics, notwithstanding the fact that near the site of the party, the President of the PRM [Partido de la Revolución Mexicana or Party of the Mexican Revolution] was deciding what to do in Puebla and whether to distance himself from San Luis Potosí where Pérez Gallardo has taken the reins of government." The implication was clear. Avila Camacho was playing at a child's birthday party while others were arranging matters of state. In response, President Avila Camacho composed a po-faced reply, which *Hoy* published the following week. The president argued that the piece was "foreign to the gravity and depth of the problems now facing the state," accused *Hoy*'s editors of displaying "malevolent intentions under the cloak of joviality," and recommended that journalists adopt an attitude of "respectful reserve."[100]

Avila Camacho's riposte was a public relations disaster. *Ultimas Noticias* announced that the president had made a mistake by writing it; and *Jueves de Excélsior* ran a front-page cartoon with the president desperately whitewashing a crumbling house. But there was worse to come. *Hoy* editor Regino Hernández Llergo's reply was a masterpiece of measured sarcasm. He sardonically thanked the president for his "lessons in journalism." He said he found nothing that violated the rules of ethics or desecrated the sanctity of the home. In short, he had not committed *libertinaje*. He claimed that it was difficult to write up a kids' party "as one would describe the representation of a work of Aeschylus." In the next section, he put forward a committed defense of satire, arguing that "Aristophanes was as serious as Aeschylus and Juvenal as solemn as the Aeneid," and that popular art, like Arias Bernal's cartoons or Novo's witticisms, were as politically important as more earnest works. In the conclusion, he focused on the president's thin-skinned reaction to the original article, deftly highlighting the government's ramshackle approach to press relations. "The Mexican people cannot understand why their president is addressing a newspaper for the first time just to discuss trivialities."[101]

In chapter 3, Miguel Alemán's press strategy was equally unrehearsed but slightly more successful, combining personal intervention with coercion and anticommunism. But it was during Ruiz Cortines's presidency that the government's spin machine changed dramatically.[102] On assuming the presidency in December 1952, the former public relations bureaucrat decreed that all official news would go through department press offices. The DGI should coordinate between them. Individual relations between journalists and officials were prohibited. Instead press officers would hand journalists press bulletins, which they were expected to modify or simply repeat. Initially, the policy caused serious resentment. On March 10, 1953, the owner of *El Universal*, Lanz Duret, published an editorial that slammed the new method of interaction. The new system, he argued, "nullified the efforts of reporters" and "converted them into mere messengers." Over the next few days *Excélsior* ran a series of cartoons that also critiqued the new government policy. In one sketch, entitled "Useless Offices," a man with a chain around his mouth put his head out of a press office. In another called "Filtered News," press offices strained news into the mouth of a reporter.[103]

Despite the complaints, the Mexican government now channeled most news through their expanded press departments in the form of bulletins. All departments now ran press offices, and the DGI expanded to 57 full-time staff. In the first year of Ruiz Cortines's presidency they produced 4,015 bulletins. By 1956 they almost hit 5,000.[104] These press bulletins changed the way stories were written, regimenting and standardizing official news. Many journalists simply typed up the press releases without further research or even putting them in house style. They even had a term for it: *refritear,* or to refry.[105] A 1958 U.S. survey of over fifty Mexican journalists found that 43 percent published bulletins "as received"; 3 percent occasionally rewrote them; 43 percent always rewrote them; and only 11 percent never published them on principal.[106] Such an approach not only made official news extremely monotonous, it also narrowed the editorial distinctions between newspapers and changed the role of the political reporter. Berta Hidalgo witnessed the shift. She explained that in the 1940s journalists took bulletins "as a reference only." Editors would not "accept a single note which only contained the facts from the bulletin." But by the following decade, reporters simply "repeated them and signed them."[107] Leduc described reporters as "*boletineros*" whose only job was to "collect a press bulletin accompanied by an envelope [of money]."[108] Carlos Monsiváis was equally damning, arguing that the press bulletin "naturalized" censorship, allowing "less space for misunderstanding."[109] The bulletins shaped what one Brazilian journalist termed the "monotonous vacuity" of the national press.[110] In fact, such was the influence of these bulletins, Pagés Llergo surmised that just as "we make chocolate without cacao and cigarettes without tobacco, we have now created journalism without journalists."[111]

Despite the increasingly professional approach there were still problems with government public relations. In an anonymous 1955 interview, a public relations insider gave his opinions on the new regime. He maintained that the government's publicity effort was still weak and diffuse. Coordination was minimal. The government was "divided, subdivided, and infradivided into dozens of different departments and decentralized companies." These each had their own press offices, which often worked on behalf of their political chiefs rather than the government as a whole. Some were relatively efficient. In the Ministry of Communications and Public Works (Secretaría de Comunicaciones y Obras Públicas, SCOP) press chief Arturo Arnáiz y Freg worked "incessantly." In the Department of Hydraulic Resources (Departamento de

Recursos Hidráulicos), the journalist turned press officer Antonio Sáenz de Miera had used his press contacts to good effect. But others were less successful. In the Ministry of the Economy (Secretaría de Economía), the bulletins were "unclear and superficial" and the press chief spent most of his time dealing with his own magazine. And the Ministry of National Defense (Secretaría de Defensa Nacional) had "no understanding of journalists' needs."[112]

During the Ruiz Cortines administration the presidential press secretary also increased in importance. Presidents had always employed personnel who had direct contact with the press. But Ruiz Cortines's press secretary, Humberto Romero Pérez, took on a new, expanded role. Romero was born in the rural Michoacán town of La Piedad, where he started as a small-town radio presenter before moving to Mexico City to gain a law degree. Here he became close to Alemán and worked as attorney general from 1946 to 1952 and as head of the Department of Work's (Departamento del Trabajo) press office in 1952.[113] Negotiating the tense relations among the state, the unions, and the press during the contentious 1952 elections gave him ample experience with the media world. On his election, Ruiz Cortines made him his press secretary. In this job, he assumed a more proactive role than his predecessors, working closely with the DGI and other departments' press offices to design custom-built, unified press strategies to control the media reaction to certain government policies. He was, in effect, Mexico's first spin doctor. Success brought rewards, and in 1958 López Mateos made him his private secretary.

To my knowledge, written evidence of only one of these plans still exists. It concerns what seems a relatively minor event, the hiking up of petrol prices in late August 1954. But it reveals a new sophistication and guile in government public relations far beyond the previous techniques. The era of the "dark arts" had begun. The ten-page document laid out a series of strategies designed to generate positive coverage of the move. First, he explained the government's essential rationale for the price rise in simple terms. Then he suggested official publicists should broadcast these ideas by approaching the editors of all the major dailies and magazines, using the government radio station, employing the services of "friendly writers" to pen favorable editorials, and putting aside PEMEX and presidency publicity funds to pay off reporters. He then expounded the details of the plan, including made-to-measure slogans, three separate press releases stressing different aspects of the price rise, and a coordinated plan for every department press office. Finally, he counseled the methods whereby different media should deliver this information. News editors were to quote anonymous members of civil society, who allegedly supported the move. The entire campaign should be couched in nationalist rhetoric. "We should use the campaign to strengthen the civic spirit of the people of Mexico." The campaign's "mystique is Mexico."[114]

But it was the plan's addendum—termed "Indirect Themes"—that was most revealing. Here, the press secretary suggested that the government invent other major stories in order to deflect attention away from the rise. "Every event has a media cycle, and in the metropolis stories normally only last two weeks. However, we can shorten the story's cycle by creating indirect themes." Among the "indirect themes" he proposed were the "capture of a millionaire criminal" (this would "reveal the corruption in the cinema industry, a theme which fascinates the public"), "the sending to Toluca of [i.e., extrajudicial murder of] the authors of some assault," "the cleansing of the political make-up of some state" and "the holding of a Ratón Macías boxing match." The public relations technique of the diversionary story has been around for some time. Luis Estrada's recent satire on media corruption, *La Dictadura Perfecta*, termed the gambit "the caja china" or Chinese box. The expression is a literary term used to denote a story within a story. But here it was used to describe a fabricated news story, which could be repeatedly expanded to fill the news cycle and obscure negative press. In the film, Estrada showed how contemporary media executives used the kidnapping of a couple of young girls to avert public attention from government corruption.[115] Was Romero's diversionary strategy the first ever Chinese box? Was this why Romero gained semilegendary status within the inner sanctum of the PRI? It seems that it was.

On September 25, 1954, a series of small bulletins appeared hidden away in the middle pages of all the major Mexico City papers. The general manager of PEMEX announced that "after a careful study of rising prices in terms of salaries, equipment, materials and exploration" the company had decided to raise prices the following week.[116] On September 27 the prices went up and a week later bus prices also rose. There were major protests.[117] But the nationals ignored them. Instead they ran the story according to Romero's plan. Editorials defended the rise. *La Prensa*'s editorial was headlined "Raising the Price of Fuel Is Today a Patriotic Imperative" (evoking Romero's "Mexican mystique"). They quoted an unnamed "distinguished economist" (Romero's anonymous member of civil society), explaining that "to maintain the rhythm of economic development of the country and to respond satisfactorily to the growing demand for fuels" PEMEX needed to make investments. The economist also claimed that refining machinery had increased in price by 78 percent. Both the quote and the figure were lifted verbatim from the government press release. The *Excélsior* editorial of the same day was eerily similar. The headline again played on nationalist sentiment: "It should be considered indispensible

that PEMEX increases its output for the good of the country." The quote
that offered the reasons for the rise was exactly the same as that in *La
Prensa*, although *Excélsior* did not claim the argument came from the mouth
of a "distinguished economist." And the fact used to support the reasons was
also identical.[118]

But in general, the petrol price rise received minimal coverage. Two events
kept it off the front page. They were exactly those suggested by Romero in his
media plan: a Ratón Macias boxing match and the arrest of a cinema impresario, Gabriel Alarcón. The boxing match took place on September 26 at the
Mexico City bullring. It was a huge event; over 60,000 Mexicans attended. El
Ratón (aka Raúl Macías Guevara) was a local hero, a poor Tepito boy who
had won ten straight bouts to become Mexico's most famous boxer. "The
crowd went wild for Macias." When he beat U.S. challenger Nate Brooks and
dedicated his victory to the Virgin of Guadalupe, "it caused a national commo-
tion."[119] Tabloids like *La Prensa* devoted ample space to the boxer. On September 27, the day Mexicans woke up to the increased petrol prices, the front
page announced "El Ratón Champion of America. The crowds go mad for his
victory over Nate Brooks" and "Ratón's boxing match will be on television and
radio." Four pages of in-depth coverage followed.[120] Over the next two weeks,
the newspaper maintained a steady stream of stories about his chances of a
world title fight, his charity work, and his welcome at UNAM. *La Prensa* even
organized a celebrity-packed public celebration of the fighter.[121]

The Alarcón scandal was more complicated. On August 10, 1954, former
Union of Workers of the Cinema Industry (Sindicato de Trabajadores de la
Industria Cinematográfica) leader Alfonso Mascarúa was stabbed, shot, and
killed outside his house in Mexico City. At first, the papers cast suspicion on
a rival union leader. But a week before the petrol price rise, the focus of the
inquiry suddenly changed. The police arrested three Alarcón associates.
They pointed the finger at the millionaire cinema owner.[122] As Romero an-
ticipated, the accusations precipitated a wave of alarmist articles. Journalists
filled the pages with stories about the murky worlds of plutocrats and hit
men, dredged up stories of previous murders, and followed the police's frustrated attempts to arrest Alarcón. The case became a veritable soap opera. It
dragged on for twenty days overlapping almost exactly with the price rise
story. First, the police acquired an arrest warrant; then Alarcón applied for an
amparo; then the *amparo* was overturned; then he escaped capture by fleeing
in the trunk of a friend's car; finally he claimed a grave heart condition that
precluded his arrest.[123] Meanwhile in the jail, the three hit men changed their
stories, got sick, and fought with one another. Editorials railed against the

"arrogant empire of impunity" previously enjoyed by the playboy business-man and reassured Mexicans that under Ruiz Cortines the law would make "no distinction between rich and poor." Cartoonists entertained readers with witty cartoons about the case. In one, two women discussed their love lives. "I want to find myself a millionaire." "Don't worry, just go and get a bus ticket to jail."[124]

So were the two stories just remarkably fortuitous events that the govern-ment cleverly exploited to dump bad news? Or was the undated press plan written after Mascarúa's murder, which Romero saw as a crime to pin on an unpopular cinema impresario? Or, most shockingly of all, did government forces deliberately murder Mascarúa to divert public attention away from the price increase? Was the Mascarúa killing a Chinese box? There is certainly evidence that the government was involved in the murder. Alarcón's lawyers argued that a hit man and fixer with secret service links, nicknamed "El Jaro-cho," had tried to frame Alarcón. He probably did the hit and he certainly fingered Alarcón as the "autor intelectual" or "intellectual author."[125] We shall probably never know the exact truth. Fortuitous, opportunist, or supremely Machiavellian, Romero's plan demonstrated that the presidential spin machine was capable of impressive manipulation.

But Romero's plan was only the beginning. Under López Mateos and Díaz Ordaz, the government's publicity machine expanded yet again. Here as in the United States, growing links between officials and private advertisers played a key role.[126] For years publicists had argued that they shared a com-mon purpose with the state. Advertising integrated Mexicans into the nation as consumers. "By teaching people to purchase," advertising ensured national growth.[127] But during the late 1950s, publicists also started to argue for adver-tising's political potential. Ads could shape social behavior as well as con-sumer patterns. For advertising mogul Eulalio Ferrer, publicity could "replace the role of education."[128] Such claims garnered official interest. In 1959, pri-vate advertisers joined with the government to form the National Board of Publicity (Consejo Nacional de Publicidad, CNP).[129] Over the next five years, the organization's members worked closely with Díaz Ordaz's Ministry of the Interior to develop social campaigns. In 1960, they tried to persuade pri-vate citizens to repair schools, pay taxes, and vote. Three years later, they ran a campaign designed to promote "Personal Improvement." The ads, which ran in the press and on the radio, cost 419,000 pesos and were designed to instill a sense of shame and guilt in parents so that they would take better care of their children.[130]

These institutional and intellectual links generated a flurry of proposals on how the government should harness advertising for broader political means. In 1963, CNP head Antonio Menéndez published *Movilización Social*, which combined a potted history of the publicity business with recommendations for the state's use of these techniques. He argued that, in order to ensure the country's economic and social development, the state needed to engage Mexicans' "voluntary, universal, and enthusiastic cooperation." To do so, he suggested using public relations techniques, employing surveys and quantitative analysis to measure the concerns of determined audiences, and then modeling media campaigns according to these concerns.[131] By the first year of Díaz Ordaz's presidency, government officials were developing many of these ideas. They started to view media policy not as a means to dilute or explain unpopular measures but as the primary means of influencing the Mexican people—a central, and perhaps *the* central, aspect of state policy. For example, in September 1965, press officer Alicio Rafael Ordoño gave a speech at the Department of Hydraulic Resources. Echoing Ferrer's words, he argued that "the education and development of the country" was not simply about schools "but about the media." "The cultural formation of a country depends on the orientation and efficiency of its informative apparatus." As a result "it is absolutely logical that the government uses the services and insights of the mass publicity industry to inform and stimulate the citizenry."[132] An internal Ministry of the Interior memo came to similar conclusions, arguing that any government was only as "effective as the amount it knows about public opinion and its procedures to influence it." To guide skeptical citizens the government needed to employ the "intensive, global, and uninterrupted diffusion of publicity through all media outlets." Bulletins were now "not enough." The government had to think beyond the "mechanical and cold" media policy of old and instead make information "attractive and didactic."[133]

In the same year, another author put together the most detailed, cogent vision of this new approach to media policy in another ministry memo. The piece started by arguing that the state needed to naturalize obedience so that citizens "adopt[ed] the expected conduct without searching for the reasons why they did so." To do this, the government needed to employ the kind of "political propaganda" that penetrated the "subconscious of the citizen" so certain actions became "mental habits." It needed, in short, to create what the author termed an "invisible tyranny." This propaganda would be constant, issued through multiple formats, adopt the language and culture of the group it sought to control, and instill a moral imperative for government support. The report also laid out detailed advice for how to influence newspapers in partic-ular. First, the author suggested moving beyond simply issuing press bulle-tins. Instead the government needed to adapt propaganda to newspapers' diverse styles. State publicists must be "descriptive in the gacetillas, reflexive in the editorials, and insinuating and suggestive in the columns and reports." Second, they had to influence newspapers' layouts, where the stories were placed, how they were headlined, and how they were presented. Third, the government could force newspapers to adhere to their demands by using debts to PIPSA and the health department as leverage. Finally, the state needed to centralize its publicity efforts rather than allow individual bureaucrats to run their own private press offices. If a magazine or newspaper attacked a par-ticular ministry, all state press officers would unite and agree to pull their funding.[134]

To what extent the document influenced government thinking, it is hard to say. Jacinto Rodríguez Munguía views it as a roadmap for future policy.[135] I am less convinced. As we shall see, some of the policies were implemented. The government moved beyond issuing dry press bulletins and used debts to leverage control. But the document seems to have been directed as much at the PRI as at the state administration, and party propaganda never acquired such sophistication. Despite government efforts, state press offices never centralized completely. Individual politicians continued to use ministry press officers and individual contacts with journalists to pursue private ambitions. (The Mexico City mayor, Ernesto Uruchurtu, used his budget to fund the highly critical fortnightly *Política*.)[136] And, the effects of the new media strat-egy were never as pronounced as the report hoped. Mexicans learned to deci-pher the new propaganda and came up with ways to undermine and counter government domination.

However overconfident the report, it does highlight how seriously the Mexican government now treated media control. This new strategic thinking generated institutional change. Under President López Mateos, the DGI ex-panded yet again. Monterrey-born law graduate and former radio announcer Luis M. Farias now employed a staff of over sixty. At least a dozen were simply employed to clip newspapers.[137] The department had the numbers and finan-cial clout to observe foreign, national, and regional publications, monitor and transcribe TV and radio programs, sponsor associations of editors and jour-nalists, set up and coordinate state-level press departments, work with adver-tising agencies, and develop close contacts with the Ministry of the Interior's DGIPS.[138] Starting in the early 1960s, the group tapped the phones of suspect pressmen, including *Siempre!* editor Pagés Llergo, and passed the information on to the DGI. But the department did more than monitor and coordinate. In 1961, the U.S. government described Farias as "the fountainhead of press guidance for the administration." He frequently called members of the press for a briefing or to give out specific news items. Journalists also called him in order to ask for information and guidance. "A simple hint by him seems to have been sufficient to kill a story and it is understood that editors generally check controversial stories with him before publishing them."[139]

Under Díaz Ordaz, the structure of the institutions dedicated to media control changed once again. The Ministry of the Interior now took over direct control of the monitoring of the press. The shift reflected the new importance given to the mass media. But it also reflected the interests of the new minister, Luis Echeverría. The future president was obsessed with the press. A former student writer and a frustrated journalist, he spent his evenings poring over the next day's proofs for *El Nacional*. He kept an eye on PIPSA meetings and newspapers' escalating debts. He even appointed his right-hand man, Mario Moya Palencia, as director general of the organization in 1968.[140] For broader reviews, he employed private public relations companies, like Informac, which gave monthly surveys and analyses of press coverage, or Metrolineaje, which tallied newspapers' sources of advertising revenue.[141] The two secret service departments, the DFS and the DGIPS, also started to devote their energies to monitoring the internal workings of both favorable and dissident publications. They had informants in *Excélsior*, *La Prensa*, *El Universal*, and popular crime magazine *Alarma*. They tapped the phones of *La Prensa* head Mario Santaella as well as left-wing journalists like *Siempre!* writer Victor Rico Galán, Cuban news agency chief Edmundo Jardón, and *Política* head Manuel Marcué Pardiñas.[142] Such intrusions allowed them to oversee companies' finances, office politics, and journalists' affairs. They provided the raw material for press harassment and dirty tricks campaigns.

Beyond increased surveillance, the ministry put Enrique Abrego Ortega in charge of the DGI. The new director general was close to Echeverría and helped coordinate day-to-day relations between the press and the ministries' press offices. As the various public relations reports proposed, these offices didn't simply issue bulletins, they now tried to influence newspapers' coverage. In 1969, the U.S. State Department reported that "the director or editor of a newspaper which carries material or is considering carrying material which a ministry dislikes is given a telephone call or breakfast meeting with the director of information of said ministry." The head is then told, "in an oblique but completely reasonable fashion" what "approach the government is taking on the issue at hand." Directors who had received this treatment "tell us that the message is always unmistakable." If the newspapers refused, Abrego stepped in. He was the "key man in policy guidance" and his interference "always carrie[d] with it the possible use of the state's police powers."[143]

Together Echeverría and Abrego also organized three new methods to deliver authorized news in a covert manner. First they established the Office of Popular Journalistic Information (Oficina de Información Periodística Popular, OIPP). This appeared to be an independent news agency. But the ministry actually used the agency to put out progovernment articles, which were then sent to provincial newspapers. The office had big ambitions. The stories were designed to "make known the work that the state is realizing to the benefit of the national community" and use "modern psychological resources" to "engrave on the public conscience the greatest mental image" of the president.[144] Second, they set up a shortwave radio news agency, NOTIMEX, in August 1968. Again, the agency claimed independence but was paid for and controlled by the government.[145] Third, they started to insert columns into the popular tabloid *La Prensa*. From January 1967 to July 1968, they placed "Política en Rocas" to push government policy, support under-fire PRIistas, and denigrate radicals. From August 1968 they changed the column's name to "Granero Político" and used the space to slander and undermine the student movement. Who wrote the columns under the pen name "El Sembrador" is still unclear. At the time, many blamed the president's press secretary. But Rodríguez Munguía holds that a UNAM philosophy professor close to Echeverría, actually wrote the majority.[146]

For the first four years of Díaz Ordaz's administration, the president's press secretary was Francisco Galindo Ochoa. Like Romero, he took an active role in press control and achieved fabled status within the infraworld of the PRI as a fixer and spin doctor. A year before he took charge, Manuel Marcué Pardiñas described him as "a rude and vain gossip-monger, the darkest, most corrupt man in the country."[147] On his death, journalist Rafael Cordona called him "the last dinosaur" and was no kinder. "Galindo, the corruptor; Galindo, the ogre; Galindo, the soothsayer of all the Caesars; Don Pancho, the true author of all the columns and all the leaks; ... Galindo, the confessor; Galindo, the analyst, the promoter, the brake, the veto and the vote, last word and initial comment; Galindo Ochoa was everything."[148]

Galindo was born in the small town of Tamazula, Jalisco, joined the party young, and became a deputy at the age of thirty-six. In Mexico City he started to specialize in public relations. He was head of the press office of the PRI twice. As deputy he was entrusted with handing out the bribes to the journalists covering the congress beat. In 1958 and 1964 he ran the PRI's presidential election campaigns. He was an imposing personality. He "chuckled loudly" at everything, smoked enormous cigars, and wore visibly expensive U.S. suits. Scherer, ever the snob, could pick out a provincial wannabe and thought his personality looked "constructed piece by piece." He specialized in getting to know the inner workings of the governing party, the personal ties, individual enmities, and the undisclosed scandals that shaped the PRI. His files of political gossip were legendary. He made his name giving corrosive tips on out-of-favor or opposition politicians to Mexico City's columnists. During the late 1950s, he teamed up with Denegri to create the *Excélsior* feature "Fichero Político," a devastating insider's column that could finish careers.[149]

As Díaz Ordaz's press secretary, Galindo was extremely industrious. Initially he was charged with simply handing out journalists' bribes. As we shall see, he took great pleasure in tailoring gifts to writers' wants. But within a year, he had built up a substantial power base inside the president's office. His employees read, scanned, and clipped both national and regional newspapers. They presented him with a long press résumé every day. These not only recounted the top stories but also analyzed editors' and journalists' attitudes in depth.[150] Like the Ministry of the Interior, Galindo was directly involved in the internal running of newspapers. In 1967, one weekly accused him of forcing *El Universal* to sack one journalist, *Ovaciones* to fire another, and trying unsuccessfully to force *El Diario de la Tarde* to cut its most high-profile columnist.[151] Galindo also meticulously controlled the reception of Díaz Ordaz's public appearances. One of his "press operations" from the president's visit to Michoacán in September 1966 remains. The plan described how his staff would entertain journalists in the national palace until the president gave his speech on TV that evening. Presidential employees would wire the text to the palace, where press staff would rapidly run up a bulletin and hand it out to the assembled reporters. A plane would fly photographs from Michoacán to Mexico City, where motorcyclists would pick them up and deliver them to the palace. Press staff would then dictate the exact subheadings to the reporters.[152]

Between 1958 and 1970, the government's public relations machine changed, and monitoring the press increased dramatically. Dozens of staff read, clipped, and summarized the texts. Secret service operatives spied on and tapped the phones of editors and journalists and planted informants in newspaper offices. In the newsrooms of the big nationals, the state knew what was going on. The aims of the government press officer also transformed. Now he was not simply charged with issuing bulletins and hoping that they were either printed verbatim or written up in a favorable manner. Now he had to make sure that journalists ran the news in a positive light. Money, in the form of bribes and gifts, obviously played a big part. But so did sophisticated press plans and constant phone calls, reminders, and threats. So did new means of delivery, like covert government news agencies and anonymous prewritten columns. In 1969, a PRI insider commented that the success of state propaganda lay in the fact that it "has stayed hidden and no one knows, or at least they don't know in detail, the existence of the organs that produce it." Unlike the old DAPP, which had openly produced clear bulletins, this new propaganda had "succeeded surreptitiously."[153] An "invisible tyranny," it was not. Some knew it, some revealed it, and many resisted it. But it was the beginning of spin.

Financial Incentives

Financial incentives also undergirded government efforts to control the printed press. They were of two types. First, state subsidies in the form of direct payments, cheap paper, low-interest loans, government advertisements, and paid news stories or *gacetillas* sustained national newspapers and magazines. They floated struggling businesses and enriched individual directors. The government employed them to extract concessions; their removal was used to sink incompliant papers. Second, at the level of the individual journalists, the government used regular payments, one-off bribes, land, houses, gifts, and administrative jobs to secure favorable copy. Attitudes to state disbursements depended on the newspaper. Some newspapers faced continual financial hardships and relied almost entirely on government largesse. But by the 1960s, other newspapers had managed to secure enough funding from private advertising and circulation to function independently.

During the period, national newspapers and magazines became bulky, costly businesses. Staff numbers grew dramatically and wages increased.[154] By 1964, *El Universal* spent well over a third of its budget on wages and other personnel costs.[155] The price of importing new printing technology from the United States or Europe was also excessive. Such high costs affected some newspapers more than others. Low-selling leftist newspapers like *El Popular* regularly confronted financial ruin. In 1951 and 1952, the paper had to sell off much of its machinery and property to stay afloat. The following year, the paper still estimated an annual shortfall of 712,456 pesos.[156] Even right-wing tabloids sometimes struggled. During the early 1950s Kawage's anticommunist *Zócalo* was also losing 15,000 pesos per week. In February 1953 he complained to the president that "everything that could be mortgaged was mortgaged, everything that could be sold, sold, everything that could be negotiated, negotiated." His debts had climbed to over 300,000 pesos.[157]

Even the big nationals struggled. From the 1950s, *El Universal* in particular faced the continual threat of bankruptcy. Increasing staff costs played an important role. The company employed six separate unions, which all pushed for higher salaries and greater benefits.[158] But poor management and falling sales also contributed to the financial problems. After Lanz Duret died in 1959, family members with no journalistic experience took over the running of the firm. They fired popular pressmen like editor Fernando Garza, hired a host of their own overpaid friends, and concentrated on recovering profits through advertising. Morale dropped. In 1963, one U.S. observer claimed that the newsroom was "the dreariest in Mexico City . . . even the colors are cold, gray-green walls, gray desks, and a blue floor."[159] The paper, he concluded, had "the heart of an adding machine." Revenue fell substantially. Sales dropped from over 100,000 during the 1950s to 76,296 in 1961 and 74,582 in 1963. In comparison, *Excélsior*, *Novedades*, and *La Prensa*'s sales were 30 to 60 percent greater. Consequently, throughout the 1960s *El Universal* hemorrhaged money. In 1964 alone, the company claimed it lost around 4 million pesos. By 1969, the acting head, Juan Francisco Ealy Ortiz, threatened that the paper would have to close its doors. *El Universal* was undergoing "the most shocking bankruptcy."[160]

Such financial problems necessitated government aid. As I argued in chapter 1, cheap, tax-free paper and the provision of debt were vital to newspapers' survival. In 1965, and again in 1969, all of Mexico City's editors pleaded with the government to keep PIPSA running.[161] But other sources were also important. Government loans were vital, especially in times of crisis. Nacional Financiera (NF), the state development bank, set up during the Great Depression to bypass private institutions, provided most of the cash.[162] In 1956, President Ruiz Cortines authorized a 300,000-peso NF loan to Kawage's struggling *Zócalo* to keep the newspaper afloat. For his next newspaper, *El Tabloide*, some insiders claimed that Kawage received between 12 and 30 million pesos in NF loans. (*Por Qué?* even estimated that state credit totaled around 62 million.)[163] Whatever the exact amount, the loans permitted the owner to build huge offices in downtown Mexico City, sell *Tabloide* at 20¢ per issue, and found and print another newspaper, *Capital*, a decade later. During the 1960s, *El Universal* survived only because of NF loans. In 1961, the owners got an NF loan of 800,000 pesos to pay salaries. In 1964, the year the paper lost at least 4 million pesos, they got a 4-million-peso loan to install a new

Goss rotary press. Within a month, they got another million-peso loan to settle outstanding wages.[164]

Government advertising also subsidized the Mexican press. There were copious advertisements for state institutions and state-run companies in all the major newspapers. On important national holidays or the anniversary of a president's election, ministries and public companies flooded the newspapers with formulaic congratulations and eulogies. Ministries provided the bulk of the advertisements. In 1969, the president's press secretary possessed an advertising budget of 200,000 pesos.[165] He also controlled the advertising for state companies. In 1967, the state's theater and the film distribution companies alone paid a total of 16.3 million pesos to the national newspapers *Excélsior, El Universal, Novedades, El Heraldo de México, El Sol de México,* and *El Dia.*[166] By the late 1950s, regional governments also contributed considerable advertising to national newspapers and magazines. Between 1959 and 1961, the government of Baja California Norte spent at least 357,229 pesos on advertising in over forty national and regional publications. They even paid *Excélsior* journalist Enrique Loubet Jr. 9,000 pesos a year to work as their Mexico City–based media consultant.[167]

These ads made up a significant proportion of newspapers' advertising revenue. Commentators repeatedly estimated that on average, the large national newspapers earned around 20 to 30 percent of their advertising revenue through government publicity.[168] But some relied on government advertising more than most. Dependence differed from paper to paper and changed over time. In 1944, government advertising accounted for 35,644 pesos or around 36 percent of *La Prensa*'s advertising. The Ministry of National Defense, which was responsible for Mexico's conscription drive, contributed nearly half.[169] But by the end of the 1960s, private advertising had grown to such an extent that big nationals received a comparatively small proportion from government departments. A private company, Metrolineaje, estimated that official ads accounted only for around 15 percent of *Novedades*'s total, 20 percent of *Excélsior*'s, and around a quarter of *El Universal*'s.[170]

Federal and state governments also floated newspapers and magazines through paid news stories or *gacetillas*. Although these appeared to be normal articles, they were produced directly by government press offices or written to order by journalists.[171] Newspapers charged government institutions for these inserts at three times the rate of normal adverts. They even published their charges in the media gazette, *Medios Publicitarios Mexicanos*.[172] Some publications specialized in their publication. Most of the second half of *Siempre!* was *gacetillas*. As photographer Julio Mayo explained, "Circulation didn't matter. Advertising didn't matter. The only thing that really mattered was publishing what government functionaries did. Every dependency had money to pay for public relations and they paid for every mention of anything that had been done and could be related to a particular functionary, for example, public works."[173] He estimated that these paid inserts made up to 60 percent of the magazine's content. When Moncada asked a *Siempre!* journalist why the magazine mixed a critical first section with a fawning second half he replied "very simple . . . whatever we make with the second half, we pay with the first."[174] But outside *Siempre!*, other newspapers also made profits from *gacetillas*. Scherer remembered during his first years on *Excélsior* bringing "adverts and adverts, *gacetillas* and *gacetillas* to the director; they were from the federal government, the state governments, the chambers of industry and commerce, the airlines, the cinema industry, the sports clubs, the banks, the rich municipalities and those that were not that poor."[175]

Finally, government funding took the form of straight payments. These expanded in scope and quantity over time. During the 1940s and 1950s, the big nationals seemed to have survived without direct funding. Only magazines and low-selling newspapers received disbursements. For example, from 1939 onward the government paid the union leader Lombardo Toledano 350,000 pesos per year to fund the Workers University of Mexico (Universidad Obrera de México). At least 75,000 went toward the maintenance of *El Popular*.[176] In 1953, the U.S. embassy reported that President Ruiz Cortines was threatening to cut all press subsidies and predicted that the move would put all the magazines in the capital out of business.[177] Two years later, an internal memo from the president's office confirmed this widespread reliance. Publications like *Mañana, Siempre!, Tiempo,* and *Todo* all received annual payments of 24,000 pesos. Struggling newspapers also got funds. Low-selling, right-wing *Atisbos* received 36,000 pesos a year.[178] By the following decade, government subsidies had started to fund the large nationals as well. In 1967, *Excélsior* received 50,000 pesos a year, *Novedades* 50,000, *El Universal* 50,000, *La Prensa* 50,000, *Ultimas Noticias* 45,000, and the *El Diario de la Tarde* 10,000.[179] Compared to annual profits, most of the sums were fairly small—but not all. In 1964, one U.S. observer claimed that the government was actually paying *El Universal* 300,000 a month to keep the enterprise afloat.[180] The amount would have allowed the paper to break even.

Such financial support curtailed free expression in three ways. First, some payments came with set expectations. According to U.S. observers, in 1941 President Avila Camacho not only promised to suppress plans to set up a rival newspaper but also handed over partial control of PIPSA to the city's big nationals. In a constricted market, *Excélsior*, *Novedades*, *El Universal*, and *La Prensa* could now channel cheap newsprint to satisfy their exclusive needs. In return, their directors offered to support Avila Camacho and the war effort.[181] Occasionally, officials made these requirements explicit. In 1956, Ruiz Cortines promised Kawage credit and favorable treatment from the city's news vendors. As a trade-off, he expected *Zócalo* to print government bulletins verbatim and "help" the state "in every way . . . as a weapon of both attack and defense." In short, the paper should become "an element of positive action in favor of the works that the president is performing for the benefit of our country." Kawage followed the president's instructions so precisely that the president's press secretary occasionally had to demand that he offer at least the illusion of debate.[182]

Second, the government cut the financial support of difficult or dissident papers. Refusing PIPSA paper (and thereby forcing publications to pay 80 percent extra on the open market) was the most commonplace method to force noncompliant publications out of business. As we shall see, the government used the tactic to suppress the 1948 satirical magazine *Presente* and the 1960s radical journal *Por Qué?* But there were other examples. In 1962, *El Popular* finally closed down, citing PIPSA's refusal of credit as the primary cause.[183] From 1960 onward, the president's press secretary, Romero, also ordered PIPSA to sporadically withhold supplies from the left-wing magazine *Política* to ensure favorable coverage. The editor, Manuel Marcué Pardiñas, described the organization as "the ignominious guillotine ready to decapitate liberty of expression."[184]

But the government withheld other funds as well. In the last two years of Alemán's term, the president suppressed *El Popular*'s government subsidy for supporting dissident unions. Only with the election of Ruiz Cortines did the subsidies return.[185] Other newspapers were less fortunate. The removal of government funding sunk the low-selling *El Diario de México* in a matter of months. On July 23, 1966, somebody switched the captions under a picture of President Díaz Ordaz and a picture of monkeys at the Mexico City Zoo. According to the editor, dissident workers executed the visual prank; others put it down to carelessness. Whatever the reason, the joke struck at Díaz Ordaz's carefully cultivated image. Street satirists had already caricatured the rather simian president as a monkey. The state immediately cut all government advertisements. Within days, all government-affiliated organizations followed suit. By November 1, 1966, the newspaper was forced to close.[186]

Third, extensive subsidies made press workers aware that their wages, benefits, and lifestyles depended, at least in part, on government largesse. The sporadic withholding of these subsidies from certain publications reinforced this perception, intensifying the fear that a handful of critical stories could put hundreds out of work. On the individual level, political journalists were reluctant to endanger their jobs, pensions, and homes in order to break controversial stories. To extend Darnton's metaphor, such acts sharpened the scissors in their heads. On the executive level, managers and editors were also unwilling to gamble multimillion-peso businesses and hundreds of jobs on antigovernment crusades. As early as 1954, writer Rubén Salazar Mallén pointed this out at a speech at the Mexican Association of Journalists (Asociación Mexicana de Periodistas, AMP). For Salazar, the industrial press had replaced the "old, bohemian, romantic period of making newspapers" when directors employed four or five collaborators. Now newspapers were "large organizations, with extensive capital and an administrative personnel that outnumbers the newsroom." Going up against the government risked ruin and "the ruin of a newspaper would now mean the sacking of hundreds of people." In fact, editors were now so concerned with ensuring government money that they often "look for new ways to flatter or try to guess the thoughts or interests of the holders of public power."[187]

Financial incentives shaped institutional attitudes to the government; they also molded those of individual journalists. The basic government payment to journalists was the fortnightly bribe, or *iguala*. The widespread custom of giving out money for favorable reports started during Alemán's presidential campaign. All the journalists that followed his national tour received "envelopes stuffed with cash."[188] Maverick photojournalist Rodrigo Moya claimed that during his presidency "the manna of pesos destined to periodicals flowed through strange sewers and circled the pyramid of directors, columnists, reporters, and assimilated intellectuals."[189] Under Ruiz Cortines, the establishment of press offices regularized the practice. Every two weeks, government publicists would hand over envelopes to the journalists who worked their particular beat, or *fuente*.[190] By the following decade, the process had developed a distinct hierarchy and rhythm. In 1961, *La Prensa* reporter Manuel Buendía explained that after the foreign correspondents left the Ministry of the Economy's press conference, a press staffer handed out cash to the Mexican reporters who were identified by two trusted journalists.[191]

These regular payments increased over time. During the mid-1950s, journalists on pretty small-scale beats like the peasants union received between 200 and 300 pesos per month, the equivalent of a week's salary.[192] By the early 1960s, little had changed. One *Ovaciones* reporter confessed to a U.S. informant that the Ministry of Public Education (Secretaría de Educación Pública, SEP) press officer paid him an extra 200 pesos a month as a salary for around four days of work.[193] But under Díaz Ordaz, the quantities of money offered, especially at the top end of the pay scale for journalists on the presidential beat or columnists, rose dramatically. In the mid-1960s the presidential office paid out over 4,000 pesos, or two months' salary, to particularly progovernment writers like Ernesto Julio Teissier.[194] According to one insider, journalists who acquired multiple beats could earn upward of 15,000 pesos extra per month.[195] By 1970, disbursements had climbed even higher. The base *iguala* was around 750 a month, and reporters on Luis Echeverría's (1970–1976) presidential tour pulled in 10,000 pesos in just three days.[196]

In fact, by the 1960s, the regular government payments were so integral to journalists' lives that they developed a distinct language to describe the process. The payments themselves were called *sobornos* (bribes), *igualas* (fees), *embutes* (bribes), *sobres* (envelopes), or *chayotes* (squashes). These terms sometimes had distinct backstories. The term *chayote* allegedly emerged after the governor of Tlaxcala invited a group of journalists to view the state's new irrigation system. The project was a disaster. The land remained dry and nothing grew. But after the governor's press officer handed out the payments, the journalists exclaimed that they could see rows of *chayotes*. Within a few years, the term had gained traction. The act of giving out cash was described as "watering the chayotes." The act of receiving payment was termed "Operation Chayote."[197] Other phrases and gags connected with these regular payments also developed. Journalists who worked as brokers between press officers and reporters were called *coyotes*;[198] the press officer's inventory of journalists and payments was termed the "talis" [an anagram of "lista," or list].[199] Jorge Joseph, a labor beat reporter during the 1950s, established the United Front of the Workers Beat (Frente Unido de la Fuente Obrera, FUFO), which used journalists' combined bargaining power to ensure that every union paid the required amounts.[200] "Sobre grande, nota chica, sobre chico, nota grande" [Big envelope, small story, small envelope, big story] revealed journalists' attitudes to the big envelope, where the press bulletins went, and the small envelope, which contained the money.[201] During the early 1970s, journalists joked that the monthly meeting between female journalists and public figures called "20 mujeres y un hombre" [20 women and a man] would be better termed "20 mujeres y un sobre" [20 women and an envelope].[202]

Journalists received other bonuses and gifts from the government. Chief among these was land. Again, President Alemán started the custom. In 1948, he donated land in the exclusive Lomas de Sotelo district west of Mexico City to a hundred journalists from the big nationals. He also organized a state loan of 730,000 pesos to build their houses.[203] Over the next few years, Alemán improved conditions, halving the interest rates on the loans and forgiving some completely. Over the next twenty years, the practice continued. The government donated more land in the fashionable Colonia Narvarte in south Mexico City to establish two more journalist neighborhoods.[204] In mid-century Mexico City's rising real estate market, these offers of free land, upmarket locations, low-interest loans, and the guaranteed provision of water and electricity were extremely popular. In 1954, five hundred journalists applied to own lands in the third colony.[205] By the end of the decade, half the journalists on the presidential beat lived on government-donated land.[206] Beyond these large-scale donations of urban lots, government officials also offered individual journalists cheap or even free houses. During the 1970s, Teodoro Rentería Arróyave was struggling to find the down payment for a new house in Colinas de Tarango just south of the expensive Lomas district. When he explained this to the Mexico City mayor's press officer, he immediately received a gift of 100,000 pesos.[207]

Government officials combined these donations of urban land with gifts of rural property. Sometimes these offers were directed at particular organizations. In 1948, President Alemán offered the *La Prensa* cooperative cut-price land in the town of Oaxtepec, Morelos, in order to build holiday homes.[208] He also donated the AMP lands in Cuautla, Morelos, and in the seaside resort of Puerto Vallarta.[209] But sometimes these donations were more off-the-cuff. In 1952, the Ruiz Cortines government awarded a group of journalists over 3,000 hectares of agricultural land in Estación Cuauhtémoc, Tamaulipas. Magdalena Mondragón headed the group, which comprised left-wing journalists who had backed the PRI candidate over his rival, Miguel Henríquez Guzmán. The planned colony was a disaster. Many journalists, including Mondragón, backed out immediately; others donated the lands to their relatives. The farmers who had previously worked the land complained that the journalists had usurped their properties. Conflicts between the local military detachment charged with defending the newcomers' lands and the previous tenants were frequent. Despite a large government loan to buy agricultural machinery, the journalists were poor farmers and crops failed regularly. In the end, the journalists simply made money by employing a private company to deforest the surrounding hills and sell the wood.[210]

Officials also offered compliant journalists well-paid government jobs. Sometimes they held these jobs in conjunction with their work at the newspapers. In 1950, Manuel Espejel ran *La Prensa*'s editorial office and worked in the president's press department.[211] Manuel Becerra Acosta balanced his day work at *Excélsior* with speech writing for the PRI.[212] During the 1970s, Carlos Moncada worked at *El Heraldo de México*, in the political magazine *Ya!*, at the

Ministry of the Interior's press office, and for the national lottery.[213] But other journalists moved in and out of government employ. Manuel Buendía shifted from *La Prensa* to the political magazine *Crucero*, then to the press offices of the Federal Electricity Commission, the mayor of Mexico City, and NF before returning to his job as a columnist at *El Universal*.[214]

Finally, press officers also gave journalists generous gifts. At times, these gifts tied in with work. Payments for hotels and bar bills were standard. When Denegri racked up a $2,200 bill at the Washington, D.C., Hilton while covering Díaz Ordaz's U.S. tour, the presidential press secretary picked up the tab.[215] But they extended to other presents as well. Sometimes they were given on the spur of the moment. When Scherer expressed his admiration for Díaz Ordaz's London tailored silk shirts, the president responded by giving him twelve, embossed with his initials.[216] Other times, the presents were carefully planned. In a tapped conversation between the PRI press chief, Galindo, and the PRI head, Alfonso Corona del Rosal, they debated what to get for the various editors. Three bottles of Chivas Regal whiskey for notorious drunk Rodrigo de Llano; a cashmere sweater for the well-dressed Manuel Buendía; champagne for the editors of *ABC*; and something silver or money for top *iguala* earner Ernesto Julio Teissier. "Best just give money to that type of people . . . it's more practical."[217]

These payments shaped individual journalists' attitudes to state power. Like the larger institutional incentives, they made journalists' livelihoods dependent on government largesse. In 1961, one *Ovaciones* journalist explained that he was the son of a poorly paid army colonel and needed to fund his seven brothers and sisters through school.[218] A decade later, another reporter explained, "I write what they tell me to write. That's the way it's done here. I have a family to support."[219] And accepting the gift carried with it certain obligations. Once paid, journalists felt obliged to follow the government line. In the 1950s, they copied out bulletins, and by the 1960s they did their best to follow the press officer's telephoned instructions. At the same time, the exchange of money and gifts cemented common cultural understandings between journalists and officials. They all indulged in the common patois and shared in the sense of being involved in a covert but normal practice. Journalists started their careers receiving envelopes and ended them handing them out.

The Limits of State Censorship

In this chapter, we have seen how the state managed to assert control over the capital's newspapers and magazines. Ideological and social links between politicians and journalists played an important role. They generated shared understandings of common national purpose and journalistic practice. So did increasingly sophisticated press policies. Strategies shifted from spontaneous interference through the mass publication of bulletins to direct attempts to control press output and reception. Financial incentives, on both the institutional and the individual level, underpinned common assumptions and assisted government strategies. The funding and manpower devoted to press censorship increased over time. Just as the ruling party became increasingly tightly controlled, so the newspapers of the 1960s were far more regulated than their equivalents in the 1940s and 1950s.

Nevertheless, even in the capital, complete control of the printed media was never achieved. Mexico was never the Soviet Union, military dictatorship Brazil, or even Peronist Argentina.[220] It lacked both a coherent, united elite and the extensive censoring infrastructure of these countries. In fact Mexican tactics resembled ramped-up, or perhaps more explicit, versions of press controls in the United States or Western Europe. Here, as in Mexico, Cold War agreements over anticommunism and journalistic practice, state financial support, and the heavy policing and occasional repression of radicals generated "media institutions" "both free of direct compulsion and constraints" that "freely articulated themselves systematically around definitions of situations, which favored the hegemony of the powerful."[221] As in these countries, room for dissent existed. Admittedly, this lessened over time as government intervention and cash disbursements increased. And, in the mainstream nationals, some themes were always strictly off-limits. Direct criticism of the president, open support for radical communism, and explicit investigation into state massacres were forbidden.[222] (Pablo Neruda claimed the president was "an Aztec emperor, a thousand times more untouchable than the royal family of England."[223]) But outside these topics, mainstream papers contained some analysis of the governing regime. Cartoons and crime pages critiqued state corruption, judicial inequality, and poorly implemented policies.[224]

Even the news pages, editorials, and columns allowed a measure of debate. The PRI was never coherent or disciplined, and diverse factions often aired grievances in the national press. Even under Díaz Ordaz, attacking cabinet members and critiquing state policies was relatively commonplace.[225] Conflict often peaked during the last years of presidents' terms, when powerful groups attempted to lever their candidates into the running for the succession or at least a position on the cabinet. These struggles often became so heated that they infringed the unwritten rules of the game. In 1957 and 1963, former president Cárdenas's public critiques of state policy fed into press debate over the acting president, the official candidate, and the very continuation of the PRI. In 1969, the fallout from the student massacre and competition between three prospective PRI candidates generated substantial, if guarded, discussion in the press.[226] Finally, as we shall see, outside the mainstream media, criticism of the government could be fierce, powerful, and influential. Here, the state used more violent means to suppress dissent.

CHAPTER THREE

The Year Mexico Stopped Laughing

The Press, Satire, and Censorship in Mexico City

On March 17, 1949, the satirical magazine *Presente* finally shut its doors. For nine months, the publication's pointed editorials, cartoons, and investigations into corruption had provided what their writers called a "space for the angry voice of the people."[1] They were not alone. During the brief period, other journalists, artists, and amateur satirists had joined in, writing articles, plays, songs, and jokes that exposed official wrongdoings and mocked the political elite. Their denunciations rocked the country's political establishment. Mexican officials confessed to the British ambassador that in summer 1948 "the flood gates of criticism were opened wide." There was a "tenseness in the political atmosphere, which seemed to render anything possible."[2] Aggressive journalism and mob fury had nearly precipitated the collapse of the administration. In the city's cantinas, barroom bookies took bets on when the Alemán government was going to fall.[3] If the magazine's brief run was a high point for satire's political potential, its closure proved a turning point for the Mexico City press. As Monsiváis argued, after *Presente* folded, "what had been the critical space of Mexican journalism restricted itself in a compulsive manner."[4] Lessons were learned. Reporters were reluctant to stoke the political unrest of the capital's crowds; political satire for a mass audience disappeared; and mainstream newspapers studiously avoided any explicit criticism of the president.

Between 1940 and 1976, gradual changes transformed Mexicans' relationship to the written word. Broad cultural, economic, and political frameworks shaped what was written. But the history of the press is not only one of long-term structures, but also one of individual moments. They comprised brief, intense interactions among journalists, officials, and readers; they linked to broader street protests; and they carried both short- and long-term consequences.[5] The year 1948 was one such moment. For a few months, readers' connections to the press changed. In the second year of Alemán's presidency, the confluence of rising prices, devaluation, and elite corruption generated serious disquiet. Journalists and members of civil society developed strong links as *Presente*'s writers and street protestors came together to produce a denunciation of the postrevolutionary regime and posit the chance of political upheaval. The crisis also changed the state's political strategies. The moment did not last long. Forced resignations and increased food subsidies severed the links between civil society and satirical journalists and coopted the capital's crowds. At the same time, attacks on the press and other satirical works were frequent; journalists thought 1948 marked "a monstrous regression in our liberties."[6] Murder, violence, dirty tricks, and propaganda closed down critical spaces and brought mainstream newspapers onside. Functionaries adapted and learned. Similar emergency measures would shape the management of future crises.

Finally, the 1948 crisis also changed the nature of humor itself. Since the revolution, political humor had flourished in Mexico City. Both satirical plays and magazines formed genuine arenas for widespread criticism. They mocked the foibles of the political elites and exposed the distance between revolutionary rhetoric and contemporary inequality. They crossed social divides, attracting audiences of both rich and poor. *Presente*'s journalists, together with the producers of the year's other satirical works, formed the culmination of this tradition. But their popularity and menace also heralded cross-class political humor's eventual demise. Over the next few years, officials moved against popular satirists, coopting the pliant and starving the more recalcitrant of space and funds. By the early 1950s, satire had lost its connection to popular protest; it had become the preserve of a political elite. Mass humor had lost its political edge, and what Mexicans laughed at increasingly became a question of social class.

Historicizing Humor

The Mexican Revolution unleashed a wave of political satire throughout the Mexican capital. Freed from the constraints of Porfirian censorship, writers now lampooned the political elite in two spaces, the theater and printed texts. On the stage, most satire comprised works of *teatro de revista* or what English-speaking audiences might term "music hall." They mixed music, dance, and political skits and were put on at both established theaters and temporary *carpas*, or tents. From 1910 onward, they achieved considerable acceptance and attracted audiences from across the social spectrum. Satirical magazines were also popular. They combined easy-to-understand cartoons with stock characters and political critique. These two satiric forms were intimately linked. Journalists often moonlighted as playwrights, and *teatro de revista* actors wrote in the press. The same stories and critiques often formed the basis of music hall sketches and printed articles.

Stage satire had a long history in Mexico. Playwrights had used works of theater to lampoon colonialism's sanctimonious idealism and critique Spanish rule.[7] But it was the revolution that introduced a popular political version of music hall to the capital. As censorship declined, writers increasingly turned to political themes. A particular brand of music hall, the *revista política*, or political revue, was born. Works now combined dances, songs, and stock characters with aggressive political critique. Initially, writers satirized the old dictatorship. In summer 1911 Luis G. Andrade and Leandro Blanco staged *Tenorio Maderista*, a parody of the story of Don Juan. Madero's partisans applauded as their hero rescued the heroine from the clutches of the thinly disguised figure of Porfirio Noches.[8] But as the revolution ground on, playwrights also turned to criticizing the country's new leaders. Two years later, José Elizondo put on *El País de la Metralla* [The country of shrapnel], in which he satirized the ambition and corruption of the revolutionary chiefs. In fact, the work was so sharp (and so transparently in favor of the dictator Victoriano Huerta) Elizondo was forced into exile in Havana.[9]

By the 1920s and 1930s, this politicized version of music hall, like corridos and mural art, had became one of the revolution's quintessential cultural forms. Satirical skits were put on in central theaters like the Apolo, the María Guerrero, and the Lírico as well as dozens of *carpas* scattered over the down-at-heel barrios of the city.[10] They started to include new fashionable dances like the danzón, the rumba, and the foxtrot, and created a new set of stock characters like the ladino Indian, the rancher, the revolutionary general, and the policeman.[11] They also maintained their political relevance. In 1936, the great comic actor Cantinflas put on a revue entitled *San Lázaro el Milagroso*, which laughed at the popular reverence for the president by comparing the distribution of land to the miracles of a Christian saint.[12]

During the 1940s, political revues underwent some changes. The violent assault on a theater entrepreneur by supporters of Maximino Avila Camacho silenced some playwrights. Cushy government sinecures mollified others. Wartime nationalism took the edge off some of the most damning political humor. But antigovernment satire continued. In a move that preempted the criticisms of 1948, writers also started to exploit the satirical potential of the distance between revolutionary rhetoric and ongoing poverty. In 1944's *El Tope de los Precios* the authors looked at the government failure to deal with escalating prices. In the first act, two prostitutes shared their experiences. The older woman claimed that life was easier during the Porfiriato. Wages were low, but so were food prices and rent. Nowadays, costs had risen dramatically "because of the politicians who hoarded" basic foodstuffs and the corrupt leaders who demanded a percentage of farmers' pay. The work even named names. In one scene, a merchant recommended to the prostitutes that if they wanted sugar they best "clean the shoes of Aarón Sáenz," head of the state sugar company. Writers also used the Porfirian comparison to emphasize the country's increasing inequality. In 1946, the two major hits were *Los Tres Pobres Millonarios*, which laid out the similarities between the Porfirian upper class and the revolution's new bourgeoisie, and *La Feria de Huesos*, which imagined bureaucrats fighting over the potential earnings to be gained through an official job.[13]

Such satire channeled popular opprobrium. Audience members were expected to join in, hurl abuse at thinly veiled caricatures, and mock politicians' sanctimonious speeches. Political revues "opened space for democratic action in which the lower classes could destroy the credibility of their authoritarian rulers."[14] In fact, foreign visitors were often surprised at the candid and critical nature of stage satire's attacks. U.S. ambassador Josephus Daniels was shocked to witness satirists like Roberto Soto and Cantinflas holding up "public officials to devastating ridicule" and compared Mexico's satiric openness favorably with that of the United States. The Spanish defense minister even warned President Cárdenas to close down satiric plays. "You ought to stop this. It was by permitting such ridicule of the Spanish Republican Government that we lost public confidence and this resulted in our downfall."[15]

Until the late 1940s, both writers and officials maintained that satire fulfilled an essential political role. For Soto, Mexicans only laughed at two things, sex and politics. The latter, he said, was "an escape valve." "When the people don't have the opportunity to express their discontent and they hear someone speaking on their behalf, it causes an outburst of joy. When they don't agree with their governors the political joke becomes a form of relief and satisfaction." The comic Jesús Martínez Rentería, aka "Palillo," agreed, calling the political joke "the only way that Mexicans can demonstrate their public spirit, a public spirit which has been forgotten by the government itself."[16] Even the victims of satire approved. President Calles offered Soto his personal protection; Cárdenas occasionally sponsored his own critics; and even Maximino Avila Camacho tolerated gags about his wealth and messy love life.[17] They recognized that being able to take a joke was a sign of confidence, power, and sympathy with the common man. Some could also give as good as they got. When Cantinflas performed at one of Maximino's parties and started to talk seriously about the poverty of the Mexican people, the San Luis Potosí strongman, Gonzalo Santos, told him to shut up. "What do you know about the people, you only know the public."[18]

Humorous magazines also provided space for satirical attacks on the regime. Like satirical theater, they had a long history. During the 1860s and
1870s their blend of cartoons and articles provided public forums for disputes
between conservatives and liberals and between different wings of the liberal
party itself. During the Porfiriato middle-class papers like *El Hijo del Ahuizote*
and working-class weeklies like *El Diablito Rojo* offered space for satire and
criticism.[19] Scholarship on satirical publications in postrevolutionary Mexico
is much thinner. Many were printed on cheap, disposable paper and surviving copies are rare. Many had extremely short shelf lives. Few lasted for more
than a couple of years. Many of the longest-running satirical newspapers were
provincial works. But in Mexico City printed satire did continue, both in
stand-alone form and in the national press. During the late 1910s and early
1920s, *Madre Matiana* used the figure of the pious female seer to mock both
the church and the revolutionary government. Caricatures of Carranza and
Obregón were frequent, and exposés of official corruption commonplace.[20]
During the 1930s, *Rotofoto* married the satirical tradition with the new fad for
glossy, photograph-heavy magazines. During its short run, it critiqued Cárdenas's policies of land distribution and petroleum expropriation and stripped
officials of their mystique, running photographs of the president in his bath-
ing shorts and the secretary of foreign affairs in his underpants.[21] During the
early 1940s, Magdalena Mondragón's *Chist* might have been more left-wing,
but played a similar role, bringing Mexico City comic writers together to criticize state programs and lampoon the governing class.[22]

During the postrevolutionary period, the worlds of satirical plays and
print media overlapped considerably. Journalists often doubled as humorous
playwrights. Elizondo, author of *El País de la Metralla*, was the society correspondent for *Excélsior*.[23] Actors often tried their hand at comic writing. Pedro
Hagelstein, editor and owner of *Madre Matiana*, started his career as an actor
and theater impresario.[24] Both Cantinflas and Palillo regularly wrote columns
in the press. In *Rotofoto*, Cantinflas even jokingly put forward his name as a
potential presidential candidate.[25] Cartoonists took figures from the stage to
illustrate their satires, and playwrights took popular comic strip characters to
flesh out their shows. Both satiric forms shared common themes. Journalists
and playwrights hung out in the same bars and cafés. (Elizondo's drinking
buddies were dubbed his *pistoleros*, or gunmen, and included future *Presente*
editor Jorge Piño Sandoval.)[26] Here, they pooled gossip, criticism, and jokes.
During the 1920s and 1930s both skits and magazines mocked the verbose revolutionary doublespeak of union leaders like Luis N. Morones and Lombardo

Toledano. During the 1940s, they compared the vast wealth of corrupt Mexican officials with the poverty of the popular classes. In 1948, these connections would come to the fore as popular satirists alternated between the genres in order to censure Alemán's regime. Subsequent government repression would also end them both.

The Satiric Moment

At first, Alemán, like his predecessors, encouraged Mexican satirists to ply their trade. He was known as the smiling president—Mr. Colgate—whose broad, toothy grin was meant to indicate a sense of humor. He confessed to Palillo that he thought "it was good that criticisms of a government occurred in a play and were designed to make people laugh, instead of building up hatred and provoking strikes, marches, and coups d'état as in South America."[27] During his campaign, he allowed playwrights to mock his riotous student days and his lack of military experience. When he came to power, he announced a new era of cultural openness by allowing the first performance of Rodolfo Usigli's righteous attack on revolutionary hypocrisy, *El Gesticulador*, at the newly inaugurated National Institute of Fine Arts (Instituto Nacional de Bellas Artes).[28] He also firmed up his friendship with Roberto Soto, publicly embracing the comic actor at the inaugural meeting of the AMP.[29]

Initially, Alemán's relations with print satirists were equally close. In 1944, he sponsored the creation of *Don Timorato*, a cartoon-heavy humor magazine. The publication was cheap, only 50¢, or half the price of most magazines. It was edited by one of Mexico's leading columnists (and future *Presente* head), Piño Sandoval. It was lavishly illustrated. The artistic director was *Hoy's* star Arias Bernal. Other cartoonists included talented youngsters like Rafael Freyre and Andrés Audiffred. In general, the magazine was only lightly satirical. A few early articles focused on rising food prices and the role of certain unnamed officials. But such pieces soon disappeared. Writers avoided direct criticism of Alemán, his allies, or members of the cabinet. Instead they focused their wit on savage depictions of Alemán's presidential rival, Ezequiel Padilla. Many were overtly racist, playing on Padilla's Guerrero roots and his close U.S. ties to employ a series of ugly racist stereotypes.[30]

But such close connections did not last long. The first two years of the administration alienated writers, workers, and the Mexico City crowds. They saw the central problem as corruption. Alemán had come to power flanked by a group of young lawyers, officials, and hangers-on. They were known as his amigos, or friends. Some held official positions. Fernando Casas Alemán was an old Veracruz ally, whom Alemán appointed as chief of Mexico City. Ramón Beteta and Antonio Ruiz Galindo were former UNAM classmates. Alemán made them heads of the Mexican Treasury and the Ministry of the Economy, respectively.[31] Others simply orbited their friend's newfound power. Enrique Parra Hernández was another UNAM buddy. Described as "the minister without a budget," he was in charge of Alemán's personal finances and, so rumor had it, his amorous affairs.[32] Jorge Pasquel was an old Veracruz friend who became an import-export merchant, baseball impresario, and media owner.[33] Others still held combined roles. Carlos Serrano was an old military contact from Veracruz who not only headed the Mexican senate but also acted as informal chief of the secret service and the president's collector of campaign contributions and general moneyman.[34]

Whatever their official roles, all the amigos used their proximity to the president to line their own pockets. Some exploited their connections to gain access to public contracts. Parra specialized in deals with state companies. In 1947, he took a 30 percent commission for selling 19 million pesos worth of rails to the railway company. Over the next year, he used his brother's position in the Bank of Exterior Commerce (Banco de Comercio Exterior) to buy vanilla, cotton, and artisanal products on the cheap and sell them overseas. He also acquired a large share of the national telephone company and multiple concessions to build Mexico's expanding road networks.[35] Pasquel employed similar techniques. In 1947, he received a contract to import all the state's construction materials through his customs brokerage offices. The following year, he got a government concession for selling petrol in Mexico City. The deal gave Pasquel the profits from three-quarters of the capital's petrol stations. He also rented planes, launches, and his private yacht directly to Miguel Alemán, charging the president 123,000 pesos per year.[36]

They also used their newfound status and consequent impunity to operate illegal enterprises. Pasquel specialized in contraband cars. This was big business. Import taxes were steep. In the United States a four-door Cadillac cost $2,485 dollars. Over the border, with import taxes added on, the same car cost around 50 percent more. Officials estimated that smugglers brought in around 4,500 illegal vehicles per year. Pasquel's customs brokerage offices in Ciudad Juárez, Nuevo Laredo, and Veracruz offered a perfect cover for the trade. He would front the smugglers the money to buy the cars in the United States, collect them at the border, issue them with fake import duty certificates, and then sell them in Mexico at an inflated price. His ranches in San Luis Potosí doubled as upscale car lots, were surrounded by armed guards, and were constantly traversed by Cadillacs and Studebakers.[37]

Others employed their status to traffic drugs. This was an even bigger business, worth $20 million a year according to the U.S. Treasury and $60 million according to Alemán's private secretary.[38] At first, Serrano attempted to monopolize the trade. As the chief of campaign contributions, he came into contact with a range of border smugglers. They agreed to pay large sums toward Alemán's candidacy in return for protection.[39] He also used these new associates to move more directly into smuggling. In June 1946, immediately after Alemán's election, U.S. customs officials in Laredo discovered sixty-three tins of opium stashed in a secret compartment of a Cadillac traveling over the border. The car was Serrano's. The driver was a nephew of one of Serrano's close associates, Juan Ramón Gurrola. Despite U.S. pressure, Serrano refused to prosecute Gurrola and even rewarded him with a leading job at the DFS. And, for the next two years, the general made repeated "very strong and rather barefaced" requests to U.S. officials to return the vehicle. In fact, in 1947 he even snubbed President Truman by refusing to attend a state banquet.[40] Serrano's effective control over the DFS increased these links. The two heads, Gurrola and Marcelino Inurreta, already had connections to the narcotics trade. After overhearing their plans for expanding the business, the U.S. military attaché concluded that they were "using the organization as a front for illegal operations to amass personal fortunes." Serrano was "fully cognizant of these sideline operations."[41] The DFS chiefs were not alone. Other agents also had shady pasts. In 1947, the U.S. Federal Bureau of Narcotics speculated that "anyone with a past record as a crooked narcotics enforcement officer needs no other qualification to be accepted as an agent in the group."[42]

In postrevolutionary Mexico, graft was nothing new. Maximino Avila Camacho's propensity for bribes was legendary; for good reason, he was nicknamed "Mr. 15 percent." Nor were illegal businesses.[43] On the border, former president Abelardo Rodríguez had a hand in gambling dens, brothels, alcohol smuggling, and the drug trade.[44] Mexicans often brushed off such corruption with a shrug of the shoulders or a shake of the head. They were politicians. What could one expect? Some even accepted it. Wouldn't they do the same in Maximino's place? But the amigos' venality was different. It caused much more widespread protest than previous efforts. In fact, it became the focus of both written and oral satire during the 1948 crisis. Why did the amigos' corruption generate such cross-class dissent?

First, the amigos rarely tried to hide their wealth. In fact, they flaunted it. Conspicuous consumption was the rule, and Pasquel was playboy in chief. He stepped out with famous beauties like María Felix. He spent months hunting wild game in Africa. He amassed huge collections of planes, boats, guns, and watches. He had a car "for every day of the week in garish colors and diverse makes." And his houses were magnificent. His Tlalpan residence was decorated with Diego Rivera paintings, Sèvres china, Louis XV furniture, and Florentine marble sculptures.[45] Pasquel's luxurious lifestyle made him the most hated of Alemán's amigos. But he was not alone. Gossip and spreads on the society pages revealed the rapid ascent of other functionaries close to the president. The British ambassador observed that Beteta had been poor. "Now he is rich but has not sufficient sagacity to camouflage his sudden accretion of wealth. The mansion he is building for himself and his bejeweled American wife has not escaped the notice of either his chief or the public."[46] Parra went from a damp house in down-at-heels Colonia Santa María la Ribera to a vast Polanco mansion and purchased a necklace for his wife that was so glitzy it "looked like a planetary system." Casas Alemán, known on the street as Alemán's "idiot prince" collected perfumes from all over the world and purchased a golden lamp for his private cabaret worth 225,000 pesos.[47]

Second, stories of high-profile corruption started to leak out in the mainstream press. For the first eighteen months of Alemán's rule, government relations with the big nationals were shaky. The government's spin machine was still in its infancy and financial incentives were irregular and weak. Many also suspected (correctly) that Alemán was behind Pasquel's 1946 takeover of *Novedades*. Such government ownership alienated rival editors and journalists, who feared such backing might put their own papers out of business.[48] In early 1948, Alemán worsened relations further by putting through stringent new copyright legislation. The law was designed to protect the rights of authors, but also included rigid articles that seemed to infringe on the freedom of the press. One backed up the old press law, giving federal authorities "the right to restrict or prohibit the publication, production, circulation, representation, or exhibition of works which are considered contrary to the respect which is due to private life, morals and public peace." Others prohibited the publication of official documents and unauthorized photographs, effectively curtailing the press's ability to corroborate an exposé.[49]

Such tensions opened up space for criticism. In 1947, *Excélsior* reprinted Cosío Villegas's venomous condemnation of the revolutionary regime, "La crisis en México." The original piece was published in an academic journal. *Excélsior's* publication brought Cosío Villegas's denunciations to a broader audience. His condemnation of "general, ostentatious, and offensive administrative corruption disguised beneath a cloak of impunity" looked like an open attack on Alemán's amigos. The government quickly silenced Cosío, threatening to spill rumors about his love life over the pages of the national press.[50] Beyond these general criticisms, a handful of high-profile scandals also crept onto the pages of mainstream press. In the first six months of 1948, the nationals explored a high-profile daylight hit on a senator, touched on the connections between political elites and the drug trade, and attacked the administration for allowing U.S. soldiers connected to the foot-and-mouth commission to carry arms and intimidate journalists.[51]

Third, President Alemán quickly managed to alienate three key groups: the military, the unions, and the Mexico City crowds. Until 1946 successive Mexican governments had sought to appease the military. Officers in particular were treated generously. They were given political power in the shape of governorships, government offices, and the autonomous command of military zones. They were offered juicy sinecures and allowed a free hand in illegal businesses.[52] But the election of Mexico's first civilian president changed this. The number of military personnel in the cabinet declined. Governors with military backgrounds were shunted from power.[53] A new generation of young lawyers now dominated official positions close to the president. Generals complained that these new bureaucrats "paid little attention to the deserving revolutionaries," made them wait in line outside their offices, and rarely answered their demands. During the 1948 crisis these aging generals would form an important opposition to President Alemán. There were even credible rumors of a military coup.[54]

Alemán simultaneously lost the support of many Mexican workers. Successive revolutionary governments had relied on workers to push through controversial policies and secure the popular vote. Even during the early 1940s, when high inflation had pushed down real wages, Avila Camacho had managed to keep the unions in line. But in early 1947 the alliance split. More moderate workers, often organized in state or regional unions, maintained their government support. More radical workers sought autonomy, wage increases, and protection from rising prices. Alemán had begun his relations with independent labor by sending the army to break an oil workers' strike in December 1946, occupying installations, and arresting leaders on the excuse of a supposed conspiracy. Within a year, they had joined together to form their own independent coalition. For Alemán's increasingly right-wing government, they presented a real threat. During the crisis of summer 1948, they would not only provide a vocal mass of disenchanted workers, but also try to harness the anger of a broader section of Mexico City residents.[55]

Finally, and perhaps most important, Alemán lost the support of the Mexico City crowd. Housing crises, university unrest, and summer floods played a major role.[56] But the key problem—the one that alienated Mexico City residents from across the social spectrum, triggered the 1948 crisis and threatened to bring down the Alemán government—was the devaluation of the peso. Within months of Alemán's accession, Mexico's balance of payments started to decline. As the United States eliminated price and export controls, the cost of Mexican imports increased dramatically. In contrast, Mexican exports barely grew. Increased postwar competition and the lowering of demand for raw materials cut into Mexico's industrial and agricultural sectors. Foreign exchange reserves dropped and the "smart money" started to leave Mexico. Large businesses, fearful of devaluation, sent their money to the United States. Foreign loans managed to keep the peso afloat during the first half of 1948. But money kept flowing out. Medium-sized enterprises started to convert their pesos into dollars as well. Finally, on July 21, 1948, the Mexican government was forced to float the peso. It immediately fell from its fixed exchange rate of 4.85 pesos to around 6 or 7 pesos to the dollar before being fixed again at 8.65.[57]

The devaluation had two important secondary effects. First, it increased the price of foodstuffs and other staples. These had been on the rise since the late 1930s.[58] But the devaluation caused a rapid upsurge. The day after the devaluation the price of some foods, like tinned products, ham, and cooking oil, rose 40 percent. Eggs and vegetables rose 20 percent. Within a week, meat was running out. Medicines, most of which were imported from the United States, also climbed in price by around 40 percent.[59] Second, the devaluation revealed an explicit causal link between high-level corruption and widespread poverty. Whatever the broader economic reasons for the devaluation, many perceived the move was the fault of the new revolutionary bourgeoisie. They had destabilized the currency by buying expensive, foreign-made consumer goods. They had undercut the peso still further by importing contraband from the United States, and they had even made fortunes from the devaluation by converting their pesos to dollars ahead of time. For the Mexico City crowd, Alemán's amigos triggered the devaluation, the price rises, and their consequent hunger. The smiling president was no longer laughing with them; he was laughing at them.

Satire in the Streets

In late July 1948, corruption, the shift in military power, antiunion policies, and price rises combined to produce serious unrest among all sectors of Mexico City society. Middle-class housewives, merchants, workers, and soldiers expressed their anger against the president and his hangers-on. This overt disquiet was picked up and recorded by agents from the Ministry of the Interior's

DGIPS. In the weeks immediately following the devaluation, they fanned out across the city, eavesdropping on conversations at market stalls, infiltrating union offices, hanging out at popular drinking dens, and picking up loose fly-sheets and songs. This was a rare event.[60] The DGIPS was a small organization, its agents mostly worked alone, and up to this point they were usually deployed to give overviews of one controversial event or infiltrate a single difficult group.[61] But for a few months, they came together and acted like the volunteers for the U.K.'s experiment in mass observation, offering up snapshots of Mexico City's public mood. The operation was a sign of government concern, which was not misplaced. The mood, they discovered, was very bad. Agents listened in as representatives from across the social classes attacked, insulted, and mocked Alemán and his amigos. Satire had taken to the streets.

In general, people used four means to express their dissatisfaction: insults, rumors, jokes, and songs. Most insults criticized those members of Alemán's administration held responsible for the current situation. They included Beteta, the secretary of the treasury, Ruiz Galindo, the secretary of the economy, Casas Alemán, mayor of Mexico City, and Pasquel, amigo and contrabandist in chief. At the markets, agents recorded "virulent attacks," "harsh commentaries," and "expressions of ill-feeling and disgust" against the amigos.[62] Such verbal assaults reflected changes in both public opinion and people's willingness to express their anger. One agent remarked that "men as well as women were more violent and less cautious and didn't hesitate to slander the government."[63] Another noticed that these insults went "beyond simple censures and constituted personal insults."[64] Ministers were described as "merchants of hunger, bandits, and thieves"; the government was labeled a "bunch of bandits starting from the top"; and crowds shouted "death to the exploiters."[65]

The president was not immune. Throughout July and early August, worried agents repeatedly noticed that Alemán was "the target of the attacks," and that some of the most vocal street critics "demonstrated a lack of respect for the president."[66] They accused him of incompetence, being incapable of "reining in the hunger merchants or the influential politicians."[67] They accused him of lacking political sense, and being unable to "glean public opinion . . . or read the papers."[68] Most concerning, they started to voice the idea that he was no better than his amigos. They whistled at his image when it appeared on cinema screens.[69] By late August, flyers doing the round of the markets read, "Death to the Spurious President Alemán, Death to the Exploiters of the People, Prepare . . . to kick the STUPID . . . BANDIT Alemán and his thieves from power."[70] For good reason, agents concluded that Mexico City's inhabitants were "losing respect for the high office."[71]

During summer 1948, rumors were also rife. Some tales were explicatory. They made the direct link between the current problems and high-level corruption. They were based on selective readings of the press and had some factual basis. They provided comprehensible, moralistic organizing narratives for complex changes and they exacerbated the overall dissatisfaction with the administration. For example, many Mexicans reduced the causes of the devaluation to illegal contraband. Smuggling in U.S. goods was illegal, involved the transfer of dollars to pesos, undercut Mexican businesses, and reduced tax income. One agent said he heard people on the buses blaming the move on the government "permitting contraband on a massive scale"; they pointed to Pasquel as "the principal contrabandist."[72]

Other rumors did not offer explanations. Instead they organized people's understanding of political instability. They expanded the parameters of the conceivable, the boundaries of what people thought could happen.[73] For the government, this looked pretty bad. In early August, a rumor emerged that assassins had ambushed Alemán on the Mexico City–Cuernavaca road, killing his driver and injuring the president.[74] It may have been started deliberately. DGIPS agents suggested that two PP activists were first overheard loudly discussing the plot on a Mexico City bus; they had done so on purpose in order to generate uncertainty and instability.[75] Some whispered that it was the start of a military coup. Among the railway workers, they claimed that "poor salaries" had driven soldiers to revolt.[76] In the U.S. embassy, they held that a dozen army generals headed by the chief of the Military Academy were responsible.[77] Whatever the rumors' origins, people believed them, and in a vicious circle they reinforced the instability that underlay them.

Mexico City crowds also swapped jokes. Most employed a distinctly black humor and mixed frustration with rumors of official corruption. In La Merced, one woman complained to a vendor about the price of eggs. "You're robbing us, I bet you came to an agreement with the inspectors to sell at this price." Then she softened her tone and followed it up with, "Well, the price probably covers the bribes you have to pay at least." Both vendor and consumer laughed. By creating a common enemy, such jokes often deflected blame away from the stall owners and smoothed over tensions with their consumers.[78] But jokes did not smooth over tensions with the leaders they named. Playing on the name of a recent U.S. film, *Ali Baba and the Forty Thieves*, street jokers started to refer to the president and his friends as Alemán and his Forty Lawyers. Such wags often invoked violence. One man, who was buying a knife in the Tepito street market remarked, "Either these things go down in price or we will have to lower them with this." "Yeah, and you'll be Juan Charrasqueado" [the macho hero of a 1948 film], the stall owner replied.[79]

The capital's residents also produced a flurry of satiric songs. In a society with a large illiterate population, they still formed a key means of condensing, transmitting, and popularizing the insults, rumors, and jokes mentioned previously.[80] They were sung in plazas, in bars, and in the center of apartment courtyards. The journalists and skit writers who wrote them made them easy to remember, lifting the melodies from popular tunes. Song sheets were printed on cheap paper and sold for a few cents by street sellers and newsboys; many were republished in newspapers and magazines. The most widespread of all, "Miguel," referred to the president. A parody of the popular Agustín Lara song "Madrid," it was catchy and easy to recite; it also neatly summarized the central themes of rising prices, corruption, antipresidentialism, and threatened violence.[81] But "Miguel" was the gentlest of the satiric songs. Other tunes, dotted with sexual references and swear words, were less family friendly. "Los Ahuehuetes" (literally the cypress trees, but used here to denote Alemán's amigos) started as follows:

Los Ahuehuetes ladrones	The Ahuehuetes are thieves.
Parra, Pasquel, y Parada	Parra, Pasquel, and Parada
Son puritos cabrones	Are complete assholes
E hijos de la chingada.	And sons of bitches.
Roban al pueblo sufrido	They steal from suffering people
Llevando putas al jefe	Taking whores to the chief
Quien después de haber cojido	Who after fucking
Los agredece y los proteje	Thanks them and protects them.[82]

Such songs concerned the listening agents. Their lyrics underlined popular frustrations, indicated a deep distrust of the president and his advisors, and threatened insurrection. They were also extremely popular. *La Prensa* admitted that "everyone in Mexico knows the jokes, funny stories, allusions, and musical parodies that freely circulated from mouth to mouth."[83] They formed a direct link between the cultural worlds of stage, print, and the street, and they fit the mood of the 1948 Mexico City crowd—halfway between carnival and revolt.

Satire and Censorship

In summer 1948, high-level corruption, political problems, and social deprivation generated an upsurge in the production of satirical cultural works. *Presente* was the most notorious, but there were also other stage plays, skits, and books. They interacted with, fed off, and borrowed from street-level humor. But they also went further. They tied together diffuse dissatisfaction to create organized narratives, offered credibility to rumors and popularized a cogent indictment of the Alemán administration. Like the slander rags of eighteenth-century France, they "reduced the complex politics of the regime into a story-line that could be grasped by any reader at any distance from the center of the action."[84] Laughter, however bleak, linked print culture and civil society. Those close to Alemán deemed such an alliance dangerous. They started to rupture the connections between satirists and the Mexico City crowd in a variety of ways. In a break from normal practice, they employed the kind of regulatory censorship more common to the country's provinces. But they also employed more subtle means. Some were aimed at the producers of satirical culture. Officials rewarded compliant writers with well-paid sinecures. They deprived stubborn journalists of paper and funds and started a mainstream campaign that attacked both professional and amateur satirists as gossipmongers. Others were aimed at the audience for satirical culture. Emergency food markets and forced resignations bought off some of the Mexico City crowd. Anticommunist rhetoric, which blamed the unions for the country's economic woes, split working-class Mexicans from their temporary middle-class allies. Finally, the production of pro-Alemán street propaganda tried to shore up the reputation of the Mexican president.

The founder, director, and editor of *Presente* was the columnist Jorge Piño Sandoval. Piño was not your average Mexico City journalist. He was not middle class, university educated, or, at least initially, right-wing. He was born in San Luis Potosí in 1902. During the revolution, he was orphaned and moved to Mexico City. Here, he moved in with the painter and communist David Siqueiros. First, he was employed as a delivery boy, hawking Siqueiros's paintings around town for a small commission. By the late 1920s he also distributed the radical newspaper *El Machete*. The job gave him a taste for journalism and he started to write the occasional story for the publication. In 1930, he was even arrested, allegedly because one of his articles directly criticized the government.[85] Over the following decade, Piño shed his links to the communists and moved into the world of journalism full time. He leveraged his friendship with another former leftist, Denegri, to gain a job at *Excélsior*. Here, he gradually climbed the hierarchy, moving from the cultural section to political news and was eventually given his own column. In 1938, he founded a film weekly, was placed in charge of *Ultimas Noticias* in 1942, and two years later directed the pro-Alemán magazine *Don Timorato*.[86] He also branched out into print entrepreneurship. But Piño's place in the newspaper establishment was always precarious. He found the social world of journalists suffocating and infuriating. Novo described him as "moody . . . always in crisis, a misfit, inflexible, always in a state of protest and rebellion."[87] The tension between his radical past and his present role as an *oficialista* columnist often caused confrontation. He was responsible for the irony-laden *Hoy* article on Cárdenas's son's 1941 birthday party and he walked out of *Excélsior* twice over differences with the editor.[88]

Such tensions also shaped his brief employment at Pasquel's revamped *Novedades*. In 1947, Piño joined the newspaper and was given a front-page column entitled *Presente*. In general, his articles were overtly progovernment. He lauded *Río Escondido*, the film in which Alemán had a small cameo, as "the best Mexican movie ever produced." He praised the president's open attitude to the press and he condemned the PP, which he viewed as a communist fifth column.[89] Letters between the journalist and the president's private secretary confirm this close relationship. In early 1948 Piño headed a group of journalists to inspect the results of the president's drive for agricultural productivity. In April of the same year he traveled to Aguascalientes, where he offered his backing to the embattled governor.[90]

But in May 1948 something changed. It is unclear whether Piño's conscience finally caught up with him or he fell out with Pasquel or another of Alemán's amigos. On May 19 his column was relegated to the inside pages. The following week, the column radically changed tone. In a strangely personal article, which seemed to reflect his ambiguous relationship with the role of the Mexican journalist, Piño interviewed himself. He explained that in order to become a columnist, he had been forced to "conquer the friendship" of "thousands of contacts." Yet such friendships came with expectations. "When dealing with public men, we [journalists] are little or nothing . . . they tolerate us and nothing more." In return for friendship, these public men wanted publicity. When journalists were unwilling to provide it, they were cut off. Liberty of the press was a sham, invented by businessmen and politicians to secure exposure. The next two columns were similarly vitriolic. Presaging his work on *Presente*, he employed rumors of government corruption to attack those close to the regime. On May 24 he exposed the president's private secretary, Rogerio de la Selva, as a Nicaraguan national. He also revealed that other officials, including Parra's brother-in-law, were foreigners. He concluded by insinuating that de la Selva was not only using his position to secure the Nicaraguan presidency but was also interfering in the election of Mexico's state governors.[91]

Two days later, he revealed the level of violence, impunity, and judicial malpractice in Alemán's home state of Veracruz. The story focused on To-ribio Vázquez, a rancher and billiards hall owner recently found hanging from a tree outside Cordoba. According to Piño, two years earlier Vázquez's ene-mies had tried to assassinate him. This precipitated a blood feud. As Vázquez started to take out his opponents, people started to disappear. Police had recently discovered fifty-eight bodies buried under a tumbledown house on the Cordoba-Huatusco road. At this point the authorities acted, but not in the correct way. They robbed the billiards hall, kidnapped Vázquez and five accomplices, tortured the prisoners, and then strung them up at various points outside the city. In a sweeping conclusion, Piño stated that "58 persons were sacrificed without the governor of Veracruz lifting a finger" and argued that "in Veracruz there is no judicial action to contain criminality." Inevitably, such revelations caused a confrontation with the newspaper's owner. Accord-ing to Piño, Pasquel offered him a round-the-world trip, the direction of a new magazine, and a substantial salary increase to tone down his column. Piño refused and was sacked. Later, he claimed that he "could not convince them that my motive was not money but a clean Mexico."[92]

Fewer than six weeks later, Piño founded the weekly satirical magazine *Presente*. His collaborators came from the world of Mexican broadsheet and magazine journalism. But like Piño, they were not from the Mexico City–born, university-educated middle class. Only Renato Leduc attended the UNAM. He was a bohemian poet and leftist who disowned his high-class upbring-ing.[93] Others were relatively low-class provincials—*gran prensa* outsiders—like the *Hoy* cartoonist Arias Bernal or Jorge Ferretis, a poet, author, and failed businessman.[94] They also comprised other writers from the world of satirical theater—Tomás Perrín was a comic actor and writer who provided the satiri-cal songs for the magazine. There were also notable female writers including Perrín's wife, the comic actress Refugio "Cuca" Escobar, and the poet Mar-garita Michelena. The start-up money, Piño claimed, was minimal and came from his shares in the *Excélsior* cooperative and his final paycheck from *Nove-dades*. Journalists were paid only nominal sums. The initial salary bill, which Piño published in the first edition of *Presente*, came to just over 23 pesos.[95]

In the magazine's first editorial, Piño explained the publication's aim. Building on his self-critique of a few months earlier, he claimed that he had started *Presente* to "liberate [him]self from political and commercial induce-ments," avoid the progovernment lies of the mainstream press, and tell the truth about what was going on in Mexico. To do so, contributors used two approaches—critiquing unpopular official policies and tying these policies directly to Alemán's amigos. Attacks on the foot-and-mouth campaign, for example, were frequent. Writers condemned the manipulation of the capital's land market for private profit and they lampooned the incompetent clear-up operation following recent floods.[96] But after July 22, like many Mexicans, they focused their critiques on the devaluation. Six days later, Piño's editorial mocked the government's theory that the lowering of the currency made Mexican goods exportable. "Mexico exports nothing, in the north we are even forced to import gasoline from the U.S." Industry was failing, and over the previous eighteen months three hundred factories had closed. In fact Mexico only "exported braceros," and all their money "goes into the hands of Spanish contractors." In a follow-up article, one of the contributors speculated that officials had hinted to bankers of the devaluation ahead of time. In the next issue, they elaborated on the claim, stating that in the days before the shift elites had moved $70 million into U.S. banks. When Beteta publicized the names of those who had transferred money, *Presente* journalists rubbished the revelations, claiming that the treasury minister had deliberately left out the principal offenders.[97]

Such criticisms were pointed, but not unusual. In summer 1948, mainstream newspapers published similar, if slightly toned down, versions of these claims.[98] *Presente*, however, went further. Rather than leaving the accusations hanging, shrouded in vague accusations against bankers, elites, or "influential people," the magazine's journalists started to name names. Like the street satirists, they connected economic mismanagement, poverty, and rising prices to high-profile corruption. In Leduc's column, he made this break with expected practice clear: "There is a tendency in the press not to personalize issues, not to name names." In contrast, in *Presente* "we will name names and we will personalize problems."[99] Another article was even more explicit. "*Presente* and the people want to know NAMES."[100] Such an approach not only smacked of *libertinaje*, it also transformed scattered rumors and murmured disquiet into a clear, antisystemic attack. Loose talk became coherent discourse. Mexico City's consumers were struggling, not because of the impersonal, uncontrollable, and impenetrable shifts of the international markets, but due to individual acts of private enrichment.

In the first article of this type, Piño, writing under a pseudonym, exposed the extent of Beteta's wealth. The article focused on his new house. The piece parodied the society pages, offering pictures of the establishment, its address (Zúñiga 205, Lomas de Chapultepec), its size (484 square meters), its price (at least 1.14 million pesos), and a description of its luxurious extent (it contained eight bedrooms, a garage, a library, an office, a kitchen, servants' quarters, a walk-in fridge, and a marble swimming pool imported from Italy). But unlike the society pages, the article also had bite. Piño claimed that Manuel Suárez, a close business associate of the president, had given the house to Beteta in a simulated sale. Suárez had also given Beteta's former boss a similar property just outside the Morelos holiday retreat of Tepoztlán. Beteta was now so rich he was doing the same, offering his secretary a house worth 70,000 pesos in return for her silence.[101]

The following week, Piño did a similar exposé of Parra, under the headline "The minister without a budget." Again, they published a picture of his magnificent new residence and publicized its address (Hegel 315, Polanco), its price (3 million pesos), and its lavish furnishings. Again, they started to investigate the origins of Parra's wealth, linking him to land fraud in Mexico City, generous state-backed loans, and special deals.[102] Other revelations soon followed. *Presente* journalists accused the secretary of the economy of using his position to obtain an exclusive contract for the furnishing of government offices.[103] They criticized the general manager of the National Bank of Mexico (Banco Nacional de México) for expropriating *ejido* land and building a luxury golf course. They repeated the criticisms of de la Selva's foreign birth and political power, and they attacked Alemán's director of the National Railways of Mexico for illegally selling off stock, filling the administration with friends and relatives, and raising the budget from 75,000 to 300,000 pesos. Most of the extra cash, they claimed, was spent on "luxury trains" for the minister's own personal use, whiskey, and "beautiful secretaries."[104]

These investigations culminated in an overt attack on Piño's former boss, Pasquel. After revealing that Pasquel had tried to bribe him to stay on at *Novedades*, the *Presente* editor started to trawl through his other business interests. He repeated rumors that Pasquel had increased the price of food by charging high rates at his customs brokerage offices. He also accused Pasquel of pushing up the price of wheat and bread by monopolizing their import into the country. Piño insulted his kin, claiming that Pasquel came from a "rancid family," a gang of Valle Nacional plantation owners whose repressive labor practices "left cruel memories in the flesh of the people." He also exposed his properties, including the cinemas in Veracruz, the offices at Ramón Guzmán 59, the "palace" in Tlalpan, and the lover's retreat in the center of the city.[105]

Increasingly aggressive cartoons complemented these attacks. They directly linked the exposés to residents' current predicaments. On the front page of the July 28 issue, Arias Bernal depicted the devaluation as a pair of scales, weighed down on one side by "$300 million pesos of influential men." Under the illustration a poor Mexican asked Beteta why the price of basic foods was so high. A sneering Beteta replied, "Not at all, it has dropped its peso" [playing on the double meaning of peso as currency and weight].[106] On the front page of the August 18 issue, Alemán was depicted running away with a note in his hand engraved with the word "Budget"; a group of voracious businessmen labeled "los amigitos" [the little friends] ran after him in pursuit.[107]

At least initially, Piño and his collaborators were keen to demonstrate that they were attacking Alemán's cronies rather than the president himself. In the introduction to the Parra exposé, Piño stressed that it was "important to differentiate between Alemanistas and Alemán." Criticisms of Alemanistas were a patriotic duty and part of the journalist's responsibility to tell the truth. Criticisms of Alemán were still off-limits.[108] For a time, such arguments had purchase. In fact, on August 11, *Presente*'s chiefs, Piño, Leduc, and Arias Bernal, managed to secure an interview with Alemán. The article headlined "An Hour and a Half with Miguel Alemán Valdés" was a real scoop. In Mexico one-on-one interviews with sitting presidents were extremely rare; critical, seemingly unmediated, discussions about failing policies, dodgy alliances, and corruption even more so.[109]

Yet this was the format of the interview. During the talks, the three journalists threw a series of increasingly hostile accusations at the president. They criticized his media policy, claiming that he had allowed commercial interests to take over and manipulate newspapers. They attacked his economic policy, arguing that rich bankers had made fortunes out of the devaluation. They denounced his plans for Mexico City, arguing that the capital was "full of potholes, rubbish, the overcrowding of stalls," and the illegal sale of poor, underserviced lots. They compared the "huge, splendid residences" of his friends with the situation of most Mexican citizens who "suffer[ed] scarcity or lack of basic foods." They followed this up by stating, "You, Mr. President, with the greatest respect, don't seem to care." They even confronted Alemán with his growing lack of popularity. His official statements might persuade the wealthy elites but, as Leduc claimed, "in the city people see things different. . . . They whistle when your image crosses the cinema screen."[110]

In response, the journalists presented Alemán as confused and weak. He batted away questions about the devaluation with the usual references to larger economic forces. He agreed with the journalists about the state of the city's press. He even approved of their condemnation of his acquaintances, calling them "friends of the second or third class" and "a disgrace or a sickness." But as the accusations piled up, he appeared less and less in control. When they reproached him for not caring about the perception of the Mexican people, the journalists claimed, "an expression of surprise, which took the qualities of a painful rictus, crossed his face." For the remainder of the interview, he appeared to go silent, allowing the journalists to pile on more complaints with little or no riposte.[111]

Presente's exposés, bold illustrations, and critical style made the magazine extremely popular. At 20¢ per issue, the publication was cheap and affordable, half the price of a Mexico City broadsheet, and a fifth of the price of a glossy magazine. In July, the U.S. embassy estimated that the magazine sold around 30,000 copies. By late August, the print run had increased to 120,000; Piño even claimed that circulation reached 182,000. Copies were changing hands for 1.50 pesos and print runs ran out after twelve hours.[112] Such figures were ten times the sales of most magazines and almost double the sales of broadsheets.[113] High circulation generated strong links with civil society. In the streets, government agents observed that Mexico City residents were reading *Presente* and weaving the printed stories into their criticisms, rumors, and jokes. In late July, one agent found that *Presente*'s piece on Beteta had generated "bitter comments" about the minister, especially among the poor.[114] *Presente*'s Parra exposé inserted the "minister without a budget" into popular comic songs.[115] And the Pasquel piece added substance to street rumors of the businessman's corrupt practices.

Furthermore, at least during these first few months, *Presente*'s readership crossed lines of class and gender. The editorial line played down partisan politics and avoided union bashing. Writers presented the conflict as between a united front of middle- and working-class Mexicans and a thin tier of the hyper-elite. Photographs of *Presente* readers showed working-class bullfight spectators holding up a placard reading "We ask for applause. Presente. The Newspaper of the People," a barber reading the latest issue, and two working-class housewives eagerly poring over a copy. Underneath, the caption explained, "The jubilation over the resurgence of Presente was equal among all social classes. But above all among the humble classes whose problems are the most important in this weekly."[116] This popularity among female readers should come as no surprise. Women were normally charged with stretching the household budget to feed the family. This role put them at the forefront of opposition to the price rises. In fact, when the magazine folded in 1949, Leduc blamed the publication's demise on the decline in female readers.[117]

Presente's funding depended on sales. Piño was a savvy publicist who knew how to reach out to the literate and semiliterate public. He actively cemented these links in two ways. On the one hand, he included the voices of Mexico City residents wherever possible. The "En la Defensa de la Calle" [In

Defense of the Street] section was key. Every week readers wrote in to denounce examples of official incompetence or corruption. Letters ranged from
mundane complaints about flooding, poor quality drinking water, potholes,
and taxes to pointed critiques of individual politicians. In August, Juan Sandalo
wrote in to complain that Casas Alemán had blocked off dirt tracks and built his
own private road to the Desierto de los Leones National Park, effectively creating his own private luxury garden.[118] On the other hand, Piño also used cultural
forms designed to appeal to a mass audience. Visual images, including photographs of palatial residences and bloody *nota roja* shots, were critical, as were
Arias Bernal's cartoons. Amusing satirical songs, some of which came straight
from the street, were equally important. After the crowd insulted Casas Alemán
with chants at a football match, *Presente* reprinted the following verses.

Ese autóctono sultán	That independent sultan
Que así se pone sus botas	Who puts on his boots like this
Ya no es Casas Alemán	Is not Casas Alemán anymore
Que hoy es Alemán Casotas	But Alemán Big Houses[119]

The magazine's resident songwriters, Tomás Perrín and Renato Leduc,
wrote others. Echoing the concerns of satirical theater, they parodied revolutionary corridos by comparing the lives of the old revolutionaries with those
of the new bourgeoisie.

Rebeldes y robavacas colgaron	Rebels and cattle thieves hung up
el 30-30	their 30-30s
Pues ya son gente popof	Now they are high society
Y hoy habrean la nación	and starve the nation
Con sus cuentas de inflación	with their bank accounts
Y sus palitos de golf	and their golf clubs.[120]

Piño's concern for reaching a broader audience even inspired his launch of
a theater revue based on the magazine.[121] He hired actors and actresses,
booked out the Lírico for two weeks, and employed Perrín and Leduc to
write the script and Arias Bernal to design the set.[122] Like the street corridos,
the songs, reprinted the following month in *Presente*, squeezed critiques of
Alemán amigos into short, memorable verses.

Era Beteta hombre modesto y	Beteta was a modest and
precavido	cautious man
Un gran patriota era el Ministro	A great patriot was minister
Don Ramón	Don Ramón

*Y gran negocio le ha proporcionado
    al pueblo
Al pueblo rubio de la vecina
    nación*

And a great business he has given
    the people
The blond people of the neighboring
    nation

Sadly, the revue was canceled at the last minute. According to Piño, the president's private secretary paid off the Lírico and other major theaters not to show the event.[123] *Presente*'s popularity made censoring the magazine a high priority.

During the period, other cultural productions shared *Presente*'s satirical coverage of the government. Just two days before the devaluation, journalist Roberto Blanco Moheno also attempted to put on a political revue at the Lírico. Entitled *El Cuarto Poder*, or The Fourth Estate, no copy of the work survives. But according to Blanco Moheno, it was "written after a bottle of rum and with a guitar" and included songs, skits, and jokes on the corruption of the mainstream press and Alemán's amigos.[124] Less than a month later, Magdalena Mondragón, the former editor of humorous magazine *Chist*, published her take on political humor, *Los Presidentes Dan Risa*. The book defended the social need for satire and offered an overview of jokes about those in power from the revolution to the present. In the final section on Miguel Alemán she trod lightly. She admitted that there were "many very cruel jokes on Alemán, some of these [were] very vulgar and intervene[d] in the private and family life of the president." These, she refused to publish. But she did print "Miguel," the parody of the Lara song "Madrid."[125] The comic actor Palillo was also busy. His "Astillas" column in the bullfighting magazine *El Redondel* made jokes at the expense of Alemán's amigos. Meanwhile his show at the Follies theater "put the government in the bin and told the truth about its worth." According to one of his fans he said the government was "a mafia of the shameless, who if they had any shame, would have already resigned."[126]

The tone and popularity of such works worried the government. And in summer 1948 the authorities brought in a raft of measures to end the popular dissatisfaction caused by the devaluation. They were a distinctly *dictablanda* blend of mass payoffs, bribery, financial pressures, threats, and deniable acts of violence. Some attacked the root causes and were aimed at grumbling Mexico City consumers. They included cheap food. On August 14, the authorities rolled out two state-subsidized markets in the upper-class neighborhoods of Colonia Ex Hipódromo de Peralvillo and Colonia Del Valle.[127] By the end of the month, they had opened four more in less salubrious barrios.[128] The markets were extremely popular. Thousands traveled to buy cheap provisions each day. The government seemed to be taking note of people's complaints. Agents noted that they "reduced the tension of the previous days" and generated "a spirit of frank optimism."[129] Even the notoriously unpopular Casas Alemán received applause when he toured the establishments.[130] In fact, Leduc blamed the subsequent decline in *Presente*'s popularity on these markets. "The uproar ceased and the people of naïve opinion dedicated themselves to eating bruised but cheap bananas."[131]

Measures also included the resignation or withdrawal of a handful of particularly unpopular amigos. In mid-August, the secretary of the economy, Ruiz Galindo, resigned.[132] Parra left Mexico City and withdrew his candidacy from the governorship of San Luis Potosí.[133] Perhaps most important, Pasquel also left the capital. On August 19 he resigned as director of *Novedades*.[134] Within a week, he had gone into self-imposed exile in his country retreat in San Luis Potosí. Such moves sated popular demands for changes at the top. Newspapers claimed Ruiz Galindo's withdrawal proved Alemán was reasserting his control over wayward cabinet members.[135] Even *Presente* praised Parra's speedy departure.[136]

A countercampaign of pro-Alemán propaganda bolstered these policies. From mid-August, government agents, probably from the DFS, started to distribute printed versions of songs that praised the president and denigrated a vague, shadowy group of unpatriotic enemies. They aped popular comic songs, were short, memorable, and based on popular melodies. "Ay Miguelito" was to be sung to the tune of the ranchero classic "Adolorido"; "Enemigos Emboscados" [Enemies lying in ambush] used the traditional song "La higuera se secó." Most were heavily anticommunist and blamed left-wing leaders for either the devaluation or the subsequent disquiet. Some portrayed the administration's Cardenistas as a communist fifth column. "Enemigos Emboscados" started, "In the center of the government / we know there are communists / enemies lying in ambush / here we have a list for you." The song continued, "Don't get scared Juquilpan [Cárdenas's hometown] / about this bad situation / these are the results / of your administration." Others denounced left-wing union leaders for taking advantage of the country's weak economic position. Despite the odd obscenity or obvious wordplay, these were relatively weak efforts.[137] They lacked the wit, vitriol, or outright vulgarity of the anti-Alemán pieces. But they demonstrated that the authorities were keen to use popular cultural forms to counter street-level dissatisfaction.

The government also gradually brought the capital's newspapers over to its side. Initially, both broadsheets and tabloids criticized the administration for the handling of the devaluation. *Excélsior* questioned the timing of the move and forced Beteta to publish the list of dollar transfers.[138] *La Prensa* even called for the resignation of the cabinet.[139] But soon the tone of the newspapers changed. Why editors and journalists started to support the government remains unclear. Perhaps shared concerns over social instability and increasing union power kicked in. But financial considerations also seem to have played a role. There were rumors that the government offered to cover newspaper losses on overseas purchases in return for more cautious treatment of the devaluation's economic effects.[140] And, it seems no coincidence that Alemán announced the donation of Mexico City real estate to journalists at the end of the year.[141]

Whatever the reasons for the change, the progovernment press campaign started in early August. Beyond highlighting and lauding Alemán's attempts to lower prices, the operation took two forms. First, writers tried to split the middle-class and working-class opposition by blaming union chiefs for the dissatisfaction.[142] Like the pro-Alemán corridos, they portrayed the popular anger as part of a communist plot. On August 10, *La Prensa* denounced miners and railway workers, infiltrated by "communist elements employed to create problems," for orchestrating the attacks on Alemán's cabinet members.[143] Before a large-scale union demonstration on August 21, *La Prensa* covered the event with the headline "Pretext for agitation by Communistoids" and claimed that the march formed "part of a campaign invented by Vicente Lombardo Toledano and Valentín Campa."[144] After the protests, the newspaper claimed the march was poorly attended, unenthusiastic, and simply a "relief for a few street agitators."[145]

Second, the papers started a campaign against what they described as *murmuración*, or gossip. In mid-August, the capital's newspapers started to publish a rash of paid inserts by groups variously calling themselves the National Orientation Center (Centro Nacional Orientador) and the Committee of Struggle Against Murmuración (Comité de Lucha contra la Murmuración). These inserts were broadly similar. They defended the devaluation using official arguments about the international economic situation and they attacked a new figure in Mexican politics, what they termed *el murmurador*, or the gossip. They claimed that the gossip was taking advantage of the devaluation to "go on to the street and spread slander and alarm." He aimed not to help and improve the Mexican economy, but to undermine it. "He leaves his machine to gossip. He leaves an urgent meeting to gossip. He abandons his children and prefers the streets to spread his gossip. He who gossips never works, for gossip needs leisure."[146] Newspaper columnists took up this idea. *La Prensa* ran an editorial entitled "Proconfidence and Against Gossip," which lauded the goals of this hurriedly assembled group. In another article, journalists claimed that those who did not receive a *cañonazo* [literally a cannon blast but actually used to denote a payoff] were indulging in a "subterranean campaign of gossip to attack the government."[147]

The *anti-murmuración* campaign rested on distinctly gendered appreciations of the public sphere. Like other words for gossip, like *chisme, habladuría,* and most notably *comadreo, murmuración* had gendered connotations. *Murmuración* was practiced by women, in the home, at the well, or in the market. It mixed the private and the public, unsubstantiated rumors and well-known facts. As such, it stood in opposition to the formal public sphere, which was held to be objective, practiced by men, and transmitted by the printed word. Campaigners embedded these understandings in their propaganda. *Murmuración* was described as "like weeping and blasphemy" and "not the brave attitude of a man." *Murmuración* was not the refrain of a "MAN OF THE STREET."[148] By attacking *murmuración*, journalists and government propagandists attempted to both denigrate the popular tales of government corruption and shore up the boundaries of what should be treated as both appropriate male behavior and proper news. Insinuating that Beteta had orchestrated the devaluation or singing songs about Alemán's romantic trysts were neither.

Beyond this general campaign to bring down prices and suffocate vocal disquiet, government agents also attacked satirical cultural productions. Measures against *Presente* started immediately. While Piño was readying the first issue of the magazine, the authorities tried to close down the venture by publishing a rival magazine with the same name. Government lawyers claimed that Piño's magazine infringed on the official journal's copyright.[149] The accusations came to nothing, but they foreshadowed the problems to come. On the publication of the magazine, the authorities used their most common strategy. They offered money for silence. The president's private secretary, de la Selva, approached Leduc and asked him, "Hey, you bastard. . . . What do you want? It's fine that Piño and Arias Bernal are fucking around, they're not friends with the president. But you are a friend of Don Miguel and I need to know what do you want to shut your mouth." Leduc replied that he wanted nothing. "So why are you shouting in that little fucking paper?" de la Selva asked again. "Because as soon you university people got to power, people started to want the military back as they stole less," Leduc responded.[150] Government agents also started to harass *Presente* staff. In an August interview with *Presente*'s chief writers, they complained that Pasquel had threatened them with death. Piño lived with three police guards outside and a machine gun trained on the door. His friends carried a pistol each. Pasquel's brother had picked up on the editor's precautions and promised to kill him "whenever his guard was down." Arias Bernal protested that gunmen had kicked down his door and trashed his apartment. Perrín moaned that his house was being watched by "suspicious types."[151]

Presente survived these attacks relatively unscathed. Costs were low; sales were healthy; income was regular; and Piño, Leduc, and Arias Bernal, at least, expected this kind of provocation. But on August 21 an attack on the magazine's printing press threatened to close the magazine for good. At 10:40 P.M. twenty *pistoleros* broke into the press where *Presente* was being printed. They held up the workers at gunpoint, smashed the presses, robbed copies of *Presente* and two other magazines, and stole watches, fountain pens, and a wallet containing over a thousand pesos. Workers called the police, but the officials did not arrive until an hour after the incident. According to newspaper reports, the gunmen did 70,000 pesos worth of damage.[152]

From the beginning, theories on who ordered the attack abounded. Many, including Piño, accused Pasquel. The evidence was impressive. He had a motive. The previous issue of *Presente* had attacked Pasquel directly. The piece precipitated a further exposé in the tabloid *La Prensa* and Pasquel's hurried resignation from *Novedades*.[153] He also had form. Pasquel's temper was an open secret. He had beaten up a worker for insulting his father and had shot a migration officer in Nuevo Laredo just five years earlier.[154] Circumstantial evidence was also strong. The day before the attack, Pasquel had published an interview in *Novedades*, which defended his business practices, rubbished his critics, and seemed to suggest he would not leave Mexico City without a fight.[155] According to Piño he had followed up this insinuation with a threatening phone call.[156] Finally, the owner of the printing press recognized one of the gunmen as Veracruz hit man Manuel Felipe Villaverde, aka "El Asturiano." She had previously seen the man hanging around the offices of Pasquel's newspaper, *Novedades*.[157]

But over the next ten days, the case against Pasquel started to unravel. Pasquel vehemently denied the charges and argued that he would not have been stupid enough to destroy the printing press on the day after his defiant interview. Villaverde was shot in mysterious circumstances in a downtown cantina. Government agents and policemen started to leak that the assault on *Presente* was not as it seemed. Journalists picked up on the rumors and hinted that the attack was actually an "auto-assault," planned and directed by either Piño or a shadowy cabal of politicians funding the magazine.[158] On August 27, *La Prensa* published a couple of articles that pointed to the holes in the case. They indicated that the gunmen clearly did not know what they were doing, as despite the damage, *Presente* was published two days later without a hitch. They suggested that "it was strange that the maneuvers of the squadron of attackers was not seen by anyone in the neighborhood before the attack."[159]

The same day, *El Universal* published an odd insert by a man calling himself Salvador Pérez de León. The writer did not explain his role, his interest in the case, or why he had decided to take out an expensive ad in the newspaper. But in the letter he suggested that either the attack was an auto-assault or a deliberate attempt to frame Pasquel. He concluded with a bizarre section on Piño's own psychological well-being. Here he argued that Piño had dubbed his group of daring reporters "The Suicide Squad," not because they were confronting the establishment, but because Piño himself was suicidal. He claimed that Piño had tried to kill himself on previous occasions. He suggested that the magazine was "an attempt to commit suicide and leave the charge at someone else's door . . . to create the myth of a sacrificed man and make himself a martyr." Out of context, the piece seems surreal. But at the time, those in the know, including Piño, probably read between the lines. Setting up fake suicides was a specialty of the Mexican secret services. During the 1930s, they had used similar techniques to kill criminals, and Alemán's DFS would use the method to rid themselves of difficult politicians and journalists. The letter was actually an indirect threat.[160]

Although government agents probably leaked the accusation that the attack was an "auto-assault," it is worth dealing with briefly. In his autobiography, Blanco Moheno laid out the charges in full. He claimed that Carlos Serrano, Alemán's moneyman, was actually funding the magazine. He was using Piño, Arias Bernal, and Leduc's satirical skills to topple his rivals, the president's law school friends. When Alemán warned him that the magazine risked stirring up the Mexico City crowd, he and Piño engineered the attack to shut up the magazine.[161] The story has some merit. *Presente*'s stories never touched Serrano's activities, and Serrano hated at least one of the publication's major targets, Casas Alemán. But Blanco Moheno is not a reliable narrator, and the theory has other serious problems. Piño's reason for holding fire on Serrano was not necessarily funding, but more probably self-preservation. It was well known that the DFS had kidnapped, beaten, and imprisoned on bigamy charges a Los Angeles–based Mexican journalist who had leaked the Cadillac story.[162] So he was probably right to be afraid. *Presente* did attack Serrano's closest collaborator and friend, Parra, and forced him into internal exile. Finally, and most important, the attack did not precipitate the magazine's demise. In fact, the publication's highest-selling issue came out the next week.[163]

So, who *did* order the attack? Pasquel was probably involved. Piño maintained his accusations against the playboy in the face of police denials, and the murdered gunman, Villaverde, was a known Pasquel associate. By late August, Piño also suggested that other "fat cats" were involved. He never dropped names. But reading between the lines of various news stories and interviews, it seems that he suspected that De la Selva might have ordered or at least approved the attack. Piño had regularly mocked De la Selva in the magazine, and De la Selva's sister had visited the printing press just an hour before the attack.[164]

De la Selva took his orders directly from Alemán. Perhaps he acted alone to maintain his own reputation. But it seems unlikely that the embattled foreign-born politician did something so risky without some kind of presidential authorization. The interview with Alemán appeared just ten days before the attack.[165] Alemán certainly sympathized with the assault's aims. In the following months, the president publicly sought to redraw the lines of acceptable journalism. On August 31, *Excélsior* reported that Alemán supported the *antimurmuración* campaign. "While the capital gossips, the rest of the country works," he stated.[166] In his September state of the union address he admitted that the "sensationalist press" could play a positive role, when it served the collective good and based its accusations on verifiable proof. But he condemned "opportunist critics" and journalists who took advantage of freedom of expression, "exaggerated" discontent, and disoriented public opinion.[167] In a letter to the AMP, he was even more blunt. He warned writers that they should base their accusations on evidence of wrongdoing rather than rumors and that the fraternity of journalists should rid their membership of less scrupulous members. Finally, he reminded reporters that "the best way to defend liberty of expression" was to avoid "pushing the limits of respect for private lives, morality, and the public peace as disgracefully has happened in some publications."[168] The point was clear. Writers needed to keep within a strict interpretation of the press law. Gossipmongering and *Presente*'s brand of satirical muckraking were not acceptable. These journalists were not the victims; they were the perpetrators.

Despite the assault, *Presente* continued. But for the average Mexico City reader, *Presente*'s time had passed. After September 1948, the price of *Presente* rose to 40¢ a copy and circulation fell to around 25,000 per issue.[169] As *Presente*'s journalists admitted, popular indifference killed the magazine. But persistent government intervention did not help. In October the government cut the PIPSA provision of paper to *Presente* by 75 percent. The magazine now received only two metric tons per week. Piño was forced to buy expensive imported Finnish paper and beg for offcuts from friends in the journalism industry.[170] Over the next few months, the magazine shrunk in size, even as it increased in price. The final issue was printed on poor quality paper and was only eight pages long.[171] There is some evidence that government agents finally made good on their threat to "suicide" Piño. Just before the closure of the magazine, Piño tumbled from a second-story balcony onto the ground below, breaking multiple bones. He survived, but only just. Many suspected he was pushed.[172]

The use of such violence to silence Mexico City journalists was extremely rare. But it was not unprecedented. In 1948, the authorities probably used it on at least one more occasion. On November 10 gunmen shot Fernando Sánchez Bretón, the director of a low-rent political magazine, *La Semana Ilustrada*, outside his car. It looked like a professional hit. Two cars trapped the journalist beside his vehicle. The assailants shot him four times. Sánchez fell to the ground but did not die right away. He was taken to hospital, where he survived for two weeks before passing away. In his hospital bed, he pointed the finger at Pasquel, claiming that the businessman had phoned his office and threatened to have him killed if he didn't shut up. But again the authorities covered up the crime. According to a handful of exposés, the DFS arrested four petty thugs, beat and tortured them, and then forced them to sign a confession. One, Roberto Batillas López, aka "el Güero," was a former amateur boxer and the bodyguard of film star Jorge Negrete. He claimed the agents drove him to the Toluca road and beat him in the stomach and the private parts. When he made a run for it, they shot him in the back. They then placed a gun against his head. The process was classic *ley fuga*. The Toluca road was a notorious spot for shooting difficult suspects. But for some reason, "el Güero" got lucky. One of the DFS men intervened, pushing down the gun aimed at his head and saying, "I don't want you to talk you son of a bitch, I come as a representative of the society of Mexico, you are a scapegoat. We know that you don't have anything to do with the matter, but you are going to pay anyway." Despite el Güero's claims, all four men got sixteen years in jail. Pasquel's name was never mentioned.[173]

The attack on *Presente*'s printing press was the most high-profile example of the top-down censorship that took place in the summer of 1948. But there were other examples of legal censorship and dirty tricks. The day before the devaluation, police raided the Lírico theater and banned the performance of the political revue *El Cuarto Poder*. Casas Alemán claimed the language and dancing was too risqué. Blanco Moheno responded that the Mexico City chief was trying to censor critical jokes about his own administration and that of the president. When Blanco Moheno cut the offending gags, the play went ahead, albeit with a reduced crowd that was unexcited by the bland rewritten work.[174] Government agents and the police also bought up or simply took all the Mexico City copies of Mondragón's *Los Presidentes Dan Risa*. In late August, gunmen visited her house, banged on the door, and, finding no one was home, shot up the outside of the building. A neighbor identified their getaway car as belonging to one of Alemán's personal bodyguards.[175] Even Palillo was gagged. His column was cut from *El Redondel* and his show at Follies was canceled early.[176]

Humor Post-1948

The short-term effects of the campaign to silence popular satire campaigns were dramatic. Publications and theaters were closed; journalists were shot at and pushed from balconies. But the long-term effects were perhaps more significant. For at least two decades, the large-scale cultural production of political satire died. Satirical magazines disappeared. Leduc's and Arias Bernal's attempt to revive the genre with 1952's *El Apretado* was markedly less successful.[177] *Rototemas*, a 1959 Cardenista attempt to coopt humor and muckraking for the Mexican left, also sunk after a few months due to poor sales, official repression, and anticommunism.[178] So did political revues. In 1953, Cantinflas tried to refresh the genre with a series of satirical sketches entitled "Yo Colón." They mocked both the Alemán and Ruiz Cortines regimes. But the reception was poor. The theater owner disowned the jokes, and reviewers reminded audiences that Cantinflas had publicly supported the former president. Two years later, a similar revival was equally unsuccessful. The shows were fined and shut down. Journalists no longer rushed to the theater's defense. Instead they pompously denigrated popular satire, claiming it "ate away the foundations of authority, making such authority appear so crumbly, so fragile, and so useless, that it is worse than rags thrown in the middle of the street so that everyone can step on them."[179]

The satirists and journalists, who had used their talents to embarrass the Alemán administration, became increasingly *oficialistas*. Piño went into enforced exile in Argentina. When he returned in the 1950s, he reverted to his job as a political columnist, earning a 2,000-peso monthly *iguala* for his silence.[180] Arias Bernal toned down his works and went back to producing anticommunist cartoons for overpriced color magazines. Mondragón became editor of the short-lived *La Prensa Gráfica* and headed the left-wing journalists to whom were donated the agricultural colony in Tamaulipas in 1952.[181]

Blanco Moheno went on to become one of the foremost supporters of the
PRI government, hawking his silence for government jobs and comfortable
columnist posts. During the late 1970s he even became a PRI deputy.[182] Even
the professional comics calmed down. Cantinflas became a government shill,
marching arm-in-arm with Alemán, acting as an electoral observer at the controversial 1952 election, and producing a series of increasingly unfunny films.[183]
Roberto Soto sank so low that he took employ as Baja California Norte governor Braulio Maldonado's clown, doing shows to offset the minister's declining
popularity.[184]

Political humor did not disappear completely. Throughout the period cartoons remained acceptable spaces for dissent.[185] But as text and stage versions declined, the audience for satire narrowed. Satirical jokes became part
of elitelore, the informal system of gossip and rules that were limited to Mexico
City's ministries, administrative offices, and newsrooms. According to Monsiváis, after 1948 a "sense of humor" was one of the rights journalists kept to
themselves. In private they were "acute and destructive commentators"; in
public they were "corny and oficialista."[186] To enjoy such jokes, listeners needed
an intimate knowledge of leaders' personal foibles, the inner workings of the
party, and the oblique language of the PRI. They also needed a shared cynicism about the actual aims of power.[187] As a result, such gags rarely made their
way onto the street. If they reached print, they were encoded in incomprehensible political columns in underread broadsheets or hidden away in limited
edition political newsletters, which not coincidentally saw a rapid upsurge after
1948.[188] As a result, most Mexicans lacked the references, the context, and the
values to make such jokes. In fact, Samuel Schmidt argues that "among the
nonelite groups not a single political joke seems to have been produced" during the period.[189] Satirizing the system became a game for the PRI's inner circle.

In contrast, popular comedy became increasingly apolitical. Armando
Jiménez's ethnography of Mexican street *picardía* [mischief] contains chapters
on flatus, excrement, sexual relations, infidelity, and drunkenness. There are
lengthy digressions on "el zorrero," the mid-century Mexico City thief who
used to mark his territory with his own shit. And there are over forty flippant
euphemisms for female menstruation. But political jokes are scarce. The only
gag on the PRI is a piece of bathroom graffiti, which describes the party as
"a total son of a bitch . . . like this cubicle, smelling of shit."[190] According to
Mexican humorologists, the two most popular traditions of gag-making also
lacked political bite. *Albures* were double entendres with obscene allusions. They
were occasionally used to mock the powerful. But they were employed more
frequently to prove superior masculinity in verbal contests of one-upmanship.[191]

Relajo was a form of nonsensical communal wordplay and mockery designed to deflate solemn situations. As such, it had satiric potential. But according to street philosopher Jorge Portillo, who wrote a book on the subject in the early 1950s, this went unfulfilled. By opposing any serious discussion, *relajo* embraced what he termed "negative liberty," an unconstructive refusal to engage with pointed criticism or suggest any meaningful change. Relajo was "conservative" and "unproductive";[192] Cantinflas, its foremost practitioner, was a harmless, sanitized version of the Mexico City working class, whose "verbal confusion . . . rather than serving to criticize the demagogy of the politicians, actually legitimize[d] it."[193]

Satire and Social Forces

This story of street jokes, satirical cultural works, and suppression helps explain the chronology of Mexican political humor, the connections between press readership and broader social and political forces, and the mechanics of state censorship. The events of summer 1948 demonstrate that under certain conditions the links between journalists and civil society could flourish even in Mexico City. Writers and readers interacted; popular complaints found an echo on the printed page; and satire became a shared language. Yet it also shows the limits of these connections in the capital. Here, the administration could deploy extensive resources, including subsidized food, press payoffs, land donations, and groups of hitmen and thugs to sever the links between print culture and the Mexico City crowd. After 1948, it still existed in some spaces, particularly in the *nota roja* of the tabloid press. But satirical texts no longer formed part of the broader public sphere.

In more general terms, the chapter suggests some rules governing the production and reception of political satire. In 1948, satire was not simply an escape valve. It was a genuine threat. By providing a narrative that linked popular suffering to elite corruption, satire provided a comprehensible, unifying language for dissent. But the popularity and efficacy of this language—the level of this threat—depended on broader socioeconomic and political processes, including, in this case, the price of basic foods and the perceived possibility of government reform. It also depended on what one might term satirical entrepreneurs, those inside the media, like Arias Bernal, Piño, and Leduc, prepared to both leak stories and organize these stories into wider discourses.

Finally the story also suggests more universal understandings of censorship. As laid out in chapter 2, censorship involved medium-term cultural processes, including the development of broad understandings of nationalism, economic progress, and the proper practice of journalism. But it also comprised impromptu bursts of multiagency repression, which included the covert use of violence. Such strategies not only stopped the immediate threat, but, buttressed by the authorities' explanations in public statements and private letters, they also provided a new manual for journalists' behavior. The story of *Presente* became an instructive myth. From 1948 onward, Mexico City's reporters learned the limits of acceptable discourse, the boundaries of their audience, and the prospective punishments for those who expressed dissent.

CHAPTER FOUR

From Catholic Schoolboy to Guerrilla
Mario Menéndez and the Radical Press

On the afternoon of September 8, 1974, twenty government agents smashed down the doors of the radical newspaper *Por Qué?* They arrested the journalists and secretaries, destroyed the typewriters, and gathered together the documents, articles, and photographs that littered the desks. The following day, gunmen kidnapped the editor, Roger Menéndez. The prisoners were taken to the notorious Military Camp No. 1 on the outskirts of Mexico City. Here, they were tortured and questioned for the next fortnight before they were finally released. For *Por Qué?*'s reporters, repression was nothing new. Government agents had refused the publication paper, stolen print runs, kidnapped and tortured its reporters, and probably bombed the offices. In fact, Roger's brother, Mario Menéndez, was still in enforced exile in Cuba. But the ferocity of the 1974 attack, the subsequent imprisonment, and the loss of machinery finally put an end to the magazine.[1] For six years, *Por Qué?* had provided a unique space for critical, investigative journalism. The magazine's reporters had traced the evolution of student radicalism from the Mexico City streets to the Guerrero jungle and the Chihuahua mountains. They had exposed the violent *cacicazgos*, crony capitalism, and rigged elections of the provinces, and they had uncovered corruption, repression, and even links to the CIA at the highest levels of the Mexican government.

Despite *Por Qué?*'s achievements, few Mexican intellectuals lamented its demise. Coverage in the nationals was sparse. Even left-wing publications wasted little ink on the closure.[2] Over the past four decades, discussion of the magazine has been similarly muted. Most media scholars ignored the publication, choosing instead to concentrate on the control of the big nationals or the rise of Scherer's more open *Excélsior*. Those who looked at *Por Qué?* dismissed the magazine as "tabloid" and "exaggerated" and depicted its denouncements as the "fruits of desperation and not careful reflection."[3] Opinions on the founder, editor, and star journalist Mario Menéndez have been even harsher. Former student leaders suggested that Menéndez was either a DFS or a CIA spy, employed to divide the Mexican left.[4] Jorge Castañeda scorned the Yucatán writer as a DFS mole, a "discredited journalist," and a "shady ... adventurer" who indulged in various "pseudo-guerrilla activities."[5] Menéndez's own post–*Por Qué?* career accounts for some of this bad press. As we shall see, when he returned from exile, he started a new magazine, *Por Esto*, and did work on behalf of the government. But it also reveals the closed, snobbish world of the capital's media to which Menéndez was always an outsider. In fact, it was probably this outsider status that prompted him to break the unwritten codes of the capital's press. Though wealthy and educated, he came from Yucatán, not Mexico City. He shunned the incestuous political gossip, conspicuous consumption, and hard-drinking camaraderie of his fellow journalists. At the height of *Por Qué?*'s success he still drove a small Renault and lived in a rented apartment.[6] His attitude to other journalists was "isolated and critical."[7] His team comprised family members, provincial reporters, or nonjournalists from the world of literature or activism. Even when he took charge of one of the major national magazines, *Sucesos Para Todos*, he rarely visited the office. He also bucked journalistic codes of conduct. His prose style was brusque and to the point. He named the guilty, and insulted the president. During the 1970s, *Por Qué?* was far to the left of most left-wing publications, which sought some kind of rapprochement with the new president, Luis Echeverría (1970–1976).

Menéndez should not be dismissed so quickly. In fact, the story of the provincial journalist and the rise and fall of Mexico's most radical magazine reveals the profound changes to the world of print journalism in the 1960s. During the period, many journalists, like Menéndez, radicalized politically. As this chapter demonstrates, this was not a simple, one-way process. Political awakenings were often long, drawn-out, and fraught activities.[8] External factors, from making contact with likeminded comrades through witnessing state repression to discovering evidence of government corruption, accelerated radicalization. Other outside pressures, from national and international governments, but also from financers, family, and friends, slowed, curtailed, and even reversed radicalization at key points. In Mexico, the process was even more tortuous. The ruling party had enemies on both left and right. And along the way opponents of the state often found allies on both sides. Such connections often led to accusations of political flip-flopping or state collusion, as in Menéndez's case.

But these personal changes did have major effects. As Menéndez and other writers shifted to the left, they rejected the old, inward-looking world of cozy state-press relations. Instead they started to see journalism as a means to uncover the networks of self-interest, corruption, and public-private links, which undergirded both political and social systems. They began to reach beyond the traditional audiences for political journalism, to workers, clerical employees, students, and even peasants. *Por Qué?*'s bold language, *nota roja* style, antiestablishment approach, reliance on investigative journalism, and focus beyond the capital foreshadowed and influenced not only the small-scale alternative press of the 1970s, but also the hard-hitting, left-leaning nationals of later decades like *Proceso*, *Unomásuno*, and *La Jornada*. The government response to *Por Qué?* also exposed the new methods of government censorship, which went beyond the employment of a few pliant journalists and ex-officio gunmen and was now institutionalized in a relatively powerful and cognizant secret service.

Finally Menéndez's own story forms part of a larger narrative of how East-West divisions affected national cultures. The Cold War was a media conflict in which both left- and right-wing groups sought control of information.[9] Like other left-wing journalists, Menéndez was, at least in part, funded by the Cuban authorities. His exposés of guerrillas, CIA influence, and official repression proved extremely influential among national and international leftists. But they also drew him into the murky world between journalism and political intelligence. The public sphere, such as it was, became even further curtailed by secret service organizations and covert groups. Here, media conflict, armed insurgency, and the dirty war met. Here, journalism mixed with radical propaganda and reporters doubled as government agents and even guerrillas. Here, secret service agents and spies joined press officers in the game of media manipulation. And here, Mexican suppression intertwined with international attempts to shut up reporters and undermine their credibility. Censorship moved out of the pressroom and into the realm of espionage and counterterrorism.

The "Death" of Mario Menéndez (1937–1965)

On February 9, 1965, a small advertisement appeared in the pages of *Excélsior*. "Mario Menéndez died yesterday in the city of Merida, capital of the state of Yucatán in the breast of our Mother the Catholic, Apostolic and Roman Church, comforted with spiritual help and papal benediction. His wife, children, uncles and other family members pray for him to find profound peace, begging God that his soul rests for eternity."

Mario Menéndez was not actually dead.[10] He had moved to Mexico City to become a national journalist. The obituary was a threat, probably improvised by angry members of Yucatán's so-called *casta divina* [divine caste] or economic elite. But it also contained a more profound meaning. By publishing his first book a few months earlier, Menéndez had severed his ties to his family, his community, and his old life. The work, *Yucatán o el genocidio* [Yucatán or the genocide], was a carefully compiled but savage piece of investigative journalism, which laid the blame for henequen growers' poverty at the feet of both corrupt bureaucrats and a smug, self-interested bourgeoisie. For Merida's upper classes, the old Mario Menéndez—Catholic schoolboy, churchgoer, society husband, scion of one of the city's wealthiest families—was dead. But Menéndez, the journalist, the editor, and the left-wing activist, still lived.

Mario Renato Menéndez Rodríguez was born in Merida on January 14, 1937. His parents were Mario Menéndez Romero and Pilar Rodríguez Cantillo. His grandfather, Carlos Menéndez, was owner of the city's foremost newspaper, *El Diario de Yucatán*. Carlos Menéndez had started his journalism career during the Porfiriato, and like many local journalists, turned against the regime. He criticized the treatment of Yucatán henequen workers and supported the anti-Porfirian candidate for governor.[11] Over the following decades, however, his radicalism declined. Like many early revolutionaries, he disliked Díaz's undemocratic dictatorship, but also feared Mexico's masses. He combated moves to undermine what he saw as the country's natural socioeconomic hierarchy and opposed both revolutionary anticlericalism and attempts to redistribute the country's wealth. Such opinions moved the journalist into alliance with his old enemies, the state's economic elite, and their vocal protectors, the leaders of the Catholic Church. By the 1920s, his newspaper was effectively the planters' paper. Such opinions generated frequent clashes with the revolutionary authorities. Left-leaning governments repeatedly held public incinerations of the paper. Perhaps the highest-profile confrontation was with the state governor Bartolomé García Correa (1930–1934) and involved an armed attack on the newspaper, its forced closure, and a long-running legal case.[12]

Over the next three decades, Carlos and *El Diario de Yucatán* settled into a less combative relationship with the government. The paper continued to support the planters and criticized the 1937 decision to divide up their estates. But Merida's old landowners soon realized that the policy barely affected their wealth. By keeping the expensive henequen shredding machines and the best lands, they could continue to dominate the industry. And *El Diario de Yucatán* followed their drift, occasionally sniping at individual bureaucrats and one-off policies, but broadly defending the new arrangement between the state and the local oligarchy.[13] In the 1940s Blanco Moheno summed up *El Diario de Yucatán* as follows: "An efficient, good newspaper professionally speaking, but directed by a reactionary egotist and written by the Garcías, Juncos and Correas, who claim that the unfortunate are worth nothing, not even being robbed . . . Señor Menéndez can't even call the people the 'pueblo' but 'the turbamulta' [mob] [or] the 'befa' [mockery]."[14]

Menéndez grew up in the shadow of his snobbish and domineering grandfather. From the mid-1960s he would sever links with *El Diario de Yucatán* and many of his family members. But despite his leftward shift, he never turned on the newspaper's founder. In fact, his grandfather remained an inspiration. Selectively commemorating the editor's career, he set aside his right-wing politics and instead embraced his contrarianism. (In *Por Qué?* he even continued to use Carlos's old pseudonyms for his own work.)[15] But such rewriting of history was yet to come. During Menéndez's early years he grew up in an elite, conservative Merida home. Supporting the planters, maintaining good relations with the government, and growing *El Diario de Yucatán's* readership offered money and status. Menéndez received the education of the state capital's upper class. He went to church and Sunday school; attended a private Catholic primary; and was then sent to the exclusive New Orleans Catholic high school, Holy Cross. After graduation he went to the University of Tulane to get a degree in the humanities.[16]

When Menéndez returned to Merida in 1958, he threw himself into two activities, the family business and the Catholic Church. At *El Diario de Yucatán*, he worked his way up from the bottom. He did stints at the warehouse, the printing workshop, and the typesetting department. By 1960, he was promoted to the newsroom. The following year, his grandfather Carlos died and Menéndez became the director of the newspaper at the age of twenty-four.[17] A visiting U.S. observer was impressed by the operation. He noted *El Diario's* commitment to editorial independence. Menéndez boasted that they refused to take government money, flagged *gacetillas* with the phrase "paid insertion," and even limited private publicity. Family members did most of the work. Menéndez's father and uncle were editors. Another uncle was the publisher, and a cousin was the mechanical overseer and business manager. Beyond Menéndez's relations, there were only eleven newsroom employees. Despite the limited staff, *El Diario de Yucatán* maintained a certified circulation of 42,705. It was the third-highest-selling regional newspaper in Mexico, unloading just slightly less than big city broadsheets like Monterrey's *El Norte* and Guadalajara's *El Occidental*. Finally, he remarked on Menéndez's ambition. The young director told the visiting American that he did not work "for money but for satisfaction" and was driven by a desire to "seek and present the truth."[18]

While Menéndez was climbing *El Diario's* hierarchy, he was also reentering Merida's world of elite Catholic groups. In the early 1960s he married the daughter of one of the *casta divina* families. From then on, he attended mass every Sunday; he went to conferences on morality and dogma; he joined lay Catholic organizations and even took "Cursillos de Cristiandad." These were short, intensive courses on Christianity, which stressed spiritual development and were designed to train lay Catholic leaders. He also grew close to the archbishop's right-hand man, Rafael Bueno y Bueno. The secretary was no liberation theologian, but he did lead the more progressive sectors of the local church.[19]

Menéndez's relatively stable balance of work and church did not last. In 1963, his roles as independent journalist and upper-class Catholic came into conflict. Within a year, Menéndez would have to choose between his drive to "seek and present the truth" and his place within Merida society. The issue that generated the dilemma was the state's largest cash crop and the source of the elite's wealth—the henequen industry. Before looking at Menéndez's rather technical investigation into the business, it is worth pausing for a moment to examine the state of Yucatán's henequen industry in the early 1960s. Henequen had been the state's major export since the nineteenth century. Vast haciendas grew thousands of hectares of agave plants. Landowners' factories turned the raw fibers of the cactus into twine, which was then exported for industrial use. The process caused the takeover of communities' lands and the employment of many villagers as debt peons. After the revolution, progressives demanded an end to the exploitation. Under Cárdenas, the government complied, distributing over 100,000 hectares of hacienda lands to 25,000 *ejidatarios*. In 1938, the state decided that the lands would be worked communally.[20] The government's ejido bank—the Agrarian Bank of Yucatán (Banco Agrario de Yucatán)—took over distributing credit among the *ejidatarios*. By 1961, the state had founded a private-public institution, Cordemex, charged with buying and exporting the twine. The state owned half the organization, and members of the *casta divina* retained the other half.[21]

Despite the changes, exploitation continued. Bank chiefs and *casta divina* shareholders got rich while the *ejidatarios* remained mired in poverty. Big profits, however, failed to eliminate interelite squabbling. In 1963 members of the *casta divina* fell out with the head of the ejido bank, Gilberto Mendoza Vargas. They suspected that the state official was trying to persuade the *ejidatarios* to turn on the *casta divina*. At this point, they decided to call on their old ally, *El Diario de Yucatán*, and its new director, Mario Menéndez. The plan was to slip Menéndez information on the bank's corrupt practices and use the ensuing public outrage to get rid of Mendoza. They assumed that

Menéndez was his grandfather's man, that he would sacrifice his commitment to journalism to maintain the status quo.[22] They were wrong.

For over a year, Menéndez investigated the inner workings of the henequen industry. He pored over complex financial documents, interviewed bureaucrats, and tracked down members of the Merida elite. He produced dozens of articles in both *El Diario* and *Excélsior*. In late 1964 he published these articles, together with details of the mechanics of the investigation, in a book bluntly entitled *Yucatán o el genocidio*. The work was much more than the simple indictment of the *ejido* bank that the *casta divina* intended. It was an indictment of an entire socioeconomic and cultural system. Through the collusion of state representatives and business elites, the domination and mistreatment of *ejidatarios* continued, and, through the hypocrisy of the ecclesiastical hierarchy, Merida's select few were excused their sins. But the work was not just investigative journalism; it was also autobiography. Hard data on henequen pricing were interspersed with the author's thoughts on economic exploitation, journalism, and the role of the good Catholic. What emerged was not only an account of corruption but also the story of Menéndez's transformation from obedient Catholic son to left-wing radical. We view how Menéndez's commitment to journalism, what he calls the "the need to speak the truth with all of its consequences . . . the naked, the hurtful truth . . . which will agitate spirits, and arouse questions, queries, and doubts," drove this journey.[23]

As the members of the *casta divina* intended, the investigation began as an attack on corrupt officials in the *ejido* bank. In January 1963 Menéndez started to hear rumors that there had been a fight at the last meeting of bank bureaucrats and Cordemex shareholders. One of the Cordemex men, Vicente Erosa Cámara, had called the bank chief, Mendoza, a liar. Menéndez vowed to find out why. After harassing a bedridden Erosa for the information, the businessman eventually handed over a folder of documents. They revealed that Mendoza was deliberately underreporting the overseas price of henequen, selling the product at a much higher value, and pocketing the difference. The journalist confronted Mendoza with the evidence over dinner. According to Menéndez he told the official, "I am going to denounce you all before public opinion. I am going to accuse you of being thieves. No more, no less." He promptly did so in a series of *El Diario* articles. In reaction to the accusations, officials tried to mollify the journalist by offering up a handful of lowly bank employees as scapegoats. But Mendoza remained firmly in place. Further investigations revealed that the bank head had powerful protectors, both in the bank's head office and the DAAC. They were not going to move him, because they were also on the take. Menéndez became frustrated. "I am not accusing them of being pendejos [stupid], I am accusing them of being thieves."[24]

At this point, Menéndez diverged from the *casta divina* script. As his investigations continued, he discovered that Mendoza's infractions "were not the worst." In fact, Merida's business elites and the national politicians who colluded with them were the "real criminals." They were the architects of a system that condemned Yucatán's *ejidatarios* to short lives of hunger and poverty. Mendoza's partner in the fraud was one of Menéndez's fellow highborn Catholics, José Trinidad Molina Castellanos. Molina may have posed as a devout believer, but in fact he was the "perfect gangster." He acted as a broker for the U.S. henequen purchasers and helped Mendoza fix the numbers. Cordemex, the organization that had initiated the inquiries, was equally corrupt. Menéndez accused the shareholders of manipulating the price that they paid the communal *ejidatarios*. As landowners, they sold their own raw henequen on the U.S. market at a low cost. This dropped the price of the product. As factory owners, they then bought the peasants' raw henequen at this low price, and charged them to process the fibers at their own private shredders. As Cordemex shareholders, they sold the completed product at a vastly inflated cost. They may have lost out on selling their own produce, but they made a fortune on processing the *ejidatarios*' henequen and selling it in the United States.[25]

Finally, Menéndez went after the church hierarchy. Throughout the book, he employed religious language and biblical allusions to argue his case. Terms like "Christian spirit," "human dignity," and "spiritual misery" dotted the text. In one section, he expressed how his understanding of moral theology drove his investigations. He argued that Christian teaching demanded that the believer denounce malpractice. Only such acts of speaking the truth would lead to the individual redemption of the criminal, the exercise of justice, and the extension of charity toward the unfortunate. But gradually Menéndez realized that the church leaders, who had taught him such beliefs, were equally immoral. When he demanded the ecclesiastical authorities sack Molina from the "Cursillos de Cristiandad," they refused. When he attacked Molina in public, a local priest berated him for forgetting his commitment to charity and his own family. When he denounced the Cordemex shareholders as thieves, his old mentor Father Bueno accused him of blasphemy. Menéndez concluded that Merida's ministers were part of the same system as the national politicians and Merida bourgeoisie. They might have been eloquent speakers, but "in the midst of such vanity and exhibitionism they justified their mercenary attitude, practicing precisely the opposite of what they taught. . . . Inside they possessed a cowardice that was pitiful."[26]

Menéndez's increasingly vitriolic attacks alienated the young journalist from the church and from upper-class Merida society. By mid-1963 he claimed he was a "social leper." People refused to greet him in the street and they moved away from his table at restaurants; fellow churchgoers avoided sitting next to his wife at mass; members of the *casta divina* even tried to upset his marriage. Cordemex representatives phoned him at home and threatened that they would spread the news of a child he had sired while at university in New Orleans. "Not even hyenas abandon their own kids." They also tried to split him from the family business. They told his father he was a communist and threatened to remove their advertising from the paper. His uncle eventually banned him from publishing in *El Diario* until he stopped attacking the Cordemex shareholders.[27]

By mid-1964 the first stage of Menéndez's journey was almost complete. He left behind the regular rhythm of church attendance and social engagements. He stopped studying religious texts and immersed himself in the teachings of Karl Marx. He rejected the family newspaper and now published in the left-leaning national magazine *Siempre!* He even moved out of his home and was "living in solitude in a makeshift native house on his property." The U.S. consulate concluded that he had "disassociated himself from the church, abandoned his friends, and sought aid from the far left."[28] Late in the year, his family tried one last attempt to bring him back onside. They teamed up with the U.S. consulate, arranged a scholarship for Menéndez to attend a journalism seminar at Columbia University, and suggested that he might start a doctoral program in the United States. Initially, he seemed tempted. The U.S. consul wrote that despite his "defection . . . there is substantial basis for hope that Menéndez will abandon his new found friends of the left." But again he was wrong. Instead Menéndez flew to the capital. On the day of the journalism seminar, he appeared on the pages of *Excélsior*, attending a party thrown by the new director of the paper. Menéndez was now a Mexico City journalist.[29]

Menéndez in Mexico City (1965–1967)

The capital was a far cry from the staid, conservative world of Merida. Here, Menéndez, the incipient Marxist, joined a host of other activists from Mexico's "new left." Over the previous five years, the Cuban Revolution had intensified the polarization of Mexican politics. Left-wing PRIístas joined with a new generation of young radicals to push for more progressive policies on U.S. imperialism, labor rights, land distribution, and democracy. They congregated around the university, in certain political organizations, and in the editorial offices of a few newspapers and magazines. The most prominent space was Manuel Marcué Pardiñas's *Política*. Here, writers started to break the old rules of Mexican journalism, exposing acts of repression, attacking the president directly, and undermining the state's discourse of revolutionary nationalism. When Menéndez took over the editorship of the popular national magazine *Sucesos Para Todos* (often shortened to *Sucesos*), he built on these shifts. But he also innovated. He emphasized investigative journalism, pushing reporters to track down and publish evidence of state corruption. He stressed the importance of visual media, using a wealth of photographs and cartoons to illustrate these investigations. And he internationalized serious coverage of left-wing movements, publishing reports on guerrilla insurgencies in Guatemala, Venezuela, and Colombia.

In the early 1960s, Mexico's "new left" rose to prominence. The members formed part of an international movement of young radicals who were disenchanted with formal politics, admired socialist movements in developing nations like Cuba and Vietnam, and opposed Western, and in particular U.S., imperialism. But they also had a distinct local flavor. They were connected to Mexico's old left, particularly the country's former president, Cárdenas. They were concerned with Mexico's specific social problems, including the repression of unions, the jailing of political prisoners, and the increasing inequality in the countryside. They focused their attacks on the ruling party's probusiness, pro-U.S. right wing, especially those close to former president Alemán and future president Díaz Ordaz. During the period, Mexico's "new left" established extensive support in Mexico City's major universities. They also founded new organizations to push for their goals. These included the catch-all left-wing group, the MLN, and the alternative peasant union, the Independent Peasant Central (Central Campesina Independiente, CCI). By the time Menéndez arrived in the capital, they had even created a political party, the Electoral Front of the People (Frente Electoral del Pueblo, FEP), which fought unsuccessfully for inclusion in the 1964 presidential elections.[30]

The new left also carved out a distinct space in the national print media. Alternative news sources played a key role. Up to the 1960s, U.S. news agencies and government press offices provided the basis for most Mexican news.[31] But after 1960 new press agencies increased their coverage and penetration. The Cuban news agency Prensa Latina led the way.[32] It poached serious Mexican journalists, like the *Siempre!* writer Edmundo Jardón and *El Diario de la Tarde*'s Juan José Morales. Initially at least, it also paid well. Morales now "ha[d] several suits made of English material, dr[o]ve a flashy English sports car and [ate] only in the best restaurants." It offered its service at a cut-rate price or even for free. It channeled what one journalist rather simply dubbed "nice things about Castro and nasty things about the U.S." to the capital's press. In 1960, recipients included *El Popular* and *El Diario de México* and a handful of magazines like *Impacto*, *Mañana*, and *Siempre!*[33] Three years later, the organization had increased the number of newspapers that published its information to twenty-four.[34] Other socialist countries joined the Cuban effort. By 1965, Soviet and Chinese news agencies operated offices in Mexico. They fed stories to the radical press, but also to more mainstream titles like *El Día* and *Siempre!*[35]

Alternative sources of funding were also important. These are more difficult to trace. Soviet, Chinese, and Cuban secret service archives still remain off-limits. But according to U.S. and Mexican sources, socialist countries all paid for favorable coverage. The Cubans especially paid *Siempre!* and *Política* to run *gacetillas* and even multipage pullouts. These covered grandstanding speeches or retold heroic narratives of socialist success. They were professionally designed and well illustrated with photographs of applauding crowds. Socialist news agencies also paid individual Mexican pressmen. The *iguala* spanned the political spectrum. In 1967, a handful of Prensa Latina reporters complained that the company offered them low wages while paying *Siempre!* editor Pagés Llergo a stipend of 2,000 pesos a month.[36]

By the mid-1960s political polarization and alternative news sources were starting to overhaul the Mexico City media. The workers' daily, *El Día*, shifted further to the left, critiquing government labor and agrarian policy.[37] At *Siempre!*, Pagés Llergo not only published *Cultura en México*—the pullout section written by "communist sympathizers" expelled from *Novedades*—but also invited radical journalists like Victor Rico Galán to join his organization.[38] At *Excélsior*, the death of the former editor Rodrigo de Llano had precipitated an internal coup. Old *oficialistas* were pushed out. Young, left-leaning journalists, like Julio Scherer, Manuel Mejido, and Manuel Becerra Acosta, now dominated the cooperative.[39] Progress was gradual. Old habits, like venerating the president and playing down state violence, died hard. Setbacks were frequent. Díaz Ordaz's government would combat these shifts with a raft of methods of press control and media censorship. But the codes of conduct were beginning to change.

Nowhere was this clearer than at *Política*, the fortnightly magazine founded by Marcué in 1960. The magazine preempted many of the changes Menéndez would bring to Mexican journalism through *Sucesos* and then *Por Qué?* It was funded by a mix of Cuban, Russian, and Chinese governments and out-of-favor PRIístas.[40] Marcué started to break the unspoken rules of the game.

Attacks on the president, for example, were increasingly frequent and direct. The secret service described the magazine as characterized by its "constant and systematic attacks on the President of the Republic."[41] When López Mateos nominated the right-wing secretary of the interior, Díaz Ordaz, as PRI candidate, the attacks became even more confrontational. In May 1963, the magazine laid bare the covert system of "tapadismo," whereby outgoing presidents directly chose their successors. Under a picture of the candidate, they placed the caption "Eminences more black than grey." Writers called his supporters "mostly large landowners and murderers." They stated bluntly if presciently that Díaz Ordaz represented "venality, caciquismo, pistolerismo, fascism and handing over the country to the U.S." They concluded that Díaz Ordaz not only "smelt of the sacristy," but that if he won he would convert the country into a "paradise for the FBI and the CIA."[42] The November 1963 front cover was even more aggressive. It held a Rius cartoon of Díaz Ordaz dressed in Catholic vestments with a Nazi swastika on his stole. In one hand he carried a bludgeon, in the other stone tablets. Rius had intended the tablets to contain a mock Ten Commandments of Díaz Ordaz's Mexico. But Marcué overruled the cartoonist and instead printed a quote from the *Wall Street Journal* that described the PRI candidate as "a vehement anticommunist who commands the powerful support of ex-president Miguel Alemán and of the Catholic Church."[43]

For seven years *Política* dominated Mexico City's radical press, tested the limits of press freedom, and shifted government approaches to censorship. The magazine's direct, confrontational style not only influenced Menéndez's approach in *Por Qué?*, but also opened the door to his first major national appointment, as editor of the magazine *Sucesos*. In the early 1960s, the owner of a successful furniture business, Gustavo Alatriste, moved into the entertainment industry. He married a young starlet, started to produce movies (including Luis Buñuel's later works), and acquired two magazines, the lifestyle-oriented *La Familia* and the political weekly *Sucesos*.[44] The latter was a low-grade version of *Siempre!*, cost half the price, sold double the copies, and mixed political commentary with crime news and scandal.[45] Up to 1965, the author and columnist Raúl Prieto ran the paper. He was left-wing but not communist. The photographer, Armando Salgado, who worked at the magazine at the time, claimed Prieto allowed his journalists to work "sin pelos en la lengua" [i.e., with relative freedom].[46]

But in late 1965 Alatriste sacked Prieto and put Menéndez in charge. Quite why remains a mystery. DFS agents could not understand why the entertainment mogul employed the communist muckraker. Alatriste was no radical. In fact, he maintained regular and friendly contact with the Ministry of the Interior.[47] But he had contacts on Mexico's new left and a more liberal interpretation of press regulations than most press owners. (In 1968, his magazine would provide relatively sympathetic coverage of the student movement; a decade later he employed the radical filmmaker Alejandro Jodorowsky to edit the magazine.)[48] According to Salgado, the owner was impressed by Menéndez's investigative work in Yucatán and wanted to push the magazine in this direction. Rius, however, gave a different account. He claimed that PCM, of which Menéndez was now a member, was trying to infiltrate mainstream media. They got *Sucesos* journalists to persuade Alatriste to sack Prieto and hire Menéndez. Whatever the direct reason, *Política*'s run demonstrated that radical magazines could survive, were popular among university students, and were able to influence public opinion.[49]

As soon as Menéndez took charge of *Sucesos*, he overhauled the publication. He allowed left-wing sympathizers to stay on and brought a group of new PCM members into the magazine. The tone changed from "populist" to "radical."[50] Puzzle pages, jokey human-interest stories, and explicit crime news declined.[51] Instead, Menéndez published a series of serious investigative pieces into state repression and corruption. Many dealt with the situation in the countryside. Some focused on old interests. He wrote pieces on the agrarian conflicts in Yucatán, called out the governor for "ineptitude, irresponsibility, and lack of firmness," and accused the *casta divina* of deliberately selling off Cordemex at a vastly overinflated price. He also published documents that indicated his old foe, the former director of the DAAC, was responsible for defrauding the *ejido* bank of La Laguna, Coahuila, of 1.5 billion pesos. But he also commissioned his team to investigate other conflicts. Immediately after taking control he sent Rico Galán to put together an article on the guerrilla uprising in Ciudad Madera. The piece criticized the army as "accustomed to repress and abuse not to fight," demonstrated a clear sympathy with the guerrillas, and flagged their summary burial in a communal grave. It was illustrated with Rodrigo Moya's graphic photos of the dead guerrillas.[52] (It was also probably the article that pushed Díaz Ordaz to punish Rico Galán with imprisonment on trumped-up charges of planned rebellion.)[53] He commissioned journalists to cover the doctors' movement in a favorable manner, blaming state officials and corrupt union leaders for causing the strike, and flagging government aggression.[54] He also sent journalists to cover urban struggles. A former *Política* reporter did an analysis of the problems at a Mexico City canning factory. He named the owners, investigated their wealth, narrated the sacking of twelve union members, and showed how the remaining laborers were coerced to work for minimal wages at gunpoint.[55]

Taken together, these were innovative. Political magazines occasionally ran investigative reports. But most were short, vague on the details, and tended to concentrate on issues in the capital. *Sucesos*'s articles were detailed, in-depth, often two- or three-part investigations. They named names and linked state officials and business oligarchs to the exploitation of the country's lower classes. They were backed up by evidence and often contained pictures of official documents to make the point. They were extremely well illustrated by Salgado or Moya's photographs. (The canning factory story even included a snap of the company's *pistoleros*.)[56] Menéndez's concern with presenting information in an easily accessible manner also affected his attitude to cartoons. *Sucesos* had published occasional Rius supplements before. But Menéndez gave the cartoonist his own regular pullout section, entitled *El Mitote Ilustrado*. Rius invited a host of young cartoonists to contribute. The supplement was a real success. Pagés Llergo admitted that their parody of *Siempre!*—entitled *Siembre!*, replete with a fake cartoon front cover—was better than the real thing. The *Mitote Ilustrado* team would go on to provide the cartoons for the first issues of *Por Qué?* and eventually set up the short-lived, but legendary, counterculture cartoon magazine *La Garrapata*.[57]

But the articles that really made *Sucesos* were his own stories of Latin America's guerrilla fighters. Menéndez claimed that he stumbled upon interviewing guerrillas in error. In 1966, he went with a group of Mexican journalists to cover Díaz Ordaz's trip to Central America. At the hotel, an anonymous informer left the reporters a message. "You have seen one side of Guatemala, if you want to see the other side be at the hotel tomorrow at seven." Menéndez and his photographer were the only ones to take up the offer. The next day they drove out to the jungle and were introduced to the forces of the Frente Guerrillero "Edgar Ibarra." The journalist and the photographer spent five days with the group.[58] The resulting articles were published between February and April 1966. Moya's photographs illustrated each piece. The first few articles examined the underlying social factors that had generated the movement. Menéndez described a "dramatic panorama of economic exploitation, misery, unhealthiness, ignorance, a lack of individual guarantees, crimes, and poor treatment." The rest looked at life in the guerrilla camp. They examined guerrilla strategies, including the use of "armed propaganda" and the everyday life and living conditions of individual fighters.[59] Menéndez's exposé of the Guatemala guerrillas provided access to other Latin American groups.

Over the next eighteen months he did similar multipart stories on Douglas Bravo's Venezuela fighters and Colombia's Army of National Liberation (Ejército de Liberación Nacional, ELN). He also went to Cuba to interview Fidel Castro.[60]

The stories had global significance. They demonstrated the extent of Latin America's early guerrilla insurgencies and the influence of the Cuban Revolution. In fact, the stories had much in common with the press coverage of the Sierra Maestra movement. In 1958 Herbert Matthews visited the Cuban camp and sent back reports that revealed Castro was alive and offered glimpses of the revolutionaries' daily lives. Within months, other reporters followed suit. By April 1958 six journalists formed what Che Guevara termed "the most exclusive Press Club in the world."[61] Such similarities suggest Menéndez had read the earlier articles; he was certainly studying in the United States when the Matthews articles were published. They also hint that by now he was taking money from the Cubans. Castro understood the benefits of positive media attention. The Mexican government certainly thought the Cubans paid him; the DFS reported that Menéndez was receiving $4,000 dollars per month from Castro's government. There were also rumors that *Política* was going under because the Cubans had shifted funding to Menéndez's *Sucesos*.[62]

Beyond the articles' international significance, they also had substantial influence in Mexico. To this point, stories on left-wing insurrections were scattered, cloaked in a virulent anticommunism, and often drawn directly from U.S. news agencies. Menéndez's action-packed articles were something completely new. They were overtly anti-imperialist. The Guatemala pieces discussed United Fruit's influence, and the Colombia articles speculated that the president was a CIA plant. They also drew the reader in. Like *Yucatán o el genocidio*, the pieces were also autobiographical. They placed the journalist-adventurer at the center of the action. Menéndez was pictured sharing the guerrillas' meals, deep in conversation with their leaders, or laughing with the foot soldiers ("The popular Juanito made good friends with the director of Sucesos" read one caption). Like a war reporter, he gave eyewitness accounts of the combat. In Colombia he observed an attack on a train; in Guatemala he witnessed a piece of "armed propaganda" in a small village. But perhaps most important, they humanized the rebels, often focusing on the personal experiences and life histories of individual fighters. They included details on the guerrillas' diet (condensed milk in Guatemala, monkeys in Colombia), their relations with surrounding villages, and snippets of overheard conversations. Finally, although the comparisons were never explicit, he also hinted at the similarities between the situation in these countries and Mexico. The background to the Venezuela story included incidents clearly designed to remind readers of events at home, including students beaten for demonstrating on behalf of Cuba and workers attacked for defending their rights. The Colombian commander was quoted as speculating that "all the countries of our continent have excellent conditions to make revolution."[63]

Such coverage had power. In terms of style, the articles closely mirrored U.S. new journalism; they were interesting, readable pieces of left-wing reporting; and they opened up the possibility of revolutionary insurgency in Mexico.[64] Soon after Menéndez left the magazine, the United States surveyed Mexico's middle classes on their reading habits. They found that *Sucesos* vied with *Siempre!* as the most popular magazine.[65] Further down the social hierarchy among high school students and labor leaders, it was the favorite publication. Over 60 percent of those surveyed browsed the magazine. Decades later, the guerrilla Alberto Ulloa Bornemann remembered being inspired by Menéndez's reports.[66]

Throughout his stint in charge of *Sucesos*, Menéndez's relations with the government were ambiguous. His editorials were sanctimonious and condemnatory. Investigative reports often directly uncovered official corruption. Like the editor of *Política*, he probably took foreign money. Like *Política*, *Sucesos* exposed government repression and undercut the mythology of the revolution. Articles highlighted the use of military force, and editorials compared the contemporary administration to the Porfiriato.[67] Such coverage caused problems. By April 1966, PIPSA withheld paper and forced Alatriste to send the formatted magazine to Texas for printing.[68] But unlike Marcué, Menéndez never broke the first law of Mexico City journalism. At *Sucesos*, he never directly insulted the president. Instead, reporters characterized their revelations as designed to help Díaz Ordaz. Corrupt officials and murderous governors were not extensions of the executive government; they were undermining and embarrassing the president. If he only knew, they implied, he would do something.[69] It is unclear who ordered the editorial line. Maybe it was Alatriste; perhaps it was Menéndez; perhaps it was even Castro, who was trying to keep the Mexican government onside. Whatever the reason, such caution would soon prove very useful.

In late February 1967 Menéndez made a fleeting round of the *Sucesos* offices. He grabbed the photographer Salgado, gave him 10,000 pesos to buy new equipment, and ordered him to take planes to Guatemala, then Panama, then Bogotá. After a few days in the Colombian capital, he met with Menéndez. They took a plane to the isolated petroleum zone of Barrancabermeja and rented rooms in a hotel. On the third day Menéndez returned and said the rebels were ready. The journalist and the photographer followed the members of the ELN into the jungle. They stayed for a month. They interviewed the leaders and the soldiers; they marched dozens of kilometers a day; they got sick; they even witnessed a successful attack on a military train. Finally, they decided to return. Salgado managed to escape, disguised as a Colombian peasant. Menéndez was less fortunate. When he arrived in Bogotá, he went directly to the Mexican embassy. But when the embassy officials realized he was going to give a press conference on the guerrillas, they handed him over to the Colombian military. He was held for three weeks. The Colombians accused him of bringing Cuban money to the guerrillas, masterminding the train attack, and covering for the rebels. Finally, following pressure from Díaz Ordaz, he was freed.[70]

Menéndez's Colombian exploits made him famous. For the next two months, *Sucesos* ran report after report of Menéndez's adventures in the jungle, his capture, and his release. The story was covered in all Mexico's major newspapers as well as the international press. But they also drew him deeper into Cold War conflicts over media control. For the left, the coverage was a publicity coup. One guerrilla called it "one of the greatest propaganda achievements of the ELN."[71] For the U.S. and the Colombian authorities, it was a disaster. It demonstrated the penetration of Cuban propaganda, humanized the guerrillas, and highlighted the capabilities of the rebel forces. To counter the reporting, both governments leaked information designed to undermine the journalist's credibility. At first, both the Associated Press and Bogotá's *El Tiempo* argued Menéndez was a Cuban spy sent to help the ELN. They claimed he held various passports, carried over $10,000 in travelers' checks, and was "a personal friend of Fidel and Che." Reporting was just a front. In fact, "he disguised his subversive activities with the exercise of journalism." It was no coincidence that violent left-wing attacks had peaked in Bogotá after his arrival.[72] But within a week, they changed tack. Newspapers now hinted that he was a CIA spy. *El Tiempo* claimed a man with an American accent had phoned their office and demanded to know Menéndez's whereabouts. Finally, after Menéndez's release, Colombian military officials dropped both stories. Instead they claimed Menéndez had betrayed the ELN, pinpointed their location, and aided the destruction of the group.[73] Taken together, the stories were contradictory; they were also probably false. But they were repeated at the time in the Mexican right-wing press and they provided the raw material for future campaigns to undermine Menéndez's next publication, *Por Qué?*

After Menéndez returned, his attitude to the authorities shifted. The change confused the Mexican left and provided ballast to accusations that he was a double agent. For the next few months, he tried to rebuild his old connections.

Perhaps he was simply playing for time. Perhaps his shift was part of a covert deal with the Mexican government. Or perhaps his stay in a Colombian cell genuinely shook the young journalist. The way in which he tried to reintegrate himself with his family and the church certainly suggest the latter. As in 1958, when he returned from his wild years in New Orleans, Menéndez, the repentant sinner, seemed to return. Again, in Cold War Mexico, the personal and the political intertwined. In his first editorial after his return, his hectoring tone disappeared. Instead he offered his "deepest thanks" to Díaz Ordaz and the Mexican ambassador in Bogotá. He thanked his father, who had denied Menéndez was a Marxist, highlighted his "solid Christian upbringing," and pushed for his release. He even acknowledged the help of members of the church hierarchy.[74] The Colombia incident brought to an end Menéndez's editorship of *Sucesos*. According to contemporaries, Menéndez's buccaneering style had caused the owner and the editor to fall out. Others claimed that Menéndez refused to renounce his support for Castro. Perhaps the pressure to toe the line and betray former comrades became too much. Whatever the reason, in October Menéndez stepped down. He visited Cuba and briefly published a pro-Cuba journal entitled *Hora Cero*. But the publication was a failure. This time he decided to set up on his own.[75]

Por Qué? and 1968

At first, Menéndez did not envisage *Por Qué?* as a radical publication. In fact, whether for financial or personal reasons, the magazine started as upmarket politics and entertainment fortnightly. He used cash from his own inheritance, a handful of wealthy Yucatán investors, and U.S. and Mexican advertisers. He employed his brothers, the *Mitote Ilustrado* cartoonists, and a few ideologically diverse freelancers to write the copy. He aimed the publication at the Mexico City elite. The price was high and the editorial line was relatively moderate. Menéndez flagged government failures, but pushed for the renovation of the ruling party, not armed rebellion. The student movement changed everything. State repression and the collusion of the mainstream media radicalized Menéndez once more. For the next six months, *Por Qué?* ran issue after issue that supported student aims, exposed government violence, and named those responsible. The format also changed. The price dropped and the magazine adopted a populist, tabloid style. The shifts generated enormous popularity, especially among students. But they also produced a government reaction, which employed a variety of dirty tricks to limit the magazine's influence.

Menéndez's original idea was to produce a highbrow fortnightly—a Mexican version of *Paris Match*. According to government agents, he had even concocted the idea with his friend, the Yucatán journalist and PRI senator Carlos Loret de Mola. Once again, Menéndez was trying to reestablish his old connections. On January 8, 1968, he set up a publishing company, Reportaje. The company's sole aim was the publication of *Por Qué?* Money came from diverse sources. Menéndez and his brothers put in 350,000 pesos. (The cash probably came from selling their shares in *El Diario de Yucatán*.) A handful of Menéndez's old friends from the Yucatán elite put in around the same.[76] But the major investor was the Yucatán film producer Manuel Barbachano Ponce, who sunk 650,000 pesos into the business. He was a media mogul from the Yucatán elite, who had made his money producing news and entertainment shorts for the cinema. But like Alatriste, he moved in the circles of Mexico City's left-wing intellectuals and had helped produce some of Buñuel's later works. At first, *Por Qué?* also attracted substantial private advertising. The first dozen issues included publicity from multinationals like Bostik glue, Superior motor filters, and high-class national real estate agents Lomas de Shangri-La. He even managed to get an agreement from a big U.S. publicity firm, Grant Advertising, to provide commercials for the magazine. But companies with connections to Menéndez made up the bulk of the copy. Advertisements for tourism in the Yucatán and AEE newspapers like *El Dictamen* and *El Porvenir* were commonplace.[77]

The initial contributors were also diverse. They included his brothers, Roger and Hernán, and leftists like the *Mitote Ilustrado* cartoonists and the university professor Heberto Castillo. But they also comprised a group of less ideologically committed writers from *Por Qué?*'s glossy rival, *Gente*. According to state agents, Menéndez had invited the group to join at a cocktail party held by the dissident former president of the PRI, Carlos Madrazo.[78] They included the author Elena Garro and the journalist Manuel de la Isla Paulín. De la Isla in particular was a strange choice. Rather like Menéndez, he started his career as a journalist, a Catholic youth group leader, and a National Action Party (Partido Acción Nacional, PAN) sympathizer. But in 1963, the PAN expelled its radical youth wing. At this point, de la Isla took an alternative course. Rather than turning to the left, he embraced the far right. He took jobs at an anti-Semitic magazine, a right-wing national, and eventually García Valseca's *Sol* chain. He also became embroiled in the world of Cuban exiles. In July 1965 he was implicated in the bombing of the Cuban cultural institute and the Mexican left-wing daily *El Día*. He spent two years in prison, where he came into contact with Menéndez and even wrote a piece for *Sucesos* describing life inside Lecumberri jail.[79]

De la Isla would not last long at *Por Qué?* He left at the beginning of the student movement in July 1968. But his initial employment does raise questions about Menéndez's state of mind. Why did a pro-Cuban communist hire a fascist sympathizer to work on his magazine? Three reasons spring to mind. Perhaps Menéndez brought in de la Isla to offer some editorial equilibrium like *Siempre!*'s Pagés Llergo? Maybe it does demonstrate CIA or DFS involvement. Did Menéndez's handlers force him to make the hire? Maybe they thought de la Isla could keep an eye on Menéndez or vice versa? Or maybe they thought the hire provided an insurance policy if Menéndez went off script: Who could trust he was a true believer if he also employed a known right-winger? But most probably, the hire reveals the strange alliances radicalization could generate. In Mexico, the PRI coopted both left and right. Those who opposed the party were pushed to the extremes. Here, even during the Cold War, they sometimes met, united by a shared goal of combating the state. Menéndez's wealthy background meant he made these alliances more than most.

On February 28, 1968, the first issue of *Por Qué?* hit the newsstands. It was glossy, packed with photographs and cartoons, split evenly between politics and entertainment, and cost 5 pesos. This was 2 pesos more than most political publications; the magazine was aimed at the wealthy. The introductory editorial revealed little evidence of Menéndez's left-wing sympathies. The usually paranoid U.S. embassy claimed the first issue gave "no inkling of any particular political orientation."[80] He offered the usual platitudes speculating that the magazine would match his desire for the "fervent and constant progress of the country." And he voiced the hope that *Por Qué?* was going to be a Mexican version of the *New York Times* Sunday supplement. Two ideas, however, were revealing. First, he described the aim of *Por Qué?* as finding the "origin, motive, and cause" of distinct situations. Such a belief in the power of investigative journalism had pushed Menéndez to seek out guerrilla insurgents in the jungle and uncover the networks of self-interest that governed the henequen industry. These ideas were now going to guide his magazine. Second, he attacked the mainstream media as beholden to "sectarian interests." Such interests not only generated vapid flattery but also ignored the nation's problems. *Por Qué?*'s journalists, in contrast, were going to speak plainly.[81]

Over the next five months, Menéndez tried to balance *Por Qué?*'s elite appeal with his commitment to investigative journalism. The attempt made for an odd mix. Cultural pieces aimed at the bourgeoisie comprised a third to a half of most issues. There was a regular column on Mexican movies and occasional pieces on European cinema. There were fawning write-ups of international movie stars, like Sean Connery and Anthony Quinn. Every fortnight Elena Garro (using her married name Elena Paz) interviewed a female TV or movie star. These lifestyle pieces focused on the actress's home ("delightful" or "grand"), her beauty tips ("brilliant" or "fascinating"), or insights into servant etiquette ("Always tip doormen in New York"). But in the first section of the magazine, there were some interesting investigations into state corruption. There were good pieces on that perennial concern of both rich and poor—the high price and low quality of foodstuffs. There were pieces on the repression of copra farmers in Guerrero, the poor provision of drinking water in Yucatán, and an extensive and detailed essay on vice and electoral fraud in Baja California Norte. Menéndez also went on the road and completed two accounts of social problems in Chihuahua.[82]

Por Qué?, the tonally discordant, reformist fortnightly, did not last long. In August 1968 the magazine changed into an alarmist, antisystemic tabloid. It seems events, rather than ideological shifts, pushed *Por Qué?*'s transformation. In summer 1968, Mexico City was preparing to hold the Olympics. For the ruling party, the games were designed to showcase Mexico's rapid development to the world. But instead they highlighted the state's reliance on repression. On July 22, a fight broke out between rival gangs from some of the capital's high schools. The government immediately responded with violence, sending in riot police to suppress the scuffle. Such acts infringed university autonomy. Within days, high school and university students united against the official aggression. There were pitched battles around the capital's high schools, and by the end of the month the government sent soldiers onto the streets to dislodge the students. Over the next two months, conflicts escalated further. The students called a strike, formed the National Strike Board (Consejo Nacional de Huelga, CNH), and made a list of demands. They held a series of marches through the city to publicize their cause. In response, the government alternated between inactivity and heavy-handed repression. Government ministers blamed the influence of foreign communists, and Díaz Ordaz refused to meet the students or answer their demands. In late July soldiers blasted open the doors of one school with a bazooka, and in September military forces occupied both the National Polytechnic Institute (Instituto Politécnico Nacional, IPN) and the UNAM.

Finally, as the Olympics approached, officials decided to put an end to the movement for good. At a student meeting at the Plaza de las Tres Culturas in

Tlatelolco on October 2, they placed sharpshooters on the roofs of the surrounding buildings and encircled the protestors with troops. At a given signal, both groups opened fire. Dozens of students were killed and hundreds were bundled into the back of waiting army vehicles. They were taken away for imprisonment, torture, and questioning at Military Camp No. 1. In the immediate aftermath, government spokesmen claimed that armed radicals had shot first. But the official line was a lie. The strategy, which both ended the student movement and confirmed accusations of covert extremism, was a PRI ploy. Officials from the Ministry of the Interior, the military, and the secret services had planned the massacre and the cover-up days in advance. In fact, government forces had used a very similar strategy to undermine the Navista movement in San Luis Potosí seven years earlier.[83]

In response, the mainstream media followed the official narrative. Monsiváis called it the "apogee of directed disinformation."[84] In summer 1968, the government employed the full force of its new, improved spin machine. Authorized press statements and bulletins flooded the newsrooms. Well-placed articles condemned students' motives and aims. *La Prensa*'s "Granero Político" used its weekly space to denounce protestors as "antinational," "reactionaries," and "saboteurs." Press officers and government ministers leaked faked documents, played on anticommunist sentiment, and called on compliant editors and journalists to support the official line. *El Sol de México* published photographs of supposed student arms caches. Mexico's top *iguala* earner, Teissier, listed the names of "dangerous communist-Trotskyites" involved in a student plot to topple the government. The government line was essentially threefold. First, newspapers were to portray protestors as manipulated by outside forces. Second, newspapers were to soft-pedal incidents that reflected well on the students. Large-scale pacific demonstrations and general demands for democracy were downplayed or ignored. Third, newspapers were to discount or excuse acts of government violence. September's takeover of the universities was portrayed as painful but necessary and October's massacre was described as an improvised response to student aggression. Teissier speculated that if soldiers had not fired back, students would have "taken the National Palace."[85]

There were some spaces for dissent.[86] But in general, the campaign was broadly successful. In the run-up to the massacre, all *El Sol de México* articles, 79 percent of *El Universal* pieces, and 59 percent of *El Heraldo de México* commentaries took an aggressive progovernment stance. Most other pieces simply recounted events in a neutral manner.[87] Even more sympathetic newspapers supported officials at key moments. After the massacre there was a "conspiracy of silence." Newspapers took government estimates of casualties at face value and frontloaded articles with officials' opinions. Of over a thousand pieces that touched on the killings over the next week, only 12 percent included student voices. Such coverage had power. Mexico City residents wrote to Díaz Ordaz to applaud his handling of the protests; and opinion polls suggested that 80 percent thought foreigners were behind the movement.[88]

In contrast to the mainstream media, *Por Qué?* adopted a strongly pro-student line. Menéndez claimed that journalistic ethics, rather than political sympathy, motivated the change. In July he started to investigate the death of a student, Federico de la O García, at the hands of the city's riot police. As government forces denied the death, the story piqued his interest and he probed further, uncovering evidence of state repression and the media cover-up. At first, he tried to disguise the magazine's change of tack. On August 15 he published a special version of *Por Qué?* The publication contained an interview with Madrazo. It lauded the dissident former PRI head's popularity among students and posited the possibility of a new party that would combine the "revolutionary and progressive" sectors of the PRI. The timing and contents of the piece were controversial. Menéndez knew it. He disguised the magazine with a false front cover for a gentleman's fashion magazine called *Cuartel de Caballeros*. News vendors could sell the issue without attracting the attention of the police.[89]

But later that month, he overhauled the magazine completely. On August 28 the magazine published an editorial, "Where Are the Dead?," that focused on police repression. Two weeks later, Menéndez put out an "extra" on the student uprising. The price halved to 2.50 pesos, the quality of paper decreased, the private ads disappeared, and the format shrank to the size of crime magazines like *Alarma*. The tone also changed completely: the culture section and the glossy photographs disappeared, and journalists like Garro and De la Isla resigned. Menéndez now wrote much of the copy. He hired a group of student activists to contribute articles and paid photographers like Salgado and the Mayo brothers to provide photographs.[90]

Finally, he brought in the Baja California Norte journalist Carlos Ortega as his news editor. Ortega was a forgotten hero of Mexican journalism. His exposés on state corruption, police repression, and the world of Mexico City journalism shaped the radical incarnation of *Por Qué?* as much as Menéndez. In fact, he had much in common with his director. He was from the provinces, came from a conservative background, distrusted Mexico City's conventional reporters, and believed in the importance of investigative journalism. Like Menéndez he saw the reporter as a civic activist who exposed malpractice and voiced discontent. He started his career in the early 1950s working for

Tijuana's PAN newspaper before moving on to learn the trade under the muckraking editor Manuel Acosta Meza. After Acosta's murder, Ortega wrote up the events in the book *Tijuana, La Ciudad Maldita* [Tijuana, the damned city]. Eventually, pistol in hand and in fear of his life, Ortega fled the city. He returned briefly to the capital, but he found journalists were more interested in the source of the next *iguala* than serious political investigations. In 1959, he returned to the north and revealed how vote rigging and military violence won the PRI the governorship of the state. He was forced to leave once more and finally found work at PAN's national magazine, *La Nación*. Here, he maintained the publication's tradition of investigative reporting. His stories on the 1968 protests were excellent. They highlighted government violence, stated student aims, and undercut accusations of foreign manipulation. They probably inspired Menéndez to offer him the job.[91] His importance again suggests that journalists from outside the comfortable world of the mainstream Mexico City press were those who actually initiated the radical changes to the capital's papers.

Between August and December 1968, coverage of the student movement dominated the magazine. In most issues, stories on the protests accounted for over half the copy. Highlighting state violence was key. To do this, the magazine adopted the forms of the *nota roja*.[92] Political coverage and crime news aligned. Traditional political journalism and wordy editorials were reduced. Instead, painstaking narratives, which recounted the chronology of police beatings or military violence, formed the bulk of the coverage. Detailed reports listed dates, times, weapons, injuries, the titles of commanding officers, and the names of the dead. In the September extra, he offered a blow-by-blow account of conflicts between students and the police from July 26 onward. The second extra, published after the October 2 massacre, offered a chronicle of the Tlatelolco killings. In contrast to lowball official figures, the report estimated that soldiers had murdered at least a hundred protestors in the square. Such an approach cut through government obfuscation and mass media hand-wringing. As Menéndez wrote, this was the time for recounting "deeds" not "words."[93]

Dozens of photographs accompanied these stories. They included pictures the big nationals were unwilling to publish. "It was to *Por Qué?*'s offices in Colonia Roma that frustrated photographers repaired, knowing there was no chance of getting their horrific pictures into their own newspapers."[94] They were shocking, bloody, and completely unfiltered. On the front page of the first extra a soldier prepared to smash the butt of his gun into the face of a surrendered student; on the front page of the second, there was the image of a dead boy; and on the inside cover, there were the mutilated bodies of three students. Inside, there was a shot of the blood-splattered shoes of women and children—the victims of the massacre. The stylistic shift was a conscious decision. In Menéndez's introduction to the first extra, he claimed that he did so not for "commercial ends" but to "give national public opinion the truth."[95] The *nota roja* had always been used to prove injustice and get at the truth. By employing the format to illustrate the student movement, Menéndez expanded the genre and made its implicit politicization explicit.

Beyond demonstrating government repression, *Por Qué?* also sought to apportion blame. Naming the men behind the structure reflected Menéndez's own journalistic style. But it was also pure *nota roja*. Calling out the "autor intelectual" of a wrongdoing was the high point of any crime page investigation. At first, Menéndez focused on the mayor of Mexico City, Corona del Rosal. He claimed that the official had used secret service agents to infiltrate the movement and provoke violence. He also attacked the capital's police chiefs, Luis Cueto Ramírez and Raúl Mendiolea Cerecero, for encouraging riot police to use extreme force. Like a good crime reporter, he dredged up the suspects' pasts—their control over Mexico City's prostitution rings, their extensive earnings and properties, and their links to corrupt real estate speculators. They were, according to one witness, "millionaire pimps." As in the *nota roja*, Menéndez employed readers' insights to corroborate claims. On October 4, the magazine published a letter from an anonymous special agent who confirmed that he had been instructed to dress in civilian clothes and provoke fights with the students.[96]

Por Qué?'s style, price, and prostudent line boosted sales dramatically. So did new commercial strategies. Menéndez handed out around 50,000 copies to students each week. They hawked issues throughout the university and the surrounding neighborhoods to the south of the city. He also signed a new deal with the city's Union of Newspaper Wholesalers and Vendors (Unión de Expendedores y Voceadores). He now sold the publication to the wholesalers at 1,500 pesos per 1,000 copies. The wholesalers then sold the issues to the individual vendors for 1,650 pesos. Vendors could now earn 0.85 pesos a copy, over double what they made on other magazines. The agreements undercut Menéndez's per issue profits. But increased circulation more than made up for the loss. The authorities estimated that most issues sold around 200,000 copies.[97] Other claims were even higher; U.S. journalists stated that the extras sold between 380,000 and 500,000 each.[98] Unsurprisingly, the publication was particularly popular among the capital's students. The U.S. authorities wrote that the "journal has gained considerable stature among students because of its undiluted support for their cause."[99] They bought copies; they shared copies; and they handed them out at meetings. They even pulled the publication apart and stuck the individual pages to walls to form *periódicos murales*, or newspaper murals.[100] In fact, the paper became part of the students' broader attempts to wrestle the narrative from the mainstream media. Menéndez encouraged the connection, speaking at public demonstrations in support of the movement.[101] But the publication also attracted other audiences. The price and style attracted factory and office workers. One media specialist rather snottily described the magazine as the "*Alarma* of the marginal press."[102] The regional focus also drew in provincial readers. Copies of *Por Qué?* were handed out at opposition rallies in Baja California Norte and Yucatán.[103]

The tone and popularity of *Por Qué?* generated a strong state response. Multiple agencies struck at each stage of the production process in what seemed to be a coordinated campaign. But the campaign also showed the limits of government repression. The Mexican government invested in press agents and organizations that could put financial pressure on newspapers, but it never completely institutionalized censorship like more authoritarian regimes. For those with capital, connections, and, it seems, guns, there were always ways around the system. First, officials tried to deprive the publication of paper. On August 22 Menéndez asked PIPSA for tons of paper from the Tuxtepec mill. In response, the organization claimed that the Olympics celebrations had cut into paper stocks. There was simply not enough. The brothers suspected foul play. "The curious aspect of the case was that all other magazines were able to count on raw material."[104] A few years later, Roger Menéndez elaborated on the theory. "They stopped selling us newsprint because we broke the taboo. We blamed the president for the student deaths. Yes the government allows . . . other critical publications to exist. But if you watch closely they will never directly criticize the president. We did."[105] It seems their suspicions were correct. In May 1969, the director of PIPSA, revealed he had ordered the organization not to sell "one sheet" of paper to the Cuban press office, Prensa Latina, "as we did in the case of *Por Qué?*"[106] To get the edition out, the brothers claimed that they were eventually forced to buy paper at double the price from the old private mill at San Rafael. (Though spy reports suggest that Scherer's *Excélsior* actually sold the magazine paper on the black market. The theory certainly explains why Díaz Ordaz took such a strong dislike to the paper.)[107]

Government authorities tried to stop companies from producing the magazine. In an interview with the U.S. counterculture magazine *Ramparts*, Menéndez explained the process. The first printer Menéndez approached showed him an official letter, which threatened to strip the press of government contracts if it printed the publication. "If I print your magazine I will be taking bread out of the mouth of all my workers in my plant." The second printer said the same. After two days of searching, Menéndez tracked down a willing press owner. But the next day the printer appeared in the *Por Qué?* offices. "Man, he was scared shit[less]" according to Menéndez. Mexico City policemen had visited the workshop and threatened to smash the press and kill the manager. Eventually, Menéndez was forced to rely on one of his father's friends, who offered to print the magazine. "Menéndez and his entire staff set up camp at the print shop armed to the teeth with .38s and carbines. Huddled around an old rotogravure press, trying to get an issue printed before the [mayor's office] found out where they were. They managed to get half a million copies off the press before the paper ran out."[108] Officials also tried to limit distribution. Masked gunmen lifted 50,000 copies of the late October issue from the back of a delivery van.[109]

Officials, probably from the Ministry of the Interior, also established a propaganda campaign to libel Menéndez. The scheme built on tactics developed to combat Marcué and *Política*.[110] Slanders mixed genuine events with inferred alliances, played on existing prejudices and paranoias, and were delivered in formats that would appeal to the target audience. The flysheet headed "Alert Students," published in October, played on Menéndez's ideological shifts. It claimed he had betrayed the Colombian guerrillas, the owner of *Sucesos*, Díaz Ordaz, and the PCM. He now worked for the CIA, which, the author claimed, funded *Por Qué?* The flyer, titled "How to Buy a Conscience," mixed a similar narrative with a broader discourse of press corruption. Again the piece recounted Menéndez's conservative upbringing, his political flip-flopping, and his recent reliance on Díaz Ordaz. But this time, the flyer blamed his job rather than the foreign influence. Menéndez was described as a "typical journalist without professional ethics or concern for his readers," who was entirely motivated by "interests ($$$) that are not of a moral character."[111]

The Journalist and the Jungle (1969–1974)

The student movement and the government response radicalized *Por Qué?* From 1968 onward, the magazine became the voice of Mexico's extreme left. Mario Menéndez, his brother Roger, and Carlos Ortega maintained their old interests and published investigative reports on corruption, repression, and electoral fraud especially in the provinces. But now they went much further. They dismissed the unifying discourse of the Mexican Revolution and

enshrined the 1968 massacre as the key turning point in state-society relations. They openly attacked the presidents, even implying that they worked
for the CIA. They censured the reformist left, which attempted to take advantage of Echeverría's call for a "political opening." They supported radicals,
who sought to bring down the government through guerrilla insurgency. But
the student massacre had more personal effects. Menéndez also radicalized.
Like many 1968 protestors, he now viewed armed revolt, rather than investigative journalism or civic protest, as the sole means to combat the Mexican
state. He fled to his home state, assembled a ragtag group of students and
teachers, and laid out his strategy for insurrection. The group moved to a farm
on the Chiapas-Tabasco border and attempted to persuade the surrounding indigenous villages to join the guerrilla insurgency. Like many of the immediate
post-1968 movements, the plan was a disaster. Big claims of food supplies,
arms, and Cuban support came to nothing. Most villagers remained neutral
or hostile to the outsiders. Soon the small group disintegrated. At this point
the state intervened, arresting the ringleaders, including Menéndez. For
over a year he was locked up with Mexico's other political prisoners. Finally, in
December 1971, another guerrilla, Genaro Vázquez, engineered a prisoner swap
to ensure his release. Menéndez was exiled to Cuba.

In the immediate aftermath of the student massacre, *Por Qué?* struggled to
stay afloat. Menéndez warned readers that the magazine "might be assassi-
nated" at any moment.[112] U.S. embassy staff flagged the magazine's "suicidal
tendencies," speculated that the editors were "courting martyrdom," and repeatedly claimed that the publication would be forced to close.[113] As government pressure took its toll, divisions over the left's strategic approach affected
the running of the publication. By early 1969, Menéndez concluded that critical journalism alone would never bring about change. He fled home to Merida and then the forests of the Tabasco-Chiapas border. He continued to
write for the magazine, but much less frequently. Instead Ortega and Menéndez's brothers, Roger and Hernán, took over the day-to-day management of
the publication. They maintained the cheap, image-heavy, tabloid style. They
wrote most of the copy, often using pseudonyms. They also employed a range
of radical reporters, student protestors, and local activists to provide the rest.
These were not the usual Mexico City pressmen. They included Menéndez's
old *Sucesos* colleague Salgado, who moved from photography to investigative
journalism; locked-up 68ers like Federico Emery; young academics like Jorge
Felix-Baez; and a handful of Prensa Latina stringers who provided most of
the international coverage.[114]

The Menéndez brothers and their new recruits continued to produce high-quality investigative journalism. Salgado, in particular, was influenced by Menéndez's and Ortega's work. In a series of reports on Chihuahua, he traced out how a major U.S. timber firm in league with corrupt bureaucrats and local ranchers had taken over communal lands, cut down vital forest reserves, and locked up the complaining Tarahumara in vast, jerry-built prisons. He also spent weeks in the Colonia Francisco Villa outside Chihuahua City, learning how poor squatters had managed to establish a functioning urban community in the face of frequent military and police harassment.[115]

But the editors also moved on to other subjects. Union corruption became an important theme. In 1969 and 1970, there were various articles on the rise of the head of the petroleum workers, Joaquín Hernández Galicia, aka "la Quina." The pieces traced his beginnings as a small-time *cacique* in the petrol town of Salamanca, recounted his move to Tamaulipas and his first campaigns to unseat crooked rivals, and concluded with photographic and testimonial evidence of his vast wealth, vicious politicking, and proclivity for sleazy orgies.[116] So did the everyday life of Mexico City's urban underclass. There were analyses of the working conditions among the capital's nonunionized supermarket workers. There were repeated investigations into police corruption, vice rackets, and the use of torture and extrajudicial killings. Such articles glossed old *nota roja* themes with a radical hue. These were not cases of a few bad individuals, but the well-designed control mechanisms of a ruling oligarchy.[117] Like the *nota roja*, *Por Qué?* encouraged dialogue between journalists and readers. Reporters followed up complaints in the magazine's letters section and readers offered updates on recent reports.[118]

Beyond these investigations, *Por Qué?*'s articles reflected and shaped the ideological shifts of the radical left. From 1971 onward, the new president, Luis Echeverría, made conciliatory moves toward the country's leftists. He announced a "political opening," released prisoners, favored unions, upped land distribution, poured money into the universities, publicly denounced state repression, and made high-profile alliances with other anti-imperialist leaders. For many, the appeasement succeeded. Critics of earlier administrations agreed to work within the new arrangement. They reasoned that Echeverría's policies were founded on the principles of the 1910 Revolution and were better than the alternatives put forward by Mexico's business elites or an anticommunist United States.[119] For leftist journalist Fernando Benítez the choice was simple: "Echeverría or fascism."[120] But for other, often younger, more Marxist leftists, Echeverría's policies were a sham. The president's rhetoric was empty and hollow; his plans offered only short-term solutions to structural problems; and his aim was not working-class rule or even democratization, but rather the continuation of control by a U.S.-sympathizing alliance of politicians and businessmen.[121] *Por Qué?*'s writers assiduously followed this new radical line. To do so, they upended journalistic conventions, going beyond even Marcué's *Política*. They critiqued the Mexican left's founding myth, the revolution, and sought to replace it with a sacralized version of the 1968 student movement. They pinned the blame for Mexico's social ills directly on the president and openly supported those who sought to use violence against the regime.

The emergence of Mexico's radicals relied on a rethinking of the country's recent past. New conceptions of the revolution and the student movement provided a counterhegemonic framework for a new, oppositional politics. These ideas would shape two generations of leftist thinkers, unleash a wave of revisionist historiography, and become formalized in the festivities of students, teachers, and peasants. They would even cross ideological divides, forming part of the right's prodemocratization narrative.[122] But they started in the pages of the marginal press. For decades, politicians had claimed inspiration from the Mexican Revolution. During the 1970s, Echeverría and the reformist leftists did the same, highlighting the parallels between the contemporary administration and that of Lázaro Cárdenas. The ex-president's death in 1970 helped the process; he was now no longer able to argue the toss.

To counter these assertions, the new radicals started to pull apart the revolution's claims to far-reaching social change. The move rested heavily on Marxist theory, which increasingly shaped the ideas (and sadly leadened the prose) of *Por Qué?*'s journalists. Menéndez and other writers started to class the 1910 uprising as a bourgeois revolution, which might have ended the old feudal arrangements but also introduced the inequalities of modern capitalism. In particular, they rubbished Cárdenas's legacy. They denied that his policies of land reform, union support, and wage rises were radical or effective. In fact, they argued, Mexico's elites supported the reforms. Limited redistribution ensured stability, investor confidence, and the future success of the bourgeoisie. They attacked the government's attempts to establish an official hero cult around the dead president. For *Por Qué?*'s reporters, state celebrations had made the Michoacán politician "the greatest saint in the altar of iconography of the dominant class." Actually, they claimed, Cárdenas was a cynical opportunist who had fought under a bourgeois general (Carranza), had been mentored by a right-wing politician (Calles), and had only embraced reform to co-opt independent popular groups.[123]

In its place, *Por Qué?*'s writers attempted to sanctify the student movement of 1968. First, they repeatedly communicated their versions of events, laying out student demands and emphasizing government repression. Between August and October 1969, the magazine published a blow-by-blow narrative and an instructive Rius comic strip that delineated the confrontations. Such descriptions not only reawakened memories, but worked to counter the government's alternative narrative of foreign infiltration, student aggression, and minimal state violence. Second, they attempted to portray the Tlatelolco massacre as the key turning point in Mexican history. As early as July the following year, Menéndez described the uprising as "more important than the Revolution of 1910." In subsequent articles, writers compared the killings to the French counterrevolution and the massacres of World War II. Finally, they also sought to commemorate the date of the Tlatelolco killings. For four years, every early October issue included testimonies, poems, photographs, and articles, which remembered the dead, demanded justice, and drew direct parallels between the killings and other more recent repressions.[124]

As well as attempting to destabilize the regime's foundations, *Por Qué?*'s journalists vilified the Mexican executive. Díaz Ordaz was frequently attacked. Writers accused the president of masterminding the student massacre, cozying up to the United States, ordering the murder of dissident PRI head Madrazo, orchestrating electoral fraud, and lying in public. The coverage of the 1969 Yucatán elections was headed "Responsible for the Fraud: Gustavo Díaz Ordaz." A September 1969 editorial declared that his penultimate state of the union address—dubbed the "Annual Theatre of the Fantastic"—deserved a prize as "the official document furthest from reality." "You need to be crassly ignorant not to know that life in Mexico is diametrically opposed to that expressed by the president." Other writers delivered even more ad hominem attacks. They called the president "a mediocre lawyer" with a "vengeful and bloody" streak. They accused him of breaking promises, serving the industrial elite, and even suffering from a strange mental "complex" that might be "interesting for psychiatrists to study." This was bad enough. But worse was to come.[125]

On October 23, 1969, Menéndez delivered a remarkable scoop. He published a front-page story entitled "The CIA in the Presidency, in the Ministry of the Interior, and in the Foreign Office. Where Else?" Again espionage and journalism overlapped. Using contacts in the Cuban administration, Menéndez leaked reports that proved that one of the staff in Mexico's Havana embassy, Humberto Carrillo Colón, was a CIA spy. He also went further. He used official Mexican documents to show that the president, Díaz Ordaz, had not only invented the staffer's position but also directly appointed Carrillo to the role. He also reprinted letters between Carrillo and his CIA handler, which indicated quite clearly that the president's private secretary and the secretary of the interior, Echeverría, were also in the pay of the organization.[126] The piece was explosive. It accused the most powerful men in Mexico of directly betraying their country and spying for the United States. It was also, it seems, mostly true. According to recent revelations, Díaz Ordaz and other members of his administration, including Echeverría, were CIA informants.[127]

The final issue of the presidency made *Por Qué?*'s position clear. The front page held a woodcut of Díaz Ordaz. Porfirio Díaz rested his hand on the out-going president's shoulder. In front lay the body of a dead student. Underneath, the headline read "See You Never, Mister Díaz."[128] For the next four years, relations between the magazine and the president failed to improve. *Por Qué?* was no gentler to Echeverría. Writers carefully pulled apart his reformist poli-cies, highlighting discrepancies in the new social security regulations, the re-gressive nature of the new fiscal law, the crony capitalism underlying housing strategies, and the poor quality of distributed lands. They interrogated his anti-imperialist credentials. They lambasted his leftist supporters—the so-called *aperturistas*—as hypocrites, sell-outs, and frauds. They accused his speeches of being "tired, monotonous and at times utterly unsupportable." They mocked his wife's folksy, nationalist style. And, most damningly, they held the presi-dent personally responsible for the violence meted out toward Sinaloa activists, Guerrero peasants, and Mexico City students. As the October 1972 editorial argued, these were Echeverría's Tlatelolcos. They were frequent, vicious, and bloody and the orders came from the top. In fact, the only difference between the Díaz Ordaz and the Echeverría regimes was the "shocking impudence" of the former and the "vomit-inducing hypocrisy" of the latter.[129]

Finally, *Por Qué?* supported groups that sought to confront the state through violence. Most were rural guerrillas, including the remnants of Ar-turo Gámiz's Chihuahua rebels, Genaro Vázquez's Civic National Revolu-tionary Association (Asociación Cívica Nacional Revolucionaria, ACNR), and Lucio Cabañas's Party of the Poor (Partido de los Pobres). Initially, arti-cles followed the template of Menéndez's earlier reports on Latin American insurgents. There were detailed surveys of the region's socioeconomic dy-namics, interviews with anonymous guerrillas, and sympathetic explanations of the uprising. In Chihuahua, "inequality was the cause of the violence." Logging companies had robbed communal lands, imprisoned troublesome *ejidatarios*, burned their houses, and murdered their leaders. Avenues of po-litical protests were systematically shut down and villagers were desperate.

Food, hygiene, and medical care were so poor only half the children survived into adulthood. Salgado's 1971 articles on Genaro Vázquez were broadly similar. They laid out Guerrero's stark inequalities, recounted the movement's attempts at political mobilization, offered the guerrilla leader space to defend his actions, and interspersed the narrative with short observed vignettes. (Vázquez, apparently, used to carry toothpaste and a toothbrush in his front pocket. "My teeth will be clean even in the cemetery.") Ample photographs accompanied the articles.[130] Like the *Sucesos* stories, they showed the guerrillas posing with guns but also engaged in everyday activities.

Por Qué? shaped the radical left and offered a new template for Mexican journalism. The magazine also encountered a shifting pattern of state censorship. The final two years of Díaz Ordaz's presidency witnessed an intensification of conventional methods. Government agents continued to monitor the magazine, opening mail and spying on conversations. (Unlike *Política*, there are no records of telephone taps. Perhaps the documents were lost, or perhaps the CIA provided the equipment and guarded the transcripts.) PIPSA repeatedly denied the magazine paper. Instead the editors were forced to buy paper on the open market or beg other newspapers for supplies. Government forces also increased attempts to disrupt distribution. The head of the postal service ordered regional postmasters to collect any copies of *Por Qué?* sent to subscribers in the provinces. In Mexico City, secret service agents confiscated particularly incendiary issues. Sometimes they bought them up. DGIPS officials purchased 8,000 copies of the July 1, 1969 release for 14,000 pesos. On other occasions, they simply robbed the publication's delivery vans: On July 9, 1969, twelve armed men held up the company's trucks and lifted 20,000 copies destined for sale in the provinces.[131] Selling *Por Qué?* soon became a clandestine activity. News vendors hid copies under other magazines or kept issues at the back of the stall.

Violence against *Por Qué?* also grew. At first, it was harassment designed to intimidate the staff. In August 1969 four agents arrested Roger Menéndez and the magazine's printer. They were kept in jail for thirty hours, accused of fraud, and then released on bail for 30,000 pesos.[132] But as armed insurgencies multiplied and the magazine offered its support, state interventions increasingly aimed to gather intelligence and discover the links between the journalists and the guerrillas. Press censorship met Cold War policing. For example, after Salgado published the Genaro Vázquez stories, three armed agents bundled him into the back of a car. When he complained he was a reporter, one replied, "You bastard, son of a bitch, we know you're a journalist, you son of a whore! You'll see what being a journalist means to us, you son of a whore mother. We're going to fuck you up, you son of a bitch." They promptly did. For the next ten days, he was waterboarded, ducked in sewage, and beaten. During the period, officials from the Mexico City police and the secret service repeatedly questioned him about his links to the ACNR and other guerrilla organizations. He survived, but only just. After the experience he suffered a prolonged illness and dropped out of journalism.[133] The *Por Qué?* reporters arrested in September 1974 received similar treatment. For two weeks, they were beaten, tortured, and interrogated about their connections to the Party of the Poor. Afterward, like Salgado, many fled the newsroom for good.

Por Qué? also faced terrorist attacks. In the early morning of September 18, 1969, a bomb exploded outside the magazine's offices. The blast smashed windows and equipment and destroyed two cars. No one was hurt. The Cold War media conflict had already caused the bombing of one newspaper. In 1965, Cuban exiles had detonated a device outside the offices of the left-leaning daily *El Día*. But the 1969 campaign was both more extensive and murkier. The assault coincided with other bomb attacks on progovernment media like *El Sol de México* and Televisa, state institutions like the Ministry of the Interior, and the relatively critical newspaper *Excélsior*. Officials accused a small, left-wing organization called the Committee of Revolutionary Struggle (Comité de Lucha Revolucionaria, CLR). Over the following year, various CLR members confessed to planting the other bombs. But no one claimed responsibility for the attacks on *Por Qué?* or *Excélsior*.[134] Questions remained. Did CLR operatives plant the *Por Qué?* and *Excélsior* bombs to put investigators off the scent or to exacerbate political divisions? Was Menéndez somehow involved? He certainly knew key members of the CLR. And, as we shall see, he was later accused of belonging to the group. Or did government agents take advantage of the CLR campaign to challenge and intimidate wayward journalists? *Por Qué?*'s writers certainly claimed this was the case. They asserted that the director of the DFS, Fernando Gutiérrez Barrios, had warned the editors to expect reprisals.[135] In an interview twenty years later, Gutiérrez pointed the finger at the Presidential Guard.[136]

The radicalization of print journalism was only one response to the repression of 1968. Some activists attempted to use the political system to generate democratic transformation. Others moved to impoverished communities where they tried to convert downtrodden villagers. But others still saw guerrilla insurgency as the only means to produce change. Menéndez chose the latter. In a conversation with one of his fellow guerrillas he claimed that he had made the decision while watching Mexican troops gun down students at the Plaza de Tlatelolco. He described it as a military coup that could only be countered by force. But the real reasons remain opaque. He was close to the Cuban government, clearly admired other guerrilla leaders, and was always adventurous. In fact, Salgado claimed he had "met few, really few who loved adventure as much as Mario."[137] But he was also ideologically flexible, had no combat experience, and was a poor administrator. At *El Diario de Yucatán, Sucesos,* and *Por Qué?* he had relied on the talents of penny-pinching managers. The group he created would become the basis for the Forces of National Liberation (Fuerzas de Liberación Nacional, FLN). The FLN would, in turn, form the nucleus of the Zapatista National Liberation Army (Ejército Zapatista de Liberación Nacional, EZLN). But under Menéndez, the experiment was short-lived. Like many of the early student-led organizations, it was characterized by "a lack of structure, disorganization, spontaneity, isolation, the absence of an adequate recruitment policy, incapacity at forming bases of support, the bad administration of disposable resources, erratic mobility, and the total dependency on a sole individual." It was, in short, a disaster.[138]

Menéndez has never admitted his involvement in the attempted insurgency, maybe out of shame at the movement's failure or perhaps out of guilt for involving family and friends. Whatever the reason, there is little doubt about his participation. In the summer of 1968, Menéndez was introduced to a host of Mexico City–based radicals. They included the former MLN member Alfredo Zárate Mota, a high school chemistry teacher, Ignacio González Ramírez, and an agricultural engineer, Eloy Cardel Aguilar. Goaded on by Menéndez, who claimed to have received guerrilla training in Colombia, they decided to start their own organization. They called it the Mexican Insurgent Army (Ejército Insurgente Mexicano, EIM). Over the next six months, Menéndez used his connections to recruit some Yucatán students, a handful of middle-class Monterrey radicals, and a friend of Genaro Vázquez. In all, they numbered around twenty. They arrived at their base of operations on the Tabasco-Chiapas border in early 1969. To disguise their intentions, they pretended to be university biology researchers, adopted code names, and set up camp in the surrounding forest. Here, they attempted to enlist disgruntled locals, received arms training, practiced jungle survival techniques, and read from Che Guevara's book on guerrilla tactics.[139]

That was the plan at least. Soon divisions started to appear. Some resented the exercise regime. González, the biology teacher, had to return to Mexico City because he was unable to cope with the long hikes, while some of the younger Monterrey radicals thought the marches were little more than "light walks." Food was scarce. They ended up using their dynamite supplies to catch fish. Enlisting locals proved tough. During the first six months, they only managed to persuade one bilingual teacher to join the group. But above all, everyone started to distrust Menéndez. He visited the camp infrequently, splitting his time between his father's luxurious Merida home and the jungle. When he was there, he boasted incessantly. He said he had met Che Guevara and picked up hints on guerrilla insurgency. He claimed he was close to Castro and could secure big arms shipments and even a B-26 bomber. He was undermined by the Yucatán students, who resented his privileged upbringing. They repeated the accusation that he was a CIA spook and called him Panfilo Ganso, or Gladstone Gander, the rich, dandy cousin of Donald Duck. By June 1969, desertions had reduced the group's number to ten. Menéndez briefly moved camp to his family home near the Yucatán port of Progreso where he declared that they would launch an attack on the town of Valladolid with Cuban backing. But when the proposal came to nothing, the remaining members fled.[140]

The Mexican security forces knew about the EIM from at least May 1969. Two Yucatán students had come forward to testify that Menéndez had tried to recruit them. In July, the editor of the *Novedades de Yucatán* newspaper confessed that he heard Menéndez was living "among the peasants" in the west of the state, training them how to use arms. "He does not take any notice of anyone and his only interest is causing problems for the government without caring about the consequences." For eight months the government did nothing. Perhaps they needed more proof. More probably, they judged the movement harmless. But on February 9, 1970, another bomb exploded at the PAN headquarters in Mexico City. The attack was the work of the CLR. Security agents immediately arrested those connected to the organization, including the biology teacher González. Under torture, González admitted to his involvement in both the CLR and the now defunct EIM. Two days later, DFS men took in Menéndez for questioning. He was accused of treason, disturbing the peace, and bomb making.[141]

The trial became a soap opera. Like earlier prosecutions of journalists, official supporters were light on the evidence and heavy on the moralizing and insinuation.[142] This was not only about insurrection, it was also about infringing the unspoken laws of the press. The government dropped the bomb-making charge and the CLR connection but continued to insist on Menéndez's involvement in the EIM. Right-wing newspapers repeated the government's accusations, adding that Menéndez was also a heroin addict. Old foes from the Mexican media trawled through his past, highlighting accusations of CIA espionage, Cuban connections, and betrayal. *Novedades* columnist Teissier portrayed Menéndez as a pampered child who had decided to go into the forest in a fit of pique. Insults were imaginative and commonplace. The *Tiempo* correspondent called Menéndez a "Saltimbanqui [charlatan] with a chip on his shoulder . . . who was in the place he should have been years ago, prison." (*Por Qué?* retaliated that the *Tiempo* writer was a leading press gangster, "an Al Capone huehuenche" [a Nahuatl term for the leader of a traditional dance], who charged extortionate rates to follow the official line.[143])

In retaliation, Menéndez's relations and allies mounted a plausible, if rather self-centered, defense. Past offenses were forgotten as family members and Yucatán elites rallied around the journalist. First, they rubbished the government witnesses, claiming González was "suffering a delirium of persecution," another was a "mythomaniac," and another was "a teacher with an exotic name." When the charge of bomb making was dropped, they accused Díaz Ordaz of masterminding a covert, secondary operation, designed to frame Menéndez as a guerrilla. Dozens of witnesses lined up to testify that Menéndez had been living peacefully in Merida during the entire movement. The defense was in vain. Menéndez received a sentence of eight years. He was placed in Lecumberri jail with other political prisoners. But his story did not end there. Once more, Cold War politics and journalism intertwined. On November 20, 1971, Genaro Vázquez and the ACNR kidnapped the rich businessman and rector of the Autonomous University of Guerrero (Universidad Autónoma de Guerrero), Jaime Castrejón Díez.[144] In return for his release, they demanded the liberation of nine political prisoners, including Menéndez. According to *Por Qué?*, Vázquez wanted to thank the journalist for offering the movement favorable press. Echeverría acceded to the demands. A week later Menéndez and the others got on a plane bound for Cuba. Menéndez would remain in exile in Havana for the next seven years.[145]

How to Lose Friends and Alienate People

Menéndez was finally pardoned by President José López Portillo (1976–1982) and returned to Mexico in 1978. In the early 1980s, he returned to journalism. He reprised his role as a war reporter, writing about the guerrilla conflicts in Central America and established his own magazine, *Por Esto*. The weekly played on *Por Que?*'s title, but was much closer to his version of *Sucesos*. It was based in Yucatán, contained ample coverage of Latin America guerrilla insurgencies, supported the reformist left, and had substantial links to the regime. DFS informants inside the offices wrote regular reports on *Por Esto*'s politics. Former president Echeverría contributed to the magazine. Menéndez even edged closer to the PRI, working as an advisor to the state's peasant union. By 1991, the

magazine had become a daily. It now formed the left-wing rival to the Menéndez family newspaper, *El Diario de Yucatán*. Commercial competition and
cozying up to the state achieved what dabbling in insurrection did not. Menéndez's family cut him off completely. The two publications now traded insults
and competed vociferously for readers. Like many counterculture projects,
Menéndez's efforts ended in hypocrisy, family conflict, and relative wealth.
The tension between individual liberation and social change was decided
firmly in favor of the former.[146]

Yet Menéndez's story illustrates the changes to Mexican journalism in the
1960s. Individual experiences, broader cultural shifts, and institutional transformations interacted to loosen the ties that bound pressmen to the regime.
Many of the earliest converts, like Menéndez and Ortega, were from outside the
capital and started out less connected to this world. But whatever the underlying reasons, during the period the rules of the game changed. Many journalists radicalized. Some, like Rico Galán, became communist ideologues. But
for others the exercise of their profession inspired their conversion. Witnessing state violence, experiencing government censorship, and investigating
corruption pushed many to begin subverting the expectations of press writing. They included *Excélsior*'s Young Turks, like Julio Scherer, Manuel Mejido,
and Miguel Granados Chapa; cartoonists like Abel Quezada and Eduardo del
Río; and lesser-known figures like Mercedes Padrés. This was a gradual, halt-
ing, and occasionally even converse process. For many, threats, financial pressures, friendships, family responsibilities, and the shock of torture or near
death served to slow down or undercut the erosion of traditional journalistic
values.[147] Only a few were prepared to go to jail for copy.

This was also a process that started to enmesh Mexican journalism in the
murky world of international espionage. This affected both censorship and
public discourse. During the 1960s, both foreign and domestic secret services
sought to manipulate the expanding media to serve their ends. Officials started
to view journalism in terms of security. Revealing small-scale insurgencies or
exposing state-sanctioned killings no longer simply affected state-society relations in the Mexican capital, but had broader transnational ramifications.
Government spies, from Mexico and beyond, got increasingly involved in
controlling published information. They now provided state censors with a
broad range of strategies including widespread surveillance, dirty tricks, and
violence. But if the Cold War proffered new restrictions, it also offered new
opportunities. New sources of finance and information emerged. Liberal de-
mocracies found it increasingly difficult to balance freedom of the press with
increasingly outspoken left-wing journalism. In Mexico, but also in the United

States and Europe, an escalating dialectic of censorship and criticism emerged. As officials used increasingly heavy-handed means of control, opponents employed increasingly radical approaches to criticism. Few took up arms like Menéndez. But invented traditions of objectivity, responsibility, and shared values declined. New or recalibrated strategies like personal testimony, satire, sensationalism, and conspiracy reentered the public sphere.[148]

Menéndez's works also shaped subsequent publications. *Por Qué?* in particular heavily influenced Julio Scherer. When he launched *Proceso* in 1976, the magazine adopted the magazine's direct, accusatory style, the emphasis on investigative journalism, the focus on the links between crime and official corruption, and even the politicization of the *nota roja*. Menéndez's pieces also encouraged the emergence of a more critical, engaged style of political column writing. During the 1970s, the insular, incomprehensible world of the Mexico City columnist declined. Instead, columnists like Buendía and Granados Chapa started to engage with the interaction of security forces, government officials, and private businessmen. Like Menéndez, they started to reveal relationships, expose corruption, and include the dialogue between journalist and reader in their columns.[149]

Part III
The Regional Press

CHAPTER FIVE

How to Control the Press (Badly)

Censorship and Regional Newspapers

On June 7, 1976, President Echeverría celebrated the Day of Press Freedom with hundreds of media representatives from Mexico City and the provinces. The event was classic Echeverría-era theatre. Waiters served up an abstemious meal of chicken soup, ceviche, and hibiscus water; officials handed out prizes to compliant reporters; and Echeverría received an award in recognition of his "maintenance of the liberty of the press." But just as the editor of the *Siglo de Torreón* got up to speak, guests heard yells from the back of the hall. The director of the *Revista Chiapas*, Manuel Velasco Suárez, shouted that two weeks ago the army had killed a group of women and children in the border town of Tapachula. State authorities had forced the local press to cover up the massacre. The governor of Chiapas then stood, jabbed his finger at Velasco, called him a liar, and claimed that the state "was at complete peace." The interjection—intended to stop further interruptions—had the opposite effect. Local journalists rose to complain about press repression in their states. The editor of Oaxaca's student rag, *El Chivo*, claimed that official thugs had beaten and kidnapped his colleagues. A Puebla journalist accused the governor and the university rector of employing a gang to destroy his press. In all, thirteen local journalists protested. The next day, the nationals published reviews of the ceremony. But the complaints, which highlighted both the prevalence and violence of regulatory censorship in Mexico's provinces, were completely ignored.[1]

Over the past thirty years, scholars of Mexican press censorship have, in general, done the same. Instead they have concentrated on censorship in Mexico City's national press (as I did in chapter 2), and have discovered a thick network of interdependent ideological, personal, and financial relations. Constitutive censorship and crony capitalism acted in unison to suppress opposition views. There was no need for direct state intervention; self-censorship was the norm. At the same time, as the 1976 ceremony suggested and this chapter argues, these depictions of national press censorship cannot be extended to the regional press. Here, power dynamics among state actors, media owners, journalists, and civil society were quite distinct from those in Mexico City. Constitutive censorship and economic backing structured some newspapers. But sporadic, regulatory, or direct censorship continued to play a dominant role. Local authorities regularly employed short-term imprisonments, beatings, the destruction of property, threats, and public humiliation to intimidate journalists and force them to bury potentially damaging stories. These measures shifted over space and time. Political confrontations increasingly generated rhythms of censorship. Some regions developed traditions of regulatory suppression that still have some bearing on the current geography of press repression. The murder of journalists was rare and relatively strictly regulated by the national government. But it still occurred and could cause considerable conflicts among state authorities, local newspapers, and the national government.

Constitutive Censorship and Its Limits

In some ways censorship in the provinces reproduced that of Mexico City. For many newspapers there was no need for violence. Self-censorship was commonplace. Press owners might have come from a broader set of backgrounds than their Mexico City counterparts, but most were relatively conservative. In general, they applauded the rightward shift of national and local administrations. Government press offices, as in the capital, started slowly. During the 1940s and 1950s, they were underfunded and understaffed. But they gradually grew and though they never reached the competence of Echeverría's Ministry of the Interior, by the mid-1960s they issued bulletins and tried to bully local editors to take the official line. As in the capital, financial support also played a major role. Some local newspapers were owned by the state. Others were effectively floated by local administrations. Bribes and soft payments to editors and journalists increased over time. But in the provinces such means of censorship also had limits. Regional owners, editors, and journalists came from across the social spectrum, held a bewildering range of ideologies, were sustained by strong links to civil society, and often ran small-scale operations that did not require major investment from the state. Furthermore, local governments often lacked the mechanisms or the coherence to impose financial penalties. PIPSA was a national, not a state, organization. Regional infighting in the ruling party regularly threw up dissidents willing to back the opposition press.

In general, owners of the big-selling regional dailies came from a broader social background than the capital's proprietors. Some, like Jesús Alvarez del Castillo of Guadalajara's *El Informador*, were from upper-class families. Alvarez's father was a prominent businessman, and Alvarez studied in both California and France. His brother was a politician and his son a successful foreign service bureaucrat.[2] Others came from more middle-class backgrounds. Rogelio Cantu, owner of Monterrey's *El Porvenir*, was a former journalist, and his rival, Rodolfo Junco de la Vega of *El Norte*, was the son of an accountant.[3] But most, like their Mexico City counterparts, were relatively conformist. In general, they had supported business and church groups during the conflicts of the initial postrevolutionary era. Some were close to the industrial elite. *El Norte* was funded by the Monterrey Group of local industrialists. (They even appointed their own censor to make sure the paper's stories aligned with the group's needs.)[4] Others were sympathetic to church groups. Even Antonio de Juambelz, the relatively liberal owner of *El Siglo de Torreón*, was so close to the local Cristero groups that the state appointed a military censor to the newsroom during the conflicts of the late 1920s.[5] Others still were straightforward right-wingers. During the early 1940s, Vicente Villasana of Tampico's *El Mundo* supported the Axis powers. Furthermore, almost all the owners of the big regionals were deeply hostile to unionized labor. During the Cárdenas administration, the Confederation of Mexican Workers (Confederación de Trabajadores de México, CTM) had held a succession of strikes against what they termed the "reactionary press" including most members of the AEE, which had left a long-lasting and bitter impression.[6]

As a result, like most Mexico City editors, the owners of the big regionals applauded the rightward drift of the country's federal government and its state administrations. They shared politicians' anticommunism, concern for economic growth, and desire for stability. As most owners also acted as editors, they were able to impose these ideas on their journalists. José Escobar Zavala, who worked in the *Diario del Yaqui* during the late 1950s, claimed that it was the owners, not the state, who were the "real demagogues" and enforced "self-censorship." "During the [political] conflicts the owner would ask, 'Who are you with, whose side are you on?' I couldn't say that I was on the side of justice or of the readers."[7] The San Luis Potosí journalist Gregorio Marín Rodríguez offered a similar story, arguing that the editor "normally did most of the censoring." On one occasion he crossed out Marín's catty remark that the official party was "revolutionary in doctrine, but institutional in practice." On another, he cut his piece on the Cuban Revolution completely. As in the capital, journalists who refused to toe the line were dismissed. Marín was sacked from at least three newspapers for refusing to sign up to the editor's policies.[8] And during the 1960s, the famously awkward Baja California Norte journalist Jesús Blancornelas found it difficult to hold down a job.[9]

Social links undergirded these ideological confluences. Provincial capitals were small social worlds and politicians and journalists often rubbed shoulders at cantinas, restaurants, and private houses. Some of the meetings were formal. The San Luis Potosí governor and former journalist Francisco Martínez de la Vega invited journalists to the gubernatorial residence every Thursday where he dished out tequila, rum, and beer as well as his favorite cigarettes. He wrote checks for journalists' social events and trips abroad and chatted with them about the running of the state.[10] Oaxaca governor, Eduardo Vasconcelos, another journalist-turned-politician, also socialized with the local writers, regularly entertaining reporters at drunken parties in the Dos Equis bar at the Hotel Marqués del Valle.[11] Such practices generated close accords. Both Martínez and Vasconcelos received relatively good press even from newspapers that had been critical of state administrations in the past. Such relations of friendship also linked governors to individual reporters. Local hack Bernardino León y Vélez Contreras was the governor of Morelos's "party friend," a womanizer and a drunk who also wrote flattering pump pieces for the local paper.[12] Baja California Norte typesetter and journalist E. Castillo sat around drinking scotch with Braulio Maldonado and his twenty-three-year-old lover. Maldonado would occasionally press 100 peso bills into his hand as he left. "We became close friends," he explained. Perhaps not coincidentally, his newspaper, *El Reportaje*, was one of the few publications to support the governor during the political conflicts of the 1950s.[13]

As the examples suggest, it was often booze that lubricated the social ties between politicians and journalists, and among the writers themselves. Perhaps even more so than in the capital, where there was a strong café culture, cantinas provided the space for fraternizing among provincial journalists. Miguel Angel Millán Peraza remembered drinking tequilas at La Corona bar in downtown Tijuana with his fellow journalists before moving on to the city's brothels. "The drinking," he admitted, "was prodigious."[14] When Marín moved to *El Sol de San Luis* in 1952, he recalled hanging out at the bars across the road from the paper's offices with his colleagues, including the political writer and soak, Salvador Cavada. "We were all generals in the cantina, but Cavada had four stars." When Cavada keeled over during one session, Marín remarked that he had "died doing his duty."[15] As in Mexico City, drinking exploits could generate reputations. *Diario del Yaqui* reporter Esteban Valle's party piece was downing half a bottle of brandy then dancing the Huapango with the bottle on his head.[16] It also cemented the very male atmosphere of the journalistic world. Arcelia Yañiz, Oaxaca City's sole female journalist, remembered celebrating her editor's birthday in the early 1950s. They ended up outside a brothel where the editor said, "You are a lady; you can't enter." Perhaps indicating how she managed to forge a career in such a masculine world, she ignored him and did so anyway.[17] These ties, like the more official get-togethers, spread self-censorship, albeit in a subtler manner. Thus, Marín described how one of his editors, who also happened to be head of the party's popular sector, "made friendship a form of religion." They used to eat and drink together regularly. Once, his editor asked him to spike a particularly critical article. "After a lazy stretch and a bit of vacillation, I ended up accepting."[18] Social pressure could breed silence.

Beyond these informal means of self-censorship, local administrations also started to establish publicity offices. At first, they were organized by the federal government. In 1938, the director of DAPP sent out instructions for state governments to establish their own press departments. They were designed to send in information to the Mexico City base about recent state achievements as well as provide a conduit for federal propaganda. They were a disaster. In Nayarit the administration simply refused to set up an office, pleading a lack of funds and citing a 250,000-peso hole in the state budget. In Queretaro and Quintana Roo they did the same, eventually just retitling the director of the tourism department head of the press office. Even in the relatively well-off state of Nuevo León, the department took over a year to set up.[19] Furthermore, after this initial push, enthusiasm (or perhaps more importantly cash) for these kinds of departments started to run out. Many were scrapped during the 1940s. At least four states, where I have done in-depth investigations—Baja California Norte, Oaxaca, San Luis Potosí, and Chihuahua—possessed no such department during the decade. Mexico State employed the governor's badminton partner in a kind of informal role. The Sonora press office was only reestablished as late as 1955.[20]

But by the late 1950s most states possessed press departments. Initially they were understaffed and limited in scope. Under Gustavo Baz (1957–1963) Mexico State's press office consisted of two small rooms, a typewriter, and two staff members. Carlos Moncada was also one of only two press specialists in the Sonora government in 1961. In Baja California Norte, there was only one official, together with the governor's private secretary, and the state secretary of the interior, who dealt with issues of the press. (Admittedly they also paid a linkman, the *Excélsior* journalist Enrique Loubet Jr., to run the Mexico City side of the operation.) Furthermore, these offices had no clear remit beyond handing out money. Moncada wrote a few government bulletins, but in general his day-to-day business involved handing over envelopes and negotiating with cash-strapped journalists. What was so bad about the job, he explained, "was that the government lacked a defined plan on how to spread news of its works or deal with journalists." In the end he resigned—"I was not born for this corruption." The Baja California Norte office also seems to have played a similarly circumscribed role. Waves of adverse publicity sometimes intensified efforts. But in general, the department was restricted to the disbursement of cash for advertisements and *gacetillas*. In 1959, they even lacked a clippings service to ascertain the effects of their cash bribes. In Mexico State, Governor Baz's department was so chaotic that between 1957 and 1959 the director changed on five occasions.[21]

In fact, more professional state press offices only emerged in the mid-1960s. Visiting Nuevo León in 1964, a U.S. academic commented that the release of information was now "highly centralized in the office of the chief of press." The director was an experienced and well-connected man who had been director of the university art school and a journalist. He sent out information bulletins every day (admittedly still only printed on mimeograph). He also published a wide range of other publications, put together by a staff of writers, artists, photographers, and clerical workers. There was a rather stiff, formal press conference between the governor and the press every day. Press management had now moved beyond sly backhanders to the full management of official events. When the governor appeared anywhere, "the state government provided complete services." Journalists were shuttled to the ceremony; the government provided official photographs; and "the press office writers prepared an official version of events."[22] In Baja California Norte, there was a similar growth in press office activity. By 1966, the office employed ten staff, including two photographers, a photograph developer, two reporters, and two typists.[23]

By the 1970s the kind of thinking that had transformed federal press strategies also started to influence the organization of these regional departments. Alfonso Sánchez García, who worked in Mexico State's press office under Governor Carlos Hank (1969–1975), admitted that it was only then that the departments were "converted into modern, dynamic organizations modeled on private publicity companies." In 1971, in Baja California Norte the press department underwent similar changes. It was now a large organization with over thirty employees. It contained six departments specializing in public relations, radio and TV, the international media, cultural ceremonies, the local and national press, and book publishing. The local media section was the largest and employed eight staff. They analyzed, cut, and condensed stories from all the state's major papers and then sent short précis to the government's departments. Even with these new, modern press departments, press control was still far from smooth. In fact Sánchez García speculated that their expansion actually caused more problems than it solved. As functionaries now presumed that the press offices could quash press stories of official malfeasance, they increased their acts of corruption. "They thought we had the press under our control like the director at a music concert." As a result, they considered the department "like toilet paper . . . or sometimes like a machine gun."[24]

Finally, as in Mexico City, financial incentives also played an important role in maintaining newspaper silence. They included direct subsidies, payments for advertisements, and *gacetillas*, as well as individual bribes and soft payments to individual journalists. Some governments owned papers directly. The ruling party in Yucatán started the *Diario del Sureste* to combat the critical, right-wing *El Diario del Yucatán* in 1931. During the following decades, they employed local university teachers and graduates to run the paper. By the 1960s, locals grumbled that most articles were actually written in the PRI head office.[25] When Blancornelas worked in Baja California Norte's *El Mexicano* during the 1960s, the editorial rule was "always emphasize the PRI, on the others parties nothing." When he interviewed opposition candidates, the director would tell him that the story "would never be published." Eventually he found out that the paper was government-owned. "They didn't pay taxes, electricity, or paper. In reality it was a newspaper of political propaganda and not information . . . it was a world of understood values, of lies, disgusting."[26]

But direct state ownership of newspapers was rare. In most cases, authorities simply used state funds to prop up privately owned newspapers. As in the capital, PIPSA played a role. By the end of 1968, some major regionals had extensive debts with the government monopoly. The García Valseca chain's debts were particularly large, but other large regionals also owed significant sums. *El Siglo de Torreón* owed 471,027 pesos, *El Mañana* of Reynosa 394,703, and *El Heraldo* of León 308,162. Veracruz's long-running *El Dictamen* owed over a million pesos. Smaller titles owed a total of 2,831,022 pesos between them.[27] But local newsmen could circumvent PIPSA, and federal debts did not preclude attacks on local governors. So most local administrations also used direct subsidies. As early as 1942, the U.S. consul speculated that the owner of the *Diario de Durango*, Mauricio L. Sánchez, charged governors between 200 and 400 pesos a month for favorable coverage. They concluded Sánchez was "frequently . . . referred to as a bootlicker without sufficient principle to sponsor any policy which has not been advocated by the state or federal governments."[28] By the late 1950s, the practice was firmly in place. Though Moncada claimed that he started working at the Sonora press office "with an absence of malice," he soon learned the rules of the game. By the end of 1961 he was paying 5,000 pesos a month to the big dailies and 2,500 pesos to the smaller concerns.[29] A 1960 government report on regional newspapers indicated similar practices extended throughout most states. *La Tribuna Tuxpeña* relied on "the advertisements and the help the council gives it"; *El Heraldo* of Hermosillo received "a subsidy from the government of the state and help from the Department of Press and Propaganda of the same government"; *El Sinaloense* of Mazatlán got 300 pesos from the council a month; and *Ultimas Noticias* of La Paz earned 400 pesos from the state government.[30]

Beyond direct subsidies, state governments also offered a range of other financial inducements. Sometimes they bought up large amounts of the newspapers. In 1960, the government of Baja California Norte handed over 35,000 pesos in return for the promise of 1,500 copies of the weekly *Baja California* magazine for the next two years.[31] On other occasions they let newspaper companies off paying specific fees. Abelardo Casanova, a columnist for Sonora's *El Imparcial*, explained that no local newspaper actually paid social security quotas. Instead they offered favorable coverage and free advertising to both federal and state institutions. If there were debts left at the end of the year, the government simply annulled them.[32] As in Mexico City, these debt cancellations provided a lifeline for economically troubled operations. From 1958, Baja California Norte's daily *ABC* was in real financial trouble. The firm was losing between 300,000 and 400,000 pesos annually. By 1961 debts included 300,000 pesos for PIPSA, 144,304 pesos in taxes, and 1,365 pesos for social security. After a lengthy economic study, the government simply canceled the commitments.[33]

State governments also spent increasing amounts of cash on advertising and *gacetillas*. As we saw in chapter 2, the Baja California Norte government spent around 100,000 per year on direct and indirect publicity. The really big fees went to the national newspapers and magazines. Between 1959 and 1961, only around 10 percent of total payments went to regional newspapers. (It is difficult to gauge whether this was a cause or an effect of the local administration's lack of support among local journalists.) But some local publications did receive substantial benefits. The *ABC de la Costa*, which supported the unpopular PRI gubernatorial candidate in 1959, received 12,312 pesos for its coverage. Others, like the weekly magazines *Radar* and *Revista Baja California*, received steady payments of between 250 and 1,000 pesos every couple of months.[34]

In the provinces these payments were subject to substantial debate. In fact Jesús Tapia Avilés, a Hermosillo journalist, summed up the entire practice of provincial journalism as a question of "bargaining." "Don't fuck me around charging 100,000 pesos for three pages, lower it. I'll give you fifty . . . running a newspaper is bargaining, it's a market."[35] (In chapter 6, we will see how the García Valseca chain developed this tradition into a system of extortion.) But most negotiations were less extreme. In Baja California Norte, local editors tried to press the government into paying higher fees by stressing their influence and loyalty. In 1961, Jorge Tomasini, the editor of *Vocero*, asked for 7,000 pesos for reprinting the governor's annual report. "I want to make it known that my journalistic collaboration and that of Vocero has been continuous and we have ... come out in defense of Baja California's functionaries against the continuous attacks of the [Mexico City] press." In return, press officials pleaded poverty, claimed ignorance of what were often verbal agreements, and tried to put off payment until the following administration. Such delaying tactics worked. Publications often took half of what was demanded in return for prompt disbursement.[36]

Beyond these institutional payments, regional government also paid out bribes to individual journalists. There is less evidence for this than for the capital. State governments simply did not have the funds for major payoffs. There are few tales of fabulously rich provincial journalists like Mexico City columnists Denegri or Teissier. (Though Rodolfo Junco Jr., the owner of Monterrey's *El Sol*, did own a Ferrari, a private aircraft, and nine polo ponies.)[37] They may have existed, but I can find no evidence of the kind of regular fortnightly payments issued in the capital by the 1950s. In fact, payments to regional journalists appear to have been more sporadic and also more liable to negotiation. When Moncada worked in the press office in Sonora, he remembered one reporter asked for 500 pesos to move the remains of his mother to another cemetery. Moncada agreed to pay. But when he approached the governor to ask for the funds, the governor laughed and showed him receipts from his private secretary, secretary of education, and treasurer who had all paid the journalist similar amounts.[38]

In fact, probably because they were substantially cheaper, local administrations preferred to favor compliant journalists with a variety of soft benefits. The most prominent gift was land. Starting in the 1940s, state governments gave out titles to dozens of journalists. In 1942, a gang of Guadalajara's reporters received rights to lands on the road to Tlaquepaque. The group included stringers for the major nationals, major regional columnists, and the combative (at least up to that point) editor of *El Redondel*. Over the next decade, in return for explicit promises to support official candidates, they received favorable government loans, 10,000 pesos in cash, and unused railway girders to build their houses. In 1953, forty Guadalajara journalists even applied for 3,000 square meters of land for their sons to establish small farms. They asked that the plots were hooked up to the electricity supply and on a main road.[39] In Aguascalientes, journalists got a similar deal. In 1952, Governor Edmundo

Gámez Orozco ceded dozens of plots to create a journalists' neighborhood. The following year the owners received a 120,000-peso loan. In 1955, they invited the president to inaugurate a mural to journalism in the neighborhood.[40] The other major soft benefits were jobs in the state administrations. They were not as well paid as federal employment but they did offer the opportunity for substantial graft. Despite what government agents described as "his extreme unpopularity," the governor of Morelos's "party friend," León, was made PRI candidate for Cuernavaca in 1965. His tenure was marked, according to later reports, by the wholesale sacking of the city's treasury.[41] Other reporters held down journalism jobs and state employment at the same time. Raúl Albertos Betancourt, the director of Río Bravo's *El Independiente*, was also fiscal advisor to the government of Tamaulipas, a member of the Reynosa council, and a board member of the state's popular sector.[42]

Constitutive censorship and crony capitalism helped discipline local papers, as they did the big nationals. Overlapping ideologies and interests, increasingly professional state press departments, and financial disbursements all combined to orient regional publications—especially the larger industrial concerns. But such strategies were difficult to extend over the regional press as a whole. Both the internal workings of the provincial press and the fractious nature of local politics militated against these softer means of control. First, regional journalists, unlike their Mexico City counterparts, came from a wide sector of society and held varied opinions. Some were wealthy and university educated. Betancourt, the editor of *El Independiente*, was a wealthy UNAM graduate.[43] Pedro F. Quintanilla, a columnist for the right-wing *El Diario de Monterrey*, was son of a lawyer and grandson of one of the city's major factory owners.[44] Leopoldo Peniche Vallado was son of a Yucatán landowner and a law graduate.[45] In fact, by the 1950s, Monterrey's *El Porvenir* and *El Norte* recruited almost exclusively from the city's law school.[46] Jorge Villegas Núñez claimed it was a wonderful finishing school for the "gente culta."[47] But unlike in Mexico City, these were the exceptions. Few wealthy provincials aspired to the poor salaries offered by regional newspapers. Even *El Norte*'s owner described the job as a "second or third rate profession."[48]

Instead, most provincial journalists came from much humbler backgrounds. Some had a degree of higher education. Especially in the heavily Catholic center west, many attended the region's network of religious schools. They included Esteban Cibrián Guzmán, who studied at the seminaries in Zapotlán and Guadalajara before going back to Ciudad Guzmán to establish the contrarian weekly *La Vigia*.[49] They included the San Luis Potosí journalist Marín, who gained his education at a small religious school in the annex of his local church.[50] Others received their education at the country's teacher training colleges. Mexico State journalist Sánchez García attended one such establishment where he learned his penmanship by writing poetry.[51] The Saltillo columnist and humorist Armando Fuentes Aguirre was also a trainee teacher, as was one of the provinces' rare female journalists, the Baja California Norte writer Dalia Nieto de Leyva.[52]

But many came from even poorer backgrounds and had only attended primary school or were even self-taught. Néstor Sánchez Hernández, editor of Oaxaca's *Carteles del Sur*, came from an extremely impoverished family before joining the army. After volunteering to fight in the Spanish Civil War, he came back, retrained as a print worker, and then returned to his hometown to establish the combative daily.[53] Sinaloa reporter Manuel González Ceniceros was an unemployed vagrant with a taste for nineteenth-century adventure stories who eventually found a job at *La Voz de Sinaloa*.[54] The Veracruz journalist Eliezer Martínez Mora spent the early 1940s earning 15¢ a day working on road construction.[55] Simón Hipólito Castro, the founder of Atoyac's *La Voz del Ejido*, was a peasant autodidact.[56] Many pursued multiple occupations before ending up in the journalism business. The *El Correo* correspondent Osvaldo Hernández was a carpenter's apprentice, a lion tamer, a trapeze artist, a bookbinder, and an accountant.[57] Tijuana writer Oscar del Campo Venegas was a child runaway, a newspaper vendor, a grocer's helper, a bakery worker, a waiter, and in and out of correctional institutions.[58]

With such varied backgrounds, provincial journalists pursued a bewildering array of interests and ideologies. Many were conservative Catholics who still resented the official party, despite its rightward shift. Unlike their Mexico City colleagues, they witnessed few of the benefits of stability or industrialization. They had grown up during the violent decades of land reform and anticlericalism, and they now focused their anger on official corruption, the lack of democracy, and the government's perceived continuation of antireligious policies. Veracruz journalist Martínez Mora lost his grandfather to a Zapatista raid, experienced the corruption of union leadership as a road builder, described his fellow workers rather unsympathetically as "prison escapees, exconvicts, drug addicts, thieves, and individuals that were not accepted in their own villages," and eventually turned to a fanatical brand of Catholicism. When he founded the *Voz del Trópico* in Martínez de la Torre in 1948, such opinions informed his writing.[59] Salomón H. Rangel, a journalist for San Luis Potosí's *La Tribuna*, was a rich merchant, a fervent Catholic, an anti-Semite, and a member of the right-wing Sinarquistas.[60] But other provincial journalists were extremely left-wing. They included Castro, the peasant autodidact who moved in Guerrero's guerrilla circles and was eventually imprisoned and tortured on trumped-up charges.[61] They included the future railway leader Demetrio Vallejo, who started his career as editor of the Coatzacoalcos workers weekly.[62] Others still were born contrarians. Alfredo Ramírez Villavicencio, the editor of Oaxaca City's *El Chapulín*, nostalgically evoked the Porfiriato and ridiculed the revolution but also supported the striking railway workers in 1959 and the students in 1968.[63]

Second, regional authorities, unlike their federal counterparts, lacked the financial or institutional means to coopt the local press. From 1940 onward, new fiscal laws and popular mobilizations saw state and municipal tax bases shrink. Many local authorities simply lacked the funds to buy off all the local press.[64] In fact, the rather paltry payoffs listed above as well as the negotiated nature of advertising disbursements stand testament to states' limited funds. At the same time, media groups, rather than local authorities, often controlled the key resources. Even the federal newsprint monopoly, which starved out critical Mexico City magazines like *Presente* and *Por Qué?* could be bypassed with relative ease.[65] In Chihuahua, the editor of *Indice*, a left-wing weekly, was in charge of the local office and distributed the product to an array of other radical publications.[66] In Merida, the PIPSA representative was related to the owners of *El Diario de Yucatán* and furnished the daily with more than a year's worth of paper in reserve. As a result, big regionals could ride out paper blockades. A black market in paper also operated in many states. *El Diario de Yucatán* and the head of PIPSA went into business together, selling extra paper to out-of-favor presses throughout the southeast.[67] The editor of Coahuila's *El Eco* used the newspaper as a front for his much more profitable business in contraband paper.[68] If governors cut off local supplies, editors could travel to bordering states. During the 1960s, the editor of Oaxaca's *Carteles del Sur* regularly avoided the hostile local dealer and bought his supplies in Puebla.[69] On the U.S. border, the practice was extremely common. In fact, smugglers even trafficked untaxed paper into cities like Ciudad Juárez, where they would sell it to blacklisted newspapers.[70]

Third, the business models of provincial newspapers differed radically from their national counterparts. Most Mexico City dailies were huge, industrial operations, employing hundreds of workers. As we saw in chapter 2, many remained reliant on the government's cheap newsprint, low interest loans, and expensive advertising contracts to stay afloat. Instead most provincial newspapers were much smaller, often family-run, affairs. Some used industrial printing techniques and specialized workers. But even these knew how to cut costs. The Menéndez family, which ran *El Diario de Yucatán*, was famously tightfisted. In the 1960s, the director, Abel Menéndez, wore the same suit every day, had no car, and walked to work. Although the newspaper hit a certified circulation of over 40,000 copies, he employed only five journalists, a wire editor, and five proofreaders.[71] Many provincial newspapers were still small-scale artisan operations. Here, journalists often performed multiple tasks. (As the cynical former reporter Alfredo Gutiérrez y Falcón commented, the provincial writer "had a work day without end, was the seller of adverts, the columnist, and the proof reader."[72]) These operations also had low capital and costs. They owned small premises (the offices of Tijuana's *Noticias* comprised an 18- by 15-foot room with seven typewriters)[73]; they used cheap, secondhand machinery (Alberto Amador's *Diario de Ensenada* plant "looked more like a garage than a newspaper plant" and employed a sixty-year-old flatbed press)[74]; they employed minimal staff (the owner of Oaxaca's *Carteles del Sur* wrote all the articles under different pseudonyms and employed only a typesetter and a part-time cartoonist)[75]; and they paid measly wages (Carlos Moncada started his career at Ciudad Obregón's *Diario del Yaqui* earning 175 pesos a month).[76] In these cases, official cash might have been welcomed, but unlike for the big nationals, it was not crucial to everyday operations. Most provincial newspapers could survive without state disbursements.

Finally, politics in the provinces was much more open and competitive than in Mexico City. At the state level, multiple elite groups competed not only for the elected positions but also for influential sinecures in state administrations. The process of nominating the PRI's gubernatorial candidate, for example, often involved bitter rivalries, demonstrations of mass support, propaganda campaigns, bribes, ballot rigging, and violence. Even when governors came to power, they often faced opposition from out-of-favor groups or relatively autonomous *caciques*. At the municipal level, politics was even more fractious. Again multiple groups competed for power, through the PRI, through opposition parties, or even through civil disturbances.[77] Taken together, such political effervescence diminished the need for newspapers to take official money. They could look elsewhere for advertising or backing from ostracized elites, competing PRI politicians, *caciques*, or rival political parties. Large provincial newspapers, like *El Informador*, *El Siglo de Torreón*, and *El Norte*, clearly benefited from the tensions between local industrialists and the official party.[78] As we shall see in chapters 7 and 8, smaller artisanal newspapers were often floated by small merchants and businessmen excluded from local politics. Even intra-PRI fights could make for a contentious and popular press. In Sonora, during the 1967 PRI primaries, opposing party grandees competed for the nomination. On one side was the official candidate and former senator Fausto Acosta Romo. He was supported by Ciudad Obregón's *Diario del Yaqui*, Guaymas's *La Gaceta*, Hermosillo's *El Diario*, and Nogales's *Acción*. On the other side was the outgoing governor's friend and newspaper owner Faustino Félix Serna. He was backed by the *Diario del Yaqui*'s direct rival, *La Tribuna del Yaqui*, his own paper, Hermosillo's *El Sonorense*, and Guaymas's *La Extra*. As the struggle for the nomination intensified, these newspapers competed to expose scandals on rival politicians. Press control was impossible.[79]

Violence and Censorship in the Regional Press

As ideological confluence, financial control, and self-censorship were less easy to achieve than in the capital, authorities often turned to more direct, violent means of censoring the press. Attacks on journalists were frequent, although they peaked at certain times and in certain places. Most of the perpetrators were members of the state or local authorities, who used the police or off-the-books hit men to do their dirty work. Their reasons, it seems, were normally twofold. First, they were concerned that certain articles or exposés damaged their personal or family honor. Second, and I think more important, they worried that targeted press campaigns destabilized their political position, either by generating civil mobilizations or by flagging corruption or unacceptable illegal activities. Means of regulatory censorship varied. The most popular method was short, sharp bursts of imprisonment, either under the official press law or on other unconnected charges. Threats, beatings, and the destruction of property were also commonplace. Some authorities employed rather makeshift versions of the federal state's dirty tricks campaigns, designed to humiliate and delegitimize opposition writers. Finally, and only as a last resort, authorities also sometimes employed murder.

Between 1940 and 1960, I have found evidence of over 200 violent attacks on provincial newspapers.[80] They are cited in complaints to Mexican presidents and in various journalistic overviews of the period. In reality, there were probably far more. The editor of Oaxaca's *El Chapulín* recounted at least eight occasions when he was beaten, threatened, or forcibly ejected from the state. But by the late 1940s, he gave up reporting the incidents as "the authorities never did anything."[81] In fact, only one complaint appears in the presidential archives. In terms of timing, attacks on the press peaked between 1945 and 1948, during the mid-1950s, and once again in 1959. The rhythms of state and municipal elections and the emergence of individual social movements clearly played a role. Many of the attacks in the 1950s occurred in Baja California Norte, where a strong PAN party faced down the governor Braulio Maldonado.[82] But national politics also played a part. During the mid-1950s, President Ruiz Cortines announced a campaign against official graft. The move generated a wave of press denunciations of corrupt local functionaries. Santiago Rivas, editor of Cananea's *El Intruso*, explained that he had published testimonies against the corrupt head of the health authorities "as part of the president's moralization of public functionaries."[83] But the move also produced a spike in reprisals against the press. Similarly, presidential candidate López Mateos's pointed remark that "cacicazgos surviv[ed] as long as the people tolerate[d] them" triggered another wave of press attacks on unpopular local authorities.[84] Again, violence followed. In 1959–1960, there were thirty-one attacks on editors and journalists. As we shall see, they included the usual threats and beatings, but also murder.

In terms of geography, nearly half the assaults occurred in the five states of Baja California Norte (thirty-one attacks), Tamaulipas (twenty-four), Veracruz (twenty-two), Oaxaca (fourteen), and Jalisco (ten). General patterns are difficult to discern. Two northern states suffered the most attacks. Here, there were high literacy rates, relatively high newspaper readership, and, especially in Baja California Norte, a functioning opposition party.[85] But the two states with the next highest levels of violence were in the center and south, where conflicts between *caciques* and civil society–press alliances seemed to have caused the high levels of repression. In Veracruz, nearly half the attacks occurred in the petrol-rich region of Poza Rica. During the 1950s, PEMEX leader Jaime Merino ran "the municipal authorities, the local and federal deputies, the schools, and even the sports clubs." It was known as the "Merinato." Gradually, squatters, teachers, and breakaway PEMEX workers coalesced into an opposition movement. Conflicts became increasingly violent. On October 6, 1958, police opened fire on the protestors and on March 17, 1959, demonstrators briefly kidnapped the Veracruz governor.[86] During the movement, journalists played an important role in stating the opposition's demands, uncovering acts of corruption and violence, and publicizing these acts through articles in the local and national press. As a result, they were heavily persecuted. In February 1957, Merino's *pistoleros* kidnapped the director of *La Voz de Poza Rica* and planned to kill him before he managed to escape. Three months later police smashed up the printing press of *Acción* and stole the entire print run. The following year, police arrested and beat a newspaper seller almost to death. In June 1958, twenty thugs attacked workers at the local newspaper

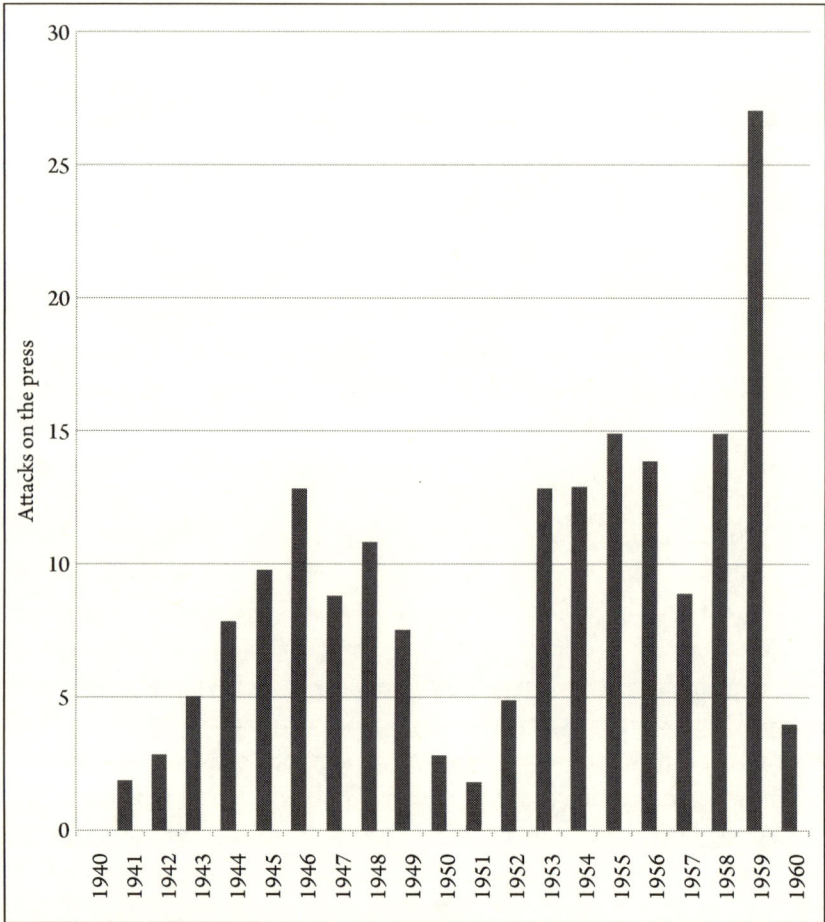

The chronology of attacks on the press, 1940–1960

La Opinión, and in 1960, assassins killed the *El Diario* journalist Alberto J. Altamirano.[87]

As these examples suggest, most attacks were directed by regional or local authorities. Obviously piecing together those responsible, what victims termed the "autor intelectual," is a tough job. Impunity was the rule. To my knowledge, only two perpetrators of press attacks were actually prosecuted. In these cases, the gunmen failed to reveal who had ordered the hit.[88] In a few cases, private companies were involved. In 1942, the Puebla weekly *Consolidación* ran a campaign against soft drink companies with poor hygiene records. Locals visited the paper with bottles containing mouse dropping, toothpicks, and "disgusting tangles of hair." In response, one of the factory owners stormed the newspaper offices, smashed the bottles, stabbed a journalist with a pen, and threatened to kill the editor.[89] But in over 95 percent of the cases where victims or their allies made direct accusations, they pointed the finger at state representatives. In 37 percent of the cases, they accused the state governor. Braulio Maldonado, the governor of Baja California Norte, and Hugo Pedro González, the governor of Tamaulipas, headed the list. Another 10 percent accused other members of the state administration, most often the secretary of the interior. Thirty-five percent of accusations were against municipal authorities. They included mayors, council members, and policemen. In November 1945, for example, the municipal president of Tuxtepec arrested the editor of *Acción* for writing negative stories about the administration.[90] Another 9 percent of accusations were against members of the military. In September 1956, *El Sol de Zacatecas* and *El Heraldo* of Aguascalientes ran articles that accused the soldiers of the thirtieth infantry battalion of murdering a peasant from the village of Tacoaleche and threatening to kill the witnesses. In return, the zone commander put the editors in jail.[91] Finally, informal local *caciques* allegedly committed around 5 percent of attacks.

Working out why local authorities acted in this way is tougher than it might seem. Asked about the rapid upsurge in journalists murdered during the 1990s, Blancornelas speculated that fewer than 10 percent were actually killed for their writing.[92] Most, he argued, were murdered for attempted blackmail, links to organized crime, or for mundane personal reasons. No doubt, there were similar cases in the preceding decades. Francisco Javier Mock, a journalist from Chiapas's *Diario del Sur*, was stabbed to death on a Tapachula street because of an old family feud.[93] State authorities often threw around accusations of extortion to excuse violence against the press.[94] But authorities attacked most reporters for their journalistic work. As the newspaper industry grew, politicians of all stripes, from governors to bureaucrats to rural strongmen, read the press. Gonzalo Santos, the San Luis Potosí *cacique*, was a careful reader of the dailies. In 1954, he sent three critical articles from the local *El Heraldo* to the president's private secretary, underlining offensive sections and scribbling the word "weak" at the top. In the accompanying letter he acknowledged that the president had advised local leaders to "Maderear" (the term was a reference to President Madero, and suggested going soft on the press). Instead he suggested politicians "Carrancear," "Obregonar," "or if you will permit me, Huastequear" the press (i.e., take a harder line).[95] Less secure politicians were even more anxious about their coverage. In a tapped phone call the senator Francisco Hernández y Hernández asked his partner about newspaper reports on his treatment of landless peasants. She replied that they had mentioned him in a positive light.

HERNÁNDEZ: "But in all of them?"

PARTNER: "Yes in all."

HERNÁNDEZ: "In *all* of them they mentioned me?"

PARTNER: "In all . . . except in *El Nacional* . . . which said the caravan [of peasants] arrived in Mexico."

HERNÁNDEZ: "But in all of the others?"

PARTNER: "Yes . . . in all of the others."

HERNÁNDEZ: "They didn't ignore us?"

PARTNER: [clearly losing patience] "No, no, no, but it is dealt with soberly . . . although it is on the front page and in all the columns . . . inside it is very sober."[96]

The reasons for politicians' concerns were twofold. At one level, old nineteenth-century ideals of personal honor still ruled.[97] Sometimes politicians felt that reporters had overstepped the boundaries of good taste, made accusations about their private lives, or unfairly involved their family members. As Octavio Paz argued, many Mexican politicians took criticism personally. "A difference in opinion" could "instantly and unconsciously become a personal quarrel."[98] Perusing the dailies in early 1947 the governor of Tamaulipas, Hugo Pedro González, revealed just these values, complaining to his friend that the accusations made by Heriberto Deandar's Nuevo Laredo "rag" were of the "highest register." "They didn't even stop at my wife," he wrote before lamenting, "I need the patience of a saint, more than I have had before, to put up with these injuries to our house by those who do this with impunity."[99] As a result, some attacks on the press were not so much acts of censorship as punishments for perceived slights.

But these ideas of honor now dovetailed with more pragmatic concerns. Top-down removal of both gubernatorial and municipal authorities was relatively common during PRI rule. Keeping local power depended on maintaining the perception of the president (in the case of governors) or the governor (in the case of mayors) that one could preserve order. Control of the public sphere was crucial to this. Print media reputations for graft, repression, or incompetence could flag problems to superiors and lead to dismissal. Marín, for example, described how the head of San Luis Potosí's health workers accosted him in the street and punched him as he feared the journalist's exposés of his illegal activities endangered his job.[100] As we shall see in chapters 7 and 8, such reputations could also feed into popular mobilizations, which could in turn force authorities from power. Often attacks were simply censorship.

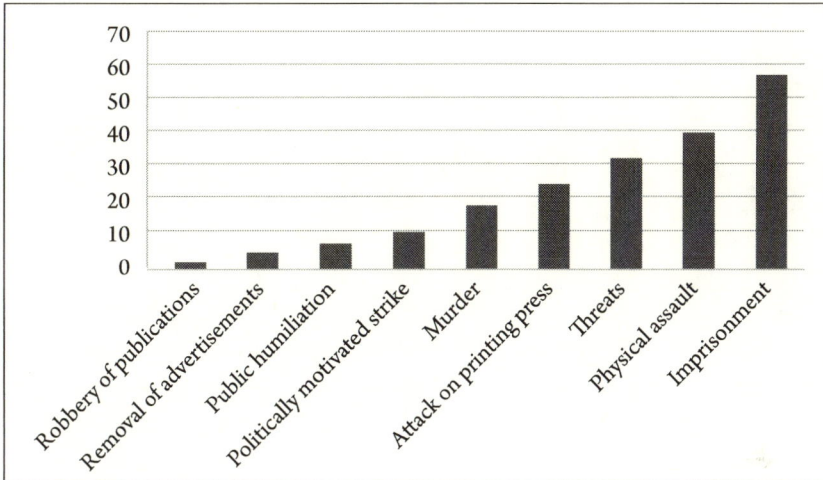

Types of attacks on the press, 1940–1960

The most common way to shut up the regional press was imprisonment. Jailing accounted for nearly 30 percent of attacks. Most fell foul of the 1917 Press Law. After 1940, this law was only very rarely employed in Mexico City. But in the provinces it was regularly invoked. Originally written to guard the Carrancista administration against press criticism, the law stunted political journalism in two ways. First, it protected the honor of citizens and functionaries from insults, libel, and slander. Even subtle pokes, or so-called *indirectas*, were prohibited. Article 34 ruled against journalists who insulted citizens or bureaucrats "covertly." Furthermore, lawyers argued that the concept of honor should be extended from the individual to the institution; badmouthing a general insulted the honor of the army. Article 350 of the Penal Code confirmed this, threatening up to six months imprisonment for slandering "the Congress, the Senate, a law tribunal, or any other official institution." Second, the law legislated against journalism that threated the public peace through "discrediting, ridiculing or destroying the fundamental institutions of the country" or "insulting the Mexican nation or its political entities."[101]

Outside the capital, the law was not only extremely restrictive, it was also regularly employed. When Reynosa's *El Bravo* accused the authorities of dishing out bribes to favored journalists, the local judge locked up the editor for slander.[102] When Cibrían's *La Vigía* accused military authorities of taking bribes to let rich kids off military service, he was also jailed.[103] In Baja California Norte in particular, the law seems to have been the authorities' principal tactic. In 1943, they jailed a journalist from *El Cóndor* for claiming that police were illegally handing Mexican prisoners back over the border to U.S. policemen. The following year, they locked up journalists from *El Imparcial*, *El Cóndor*, and *Cine al Día* for revealing the links between state authorities and the Tijuana prostitution racket. In 1948, they detained another journalist for claiming that certain influential businessmen owed him money.[104]

As the Baja California Norte examples suggest, legal methods to silence the press shifted over time and from state to state. By the 1950s, most administrations only very occasionally invoked the press law. Instead, local authorities increasingly employed Cold War laws designed to prosecute political rebellion. In Chiapas, during the mid-1950s, state authorities frequently used Article 145 of the Penal Code, the law of social dissolution. Though it was designed primarily to prosecute left-wing activists and union leaders, the state governor now extended its use to journalists. In 1956 alone three journalists were prosecuted under the law. The most unfortunate, a photographer called Ernesto Mendoza, was not only charged with social dissolution, but also sedition, damage to private property, robbery, and homicide. His union representative wondered how "such a large number of crimes could be committed by just one person, who with his . . . camera simply goes around complying with his journalistic duty."[105] Other local governments turned to accusations of outright rebellion. In 1960, the police arrested the Hermosillo journalist Jesús Tapia Avilés on charges of planning to take up arms against the local governor. To cement their case, they locked him up indefinitely in Guaymas prison, gathered together a bunch of false witnesses, bribed his lawyers to present no defense, and eventually sentenced him to fifteen years. He got out only after he called on contacts in the federal government. Even then he was forced to post a bail of 15,000 pesos.[106]

As the examples suggest, local authorities also simply invented crimes and pinned them on difficult reporters. In 1965, for example, the press officer for Ciudad Juárez's council teamed up with the police to frame two journalists who worked for the contentious *Crónicas* newspaper and freelanced for the national crime magazine *Alarma*. They had been investigating collusion between the local health department and the police in covering for the vice trade. To stop their exposés they were accused of robbery, causing injuries, and resisting arrest. One got out after paying 25,000 pesos in bail; the other received a five-year sentence.[107] Other reporters received similar treatment. In 1945, Guillermo H. Ramírez, author of the account of provincial journalists, *Los Gangsters del Periodismo*, was imprisoned for the "corruption of minors."[108] Despite the high level of imprisonment, the strategy usually served as a warning rather than a long-term solution. On most occasions, authorities incarcerated journalists for brief periods, often no more than a few days. Raúl Aceves, a freelancer from Ciudad Victoria, was arrested six times under the law in just five years.[109] In the most extreme situations, accusations of infringing the press law sometimes reached the Supreme Court, where they were normally quashed.[110] But this was not always the case and some journalists had neither the contacts nor the cash to post bail or undertake long court cases. The editor of San Andrés Tuxtla's satirical *Pica Pica* languished in jail for eight months before he even faced trial.[111]

As well as employing the law, local authorities often turned to more extra-legal methods to assert control. Nearly 21 percent of attacks comprised physical assaults. At times, they were spontaneous acts of aggression. In Tamaulipas the chief of police beat a journalist from *El Diario de Nuevo Laredo* in the street. The reporter had asked the former colonel to comment on accusations that he was protecting his son's car theft racket.[112] But on other occasions, authorities planned in advance and used police or, if possible, deniable thugs, to commit the attack. In March 1955 police kidnapped, beat, kicked, and shot two Guerrero crime journalists before dumping them down a gully outside Cuautepec. Their crime, the reporters wrote, "was to follow the moralizing campaign of President Ruiz Cortines" and expose police corruption.[113] Again traditions seemed to develop in certain areas. By the 1950s, beating trumped imprisonment as the main official strategy in Baja California Norte. In 1954, officials in Tecate goaded the police to beat up *ABC*'s correspondent for accusing a local cock-fighting promoter of shaking down customers. The mayor threatened that if he continued he would be hanged. There were "a few trees outside the town, where we can balance the accounts." Four years later, state police officers working for the governor beat up four local journalists in just four months. Luis Lelane, an editor of *Prensa Libre*, was taken into the desert, beaten, and left for dead; José Parra, another editor of *Prensa Libre*, was clubbed and then left by a local dam; Eduardo Guzmán, a political cartoonist, was attacked as he left a TV station; and Carlos Estrada Sastre was beaten over the head when he entered his hotel room.[114]

Threats were another popular way to curtail the press and comprised around 16 percent of attacks. The San Luis Potosí journalist Marín was threatened on four occasions; the Oaxaca satirist Alfredo Ramírez Villavicencio on at least three.[115] Again some threats were spontaneous—chance meetings that turned nasty. Many played on ideas of honor. In February 1957, freelancer

J. Alberto Rosales bumped into former federal deputy José Ricardi Tirado in the bathroom of a Tijuana hotel. After the journalist "replied like a man" to Ricardi's insults, the conversation went as follows:

RICARDI: "Anyone who speaks about me dies."
ROSALES: "I know you could perfectly easily order someone to kill me because you have loads of money and power and you are surrounded by pistoleros."
RICARDI: "I don't need pistoleros to kill a little man like you."
ROSALES: "So give me an opportunity to defend myself."

Ricardi suggested a duel. They went outside and walked toward Ricardi's car. Just then two policemen approached and asked what was going on. Rosales replied, "Señor Ricardi wants us to kill each other in the desert. As I don't known how to use a firearm, he has given me this one." When the police asked Ricardi to leave, he screamed at the journalist that he "would pay."[116] Other threats were more formal and considered. In 1953, various journalists in Guerrero complained that they had received death threats through the post. They alleged that the threats probably came from the local tax chief, who had been repeatedly accused of corruption.[117] Similarly measured threats also confronted León Barradas, the director of Jalapa's *El Comentario*, when he went to the state attorney general to demand guarantees. The attorney general calmly replied that "if the newspaper kept coming out and criticizing the governor, the paper would not circulate, the press would be destroyed, and he wouldn't say what would happen to me personally."[118]

Around 13 percent of the attacks involved the destruction of printing presses. As we saw in chapter 1, buying a print press in the provinces was relatively cheap. But for small concerns, the press still represented the vast bulk of investment. Destroying the press put locals out of business. In June 1945, the governor of Sinaloa's thugs burst into the workshop of Culiacán's *El Regional*. They destroyed the press and burned the archives. According to the editor, they did this to keep the paper from printing stories hinting that the governor had ordered the murder of his predecessor.[119] In May 1955, the police entered the offices of Veracruz's communist newspaper *Noviembre*. They stole all the copies of the last issue and dismantled and smashed the press. As a result the newspaper folded.[120] A year later, masked thugs attacked and destroyed the machinery of Toluca's *El Mundo* newspaper for waging a campaign against the governor. Years later the editor bumped into one of the culprits. He explained that the governor had recruited the gang through contacts in Mexico City.

One was a DFS officer, another was one of President Alemán's hit men, and the third was a "huge man they called El Estupido."[121]

Around 5 percent of attacks were politically motivated strikes. Again, these are sometimes difficult to discern. Local newspapers often paid risible wages, so strikes by print workers were frequent. But in many cases local authorities encouraged workers to interrupt printing or if necessary bankrupt the publication. In 1954, for example, a group of young men formed a print workers union and attempted to get jobs at Matamoros's three critical newspapers. When they failed to do so, they proceeded to disrupt production of the newspapers through a series of wildcat strikes. Though the strikes had the whiff of legality, the governor's prints were all over the campaign. As one established print worker explained, the strikers were an "apocryphal union" comprised of "young men who don't know anything about our specialty." They received wages from the local tax collector and were backed by the head of the local labor board, who was also a close friend of the governor. As one concerned citizen explained, the strikes were "trying to silence the press. They [were] acts of government censorship."[122]

Local authorities also employed deliberate acts of public humiliation. These were often imaginative, impromptu versions of the kind of dirty tricks used to undermine national journalists like Marcué and Menéndez. But whereas in the capital they often relied on slandering writers with accusations of political duplicity or hypocrisy, in the provinces they were based on the continuing link between journalists' personal honor and their right to speak on behalf of public opinion. As a result, such plots often sought to rob reporters of public credibility. Perhaps the most obvious example of one of these schemes involved Aristarco Montiel, the editor of Apizaco's combative weekly *Don Roque*. As I outlined in chapter 1, within a year of *Don Roque*'s publication, the newspaper had shifted from a rather dull chronicle to a critical space for public complaints over corruption, sex trafficking, commercial exploitation, and state-backed murder. The paper was a classic small-town artisan paper of the mid-1940s and, like Oaxaca City's *El Chapulín*, which I shall look at in chapter 7, it had an impressive following and considerable links to civil society. But such attitudes bred powerful opponents and in early 1947 eight gunmen grabbed Montiel and bundled him into the back of a waiting van. They threatened him with their guns, forced him to down a bottle of liquor, and dressed him in women's clothing. They then kicked him out into the street where he was immediately arrested by the local chief of police. The following morning, the local authorities assembled a large crowd outside the police station and let Montiel go. As he staggered out, terrified, bleary-eyed, and still robed in a woman's dress, the crowd shouted a "torrent of insults." The plot clearly played on the masculine ideal of the public sphere. Montiel was not a journalist; he was a gossip and a rumormonger and hence deserved to be treated as a woman.[123]

Not all public humiliations were quite so elaborate. Some, like the Montiel scheme, played on gendered ideas of proper behavior. During the early 1950s, one of the very few female press owners, Natalia G. de Joch, who ran the Ciudad Victoria daily *Noticias*, endured advertising boycotts, deliberate electricity stoppages, the destruction of her press, and tailing by government agents. She also suffered attacks on her reputation when the official newspaper hinted that she had murdered her husband and hooked up with a younger lover.[124] But other plots were rather more anodyne and simply sought to implicate journalists in criminal activity. Just as ties to the drug trade were used to undermine left-wing activists, similar accusations were employed to undercut journalists' credibility.[125] According to the Tijuana editor José Garduño Bustamante, state agents strapped a package of marijuana underneath his car just before he was about to cross the border. They also notified the U.S. police, who searched the vehicle and found the bundle. Garduño got off only when he pointed out he was too fat to get under his car and place the dope.[126]

Unlike today, the murder of journalists was relatively rare. But it was not unknown. Carlos Moncada estimates that local authorities murdered eleven journalists during the period. In fact, twenty provincial journalists were killed between 1940 and 1970.[127] The practice of murdering journalists rather stood apart from other forms of press violence, had its own rhythm and dynamics, and was as dependent on the actions of the national government as local authorities. In general, murdering journalists was an extremely high-risk strategy. It was widely reported, could cause popular outrage, and often brought the unwelcome attention of a national government that was keen to maintain at least a veneer of press liberty. Governors understood that murdering journalists was a last resort and could lead to their dismissal. Finally, journalist killing, as it does today, also intertwined with attempts to suppress public knowledge of the connections between the state and organized crime.

The 1947 killing of Tampico's *El Mundo* editor Vicente Villasana is particularly instructive. Villasana was a famously combative local editor. He was originally from Queretaro and cut his teeth attacking Saturnino Osornio's state *cacicazgo* before fleeing north to establish *El Mundo*. Here, he proceeded to campaign against Tamaulipas's strongman Emilio Portes Gil and his succession of handpicked governors. Portes Gil loathed the journalist. In late 1946 he gave a speech in which he accused Villasana of venality, blackmail, extor-

TABLE 1 Provincial journalists murdered, 1940–1970

Date	Journalist	State
1944	Salvador Guerrero González	Coahuila
1947	Vicente Villasana	Tamaulipas
1949	José María Jiménez Rubio	Sinaloa
1953	Raúl Parra Molina	Oaxaca
1956	Manuel Acosta Meza	Baja California Norte
1956	José Sánchez Trigueros	Baja California Norte
1956	Fernando Márquez Sánchez	Baja California Norte
1959	Jorge Salinas Aragón	Veracruz
1959	Raúl Beltrán Reyes	Veracruz
1959	David Meave	Puebla
1959	Fernando Esteban Jiménez	Veracruz
1959	Arturo Ramos	Chiapas
1959	Flavio Pérez	Chiapas
1959	Francisco Mock	Chiapas
1960	Alberto J. Altamirano	Veracruz
1960	Rubén Corona	Sonora
1961	Carlos Estrada Sastre	Baja California Norte
1964	Facundo Génico Salinas	Oaxaca
1968	Juan Muñoz Flores	Morelos
1970	Ernesto Espinosa Hernández	Chihuahua

tion, opportunism, and Nazi sympathizing. The following year, the governor, Hugo Pedro González, made similar accusations, claiming that Villasana was criticizing his administration because he refused to hand over cash. In response, *El Mundo* increased the pressure on the local government. On March 12, the paper revealed that the Llera authorities had gunned down at least three peasant protestors outside the municipal palace. The following week, the paper ran a series of stories on the sacking of a local government treasury. Finally, on March 21, *El Mundo* published an explosive article that not only revealed that the authorities of Nuevo Laredo allowed the notorious drug trafficker Alfonso Treviño to leave his prison cell every night to visit the city's cabarets (he used the prison, they claimed, as a "dormitory"), but also stated that he was protected by the governor and in business with the governor's brother. The piece would have been damaging at any time, but in early 1947 it was particularly harmful. As we saw in chapter 3, the Alemán government was under increasing pressure from the U.S. government to stamp out collusion between officials and drug traffickers. Over the following week, the paper refused to let up, covering the federal investigation into the drug accusations, the imprisonment of more Llera protestors, and the jailing of a local journalist.[128]

Finally, on the evening of March 31, Villasana traveled to a Ciudad Victoria hotel to meet his lover. At 7 P.M. there was a knock on the door, which Villasana answered. The state chief of police, Julio R. Osuña, entered the room and shot the editor dead. The murder caused substantial outrage. In Ciudad Victoria and Tampico, opposition groups from the right-wing PAN to left-wing unions joined together and took to the streets, demanding the prosecution of the murderer and the resignation of the governor. In Tampico thousands attended his funeral. In *El Mundo* and the national broadsheets journalists started to publish details of the crime. They traced Osuña's bloody heritage. According to reports, his father was a famously unstable revolutionary general, his brother had shot his best friend then committed suicide, and his sister was in prison. They revealed that in the hours before the murder, Osuña had been drinking with Portes Gil and other members of the governor's coterie. They had denounced Villasana in violent terms, goading Osuña to make an attack. Finally, they disclosed that after the killing Osuña had fled to see the governor, who agreed to hide him on his own ranch. On April 3 they arrested Osuña; a week later President Alemán dismissed the governor.[129]

For almost a decade, lessons were learned. There would be no impunity for killing journalists. For governors, murdering members of the press was strictly off limits. Alemán had made his position clear. His successor, Ruiz Cortines, had ordered local leaders to "Maderear" the press. As a result, killings dipped and only two provincial reporters were killed over the next nine years. One was murdered in a fracas with a local police chief far from the state capital in the Oaxaca port of Salina Cruz. The other was poisoned in mysterious circumstances, probably by Sinaloa drug traffickers.[130]

But in 1956 the practice of murdering journalists returned. On July 26 a young man knocked on the door of Tijuana editor Manuel Acosta Meza's house. When Acosta answered, he was shot three times. He died immediately. Acosta was another of the provinces' difficult, crusading journalists. He had started his career in the early 1940s, editing the critical Tijuana weekly *El Imparcial*. He also held down jobs as the *San Diego Union*'s Mexico correspondent and a stringer for the United Press. His exposés covered police incompetence, official corruption, and state links to the drug trade and the vice industry. As the *San Diego Union* approvingly wrote in his obituary, "There are few if any public officials in Tijuana who have not found mention in Manuel's newspapers if he thought them guilty of misappropriation of public funds." He also had close relations to the city's civic organizations, had helped set up a polio clinic and a homeless shelter, and was on the committee that successfully pushed for Baja California Norte's status as an autonomous state. Such writing generated a series of run-ins with the authorities. In 1944, he was imprisoned for infringing the press law; in 1950 and 1954 he was beaten by unknown assailants; and in early 1956 the authorities had forced local businesses to withdraw ads from *El Imparcial*. But around June 1956, he managed to find the funds to restart the belligerent weekly. He immediately began to reveal the arrangements between the governor, Braulio Maldonado, and the city's prostitution racket. He disclosed that Maldonado had teamed up with various members of the mafia (or what Acosta termed the "Union of Pimps") to establish an out-of-town zone of brothels called Los Kilometros on the road to Ensenada. The zone's shacks and bars allegedly employed 8,000 women. Furthermore, Acosta claimed that Maldonado's wife had established a charity organization where she laundered the funds for the set-up. The stories caused a national scandal. The capital's broadsheets sent correspondents to the border and U.S. newspapers started to take an interest. Days before his murder, he announced that in the next issue of *El Imparcial* he would offer a full list of not only the "Union of Pimps" but also the local politicians who supported the prostitution and drug trades.[131]

Both contemporary and subsequent investigations all indicate that one of Maldonado's private gunmen (the so-called Chemitas) committed the murder to prevent publication of the list. For a while, Maldonado's position looked untenable. National, local, and U.S. newspapers all pointed the finger at the governor. But Maldonado managed to escape implication. First, he started a moralization campaign, closed down Los Kilometros and a handful of pay-by-the-hour hotels, and arrested some low-level mafiosi. Next, he found a convenient patsy for the crime, Manuel Dueñas. Dueñas was a former policeman from Jalisco who had found employ in the border city as a gun-for-hire. The case against him was simple. Police claimed that they found a gun matching that involved in the crime hidden at Dueñas's house. Unfortunately for Maldonado, the case against the gunman started to unravel almost as soon as it began. In August, national newspapers named the probable killer as one of Maldonado's bodyguards. In the same month, the state authorities admitted that they lacked ballistics evidence as they had failed to dig the bullet out of the cadaver during the autopsy. In September the judge resigned and in the same month a famous local lawyer took over the defense. The lawyer immediately called in experts from the Los Angeles Police Department, who categorically denied that the bullet (now extracted from Acosta's body) could have been fired by Dueñas's gun. In February 1957 the police chief in charge of the murder inquiry was charged with committing multiple irregularities. The following month the lawyer started to implicate a notorious local politician close to Maldonado, the former congressman José Ricardi Tirado. The trial was, in short, a farce. Yet despite all the anomalies, the judge found Dueñas guilty and sentenced him to six years in prison.[132]

The Acosta case changed the rules of the game. Unlike nine years earlier, the president had not stepped in and dismissed Maldonado. This was probably due to the growing force of the state's PAN party. Governors and other politicians now understood that it was possible to kill journalists, if one managed to cover up the crime. Over the next five years, the assassination of reporters increased. Twelve of the twenty murders occurred during this period. Maldonado started the trend. Months after Acosta's death, his close colleague and friend, *El Reportaje* journalist José Sánchez Trigueros, met his end in a mysterious car crash, and the printer and part-time journalist Fernando Márquez Sánchez was shot dead by one of the governor's bodyguards.[133] But it was the civic movements and political contests of the first two years of President López Mateos's term that really popularized the practice. In the atmosphere of increasing instability, press exposés could not only generate scandal but also topple governors and *caciques*. Impunity and insecurity combined to increase the rate of press murders. Seven journalists were killed in 1959 alone. At least four—Fernando Esteban Jiménez, Jorge Salinas Aragón, Raúl Beltrán Reyes, and Alberto J. Altamirano—were murdered while covering political conflicts in Veracruz that pitched civil organizations against entrenched *cacicazgos*.[134]

During the 1960s, the murder of provincial journalists declined once again. Between 1962 and 1969 there were only two killings: one of the Tehuantepec editor Facundo Génico Salinas and another of the *Alarma* correspondent, Juan Muñoz Flores.[135] Professional press departments and larger bribes probably played a role; so did more sophisticated dirty tricks campaigns; and so did presidential politics. Unlike his predecessors, President Díaz Ordaz was notoriously reluctant to remove governors or even unpopular mayors. As a result, few local politicians felt under pressure from journalistic exposés. As we shall see in chapter 8, governors like Práxedis Giner Durán endured years of press revelations and attendant civil movements. Yet the central government did nothing. Ironically, increasing authoritarianism removed the need to kill members of the press.

From 1940 onward, violent attacks on the local press were commonplace. Most assaults involved short imprisonments, beatings, and threats. Though murders were relatively rare, many local editors and reporters endured a brutal and unrelenting rhythm of intimidation and violence, redolent of the present day. These attacks could break all but the hardiest of writers.

I finish this section with the story of Ignacio de la Hoya, the leftist editor of Acapulco's *La Verdad* newspaper. Between 1956 and 1969, his newspaper published a series of exposés on the corruption and repression practiced by both state and local governments. In 1958 alone, he printed stories on extrajudicial murder, the exploitation of squatters, the illegal sale of the city's town hall to a private company, the state protection of brothels, electoral fraud, tax farming, and the misapplication of public funds. Such articles generated repeated reprisals. Individual acts of censorship or punishment developed into a long campaign of harassment. In 1956, he was beaten by unknown assailants; in 1957 the state government brought a law case against him claiming he was a Nicaraguan national on a false passport; in 1958 thugs beat a couple of *La Verdad*'s newspaper vendors and killed the son of one of the paper's writers. At the end of the year a dozen gunmen shot up the publication's offices and forced the editor into hiding.[136] When he reappeared in 1960, he was immediately beaten again by unknown attackers. Two years later the local authorities organized a strike inside the newspaper and federal agents beat de la Hoya once again.[137] Finally, in 1969, de la Hoya's luck ran out. In November the journalist wandered into the offices of Mario Menéndez's *Por Qué?* He was completely delusional and kept asking for the article on the death of the Guerrero governor. *Por Qué?*'s journalists tried to calm him down, repeating that the governor was still very much alive. Over the following days, they pieced together what had happened. The state government had paid a colleague of de la Hoya's to bring false charges of damaging property against the editor. The state police then arrested him. Over the next month, they tortured de la Hoya intensively. When he finally cracked, they released him in the middle of Mexico City. The Acapulco editor would never recover from the experience and was in and out of mental institutions for the rest of his life.[138]

Breaking the Rules

So far we have examined how increasing financial payoffs and professional press departments combined with the regular use of violence to attempt to silence Mexico's regional newspapers. But the question remains—just how censored was the provincial press? The sparse quantitative studies of the regional press seem to indicate a much lesser degree of censorship than for the national newspapers. Louise Montgomery's extensive analysis of newspaper columns and editorials written between 1951 and 1980 concluded that

49.9 percent of Guadalajara's *El Informador*'s articles and 60.1 percent of Monterrey's *El Norte*'s articles were critical. In comparison, only 10.2 percent of the national *Novedades*'s pieces were similarly barbed.[139] Paul Gillingham quotes a 1960 government study that found that only 21 percent of regional publications took direct subsidies. In contrast, 21 percent were critical, 17 percent were sensationalist moneymaking enterprises, and 41 percent had no clear affiliation.[140] Probably, regional newspapers did become more *oficialista* over time. New strategies seemed to work. A similar, if more extensive study of political affiliation completed in the mid-1970s indicates that around two-thirds of regional papers now generally supported the government. A few were directly flagged as "receiving a government subsidy." But still another third were described as opportunist, sensationalist, or antigovernment. In some states, with long traditions of combative media, like Chihuahua and Nuevo León, the majority of the papers were broadly critical. Here especially, press debate still existed.[141]

More anecdotal evidence seems to confirm this thesis. Regional newspapers broke the unspoken rules of the national newspapers. Even respectable broadsheets criticized the president openly, often blaming him directly for policy mistakes or repression. For example, in 1946 Monterrey's *El Norte* laid blame for electoral fraud firmly on the president, who, they claimed, had used "lying and high-sounding phrases" to "ignobly make use of the democratic enthusiasm of the masses and the services of the armed forces to camouflage an electoral farce."[142] Less prissy tabloids were even more explicit. In 1948, Ciudad Juárez's *La Jeringa* censured President Alemán "for surrounding himself with those who get rich from the blood of the people. . . . What has he done except issue florid phrases? Nothing."[143] Two years later, the *calavera* poem of Oaxaca City's satirical *El Chapulín* was equally dismissive. "Lawyer Alemán / If we could count how many trips you made / we would know how many lies you said."[144] Other tacit understandings were also widely infringed. Army generals and soldiers were regularly criticized. In the *El Norte* article previously noted, the columnist directly accused military representatives of "robbing ballot boxes and expelling the representatives of other parties" from the voting booths. In 1955, after one particularly bloody Chiapas commander had pursued a group of dissident peasants, decapitated them, and displayed their heads in front of the town hall, local journalists broke the story and pursued it even after the nationals had denied it.[145]

Furthermore, controversial national conflicts, which rapidly brought even the most independent Mexico City journalists into line, were treated more openly by the regional press. In 1959, San Luis Potosí's newspapers supported the radical railway workers, albeit for local reasons rather than for any great ideological sympathy.[146] Both Hermosillo's *El Pueblo* and Nogales's *El Noreste* also criticized the state for sending in troops to remove strikers.[147] Far-sighted attempts to introduce more transparency to the press were introduced by regional newspapers far before the big nationals. For example, during the 1960s, *El Informador*, *El Diario de Yucatán*, and *El Norte* all marked *gacetillas* with an asterisk or the letters IP (Paid Insertion).[148] As we saw in chapter 4, during the 1960s it was provincial journalists like Mario Menendez and Carlos Ortega who took such practices to the capital. Finally, and most obviously, most regional newspapers took a critical line toward local politics. As contemporary U.S. analysts observed, publications in the localities "enjoy[ed] a certain measure of freedom, often not exercised in the national capital, to criticize local politics and politicians. They [could] be a real force by drawing national attention to local events."[149] As we shall see in chapter 6, sometimes the motive was money. Bad press was the easiest way to push hard-up administrations into coughing up cash. But, as described in chapters 7 and 8, often local journalists joined together with members of civil society to push for real change.

CHAPTER SIX

The Real Artemio Cruz

The Press Baron, Gangster Journalism, and the Regional Press

In December 1950, the U.S. magazine *Newsweek* ran a special report on the Mexican press baron José García Valseca. In less than fifteen years, he had gone from "boy recruit" and failed journalist to owning the biggest chain of newspapers in the Americas. According to the article, he now ran twenty local newspapers from Puebla in the south to Ciudad Juárez in the north. He even owned a paper over the border in El Paso. Together they accounted for one in five of Mexico's dailies. In 1948 alone he had "gone on a buying spree" and bought five papers. He kept some of his old habits and still carried a .38 pistol under his double-breasted suit. ("I don't need it . . . it's just a habit, like a watch.") But now he was a member of the media elite who owned a fleet of three Cadillacs, two Buicks, a Packard, a Cessna airplane, and a private railroad car "for personal appearances." The article compared García Valseca favorably to William Randolph Hearst who "even in his heyday" only managed twenty-three dailies out of a total of 1,900 papers in the United States. *Newsweek* concluded that if the magnate continued at this rate of purchasing he could "theoretically own all of Mexico's papers sometime in 1965, at the age of 63."[1]

García Valseca never did manage to monopolize the Mexican newspaper industry so completely. But the mythology around the press baron grew. For his biographers, he was the epitome of the postrevolutionary capitalist, a poor-boy-done-good, whose unswerving Catholic faith, hard work, and commercial savvy had created a media empire. By the late 1960s, this included comics, the country's most popular sports daily, thirty-seven regional papers, and a broadsheet national. As a revolutionary, he was a hero who had fought in more than seventy battles and suffered multiple wounds. As a businessman he was a genius. He only slept five hours a day; he never took holidays; he had a prodigious memory; and he possessed an extraordinary organizing capacity. He also employed thousands of well-paid workers not only in his newsrooms and printing presses but also in his bicycle factories, cattle farms, and pasteurization plants. As an editor, he changed the face of Mexican journalism, introducing technological innovations, training a generation of young reporters, and bringing cheap, readable news to the country's provinces.

Salvador Borrego played down the Hearst comparison and instead equated him to the U.S. press giant Joseph Pulitzer.[2]

But for many, García Valseca was far from heroic. During the same period, a black legend of the magnate emerged. For rival newspapermen he was a "gangster," "a mercenary," and a "blackmailer."[3] The U.S. embassy called him an "unscrupulous moneymaker, always surrounded by pistoleros" who traveled around Mexico in a private train stocked with his numerous young girlfriends.[4] *Siempre!* editor Pagés Llergo described him as a "monster," "a thousand times worse than Hearst."[5] For Puebla journalist Manuel Sánchez Pontón he was an illiterate Catholic fanatic "obsessed by accumulating more money and power. . . . a financial genius, a megalomaniac buffoon, a powerful organizer, and a businessman without a conscience."[6] Former employee Daniel Cadena Z. claimed he displayed a "euphoric drunkenness with his own power . . . was subject to no law," and "never had to answer to anyone."[7] He even published a thinly veiled parody of Frank Capra's *It's a Wonderful Life* in which a ghostly García Valseca wandered the earth observing the misery his actions had wrought.[8] For Monsiváis, he personified Mexico's sold-out press. Far from opening up the public sphere, his chain merely offered "a sponsored illusion which blocked any close up of reality."[9]

In fact, the story of García Valseca was so infamous, it formed the raw material for Carlos Fuentes's 1962 novel about the dying Mexican press baron Artemio Cruz. Scholars have suggested that Fuentes's narrative of lost hopes and betrayed ideals was based on the life stories of any number of corrupt, postrevolutionary moguls, including Rómulo O'Farrill, Gabriel Alarcón, Martín Luis Guzmán, and even Miguel Alemán.[10] Yet the book's details rely heavily on García Valseca's own biography. Like the real-life baron, Cruz is born into poverty. He joins the revolution and fights for the Carrancistas in Puebla. He becomes rich by marrying into a wealthy Porfirian landowning family. He uses his newspaper empire to express his visceral anticommunism, libel business rivals, and sustain his other economic interests. As in his other novel, *Where the Air Is Clear*, newspapers either symbolize the concealment of reality (again and again Cruz's relations hide their expressions behind an open broadsheet) or form material waste, to be used as tablecloths or food wrappers.[11] If García Valseca was Mexico's Hearst, Cruz was Mexico's Citizen Kane.

This chapter explores the rise and fall of García Valseca's media empire, weighs up these rival visions, and tries to get at the truth behind the competing mythologies. But it also goes further, using the story of the press baron to draw out some more general points about the relationships between business and journalism, regional editors and state governors, and the printed word and public opinion. The growth of García Valseca's newspaper business depended on state funds, including a one-off payment from the president's brother, loans from state banks like the NF, and extensive PIPSA debts. As a trade-off, coverage of national politics was both resolutely anticommunist and unerringly positive. The *Sol* chain was *prensa vendida* incarnate. But at the regional level, state-press relations were much more fluid. Here, both García Valseca and his editors practiced extortion or what Mexicans termed "gangster journalism." Media met mafia. In return for subsidies, they gave governors protection. Coverage of their achievements was effusive; corruption, incompetence, and repression were ignored. But if they refused to pay up, the newspapers' attacks were savage. Muckraking journalists uncovered corruption, insulted officials, and deliberately incited citizen protest.

The chapter ends with one of the most extraordinary stories of government interference in the mass media. The plot reads like literature, albeit of the spy novel variety, and touches on espionage, drug trafficking, and state assassination. By the early 1970s, the chain's finances started to dry up. Falling advertising revenue and the state's refusal to sustain the company's debt caused the chain to descend into insolvency. Initially rich industrialists from the Monterrey Group tried to save the enterprise. But in 1973, their leader, Eugenio Garza Sada, was murdered, apparently in a bungled kidnapping attempt. According to some journalists, it was actually a deliberate killing performed by an undercover hit man and organized by those at the top of the Mexican government. The hit not only prevented the private takeover of the chain, but also opened up space for President Echeverría to usurp control of the business three years later.

The Birth of a Newspaper Chain

José García Valseca was born on January 7, 1902, in the provincial city of Puebla into a struggling middle-class family. His father's business ventures had struggled to take off. His first enterprise, a cigarette factory, had burned down in 1870. His next, a match factory, had also closed. Despite these setbacks, the young García Valseca grew up with the Catholic values of the Puebla bourgeoisie. His mother was a religious woman and he was sent to a small Catholic private school and attended mass at the Sagrada Familia church. According to Borrego, these experiences marked his later life. "He always conserved the Catholic faith in which he was educated," would often walk around his garden praying, and erected a private chapel in his luxurious Mexico City home.[12] Though pious, García Valseca was not an academic boy. Opponents repeatedly claimed that he was only partially literate, never read books, and insisted that his assistants hand over documents no longer than a page.[13] Such accusations smack of Mexico City snobbery. But he did leave school around the age of ten to start work, first as an assistant in a pharmacy and then as a trainee tailor. Neither job interested him. In 1913 he joined the revolutionary forces of the Carrancistas. According to his biographers, he was involved in over seventy clashes, mostly in the north of the country. His career lasted a decade. Eventually, after the fighting in the federal army against the Delahuertista rebels, he resigned his commission. He had reached the rank of colonel, a title he would insist on being addressed by throughout his career.[14] His critics were less impressed. They claimed he made up his own service record and falsified the signatures. President Alemán eventually forced one of his generals to give him a military rank "as a gift."[15]

After leaving the army García Valseca made repeated attempts to make his fortune as a merchant. But most ventures were brief. By the late 1920s, he decided to switch jobs and get into the newspaper industry. He had tried journalism before. He and his brothers had set up a short-lived paper in Puebla during the revolution. This time he was more successful. He got contracts with the government newspaper *El Nacional* and the tabloid *La Prensa* to cover news in the south of Mexico. He also tried to set up a regional weekly in Oaxaca City. After a year, the project shut down. But García Valseca refused to give up. Using the money from his first wife, a rich widow, he established a printing press in Mexico City where he started to put out another weekly, *Provincias*. As the title suggested, the magazine covered news in the provinces and was designed to appeal to the city's recent immigrants. The publication was cheap but never managed to break the capital's newspaper market.[16] Circulation only reached 3,000 copies. But the project did suggest García Valseca's future business strategies. According to Cadena, who joined the company in 1934, *Provincias* was "pirate journalism." The only way the magazine made money was by falsely claiming that it was an official government organ and demanding advertising from intimidated local politicians, merchants, and industrialists.[17] In later years rumors spread that one government official had rebuked García Valseca by saying "real radicals" did not need "the little newspapers of individuals of dubious sexuality to honor them." The Tabasco governor, Tomás Garrido Canabal, rather more colorfully threatened to skin García Valseca alive and use his hide to make a chair cover.[18]

Other ventures were more successful. He soon realized that to make real money, he needed to reach an audience beyond the elites. So he moved into the emerging comic market. First, he put out *Paquito* and then the follow-up

Pepín. These were colorful, entertaining, cheap, and easy to comprehend. They were printed on inexpensive, poor quality newspaper. They cost around 5¢ to print and they were then sold for 10¢ in newsstands, barbershops, markets, apartment blocks, and villages. Those who were unable to understand all the words could appreciate the narrative by following the pictures. They were fabulously popular. Sales of *Pepín* hit a high of 350,000 copies per week.[19] If comic books made García Valseca's fortune, sports established him as a major figure in the national newspaper industry. In 1941, he took advantage of the growing interest in professional sport and started Mexico's first standalone sports weekly, *Esto.* Again, it was cheap (10¢), accessible, and loaded with photographs. It contained ample coverage of Mexico City's most popular sport, bullfighting. The enterprise reflected a perception, especially among certain political elites, that sport, like cinema, could entertain and to a certain extent depoliticize the Mexican working class. García Valseca told one wordy intellectual that it was not "his job to politicize the masses. Just give them more sports news." He was fond of quoting Franco's dictum for keeping the peace in fascist Spain: "football and bulls."[20] Such ideas were wishful thinking. Over the next few years, both bullfights and football matches would also become sites of vitriolic popular protest. But the market for sports writing increased. In 1943, *Esto* became a daily and outsold all the other Mexico City tabloids.[21]

Just two years after establishing *Esto,* García Valseca started his chain of regional newspapers. In 1943, he founded the Ciudad Juárez daily *El Fronterizo.* By the end of the Avila Camacho presidency, he owned five more. Why did the successful publishing entrepreneur move back into the risky world of provincial newspapers? According to his supporters, it was his noble sense of nationalism. In late 1942 he suffered a series of stomach complaints. On the advice of his fellow Puebla businessman, O'Farrill, he went for tests in the United States. He was diagnosed with severe gastritis, a condition for which he would remain on medication for the next four decades. But he also picked up some gossip from one of the other patients. William Randolph Hearst was thinking of establishing a newspaper chain in Mexico. His first purchase would be in Ciudad Juárez. García Valseca decided it was his patriotic duty to stop the U.S. press baron. The story could be true. In the early 1940s an El Paso businessman owned a Spanish language newspaper, *El Continental,* which he marketed on the other side of the border. The paper sold relatively well, Ciudad Juárez had a booming, relatively literate population, and there was room for expansion. Maybe Hearst was considering taking over the enterprise? His father had bought vast land holdings in Chihuahua and the media mogul maintained a keen interest in the estates.[22] Perhaps García Valseca was simply trying to ward off the U.S. investor?

More probably, the creation of the chain was a matter of elite politicking. His new wealth brought influence. By the late 1930s, he had become part of the Puebla strongman Maximino Avila Camacho's inner circle and in 1940 he was elected substitute senator for the state.[23] Maximino was one of a new breed of postrevolutionary politicians and had little interest in using social programs or economic concessions to attract the support of workers or peasants. Instead he sought alliances among middle-class city dwellers and business elites.[24] To do so, he set great store by positive coverage in the regional press. During his tenure in charge of the state, he founded and subsidized *El Diario de Puebla* and used a blend of bribes and threats to bring the more independent *La Opinión* onside.[25] When his brother made him secretary of communications and public works he brought his concern over his public image to the capital.[26] In fact, Maximino, more than Miguel Alemán, was the first political celebrity of Mexico's mass media age. Over the next four years he secured unfailingly positive exposure in the national press. The effort bordered on a "personality cult." Journalists covered his birthday celebrations in depth, published photographic essays on his charity work, and covered his visits to the provinces like a presidential candidate's tour.[27]

Maximino also sought to purchase his own newspaper. On this matter, his brother probably offered his backing. Supporters of former president Cárdenas dominated the official newspaper, *El Nacional*, and Manuel Avila Camacho sought a platform that was sympathetic to his more right-wing policies. In February 1941 the brothers attempted to buy a secondhand press from *El Universal*. Later that year, they made an approach to acquire an interest in the tabloid *Novedades*. The U.S. authorities reported that the national government had donated a million pesos to the owner. Rumors went around that he had gone to the United States to buy a newer, faster press. Eventually, both efforts failed. The editors of the big nationals came together and persuaded the president to drop his plan to form a rival national in return for their support.[28]

The deal satisfied the president, who was gearing up to take Mexico to war. But it scuppered Maximino's plan to use his own national newspaper to back his bid for the top office. At this point, he turned to the Puebla publishing mogul. García Valseca had already helped shape one key element of Maximino's public image, publishing repeated pump pieces on his patronage of bullfighting as well as favorable glosses of his own limited skills.[29] Now, he offered García Valseca the money to start a chain of regional newspapers. Exact figures on dates, finances, and ownership structures remain hazy. The plan was not for public consumption, it went against the president's deal with the nationals, and Maximino was no stickler for fine print. But some details started to leak out. As early as July 1941, the U.S. authorities reported that García Valseca was trying to take over a Ciudad Juárez paper. When asked where the money came from, he answered, the Avila Camacho brothers.[30] Four years later, the entrepreneur talked to the U.S. authorities again and confessed that he was acting on behalf of Maximino, who wanted him to buy up or establish newspapers throughout the provinces. The embassy's media expert explained, "If the declarations of García Valseca can be taken at face value, they seem to indicate that the president and his brother are trying to obtain the control of various newspapers in the great cities to prepare for the upcoming presidential elections."[31] The press baron's critics offered more details. One estimated that the original funding totaled 10 million pesos and was taken directly from the SCOP budget. Most concurred that Maximino refused to hand over a receipt with the cash. "I don't need receipts. Anyone who plays or betrays me, I kill . . . to kill a traitor I don't need notaries, books, or protocols."[32]

The outburst may have made good copy, but it made poor business. Between 1943 and 1945, García Valseca used the money to expand beyond Ciudad Juárez and start up publications in Chihuahua City, Puebla, Aguascalientes, and Toluca. In February 1945 his patron died of a heart attack. For months afterward, García Valseca worried that Maximino's heirs would try to lay claim to the incipient chain. But no demands were forthcoming. Later that year, the press baron took over full ownership of the business and changed the title from the deliberately anonymous National Chain of Newspapers to the Chain of Newspapers García Valseca.[33] By 1946 he owned Mexico's two most popular comics, its most popular sports daily, and a chain of six local newspapers.

How to Build a Newspaper Chain

In the decades that followed Maximino's death, García Valseca's newspaper chain grew exponentially. By the end of the Díaz Ordaz presidency he ran thirty-seven dailies. Like many postrevolutionary capitalists, García Valseca's ascent relied on both state aid and modernizing, entrepreneurial strategies. Special privileges, NF loans, and favorable deals with the state paper company undergirded his empire and allowed the Puebla businessman to take risks. At the same time, García Valseca used these advantages to good effect, choosing markets carefully, identifying weak or failing competitors, pushing unions out of power, and employing aggressive pricing and production strategies to create regional monopolies. Such arrangements, which were prevalent in the media industry, formed part of what Andrew Paxman terms the "symbiotic imperative" of Mexican business, which bound postrevolutionary capitalists and politicians.[34] García Valseca got rich and the national government acquired a network of sympathetic, anticommunist newspapers that penetrated the country's provincial towns and cities.

Between 1946 and 1970, García Valseca added a host of new regional newspapers to his chain. In the early years of President Alemán's tenure he solidified his control of Ciudad Juárez, purchasing two more newspapers, and expanded into the west of the country, establishing a business center in Guadalajara and branches in Mazatlán, Culiacán, and Durango. In 1949, he visited postwar Europe and witnessed the boom in the local press. Convinced that Mexico's smaller cities could also sustain cheap dailies, he now combined his push for big markets, like Tampico (1950), with expansion into traditionally underserved cities like Pachuca (1949), Celaya (1949), and Fresnillo (1955). He also complemented his morning broadsheets with cheap, crime-heavy evening tabloids, designed to appeal to working-class readers. In 1953, he opened *La Voz de Puebla* and, four years later, the *Noticias* of León. After 1957 the process of expansion halted. Instead García Valseca focused on improving printing quality and founding a major national. In June 1965, *El Sol de México* hit the Mexico City newsstands. By the end of the decade, Borrego claimed that García Valseca's sales accounted for as much as 22 percent of the newspapers sold in the country. In comparison, even at the height of Hearst's influence, his chain never accounted for more than 10 percent of U.S. newspaper sales.[35]

The regional newspaper business made García Valseca an extremely rich man. Like Alemán's amigos, he was not afraid to flaunt it. In fact, according to his daughter-in-law, he "plastered over every surface with the veneer of money." He had a luxurious house in the fashionable San Angel district, another in the equally exclusive Lomas de Chapultepec, another in the tourist resort of Cuernavaca, and a penthouse on the top of *Esto*'s downtown offices. The San Angel residence was extraordinary. It was 8,000 square feet, contained a swimming pool, a private bicycle trail, and a movie theater and employed forty-two staff. His travel arrangements were the stuff of legend. He owned four railroad cars, which he used to visit his newspapers throughout the country. They contained a bedroom, office, bathroom, restaurant, private barbers, and a manicurist. He also owned a fleet of Cadillacs, Lincoln Continentals, and rare six-door Mercedes Pullmans. All were chauffeur driven, and police motorcycles accompanied him wherever they went. Gossips claimed that on one occasion, he was informed that his favorite Mercedes was too big to enter the courtyard of a Mexico City residence. He was asked to get out and walk. He refused and instead ordered his bodyguards to pull down the front wall of the house.[36]

García Valseca's wealth and influence relied, at least partially, on government support. Maximino's death only slowed down the chain's expansion for a year. During this brief respite he solidified links to remaining members of the Avila Camacho group, like the U.S. cinema tycoon William Jenkins and the *Novedades* owner Rómulo O'Farrill Sr.[37] He also made alliances with the incoming president. After the upsurge of state censorship in 1948, Alemán needed to rebuild relations with both the national and the regional press. García Valseca became his key broker. At first, he acted as a linkman between the executive and the provinces. From 1948 onward, he and his reporters held regular meetings with the president and kept him up to date with both provincial political problems and the publishing industry.[38] Then he turned to building links between the president and the capital's leading editors. In 1951, he organized a major banquet in honor of Alemán. Over a hundred press owners and directors attended. The festivities were designed to thank the president for increasing the supply of paper. But the following year, García Valseca institutionalized the occasion and persuaded the president to name the celebration the Day of Press Freedom.[39] The banquet became a major annual event. It was attended by the president, dozens of functionaries, and hundreds of media owners and reporters. It was always heavily covered in the capital's broadsheets and tabloids and came to undergird, confirm, and symbolize the reciprocal relations between state and press. Every year, presidents detailed their vision for Mexican journalism. In reply press owners attested to the existence of a free press. Or as Monsiváis put it, each year "the press confirmed the government's infallibility and the government ratified their credibility."[40]

For the next two decades, García Valseca maintained these extremely close relations with Mexico's powerbrokers. In part, he shared their ideology. In a rare interview, García Valseca confessed that "the government and I have the same philosophy."[41] As we shall see in all national matters, his newspapers always followed the government line. Social interaction buttressed this political support. García Valseca's parties, in particular, were well renowned. In 1964, he invited five hundred guests including media moguls, state governors, ambassadors, government ministers, and former presidents. After the U.S. ambassador left and the wives followed, hundreds of female secretaries, film starlets, and extras streamed in. According to one entertaining semifictionalized account, Irma Serrano "la Tigresa," the singer and Díaz Ordaz's lover, belted out her latest hits. García Valseca took to the stage, launched into his favorite tune, forgot the words, and waved a gold-plated gun in the air. Denegri danced on a piano with a topless model, Alemán talked media with O'Farrill, and the director of the DFS delivered a kilo of cocaine, which was consumed in the "Salon Popo-catépetl" (so called because, like the volcano, it contained a pile of snow). At the end of the night, when one of the musicians ended up dead from an over-dose, García Valseca paid the police to cover it up.[42] Such events not only ce-mented friendships but also locked guests into conspiracies of complicity and embarrassed silence.

Close links brought financial rewards. Just three months after his patron's death, García Valseca sought special favors from the government. In a memo-randum to the president, he asked for free telephone and telegraph lines, the extension of the free postal service to his Sundays and supplements, and an exemption from social security payments. Avila Camacho consented to all his demands, except the social security exemption, which, he pointed out, had only been introduced in Puebla.[43] For over two decades, the chain would maintain these privileges. Over time more were added. Low-interest NF loans, totaling (it was rumored) as much as 12 million pesos, were used to construct flash new offices in Guadalajara and Ciudad Juárez.[44] The state bank also guaranteed large loans with U.S. private banks to buy up modern printing presses.[45] In fact, García Valseca was so close to the Mexican government he was allowed to travel on a diplomatic passport.[46]

But the most important government subsidy was paper. During the 1940s, regional owners repeatedly complained that they were unable to expand because nationals monopolized the product.[47] Together with the government, national newspapers owned most of the PIPSA shares. Consequently, they dominated distribution and rarely left more than a third of imports for the provinces. García Valseca broke the cycle. Under President Alemán, he bought into PIPSA's share structure. Only three old members—*Excélsior, La Prensa,* and *Novedades*—now owned more shares. He also joined the board. He was ap-pointed as a "neutral" broker. His job was to decide on the distribution of paper, settle the disputes between rival nationals, and balance the demands of Mexico City and the regional press.[48]

Over the next two decades, García Valseca gained a competitive advantage from his position. Unlike most regionals, his newspapers never suffered from a lack of paper. Before PIPSA established branch dispensaries, free trains de-livered paper from the company's Mexico City warehouse direct to the chain's regional workshops. At particular moments, he was able to stockpile vast quantities of paper before releasing it onto the market. He also negotiated his own special deals with the government organization. From the 1950s, the chain was allowed to introduce its own paper from the United States without paying tariffs. This was strictly illegal. Only PIPSA was allowed to make tax-free imports. But the press entrepreneur used his leverage to bend the rules. Twice a year ships carrying the paper went down the Pacific coast and landed their cargo at Manzanillo. The paper was then brought to the García Valseca warehouses in Guadalajara and distributed throughout the west coast publications.[49] This allowed him to release newspapers cheaply and in vast quantities. When Guadalajara's *El Sol* was released, it swamped the market of the established competitor *El Informador*.[50] Finally the press baron used his influence to run up enormous debts. Again, most newspapers did this to a certain extent. For most newspapers there were limits, but not for the García Valseca chain. By the end of 1968 the total debt of all Mexico's newspapers to PIPSA was 71,391,688 pesos. Major national newspapers, like *La Prensa, Excélsior,* and *El Heraldo,* owed between 2 and 5 million pesos. Major regionals, like Veracruz's *El Dictamen,* owed around 1 million each. García Valseca's chain owed 23,971,183 pesos or a third of all PIPSA debts.[51]

State disbursements and special favors underlay the successful expansion of the chain. But García Valseca also used these benefits to his advantage. He chose the markets for his newspapers very carefully. In general he avoided cities, where reputable dailies with loyal readerships dominated. He never launched businesses in Torreón, Merida, or Veracruz. He left the overstocked Tijuana market as fast as he could. Instead he preferred fast-growing towns, with limited press traditions like the factory town of León, the trading center of Culiacán, or the petroleum hub of Salamanca. On the rare occasions he did challenge established papers, he linked up with elite groups that had fallen out with the dominant newspaper. In Guadalajara, he took advantage of the divisions between *El Informador* and a group of local industrialists. In 1942, they had opened *El Occidental* to break *El Informador*'s monopoly. The newspaper had failed. But six years later, García Valseca resuscitated the brand using a mix of his own strategies and the disaffected industrialists' advertising revenue.[52] Or he made sure that the established newspapers were on the slide. After Villasana's death, ownership of his small chain passed to his widow. She remarried a shady Argentine businessman called Mauricio Bercún, who took over day-to-day running of the enterprise. Bercún had no experience in the press business, and initially the new company was a disaster.[53] García Valseca moved into the vacuum, opening the rival *El Sol de Tampico* in 1950 and *El Sol de San Luis* in 1952.

Initially at least, García Valseca also exploited the burgeoning postwar market in secondhand printing presses. Especially in cities with limited competition, old machinery was more than sufficient. For *El Sol del Centro* in Aguascalientes, he purchased an old duplex press and four old linotype presses. For *El Sol de León* he employed only two old duplex machines.[54] He also actively sought out failing newspapers and bought them up on the cheap. In 1944, he purchased *El Heraldo*, which was on the brink of bankruptcy.[55] The following year he obtained the infrastructure of Mazatlán's *El Correo del Occidente*. Again, the paper was about to go under due to an ill-fated campaign against the Sinaloa governor. García Valseca persuaded the editor to lower the price for the newspaper's property and machinery from 200,000 to 36,000 pesos.[56]

Having established a newspaper, García Valseca used tried-and-tested tactics to minimize costs. From 1946 onward, he prohibited print workers, journalists, and even news vendors from joining official unions. At first this policy caused considerable disruption. In May 1946 he refused to sign a contract with unionized workers at *La Voz de Chihuahua*, closed down the workshop, and moved the machinery. In December he fired fourteen members of the press workers union from the workshop of *El Sol de Puebla* and replaced them with members of a company-controlled group. The move precipitated a long-running strike. By the end of the year, this had expanded to encompass García Valseca's workers in Chihuahua, León, and Aguascalientes. But the press magnate refused to give up. He moved production to his workshop in Mexico City, sacked more workers, and also established a rival group of non-unionized news vendors to sell the newspaper. In June 1947 President Alemán had started to bring in a series of antiunion policies. García Valseca took advantage of the shift in political mood. The government declared the strikes illegal and canceled the registration of the news vendors' union.[57] Again, state and business aligned. For the next three decades, the company administration guarded against any union involvement in the chain. In 1953, García Valseca sacked five reporters from *El Sol de Toluca* for joining the journalists' union.[58] In 1962, he closed down Queretaro's *El Amanecer* because workers started a union.[59] In fact, he was so paranoid about the infiltration of organized labor he even prohibited journalists in Ciudad Juárez from joining the local press association.[60] On the most basic level, such actions drove down wages. At the García Valseca chain, skilled press workers often earned around the same as unskilled laborers. Journalists' salaries were also comparatively low. In 1948, *El Occidental* journalists were paid a miserly 10 pesos a day.[61]

Finally García Valseca also tried to maximize initial sales. This not only cemented large readerships, but also broke or bankrupted rivals. His strategies were threefold. Most important, he used his stock of cheap PIPSA paper to keep introductory prices extremely low. When he launched *El Fronterizo* in 1943, copies were sold for 5¢. Five years later, he put out Guadalajara's *El Sol* at the same price; in contrast *El Informador* cost 15¢. The pricing strategy took its toll on competitors. In Durango, *El Sol de Durango* put the old *El Diario de Durango* out of business in just two months. García Valseca immediately bought up the failed enterprise at a bargain price and reissued the daily as an evening paper.[62] In 1948, Blas Rojo, the editor of *El Sinaloense*, complained that García Valseca's push into small provincial markets had caused a "collapse" of traditional newspapers. "The García Valseca chain seems to have an infinite source of paper and does not care about losing money."[63]

He also bolstered early sales by carefully selecting the editors of these start-up ventures. In regions with limited competition, he poached editors and journalists from low-selling or insolvent rivals. These locals understood the market, knew the advertisers, and had a good rapport with politicians and industrialists. In Chihuahua, for example, he kept on the affable former owner of *El Heraldo* who was close to the state's business elite.[64] But in cities with more established opposition, he parachuted in teams of aggressive muckrakers. As we shall see, these drew readers in with alarmist crime stories and campaigns against political corruption. In Guadalajara he employed the former editor of the national tabloid *Ultimas Noticias*, Miguel Ordorica. Ordorica was an uncooperative and difficult editor. The U.S. consul claimed that "the tool he uses most frequently is abuse, not commendation or constructive criticism. If he does not abuse you, he expects you to regard that as support of your policy." But for the first few years, García Valseca gave him a long leash. (Ordorica explained to the U.S. consul that he took the job only "with the understanding I would have complete authority.") Ordorica's independent style proved the making of both *El Sol* and *El Occidental*. Sales were impressive and advertising increased.[65]

Reading Gangster Fiction

The tone of García Valseca's newspapers depended entirely on subject matter. Around a third of front-page news concerned international or national issues. These stories were centrally produced in the company's Mexico City base and then sent out to the company's branch offices. They were heavily formulaic, often pulled directly from official press releases. They always supported the Mexican government. They demonstrated a strong anticommunist slant. But stories about local politics varied hugely. Some of the time, they supported local administrations without question. But occasionally, controversial exposés, popular campaigns, and criticisms of regional politicians interrupted the favorable coverage. Discerning the balance of commercial concerns, political interests, and blackmail that underlay these shifting approaches is a tough job. The chain's own employees were often bemused by the rapid swings in tone. Motivations overlapped and blurred. Decisions were made in secret at the very top level. Like resolutions over the drug trade, their exact details were probably only known by a few high-ranking insiders.[66] But by taking a handful of case studies and triangulating newspaper stories, secret service reports, and autobiographies, some insights can be gained. Some operations, especially in the early stages of a newspaper, were primarily designed to build circulation. Like the 1944 *El Fronterizo* campaign over the murder of a Ciudad Juárez teenager, Elvira Anchondo, they imported techniques from the national *nota roja* and sought to build interactive communities of readers. Others were pure extortion. The 1963–64 campaign against the Chihuahua governor lacked both mainstream and presidential support. Instead, García Valseca used petty slights, exposés of corruption, and hastily manufactured "popular campaigns" to force the governor to hand over funds and exclusive advertising contracts to the chain.

At one level, the editorial policy of the *Sol* chain was extremely centralized. All national and international news was written at the offices in Mexico City. Formatted reports were then sent out to the various regional branches. As the U.S. embassy observed as early as 1954, "most material published outside of local news is supplied by the García Valseca central wire service."[67] From 1949 onward, chain journalists were all given uniform in-house training at the García Valseca academy in Mexico City. García Valseca himself maintained an almost obsessive watch over his local papers. He toured the country frequently in his private train, often making surprise visits to his startled editors. When he was in Mexico City, he still kept in touch, thanks to Avila Camacho's free telephones. From his mansion in San Angel he had a twenty-four-hour direct line to his downtown offices. In his home office he had another fourteen phones, another six by his dining room table, five by his bed, and one on the door of the bathroom. García Valseca's hands-on management style extended to the day-to-day running of the individual newspapers. The U.S. embassy commented that the Puebla magnate "exercised rigid control over all his newspapers." The chain comprised a "bewildering succession of editors, none of whom managed to survive more than a few months."[68] His interference even extended to non-newspaper issues. Sánchez García, who briefly edited *El Sol de Toluca* in the mid-1950s, remembers his role also included ordering produce from his boss's Queretaro hacienda. García Valseca would phone him at 10 P.M. demanding 10 kilos of beef, fresh milk, and vegetables for his Mexico City residence.[69] Such an attitude generated substantial cynicism. When Blanco Moheno attended a speech in honor of García Valseca that claimed he loved his journalists "like a father," he turned to his friend and said, "Come on, it's not worth three tacos to hear these fucking lies."[70]

García Valseca complemented this editorial control by appointing employees with similar views. This was what media specialists term "anticipatory compliance" and ensured writers instinctively framed articles in accordance with his interpretations.[71] There were a few exceptions. The left-leaning writer Renato Leduc produced a regular column for the sports daily *Esto*.[72] But in general, his editors and journalists were strongly right-wing. His right-hand man was Clive Smith, a British mercenary and journalist who had previously worked for the *Daily Mail*.[73] The editor of his Guadalajara newspapers, Ordorica, and the head of his Mexico City academy, Borrego, were both Axis supporters.[74] In the 1960s he employed several of the right-wing refugees from *Excélsior*, including the Franco sympathizer Ponce.[75] The editor of *El Heraldo* of Chihuahua was in business with the state's landowning plutocracy.[76]

Centralized control and ideologically uniform employees guaranteed a firm and constant editorial line on national and international issues. Support for the Mexican government and particularly the president was unwavering. Visual and written coverage of state of the union addresses, presidential tours, and diplomatic meetings was copious and fawning. Image-packed *gacetilla* pullouts were frequent.[77] The *Sol* newspapers were also extremely anticommunist. On international subjects, they took most articles from the U.S. news agencies, United Press International (UPI) and Associated Press, as well as the U.S. government. In 1967, for example, they included a free USIS supplement on the Vietnam War in both their national and regional papers. They also acquired information from other right-wing organizations including Cuban exile groups, Franco's news agency, and the U.S. conservative group the John Birch Society.[78] Such articles not only disparaged the communist bloc but also presented the outside world in simplistic binary terms. Governments or groups sympathetic to the United States were supported and praised. Opposition, of whatever stripe, was deemed dangerous, "communistic," or "communistoide." In fact, some *Sol* writers clearly felt that these foreign sources did not go far enough and rewrote agency pieces in more condemnatory ways. In 1960, they substituted the language of a UPI report on protests in

Turkey. "Students opposed to the government" was changed to "rebellious students"; "a crowd of young people" became "a mass of gandules [slackers]"; and the headline switched from the rather dry "Army and students clash in Turkish cities" to the defiant "[President] Menderes will not be intimidated by a bunch of slackers."[79]

If centrally produced, anticommunist national and international news occupied around a third to a half of *Sol* front pages, the remaining stories concerned regional events. Here, the degree of top-down control seemed to waver. At times, García Valseca took a very detailed interest in this level of reporting. As we shall see, he often used his papers to bully governors for cash or simply out of personal enmity. At times he even went as far as writing the local news himself. But at other times, branch editors seem to have taken their own initiative. Various insiders claimed that the management of the chain differed from other large press enterprises. Rather than relying on a complex bureaucracy or a definite chain of command, García Valseca mixed autocratic centralization with high levels of decentralization. To maximize paper, save on taxes, and limit risk, branch newspapers actually operated as separate financial units.[80] Individual editors had to use their publication's income to pay the main García Valseca company for rent and for centrally produced stories. But outside these commitments, they were free to make money as they saw fit. Means included increasing circulation, growing advertising, or, if necessary, extorting local politicians and businessmen.

Sánchez Pontón compared the set-up to the mob. García Valseca was the kingpin and his editors were his lieutenants. They were entrusted with a particular plaza and expected to make money. There were certain laws and limits. Some targets and approaches remained out of bounds (never insult the president, never support a communist group). But in general, these local managers were relatively free as long as they kept up their monthly kickbacks to the boss.[81] Perhaps more accurately, the shape of the enterprise paralleled the structure of the Mexican state. It was a newspaper *dictablanda*, the PRI made press. García Valseca was the president and the local editors the governors. On the surface, the magnate possessed unlimited power. By right, he dominated control of key national and international issues and by custom he could interfere in local news way beyond his remit if he so wanted. But often he did not. In fact, like the Mexican president, having set down the boundaries, García Valseca often left the running of the provinces up to his underlings. They were entrusted with making money and passing a percentage up the hierarchy. If they became too unpopular, García Valseca simply swapped them out.[82]

Whether the García Valseca system was decentralized or not, local news differed from the chain's national coverage. Much of the time, local *Soles* supported the political and economic elites. But occasionally, local coverage became extremely critical. Articles exposed corruption, attacked business leaders, and angered politicians. Motivations varied. But, particularly in the first few years of a chain publication, such reports were primarily designed to attract new readers and cement loyal customers. Many were crime stories. Though local papers had occasionally employed the forms and discourses of the *nota roja* during the early postrevolutionary decades, the García Valseca chain really introduced the genre to the provinces. Much to the disgust of the U.S. consul, *El Occidental* devoted "inordinate space to crime news."[83] And García Valseca's launch of afternoon tabloids like Ciudad Juárez's *El Mexicano* and Tampico's *El Sol de la Tarde* pushed the focus on crime even further. At a basic level, crime news guaranteed circulation. It also created a community of reliable readers who wrote in, commented on the crime, offered their theories, and interacted with the newspaper and each other.

The chain's first paper, *El Fronterizo*, found an audience in this way. García Valseca launched the publication in late 1943. The auspices were good. Ciudad Juárez was a growing city; the population was increasing by around 15 percent annually.[84] Advertising revenue, from both sides of the border, was readily available. Managers had also succeeded in drumming up enthusiasm for the newspaper with a radio competition to name the publication.[85] But it was the coverage of the murder of a teenage girl that cemented the newspaper's circulation among the city's residents. On December 20, 1944, pedestrians found the body of fifteen-year-old shop worker Elvira Anchondo slumped in the back of a car. After failing to wake the girl, they called over a passing policeman. He found that Elvira was dead. Suspicion immediately fell on Elvira's boyfriend and the owner of the car, Héctor Bailón Acosta. Unlike Elvira, he came from a respected and wealthy family. According to the police who arrested him, he immediately confessed to the crime. He claimed that after drinking a few beers with Elvira, he took her to a secluded spot by the agricultural college where he tried to rape her. She fought back. He beat, strangled, and killed her. The police chief claimed that there were bruises on her face, neck, and body. Her underwear had also been found outside the car. Bailón repeated the confession in front of six witnesses at the local hospital. But at this point, the murderer's well-connected relatives got involved. One uncle—a lawyer—took charge of his defense, arguing that police had fabricated the confession. He also claimed that his nephew was suffering from "mental paralysis" and should be moved to a private room in the psychiatric ward of the hospital. Another uncle—a doctor—called in medics to do a postmortem examination of the body. They now claimed that there was no evidence of rape and that Elvira had died from carbon monoxide poisoning.[86]

In the hands of the *El Fronterizo* journalists, the case became a cause célèbre. They gave the murderer a name, "El Chacal" [the Jackal]. For three weeks, coverage dominated the newspaper. Between December 21, 1944, and January 14, 1945, over half of the articles touched either directly or indirectly on the murder. Front-page new stories updated readers on the facts of the case; editorials lamented the state of Mexican justice; and an extended letters page allowed border citizens to offer their sympathies, voice their anger, and set out their theories. In the days immediately following the death, reporters were sent all over the region to collect details about the case. The principal crime reporter found a witness from El Paso who claimed that Bailón had also tried to rape her thirteen-year-old daughter. According to the anonymous source, Bailón had driven her to exactly the same place as Elvira was found, grabbed her by the wrists, and tried to force himself on her. Fortunately she screamed, scratched him, and managed to escape. When her mother found out about Bailón's behavior, she grabbed a gun and approached the young man. He got down on his knees and begged for forgiveness. Before she could shoot him, a neighbor intervened and disarmed her. "Don't bother. . . . Don't lose yourself over a disgraced Casanova who's not even worth the price of a bullet." Another reporter tracked down the grieving family and interviewed the mother. Comforted by a group of female neighbors, she eventually managed to hold back her tears long enough to describe her daughter as a "virtuous and well-educated" young girl, who had tried to rid herself of Bailón on multiple occasions. Another journalist found Elvira's employer at a clothes shop on the main drag. Her boss praised the girl's serious and hardworking demeanor and disparaged her boyfriend as disrespectful.[87]

El Fronterizo's coverage was very deliberately designed to appeal to Ciudad Juárez's masses. To do so, the editor and his journalists employed a series of techniques. From the beginning, they played on the city's class divisions. Struggling to write letters of protest, weeping in their shacks on the edge of the city, or traipsing down the muddy tracks to go to work, Elvira, her relatives, and her neighbors were described as honorable and industrious members of the city's recent immigrant class. They were hard-working men and women with few advantages who sought better lives for themselves and their children. Bailón, on the other hand, was described as one of the city's privileged few. He was a lazy good-for-nothing. He spent his life in bars and brothels. He had got his job through family contacts and received his car as a birthday present.

He was a "good-looking boy, with money and political influence in his pocket." He preyed on "young, adolescent girls of the lower classes . . . assured of his own impunity."[88] As such, the journalists presented the murder as the culmination of everyday tensions between poor, honest workers and an immoral, predatory elite—class oppression condensed into a single, violent act. His relatives, with their good connections, ostentatious job titles, and pretentious prefixes, were also part of this elite. The subsequent cover-up was simply evidence that the political and judicial systems favored this class.

El Fronterizo's journalists also placed their own work at the center of the narrative. They were, in the words of the editor, "in solidarity with the people." They, like the city's honest policemen and judges, were trying to find evidence against Bailón. They, like the victim's family, were also facing intimidation and violence. At times, this tale of attempted censorship became the main story. Two days after the murder, Bailón's uncle turned up at the *El Fronterizo* office threatening to bring a lawsuit against the newspaper. Over the next few weeks, *pistoleros* in a gray car tailed a journalist and a copy editor. The editor received anonymous death threats over the telephone. One of the reporters was kidnapped and beaten by thugs. Lawyers close to the family questioned the paper's focus on "graphic and violent nota roja" and hinted at suing the paper either for defamation or infringing public morals.[89] Such stories intensified the link between reporters and newspaper purchasers. *El Fronterizo* readers were asked to empathize not only with Elvira's grieving mother, but also the brave journalists who were confronting the system and risking their lives to bring Bailón to justice.

Finally and perhaps most important, *El Fronterizo*'s editor opened up the paper to the newspaper's readers. During the coverage of the case, readers' letters accounted for up to half of the newspaper's space. The journalists recognized their importance and changed the name of the letters page to the unashamedly populist "The people are the voice of God." Many of the letters praised or echoed *El Fronterizo*'s coverage and reiterated the newspaper's understanding of how the case exposed issues of class and gender. Some were from poor fathers. J. Torres and the workers of a small garment factory attacked the "rich men who exploit our women" and threatened to lynch Bailón if he was not put in prison. Others were from working-class women. Josefina R. Pérez was a shop assistant. She commended the paper for speaking out on behalf of "those of us who do not have influence or money but live from our honorable work." Others went beyond expressions of sympathy or anger. A handful of amateur sleuths joined the journalists in picking apart the case for the defense. In one letter, a car mechanic used his experience and his close reading of a biology textbook to conclude that Elvira could never have died from carbon monoxide poisoning. "In order to die, the blood would have had to contain 845 milligrams of gas, which is impossible to concentrate in a car of that size."[90]

El Fronterizo's coverage of the case generated a rapid surge in circulation. By early 1944 the paper claimed to sell nearly 15,000 copies a day. Cross-referencing sales and population figures, it seems that by the mid-1940s most households purchased a copy. But the Elvira Anchondo case also did more. It not only increased the number of consumers, it also created a community of readers.[91] On one level, the links between the newspaper and these readers were political. Ciudad Juárez's nonelites now felt that they had a newspaper that defended their rights and was prepared to take on the establishment. The newspaper was, as one letter commented, "a guarantee of our interests." But these links were also emotional. Reading a paper was a sentimental activity. *El Fronterizo*'s readers sensed that the journalists experienced the same feelings of frustration, outrage, and intimidation as them. Finally, this relationship was reciprocal. If *El Fronterizo* depended on its purchasers for income and copy, Ciudad Juárez's poor classes now relied on the paper to voice their opinions. Such links generated loyalty. Despite increased competition, eight years later the United States confirmed that sales were over 20,000 for the daily and 25,000 for the Sunday edition.[92]

If some local news campaigns were built on genuine popular concerns and designed to extend readerships, others were motivated by blackmail. Critics frequently accused the García Valseca newspapers of the practice. Monsiváis claimed that the chain was "built on the blackmailing of governors" and voiced the rumor that one governor had inaugurated a school with a plaque that read, "This school was constructed with the money that was not given to the García Valseca chain."[93] Sánchez Pontón made similar, more detailed accusations. He asserted that the *Sol* newspapers often started "savage and at the time inexplicable press campaigns designed to intimidate or in the parlance of the times ablandar [soften up] local authorities." To stop the campaign, politicians were forced to sign publicity contracts for thousands a month. Those who refused were put on a black list and the campaign continued.[94]

The practice of blackmail by journalism probably dated back to Mexico's first newssheets and flyers. But the growing postrevolutionary market for the printed press certainly extended the practice. Throughout the period, accusations of "gangster journalism" became commonplace. Yet beyond offering moralistic condemnations, commentators rarely sought to disaggregate this practice or figure out its extent, mechanics, or effects.[95] Doing so is a tough

business. Untainted evidence is sparse. Only a handful of governors, press secretaries, and editors were probably aware of the exact transactions. Explicit
paper trails that detailed payments in return for silence probably never existed.
Personal confessions are similarly rare. Though official accusations of gangster
journalism were frequent, they were also suspect. Many simply served to excuse press accusations of corruption and clear officials of any wrongdoing.[96]

We also lack a conceptual framework for understanding the subject. Gangster journalism surfed the limits between liberal ideals and the *prensa vendida*.
What was the difference between the extortion part of the campaigns and
good journalism? They both critiqued the powerful, exposed corruption,
and voiced popular concerns. Many extortion campaigns were not entirely
fictitious but rather relied on real events or at least partly substantiated rumors. Was it simply a question of the underlying morality of the eventual
aims? And if only a handful of people knew these aims, did it matter? Even
journalists involved in the practice found the division difficult to discern.
Marín, who was involved in a shakedown campaign for the *El Sol de San Luis*
in 1952, remembered that at the time he and his fellow journalists "were
prepared to sacrifice ourselves as we thought we were defending liberty of
expression and the rights of the Potosino people. We attacked the government,
the cacicazgo, the abusive authorities, and the thieves and we spoke out in
favor of the dispossessed, the disinherited, and the victims of injustice."[97] In
fact, he only suspected it was all part of an extortion racket when, six months
into the campaign, he was told to remove all criticism of the government. But
if gangster journalism was about maintaining silence about controversial or
criminal acts, what was the difference between the practice and the orthodox
government payoff?

Other questions also arise. What did gangster journalism mean for the relations between national and regional governments? Were presidents and
their press secretaries aware of the tactic? Did they tacitly accept the practice,
much as they allowed a degree of competition between local factions of the
PRI? Or did they secretly encourage or even manipulate the practice to unseat or unsettle out-of-favor regional powerbrokers? What did the practice
mean for press violence? How many assaults on journalists were actually attacks on blackmailers? Finally, what did extortion campaigns mean to the average Mexican reader? Could they discern the practice? Did they simply
applaud the criticism and berate the silence? Or did they view the alternating
approaches cynically as part of an overall ploy?

Answering all of these questions is beyond the scope of this chapter. Instead, in this section I want to lay out a definition of gangster journalism, out-

line a basic chronology, examine the mechanics of a particular case study, and suggest ways in which readers reacted to the practice. In essence gangster journalism involved two interrelated practices. These are perhaps best explained in Durango journalist Guillermo H. Ramírez's semibiographical novel about provincial reporters, *Gangsters del Periodismo*. The first tactic we could call "preemptive extortion." When journalists got hold of a story of malfeasance, they demanded money not to publish it. "They blackmail the author of a crime to alter the actual information; they blackmail the venal functionary not to show him up to be a vulgar thug; and they blackmail the industrialist not to reveal the petitions of his workers."[98] The second tactic we could term "reactive extortion." When dignitaries refused to pay, journalists started campaigns of truths, half-truths, and complete fiction. "The perverse journalists took strategic positions to attack the politician that refused to give them publicity, the restaurant owner that didn't allow them free food, or the cinema owner who did not give their families free passes."[99] After a few weeks or months of intense criticism, the targets usually paid up.

García Valseca's newspapers alternated the techniques. Finding evidence of "preemptive extortion" is difficult. Payments for silence overlapped with standard compensation for positive coverage. But examples of "reactive extortion" campaigns are more common. They bucked the trend and came to official attention. There were denunciations of these campaigns in Puebla in 1946–47 and in San Luis Potosí in 1952.[100] Accusations, however, peaked in the period 1957–59. This seems to have been the turning point for García Valseca's practice of gangster journalism. What had been a series of one-off shakedowns now became a general trend. Political developments played a key role. These were years of unusual political instability in Mexico's provinces. The incoming president had spoken out against regional *cacicazgos* and effectively encouraged popular movements designed to topple these power-brokers. There were civic uprisings throughout the provinces, most of which concerned municipal elections and were often accompanied by upsurges in critical journalism.[101] But they also seemed to have provided cover for the García Valseca chain to increase the rhythm of extortion campaigns. During the period, popular protestors and gangster journalists entered into a set of symbiotic relationships. While newspapers offered space and support, social movements offered circulation, legitimacy, and easy deniability. According to local editors, they were not maneuvering for a big payoff, but were simply reflecting their readers' demands. And perhaps they were. Perhaps they did not realize the endgame until García Valseca received the payoff and they were ordered to stop.

Whatever the exact mechanics, during the period accusations of deliberate extortion campaigns increased. In San Luis Potosí, the normally *oficialista El Sol de San Luis* suddenly swung its support behind Salvador Nava's fight for the local mayorship.[102] Queretaro's *El Amanecer* backed a student movement to unseat the governor's chosen candidate for the university rectorship.[103] In Chihuahua, local journalists and politicians complained that the chain's chief muckraker, Carlos Loret de Mola, was deliberately sowing "a situation of alarm, social dissolution, and terror." He was publishing "slanders and blackmails and sacrificing friends" in order to extract more cash from politicians and local businessmen.[104] In Sinaloa, another local politician complained that the attacks on the Ciudad Juárez mayor and the mockery of the governor of Coahuila were part of a coordinated campaign—a "malevolent plot which the journalist chain of José García Valseca was developing throughout the country." He speculated that the victims' only mistake was "not allowing the chain to sacar el jugo [literally 'squeeze the juice' but also used to denote extorting money] to which it was accustomed."[105]

During the 1960s, these campaigns were less frequent but more visible. On the one hand, expanded security forces started to take an interest in the practice and compiled reports that outlined their motivations and techniques. For example, in September 1960 members of the DFS presented an account of the Queretaro press. They claimed that the García Valseca newspaper *El Amanecer* repeatedly attacked the local governor, Juan C. Gorráez. Some locals supported the attacks and felt they were justified but did not know why they were sustained. According to the DFS, the motives were both financial and personal. García Valseca was demanding an annual payment of 800,000 pesos a year to stop the attacks. He also wanted a seat in the senate and a federal deputy position for one of his friends. The governor refused so the criticism continued. According to *El Amanecer* editor, the campaign had roots in the local gossip mill. Revenge and financial motives intertwined. Five years earlier the daughter of one of García Valseca's friends had run off with a young member of the Queretaro elite. The magnate demanded that the governor intervene, split up the union, and send the daughter back home. The governor refused. At this point García Valseca approached the editor and gave him explicit orders. "Don't say Gorráez does anything well . . . only averagely or badly."[106]

On the other hand, provincial politics also changed. Multiclass, cross-ideological movements like those of the late 1950s declined. Instead they were replaced by more radical left-wing movements, often inspired by the Cuban Revolution. This robbed the campaigns of the cloak of popular legitimacy. The unstable symbiosis between gangster journalism and social movements declined. Even when an extortion campaign overlapped with widespread protest, as it did in Chihuahua from 1963 to 1964, it was often radically out of step with popular convictions or complaints. This Chihuahua campaign was perhaps the most evident of the García Valseca extortion rackets. It focused on the administration of the unpopular governor Práxedes Giner Durán and lasted over a year. It was discussed by visiting secret agents and repeatedly flagged by the critical local press. Because the writers wanted to avoid the genuine grievances of left-wing protestors, it was fantastically petty and often rather comic.

Giner took over the governorship of Chihuahua in October 1962. In terms of policy, he should have been close to García Valseca. But Giner himself was not part of the state's elite. In fact he was a gruff and foulmouthed former Villista who clearly disliked the prissy formalities, time-consuming negotiations, and endless payoffs that comprised the everyday business of a PRI governor. Almost immediately he fell out with the mogul. According to the DFS, Giner's predecessor had paid the chain a base rate of 80,000 pesos a month. Government offices also signed up to an exclusive advertising contract with the chain. In return the chain's papers "praised the works of the government, treated the errors of the local functionaries with a light touch, and [avoided] alarmist or disorientating news." Giner, however, declined to pay. In response, García Valseca approached the governor and claimed that the state government still owed the chain 65,000 pesos for past advertising. Giner said he would pay as soon as he saw the receipts. Rather disingenuously, García Valseca then claimed that the economic question was of no interest. He was simply interested in making sure that the governor abided by the principle of paying one's debts. In fact, he suggested that the governor could give the money to a good cause. Giner called his bluff and donated the cash to build a nursery school.[107] (Perhaps this is where the Monsiváis story originated.)

At this point, García Valseca started a press campaign against the governor. According to the DFS, the press magnate took over the running of the four dailies and organized the operation from his base in Mexico City.[108] The campaign consisted of three main elements. First, all the chain newspapers refused to print photographs of the governor or use his name or official title. Instead they insisted on employing wordy phrases like "the man in charge of the executive" or the "depository of the executive power."[109] In one conference with the state's livestock owners, *El Heraldo*'s journalists even highlighted the snub by neglecting to mention Giner at all but listing all forty-eight farmers instead.[110] Second, the reporters started to expose examples of official corruption. They started by flagging the Camargo-Ojinaga Road, which they claimed Giner had deliberately diverted to pass his own ranch. They then moved on to his cabinet members, accusing his secretary of the interior of linking up with large logging companies to defraud the state treasury and his treasurer of exploiting workers in his sawmills.[111]

Third, the chain's newspapers manufactured a handful of "popular campaigns" designed to inflate the perceived power of the newspaper and make the local government look weak. At the time, Chihuahua was overwhelmed by genuine popular movements. They included land invasions, teachers' strikes, and protests at the local teacher training colleges. All these were ignored. Instead his newspapers chose to canvass against small-scale irritants. In January 1964, for example, the newspaper backed a group of well-off farmers who were refusing to pay the "exorbitant price" of 30 pesos for their license plates. For the next month, coverage of the campaign dominated *El Heraldo*'s front page. Reporters published multiple interviews with outraged tractor owners, held polls with discontented citizens, and claimed that the national government was about to pull the state's share of petrol taxation because of the price rise. Eventually, the state gave way and returned license plate charges back to their 1962 levels, an annual drop of less than 5 pesos. García Valseca's journalists championed the change, which they pompously claimed was due to the "massive protests of all motor vehicle owners expressed in a virile way in the columns of El Heraldo."[112]

Such attacks had weight. They not only attracted the attention of the DFS, but also generated space for other left-wing groups to attack the unpopular governor. Without García Valseca's backing, the governor had no supporters in the local press. As we shall see in chapter 8, by 1964 protestors had coalesced to form a powerful opposition to the governor. In April 1964 this came to a head. Protestors barracked and then attacked the visiting PRI presidential candidate, Díaz Ordaz. The meeting dissolved into a running street battle between policemen and demonstrators. Both sides were forced to compromise, probably at the behest of the federal government. According to exposés in the left-wing press, García Valseca and Giner met in Mexico City and held a "black wedding." The governor agreed to pay the chain 60,000 pesos a month. In return, the magnate agreed to stop the campaign. The next week, *El Heraldo* "suddenly remembered the name of the governor of the state" and published a front-page photograph of a beaming Giner.[113]

The question remains—how did the chain's blend of anticommunism, crime stories, and alternating periods of sycophancy and criticism move provincial readers? Contrary to Monsiváis's assertion, García Valseca did not so much "block a close up of reality" as force readers to view it through a spinning pinwheel that interspersed phases of clarity and darkness.[114] How did readers react? In general, García Valseca's newspapers were relatively popular. According to stated sales in 1967, the chain's thirty-two morning and afternoon dailies comprised 13 percent of regional newspapers. They claimed to shift a total of 608,817 copies a day or 23 percent of total sales. The aggregate total failed to include big-selling competitors like Guadalajara's *El Informador*, and the chain's figures were probably inflated. But so were the circulation figures for the other newspapers. Even after the extortion campaigns of the early 1960s, the *Soles* still dominated the regional press. In fact, though García Valseca had no titles in the lucrative Monterrey, Tijuana, or Merida markets, four of the top ten and ten of the top twenty most popular regional newspapers in Mexico were from the chain.[115] U.S. surveys supported this view. The 1958 review of Aguascalientes readers discovered that the circulation of *El Sol del Centro* dwarfed that of the rival *El Heraldo*. Seventy-six percent of the city's inhabitants read the chain newspaper. The 1967 survey of thirty cities demonstrated similar results. In Toluca 70 percent of inhabitants read *El Sol de Toluca*, in Pachuca 72 percent read *El Sol de Hidalgo*, and in Mazatlán 77 percent read *El Sol del Pacífico*. In these cities rival newspapers struggled to obtain 20 percent of the market.[116]

Such high readerships perhaps help explain the heavy anticommunism that influenced many provincial cities during the 1950s and 1960s. But not all readers faithfully followed the García Valseca editorial line. On the left, particularly among students, the chain came to symbolize the repressive right-wing tone of the Mexican press. In 1961, pro-Cuba students threw stones through the windows of Chihuahua's *El Heraldo*. For the next month, the governor was forced to station troops around the building.[117] In 1966, nearly a thousand teachers and peasants surrounded *El Sol de Durango*'s head office, reprimanded the journalists for refusing to publish anything about the state's landless movements, and shouted jeers of "bootlicking capitalist press."[118]

Blackmail rackets could also cause fluctuating relationships with readers. These often culminated in strong feelings of anger and betrayal. Between 1958 and 1961 *El Sol de San Luis* supported the popular local politician Salvador Nava in his confrontations with the state's notorious *cacique*, Gonzalo Santos. According to the paper, Santos ran a "fatal cacicazgo" full of "fear, decadence, and agony." His governor was a "violent scared man" and "a useless puppet" and his candidate for the municipal presidency was not only "unpopular" but also part of a "Santista plot against López Mateos."[119] But in early 1961, Nava attempted to run for the state governor again as an independent candidate. This time, *El Sol de San Luis* withdrew its support, as a result of political pressure and financial donations.[120] For six months, the newspaper only ran ads supporting the official nominee. Journalists either ignored the Nava campaign or downplayed its importance. In July 1961 the newspaper backed a government plot to finish the Navista organizations for good. In an afternoon extra, *El Sol de San Luis* claimed soldiers had discovered a "gigantic arsenal hidden in the homes of elements of navismo." The arsenal, plastered over the front page in a grainy photograph, allegedly consisted of "2,500 homemade bombs, fireworks, and fuses."[121] The story was a complete sham. In fact, the local battalion had raided the workshops of San Luis Potosí's firework makers, arrested the workers, confiscated their wares, and falsely claimed they were part of a Navista plot. But *El Sol de San Luis*'s credulous coverage legitimized the accusations.[122]

The rapid and unexplained switch in support produced considerable resentment. In 1958, Navistas had celebrated their victory outside *El Sol de San Luis*'s offices. Now they only approached the building to shout abuse at the editor and journalists. Corridos, which blamed government payoffs for corrupting the newspaper, did the rounds.

El periódico El Sol	The newspaper El Sol
Al pueblo traicionó	Betrayed the people
Cómo un Judas Iscariote	Like a Judas Iscariot
Al gobierno se vendió	It sold itself to the government

Another song made the financial reasons for *El Sol*'s change even more explicit.

El Sol es un empleado	El Sol is an employee
Del presupuesto estatal	On the state budget
Y por cierto, el mejor pagado	And of course, the best paid
Por un fulano de tal	By some fellow or other
En él residen las ratas	Inside reside rats
Sin vergüenza y sin honor	Without shame or honor
Que se arrastran a las patas	That crawl up the legs
Del señor Gobernador	Of the governor.[123]

El Sol de San Luis's popularity would never recover. Just as supporting popular movements could generate reader loyalty, backsliding so overtly could also lose it. Circulation slowed down, commercial advertising shrank, and for over a decade the paper became a hollowed-out organ of the state government.

Bankruptcy, the "Deep State," and the End of the Chain

The fall of the García Valseca chain was as controversial as its foundation. Though it postdates Fuentes's novel, the story reads like fiction and affirms Sergio Aguayo's contention that reading the country's security files captures the magical realism of Mexican politics.[124] (Better perhaps, they read like Rafael Bernal's Cold War noir *a la mexicana, The Mongolian Conspiracy*.) On the surface, the enterprise was simply unable to service its mounting debts. In 1972, a government-controlled bank took control of the business. The following year, the Monterrey industrialist Eugenio Garza Sada tried to buy up the chain. But before he could complete the transaction, he was killed by guerrillas from the Liga Comunista 23 de Septiembre in a botched kidnapping attempt. Instead, in 1976 the bank sold the chain to the Mexican Publishing Organization (Organización Editorial Mexicana, OEM), a coalition of businessmen led by furniture tycoon Mario Vázquez Raña.

Yet peering beneath this basic narrative, the story becomes much murkier. Over the past forty years, Mexican journalists have started to ask why the Mexican government suddenly decided to call in its debts. Was the move driven by personal animosity between President Díaz Ordaz and the Puebla magnate? Or was it a concerted effort by President Echeverría to usurp control of the chain? Such questions have, in turn, led to further inquiries. These have started to delve into what might be termed Mexico's "deep state" and the shadowy links connecting secret agents, drug traffickers, and urban guerrillas.[125] According to one journalist, the Echeverría government not only knew about the planned kidnapping at least a year in advance, it also planted a hit man connected to the drug trade in the organization to make sure Garza Sada was killed. The aim was simple—to prevent the Monterrey businessman from saving the García Valseca chain and leave the way open for Echeverría to purchase the enterprise. Just like the 1976 *Excélsior* takeover, the García Valseca sale was a state-backed coup.

García Valseca's business was built on debt. During the mid-1960s, the Puebla magnate added to these liabilities. In order to roll out his major national newspaper, *El Sol de México*, he started to buy up rotary offset presses from the Miehle-Goss-Dexter company in Chicago. Gradually he replaced his old presses with this up-to-date technology. By 1971, he had purchased 143 machines for his local newspapers.[126] To cover the expansion, in 1966 he took a 125-million-peso loan from a U.S. investment company with NF acting as guarantor.[127] The following year, he took out another 75-million-peso loan entirely from NF. This time he used his properties in Mexico City as collateral.[128]

Even with government backing, the company struggled to pay back the loans. In July 1969 the U.S. embassy reported that the chain was "in serious financial difficulty." *El Sol de México* had failed to secure sufficient advertising revenue and was bleeding money. The general manager blamed U.S. companies, which, he claimed, still preferred to advertise in the left-leaning *Excélsior* rather than the pro-U.S. *El Sol. El Sol*, he argued rather desperately, "was the best friend North America has in Mexico."[129] To make matters worse, the government started to withdraw its financial support. In 1970, Díaz Ordaz refused to buy García Valseca's vast Queretaro cattle ranch to cover the interest on the private loan. Instead he suggested asking his successor. But Echeverría was no more accommodating. He refused to purchase the property or rewrite the terms of the NF loan. By early 1972, García Valseca was unable to unload his assets or service his debts. In response, the government took charge of the chain and placed it under the control of the state's investment bank, Mexican Society of Industrial Credit (Sociedad Mexicana de Credito Industrial, SOMEX).[130]

Quite why the Mexican government declined to prop up the company remains a mystery. It had done so for decades: Why change now? Theories abound. Many pointed to the personal antagonism of President Díaz Ordaz. Some claimed the hostility went back decades and hinged on old rivalries over political positions in Puebla.[131] Others identified growing tensions between the two men during the actual presidency. Borrego argued that *Excélsior*'s new left-wing leadership spread unfounded rumors about the Puebla magnate to punish the *Sol* chain for employing a handful of former *Excélsior* journalists.[132] Leduc claimed that Díaz Ordaz was angered by the unlicensed publication in *El Sol de Puebla* of a photograph of him drinking liquor. (Apparently, the president was never allowed to be seen imbibing alcohol.)[133] According to the García Valseca family, the slight was even more trivial. In early 1970 the press baron bragged at a party that he had outlasted his former Puebla rival. One of Díaz Ordaz's relatives overheard the boast, passed it on to the president, and effectively started the bad blood.[134]

Others accused Luis Echeverría of engineering the bankruptcy. There were certainly rumors of strained relations between García Valseca and the new president. In 1971, a Mexican society woman, Gloria Novoa, wrote to Echeverría's wife. She claimed that she had heard a handful of military men discussing a plot to assassinate the president at an upscale Mexico City restaurant. After questioning by the DFS she denied the story. Instead she claimed that she had recently bumped into García Valseca's son at a high society party. He had drunkenly confessed that he and his father were preparing a coup against the incumbent president. The DFS eventually concluded that Novoa was a "paranoid schizophrenic" with an overactive imagination.[135] Unsubstantiated or not, the idea was at least conceivable. García Valseca's conservative anticommunism ran contrary to Echeverría's new left-wing agenda. Though the *Sol* chain continued to hold a solidly progovernment line, the owner's commercial links to the Monterrey Group of industrialists placed him on the right of a growing division between the country's business leaders and the left-leaning government.

In fact, it was these ties to the Monterrey Group that may have precipitated one of the most controversial events in the country's recent history, the murder of Garza Sada. Before presenting the evidence for the plot, it is worth outlining the connections between the Monterrey Group and García Valseca's business and describing the tensions between the group and the Echeverría government. The Monterrey Group comprised an alliance of factory-owning families from the northern state of Nuevo León. They had survived the revolution through links to national powerbrokers, the cooption of pliable unions, and the establishment of Catholic charity organizations.[136] They also depended on their control of Monterrey's major newspaper, *El Norte*, which they had helped establish in 1938. Though the Junco family theoretically ran the paper, the Monterrey Group kept a firm grip over all aspects. They placed a censor in the newsroom who controlled the editorial line and cut unfavorable stories.[137] Articles that questioned the group's business decisions or revealed pro-union sympathies were scrapped. "If a crime is committed in the city's factories, it is ignored . . . if a crime is committed in a rival business outside Monterrey, it immediately arrives on the editorial pages."[138]

During the 1960s the connection between the Monterrey Group and *El Norte* started to disintegrate. The motives were both ideological and financial. The social provisions of the Second Vatican Council divided the city's Catholic elite. While those close to the Monterrey Group, including Garza Sada, took a disapproving line, the paper's director Rodolfo Junco de la Vega supported the church's new policies. Political differences soon overlapped with economic conflicts. Rodolfo used underhanded tricks and his influence among minority shareholders to buy out the businessmen. The ploy generated an advertising boycott and an expensive legal battle. But by 1966 the newspaper was fully independent. At this point, Monterrey Group looked around for another ally in the newspaper industry and chose the Puebla press baron. García Valseca had always coveted the lucrative Nuevo León market and shared the industrialists' conservative politics. In 1968, they joined up to launch the Monterrey daily *La Tribuna*. It was pitched as a direct rival or what one journalist termed "a punishment" of *El Norte*. The paper poached many of *El Norte*'s local advertisers as well as some its best reporters.[139]

The Monterrey Group not only clashed with the owners of *El Norte*, but also came into conflict with the new Mexican government. Echeverría's policies of releasing political prisoners, expanding land distribution, and increasing education spending struck at the group's conservative instincts. Echeverría's rhetoric, which termed business leaders "emissaries of the past" and blamed them for Mexico's contemporary inequalities, was inflammatory. Other strategies, including increasing corporate tax, placing a levy on luxury goods, and removing some of the protectionist tariffs that shielded Mexican industry, directly confronted rich industrialists like the Monterrey Group. The president also started to interfere in Nuevo León politics. In 1971, he settled a dispute between university students and local entrepreneurs in favor of the former. He dismissed the group's handpicked governor and replaced him with his own left-wing appointee. In response, the Monterrey Group moved closer to the PAN, even appointing their own probusiness candidate to become head of the opposition party.[140]

During these escalating confrontations, Garza Sada attempted to bail out the García Valseca chain. There had been rumors of a takeover for years. As early as 1969 the U.S. embassy suggested that "a group of Monterrey bankers" were going to purchase the chain.[141] But the annexing of the company by SOMEX accelerated the process. According to Borrego, in mid-1972 a García Valseca representative visited Monterrey to present the company's balance sheet to Garza Sada. A few months later, he signed an agreement to acquire the firm and pay off its debts, taxes, and other outstanding expenses. For nearly a year, the agreement was put on hold as the press baron tried to negotiate more favorable terms with NF. But by September 1973 a deal was close. Again according to Borrego, Garza Sada signed a promissory note for 175 million pesos to pay off NF and the private creditors. The government trustees of the chain were not happy. "It's just not possible that the chain remains in the hands of the most reactionary and backwards looking businessmen. You should take action to avoid this happening," one trustee warned the García Valseca accountant.[142]

In the end the warning was irrelevant. On September 17, 1973, an urban guerrilla organization, the Liga Comunista 23 de Septiembre, attempted to kidnap Garza Sada. His bodyguards returned fire and in the ensuing struggle the Monterrey industrialist was shot and killed. For years García Valseca and

Borrego whispered that the bungled kidnapping was actually a state plot to stop the Monterrey Group from saving the chain. They indicated the government's reluctance to allow the sale. They pointed to the unexplained murder of another potential investor who had shown a strong interest in purchasing the firm. They revealed that the chain's Guadalajara offices had received anonymous calls that warned that García Valseca would be "victim number three."[143] If Borrego's and García Valseca's accusations were the only proof, this would be easy to dismiss. Most evidence is circumstantial. The entire argument is cloaked in a paranoid anticommunism, and if there is any hard and fast rule of weighing up historical proof, it is to always ignore anything written by an author who has also written a book in praise of the Third Reich. But Borrego's work is not the only evidence. In 2006 journalist Jorge Fernández Menéndez published *Nadie Supo Nada*, an investigation into the murder of Garza Sada. The work combined Borrego's allegations with secret service files, press reports, and interviews with drug traffickers. Together it presented an intriguing, if still extremely improbable, version of the conspiratorial thesis.

Fernández's new evidence was essentially threefold. First, he discovered that the government had agents within the Liga. One of these agents overheard the Monterrey branch of the organization planned to kidnap Garza Sada as early as 1972. Despite this, the government did nothing, neither arresting members of the group nor warning the industrialist to seek better protection. This alone is not terribly convincing. Incompetence, imperfect communications, or a straightforward understanding that student boasts often came to very little could all explain the inaction. But the other evidence is less easy to ignore. Using the DFS reconstruction of events, Fernández concluded that the Liga member who actually shot Garza Sada was a trainee agronomist called Elías Orozco Salazar. Move forward twenty years and Fernández was interviewing a major drug trafficker called Oscar López Olivares, "El Profe." López was a founding member of what became known as the Gulf cartel. After falling out with the kingpins, he fled to the United States and turned state's evidence. His testimonies served to put away about eighty traffickers on both sides of the border. After discussing the mechanics of trafficking and the cartel's alliances with corrupt officials, López somewhat inexplicably turned to the subject of Garza Sada. He claimed that Echeverría asked his brother-in-law, Rubén Zuno Arce, and a corrupt police official, Florentino Ventura, to exploit their contacts in the underworld to kill Garza Sada and frame leftist guerrillas. According to López, Ventura placed a hit man connected to Tamaulipas traffickers in the Liga to do the job. His name was Elías Orozco Salazar. López hinted at the accusations in his self-published autobiography and even claimed that he had approached the FBI with the information.[144]

If this was not strange enough, as Fernández started to investigate the claims, things got weirder. Zuno was a well-known associate of drug traffickers both in Tamaulipas and in the emerging Guadalajara cartel.[145] Ventura was even shadier. He was employed in the government's counterinsurgency and anti-narcotics campaigns during the 1970s and 1980s. He headed up a special unit devoted to making high-level arrests and helped detain cocaine kingpin Alberto Sicilia Falcón and Guadalajara cartel head Rafael Caro Quintero. By 1985 he was the head of the judicial police and Mexico's Interpol taskforce. But rumors of Ventura's contacts to the Gulf cartel were frequent. He was even accused of being part of a narcosatanic cult associated with the organization. Many suspected that his busts were designed to aid the rival organization by taking out the competition. His methods were extremely questionable. Described as "cold, cruel, and implacable," he was known to torture detainees; even the Mexico chief of the Drug Enforcement Administration described him as "the most brutal man I have ever met."[146] On September 17, 1988, exactly fifteen years to the day after the Garza Sada killing, Ventura got into his car with his wife, the former Liga member Salazar, and Salazar's wife. Salazar later claimed that he and Ventura had become acquaintances because their two wives were old school friends. After getting out to do some shopping and visit a bar, they got back into the car. At this point, according to Salazar's testimony, Ventura got into an argument with his wife. The arguing couple exited the car. He then pulled out his gun, shot her, shot her friend, and shot himself. All three died instantly. Salazar then also got out of the car, handed himself to the police, and was released without charge after three hours.[147]

The coincidences were bizarre to say the least. The involvement of Salazar, the date, the rumored links to the Gulf cartel, the fact that the police released Salazar—a former guerrilla—within hours of his arrest all undermine the official version of Ventura's death. At the time, a handful of journalists probed the official version, interviewing waiters who claimed that Ventura was neither drunk nor arguing with his wife, questioning why the case was shut so swiftly, and inquiring why Ventura's body was cremated the day after the murder. In Fernández's interview with López, the former Gulf cartel member substantiated such suspicions. According to López, Salazar was still a Gulf cartel plant, sent to kill Ventura because the judicial policeman was threatening to set up on his own. The subsequent police cover-up also dovetails neatly with plausible accusations that the incoming government of President Carlos Salinas de Gortari had links to the Gulf cartel.[148]

Despite the extraordinary coincidences, there are still extremely large holes in the story. López was not a reliable witness and Fernández has never published a transcript of his interview with the former trafficker. Furthermore, the interview was subject to some fairly murky negotiations. Even Fernández hints that he may have paid for the information. Salazar, perhaps understandably, has always maintained the official story. Neither the journalist nor the trafficker can explain why Salazar endured a decade in jail if he was a government plant. Salazar's subsequent career as a representative of Tamaulipas's Party of Work (Partido del Trabajo, PT) seems to bear out his leftwing credentials. (Although former secretary of the interior Manuel Bartlett's membership in the party indicates that the PT is not averse to admitting PRI insiders with suspected links to drug trafficking.)[149]

If true, the case suggests that during the 1970s Echeverría, together with members of the DFS, were establishing what we now might call a "deep state," a clandestine alliance of political elites, security personnel, and criminals prepared to undermine judicial norms in order to maintain what they deemed social and political stability. Perhaps, by the early 1970s, Echeverría or at least those close to the president felt that Garza Sada's takeover of the García Valseca chain risked giving the hostile business sector an influential mouthpiece. They were prepared to murder the industrialist and face the inevitable fallout in order to prevent the purchase. Three years after the Garza Sada killing, OEM purchased the chain from the government bank. The manner of the sale did nothing to dampen speculation about Echeverría's interference in the company. OEM's two prominent board members were Vázquez Raña and *El Universal* owner Ealy Ortiz. They were both close to Echeverría, and Vázquez was even rumored to be a distant relative. The two men OEM chose to lead the chain were Echeverría's closest collaborators, his press secretary Fausto Zapata and his secretary of the interior Mario Moya Palencia. Even the U.S. embassy concluded that OEM was probably a front for the president. Expelled *Excélsior* editor Julio Scherer confirmed their view, confessing to a U.S. informant that the company had asked him to work for the *Sol* chain. "I would never do that. I would never work for those people. I'm not a prostitute."[150]

The Survival of Gangster Journalism

The purchase of the *Sol* chain brought to an end García Valseca's dominance of the regional newspaper market. It had lasted three decades. The Puebla press baron had brought industrial newspapers to Mexico's regions, especially in the center and north. He had trained hundreds of journalists, introduced the large-scale use of the *nota roja* to the provinces, and established a reader-ship of professionals, white-collar clerks, shopkeepers, and workers. Whether inadvertently or not he had sided with cross-class social movements, helped popular mayors get elected, and brought down unpopular governors. But he had also spread anticommunist propaganda to the same audience. In doing so, he had helped vaccinate many of the provinces' petit bourgeoisie against radical change. He had also introduced gangster journalism or extortion by newspaper to these same areas. In San Luis Potosí and Chihuahua, the prac-tice generated a distinct cynicism about the printed media. Thanks to García Valseca, few readers in these states believed in the liberal ideal of the public sphere.

In 1982, García Valseca passed away. But his legacy lived on, although not in the places one might expect. A year after OEM took over the magnate's com-pany, a DFS agent was instructed to complete a review of the country's newspa-pers. After going through the publications state by state he finally came to the newspapers of Mexico State, that alternating ring of factories, shantytowns, and farmland that surrounded the capital. He claimed there were 431 publications, or the same quantity as the rest of the country combined. Ciudad Nezahual-cóyotl alone housed 120 newspapers. The recently erected squatter commu-nity was a hive of journalistic community, a Mexican version of England's eighteenth-century Grub Street. Writers from across the social spectrum in-cluding "the teacher, the laborer, the ice cream seller and the pimp" had pur-chased black market press credentials for between 500 and 1,000 pesos each. These writers had set up newspapers and started to use the threat of exposing corruption or vice as an "instrument of extortion." It had become the "modus operandi of hundreds, perhaps thousands of individuals."[151]

Initially, they focused on merchants, brothel owners, and politicians in the surrounding area. But they had also started to use the technique to squeeze money from more highly placed officials. Sánchez García, who joined Gover-nor Hank's press office in the 1970s, was in charge of making monthly pay-ments to Ciudad Nezahualcóyotl's prefab journalists. Echoing the DFS agents, he said, "ninety percent were picadores [people who made up stories] and the rest were pimps, cantina or pulqueria owners or brothel keepers." One of the journalists, called Dr. Bordes (although "he knew about as much about medicine as a frog knows about singing") explained the practice. "If you tells us loads of fibs, but give us no money, we go away annoyed. But if you give us money, you can lie your arse off and we will go away happy."[152]

CHAPTER SEVEN

The Taxi Driver

Civil Society, Journalism, and Oaxaca's El Chapulín

Late in the afternoon on February 15, 1943, the taxi driver and part-time journalist Alfredo Ramírez Villavicencio, aka "El Chapulín" [the Grasshopper], was walking back home through the center of Oaxaca City. A few blocks from his house, a Chevrolet with tinted windows pulled up beside him. The local mayor poked his head out of the window and beckoned him toward the vehicle. As he approached the car, the politician began to harangue the writer and his fellow journalists from the city's weekly satirical magazine *El Momento*. Citing a recent article on the maladministration of the national conscription campaign, the mayor declared they were all "traitors to the country," got out of the car, and started to punch the reporter. Spying the mayor's bodyguard cradling his weapon in the front seat, Ramírez decided the best policy was to flee. He ran straight back to *El Momento*'s offices, where he immediately put together a one-page extra on the confrontation, headlined sarcastically "Democracy Continues, the Mayor of Oaxaca, Champion of Democracy." The revelations sparked a wave of popular support. Hundreds of citizens sent telegrams and letters to the newspaper to declare their backing. A group of young men offered to act as bodyguards for the publication. When Ramírez crossed the playing fields where conscripts were practicing military exercises, they put down their wooden weapons and gave the journalist a spontaneous round of applause. According to the paper, the outpouring demonstrated *El Momento*'s masthead claim that it was "for the people by the people."[1]

So far, this book has examined the rise of Mexico's industrial press—the big, complex national newspapers and provincial chains that came to dominate both circulation figures and contemporary estimations of the Mexican press. I now turn to the country's artisan newspapers, the small, local operations often based around a single printing press where labor specialization was weak and often fewer than half a dozen employees did multiple jobs. In most studies of the Mexican media, commentators ignore these types of publications or dismiss them as intemperate and irrelevant "reform sheets, critical, carping, bitter, crusading organs, with axes to grind and personal grudges to nourish."[2] Yet as I argued in chapter 1, despite the financial ascendancy of the larger operations, increasing literacy, cheap paper, and the emerging market in secondhand presses allowed these types of newspapers to grow and even thrive. By the 1940s even a taxi driver could afford to run his own newspaper. Though their limited personnel, journalistic rhetoric, and production values harked back to the *periódicos de combate* of the nineteenth century, they were not simply relics of a bygone age. In fact, their combination of low running costs and close relations with their readers made them a crucial part of provincial Mexico's independent and confrontational civil society. As Ramírez claimed, they were often "for the people and by the people."

Up to this point, I have only dealt with the relations between Mexican newspapers and civil society in passing. In 1948, a socioeconomic crisis generated bonds between satirical productions and the capital city's crowd before food subsidies, anticommunism, and censorship curtailed these connections. During the late 1960s *Por Qué?* used *nota roja* techniques to create a community of readers. And in the late 1950s García Valseca's practice of gangster journalism occasionally overlapped with the demands of provincial populations. But as I argue in this chapter and the next, links between the press and civil society could be more permanent. In thinly industrialized trading hubs like Oaxaca City, the official party had yet to coopt the merchants, artisans, and household servants, which comprised the majority of the population. Neighborhood networks and unofficial associations remained relatively autonomous and free from state power. For a few decades at least, such voluntary interaction produced high levels of trust and cooperation. Civil society came together to challenge unpopular economic and political policies. During this period, publications like *El Momento* and its successor *El Chapulín* were key to this function of civil society. They not only provided a forum for local citizens to make interpersonal connections, they also offered space for critics to unmask official corruption and develop counterhegemonic discourses. As such they were at the forefront of confrontations with political power. In places like Oaxaca City there was a geographically limited but functioning public sphere, and satirical journalism operated as a relatively effective bridge between civil society and the state.

Civil Society in Oaxaca City

During the postrevolutionary period, particularly in provincial cities, social interaction generated strong links between citizens. Civil society flourished. On the one hand, in these spaces the institutional power of the state was still relatively weak. On the other hand, other areas for interpersonal communication and the forming of alliances thrived. They comprised both informal networks like the *vecindad* and the market and formal associations attached to church, commerce, and charity organizations. They, not the state, often provided housing, services, and health care. Over the years, the official party successfully coopted many of these groups. But such attempts were still in their infancy. During the 1940s and 1950s such groups remained relatively independent of political control.

In the immediate decades following the revolution, Mexico's regional governments struggled to assert their authority. On the most basic level, they were extremely impoverished. Even combined with federal subsidies, such a low income limited state capacity or what Alan Knight has termed "the weight of the state." Throughout Mexico, bureaucracies remained chronically shorthanded.[3] Underfunded and understaffed, state administrations found it extremely difficult to build broad bases of support, especially in less industrialized cities like Oaxaca City. Here, the traditional bulwarks of Mexico's revolutionary governments were limited. Peasant recipients of land grants existed, but only on the outskirts of the community. Supportive unionized workers were equally sparse. Most of the city's inhabitants still labored as artisans, small merchants, and household servants. These groups perceived that they were poorly served by the revolutionary government's policies. Land reform and unionization were blamed for pushing up the prices of consumer goods. Administrative corruption was held accountable for raising taxes, creating commercial monopolies, and damaging the provision of public services. From the mid-1940s, the state would try to coopt these groups into the official party's popular sector, the National Confederation of Popular Organizations (Confederación Nacional de Organizaciones Populares, CNOP). But this was a long, drawn-out, and conflictive process.[4]

If the socioeconomic means of coopting Oaxaca City's inhabitants were limited, so were cultural methods. In the state capital, revolutionary hero cults and secular celebrations failed to make the same impression that they did in other parts of the country or even the state. In the birthplace of Porfirio Díaz, allegiance to the old dictator died hard. Hindsight persuaded many citizens to commemorate the Porfiriato as a period of administrative stability, low prices, and regional power.[5] Over time, state authorities eventually found a means to incorporate the city's inhabitants in the annual celebration of Oaxaca's ethnic groups, the Guelaguetza. But again, the process was protracted, controversial, and costly. One-off celebrations of the state's ethnic diversity in 1933, 1935, and 1941 were not followed up by regular events. The state's intellectuals derided the jerry-built traditions, which stood in for real indigenous culture. As late as the 1960s local consumers still baulked at the price rises generated by the yearly influx of hundreds of rural peasants.[6]

The weakness of the state administration and its struggle to win the support of the capital's inhabitants made for unusually unstable politics, even for postrevolutionary Mexico. But it also offered room for the growth of civil society, relatively free from state interference. Two spaces in particular provided opportunities for the building of informal networks between citizens. The first was the tenement building or *vecindad*. These were complexes of rented single apartments facing onto a central patio. Most were located to the south and the west of the main square around the major markets. Before the 1960s, when settlers started squatting on lands on the edges of the city, most inhabitants, from poor rural immigrants to middle-class teachers and merchants, lived in these types of accommodation. They provided space for the sharing of information and the making of friendships and alliances.[7]

The second network was the market. Oaxaca City had always been the commercial center for the towns and villages that dotted the Central Valleys. But during the 1940s, the proportion of residents involved in commerce doubled from 7 to 15 percent.[8] Most vendors were based in the city's five principal markets. Those who were unable to purchase a spot were forced to make do with selling their wares in the streets outside. In addition to these established shops, every Saturday there was a major market in the main square. As locals from across the social spectrum met in the markets and haggled over the prices of artisan products, agricultural crops, and prepared foods, they also formed social networks. Such networks not only involved interpersonal relationships and commercial understandings, but also the discussion of politics.[9] During the 1952 movement against the governor, one visiting journalist remarked: "The fact that everyone visits the market makes this commercial center the vital nerve of the politics of the state. Here is where all the indigenous people of all the regions of the state know the news and discuss what affects their interests. Any Oaxacan knows that before the governor can govern with the Congress, he must first come to an accord with the plaza or the market."[10]

If the strength of civil society was based on a handful of informal networks, it also rested on a proliferation of nonpolitical associations. Many were connected to the Catholic Church. These lay organizations had a long history, going back to colonial *cofradías* and the expansion of the church's social role in the late nineteenth century.[11] After a brief hiatus during the confrontations of the late 1920s, church leaders once again sought to reach out to a broader social base. By 1938 priests had established branches of Mexican Catholic Action (Acción Católica Mexicana, ACM) in the city's parishes. The organization gradually moved into social work. By the early 1940s they built a workers' center with 2,000 male and 500 female associates. These were impressive numbers. In fact, membership accounted for over a tenth of the city's working inhabitants or a quarter of households and trumped membership of official unions around ten to one.[12]

The church provided the largest space for these nonpolitical associations. But during the 1940s other organizations—often linked to existing networks—also emerged. Some concerned the provision of public services, like the non-affiliated union of electricity consumers or the Resistance League of Users of Water of Oaxaca (Liga de Resistencia de los Usuarios de Agua de Oaxaca, LRUAO).[13] Other independent organizations acted on behalf of particular interest groups. Small merchants were represented by two organizations. The first, the Committee for the Defense of Market Vendors (Comité de Defensa de Expendedores de los Mercados, CDEM), was established in 1944, was linked to the church, and was connected to other public service pressure groups. The second organization, the Union of Market Vendors (Unión de Expendedores de Mercados, UEM), was established by a break-off group of the CDEM and was more secular in outlook. Despite their differences, both associations played similar roles, demanding subscriptions from their members, providing space for debate at weekly meetings, and refusing to ally with any of the state's political parties. On this point, the CDEM leader was particularly firm. He turned down PRI membership repeatedly and frequently refuted accusations that he represented the PAN or the Sinarquistas. "All the governors and people that call themselves revolutionaries are bandits and I have the backing of the Oaxaca people," he told one U.S. anthropologist.[14]

Without a doubt, there were government attempts to coopt some of these civil organizations. But most efforts were ad hoc, costly, and unpopular. For example, in early 1945 Governor Sánchez Cano made a handful of civil leaders part of his own municipal development team. Within six months, they had all left, claiming the governor had little interest in constructive dialogue.[15] Between 1947 and 1950 Governor Vasconcelos went even further, lowering commercial taxes, spending lavishly on reconstructing the markets, building schools for vendors' children, and even allowing one of the most difficult stallholders, Dolores "La Diabla" González, to lead the city's annual celebrations. By 1949 the majority of the UEM had joined the popular sector of the PRI. But the alliance was limited and short-lived. The CDEM, which claimed at least twice as many members, refused to make any alliance with the government. The following year even the UEM voted to separate from the PRI and retain its autonomy.[16]

The Press in Oaxaca City

If *El Momento*'s role relied on the publication's intense interaction with civil society, it also depended on both the city's journalistic traditions and the contemporary shape of the public sphere. Though Oaxaca City was the third municipality in New Spain to begin printing its own publication, the state as a whole was never a center of the publishing business. For the nineteenth century and a large proportion of the twentieth, the majority of the population consisted of monolingual speakers of indigenous languages. During the final years of the Porfiriato, the literacy rate edged up from 7 to 9 percent of the population. But the state was still one of the most illiterate regions of Mexico, second only behind Chiapas. Despite these difficulties, the state still sustained a relatively strong, critical newspaper industry. In the capital city the concentration of secular and church schools and the growth of the state university boosted literacy rates far above the state average. By the end of the Porfiriato, the rate was around 53 percent of adults; and by 1950, it had risen to nearly 80 percent. Such high rates encouraged the production of numerous papers. Between 1813 and 1953, the state produced 463 titles. By the end of the dictatorship there were over a dozen print shops in the city. In 1907, there were thirteen weekly, bimonthly, and monthly newspapers in circulation.[17]

Many publications were printed by the government or publishers close to the administration. They included official or semiofficial papers like *El Eco Mercantil* (1891), *Oaxaca Progresista* (1910), and *Oaxaca Moderno* (1911), the pro-reelection newspaper *Voto Público*, and the English-language *Oaxaca Herald*. They were aimed exclusively at the political and economic elite and were unapologetically supportive of the status quo. But beyond these *oficialista* organs, Oaxaca also had a tradition of independent opposition newspapers that arrived in two waves. During the early years of the Porfiriato, as in many regions of the country, local journalists maintained the tradition of the Restored Republic's *periódicos de combate*. In papers like *El Cometa* (1878) and *El Amigo del Pueblo* (1879) they continued to write argumentative and antagonistic pieces that critiqued those in power. The second wave coincided with the rise of radical liberal opposition to Porfirio Díaz's reelection during the first decade of the twentieth century. Publications included *El Bien Público* (1905) and *La Voz de Justicia* (1907).[18] Many of these critical newspapers were heavily satirical. Invective and ridicule not only skewered political elites but also helped to expand the reading audience beyond the university-educated upper classes. Such efforts began the custom of popular, humorous political publications, which would culminate with *El Momento* over half a century later.[19]

After the revolution, the literate public grew. By 1954 the state had eighteen publications, including five dailies and six weeklies. Compared to predominantly urban states, this was not many. But the basic figures tell only part of the story. Oaxaca may have suffered a scarcity of cultural, entertainment, or religious publications, but it had more news publications than two-thirds of the states. The penetration of newspapers in the state capital was relatively high. The city's publications were still cheap, between 20¢ and 30¢. According to both stated sales and insider government reports, by the 1960s the circulation of the city's newspapers totaled 25,500 or about twice the number of urban households. The forms of the city's newspapers, however, changed relatively little. In fact, the structure of Oaxaca's postrevolutionary press suggests the high degree to which local traditions, rather than technological innovations, business shifts, or national processes, shaped local public spheres. As in the Porfiriato, non-news publications were sparse or fleeting. What was the use of an entertainment weekly when there were only two cinemas and one radio station?[20] And large chains avoided the state. (In 1950, a Michoacán entrepreneur, Juan Abarca Pérez, tried to enter the market by establishing the daily *Nuevo Diario*. As we shall see, readers violently rejected the effort.)

Instead, as during the dictatorship, progovernment broadsheets, which imitated the style if not the circulation of Mexico City's industrial papers, dominated the local market. Some were entirely official and attached to particular governors. These employed state bureaucrats as writers, ran minimal or no ads, and were printed on the state government printing press. They were predominantly aimed at the state's bureaucrats and had few readers outside these offices. This local variation on the template of the party newspaper *El Nacional* was a relatively original Oaxaca custom, only occasionally practiced in other states. Examples included Manuel García Vigil's *La Patria* during the 1920s, *Oaxaca Nuevo* under Constantino Chapital (1936–40), *Antequera* under Vicente González Fernández (1940–44), *La Voz de Oaxaca* under Edmundo Sánchez Cano (1945–47), *Provincia* under Eduardo Vasconcelos, and *La Prensa* during the 1960s. Others were privately owned but relied heavily on state backing. They included Marcelino E. Muciño's *El Mercurio*, which ran between 1920 and 1932, local intellectual Mateo Solano's short-lived *El Globo*, and Eduardo Pimentel's *Oaxaca Gráfico*, which was founded in 1953 and continued the custom of elite focus and government support.[21]

But not all postrevolutionary newspapers were progovernment. In fact, it seems the unconcealed nature of the official newspapers also generated a complementary market in critical newspapers. Many readers still demanded press autonomy, and the tradition of publishing independent publications remained. Some were serious critical newspapers. Between 1947 and 1950 Governor Vasconcelos made a concerted effort to encourage the establishment of more local papers. According to his supporters he ended the practice of "putting a black flag over all the newspapers that were outside the camarilla," shared official advertising revenue around multiple publications, and encouraged debate in the printed press. In just three years, such support led to the founding of at least half a dozen dailies and weeklies. They included ephemeral cultural publications, newspapers connected to opposition parties like the PP-backed *La Opinion*, and regular information papers like *La Tribuna del Sur* and *Oaxaca Popular*.[22] The campaign culminated with the establishment of *El Imparcial* a year after Vasconcelos stepped down in 1951. Like many of the best regional dailies, *El Imparcial* was owned and run by one family. A rich Guanajuato widow, María de los Angeles Pichardo García, arranged the financial backing; her eldest brother, Manuel Pichardo, acted as editor; and her three other print worker brothers provided the technical expertise and much of the content.[23] The newspaper gained substantial initial readership by providing supportive daily coverage of the 1952 movement to unseat the governor. But even after the governor was removed, the paper maintained a critical stance toward local politics. Exposés of corruption and violence were commonplace. Editorials often strongly critiqued governors, local congressmen, and rural *caciques*.[24] Such autonomy also appealed to the reading public. In 1962, the newspaper claimed a circulation of 8,500 copies or over three-quarters of the city's households. Even a visiting U.S. pressman admitted the paper was popular, and state security officials claimed it was "well accepted among the public."[25]

Other independent postrevolutionary newspapers, like *El Momento*, mixed humor and politics. In Oaxaca, the tradition of the nineteenth-century satirical press lived on. Many of these publications were short-lived. They included the 1927 newspaper *El Brujo*, dedicated to "information, combat, and comedy," and the 1929 caricature magazine *El Ciclón*.[26] In fact, some were deliberately ephemeral, like the flurry of *calavera* flysheets published to coincide with the Day of the Dead. These were two- or four-page collections of short verses accompanied by small cartoons. The custom went back to the dictatorship, and the publications formed acceptable, transient spaces for local poets to critique and mock political and commercial elites. National newspapers had ejected the practice long ago, but they still existed in the provinces where they acted as "an escape valve, on the pretext of the dead to shoot down well-known people above all politicians and the heads of businesses."[27] In fact, Ramírez and his fellow *El Momento* journalists, Alfonso Saavedra and Guillermo Villa Castañeda, cut their teeth as *calavera* writers. But other humorous papers survived for years and demonstrated the continuing appeal of political satire. They included Ernesto Hernández's 1930s newspaper *El Argumentado*, which contained biting criticism of both secular and ecclesiastical leaders and was often printed in Mexico City to avoid state censors.[28] They also included Manuel Llaguno's *El Zancudo*, which ran regular weekly issues between 1922 and 1929. Like the earlier satirical newspapers, *El Zancudo* used humor to draw in an audience beyond the educated elites and claimed on its masthead to be "the defender of the humble people." Like *El Momento*, the paper mixed stories of government corruption with satirical songs and parodies. And like *El Momento*, the publication sought to bridge the divide between print criticism and street protest; it even published collections of offensive rhymes to accompany the annual Easter Judas burnings.[29]

El Chapulín: Oaxaca's Satirical Weekly

On May 8, 1937, the print worker Guillermo Aguilar Varela published the first issue of the satirical weekly *El Momento*. Over the next thirty years, the newspaper went through various guises, was forcibly closed down on at least two occasions, and changed its name three times. However, the staff remained constant. The same half dozen part-time journalists provided copy for the newspaper until its eventual closure in 1969. During the period, they built on nineteenth-century journalistic traditions, placing considerable stress on their own honor. But they now linked this value code to the new postrevolutionary era of civic politics. Honorable journalism not only signified telling the truth, it also meant supporting the demands of the masses. They did this in a variety of ways: They developed a range of methods to expose official corruption, which carefully trod the line between acceptable coverage of public maladministration and unacceptable reporting of private misdeeds or *libertinaje*. They used a variety of parodical forms to mock the revolution's redistributive and democratic pretentions. They opened up the pages of the newspaper to the city's inhabitants. For at least two decades, letters to the newspaper became the key avenue for citizens to communicate with each other and with the government. Finally, the newspaper supported the city's civic associations and linked discursive demands to street protests.

Piecing together the publishing history of Mexico's artisan newspapers is no easy business. Many were printed on cheap, disposable paper, were rarely registered with the federal post office, only circulated in a particular town or city, and were only irregularly sent to the national newspaper library in Mexico City. Fortunately, there are more copies of *El Momento/El Chapulín* than most.[30] Together the issues reflect the newspaper's occasionally fraught relationship with the local authorities. *El Momento* hit the city's newsstands in 1937. At first, it was a relatively standard independent paper that mixed local and national news. Ramírez was limited to writing a gossipy political column under his pen name *El Chapulín*. Within two years, Ramírez had run into trouble and the newspaper was closed down. In 1940, however, it reappeared, this time using Ramírez's pen name as its title. *El Chapulín* ran for another year before switching back to its original moniker, *El Momento*. Between late 1940 and 1947 the newspaper modified its form, ditched the orthodox news, focused on gossip, satire, and campaigning, and put out weekly issues uninterrupted. But during a 1947 social movement, *El Momento* was closed down again. When it resurfaced in March 1947 the paper had changed its name back to *El Chapulín*. For the next twenty-two years, the publication would keep the nickname of its foremost journalist as its title. The state authorities, however, still had one disruptive strategy left. In 1948, they published a rival version of *El Chapulín*, confusingly called *El Momento*. The newspaper used the same poor quality paper, the same type, and the same jokey language but removed all criticism of the administration. It was designed to hijack and confuse the real newspaper's readers and disappeared after only six months.

Despite the publication's shifting nomenclature, the newspaper's staff remained relatively constant throughout its existence. They came from diverse backgrounds and pursued varied jobs. Despite these differences, they shared a sense of humor, a critical appreciation of the ruling party, and a set of journalistic values. Together, they also revealed how the revolution democratized the practice of journalism, especially in the country's provincial cities. At the center of the gang was Alfredo Ramírez Villavicencio. For a journalist who remained in the city's spotlight for over three decades, we know remarkably little about him. He was probably born in Oaxaca City in 1901, the son of Ezequiel Ramírez and Juana Villavicencio. It is possible his father was head of the city's police force (which might explain Ramírez's later links to the city's legal fraternity).[31] In a rare interview, Ramírez explained that he only attended primary school before joining the military forces of General Rafael Eguía Lis. After the revolution, he lived a peripatetic existence, working as a miner, an electrician, and a railway worker before returning to Oaxaca City in the late

1920s. By this time, both his parents were dead and he used his inheritance to purchase a car and set himself up as the city's first taxi driver.[32] Though he gained fame as a journalist, he continued to practice the job well into his sixties. The trainee print worker Gabriel Quintas remembers that he used to proudly display his taxi license, which was marked with the numbers oo1.[33] While he established his business, Ramírez also moved into the household of the local lawyer and university professor Alfredo Castillo. As Ramírez never married or had children, the Castillo residence would form his permanent home. He would remain there for the next thirty years, paying his way by also working as the lawyer's private chauffeur.[34]

Unlike many journalists, Ramírez had no family connection to the publishing industry. He had a limited education. Though his patron Castillo was a well-known lawyer, he was not a public writer. Instead Ramírez seems to have broken into the business simply through his comedic skills. All the biographical references portrayed him as a "vernacular poet" and "genuinely popular writer" with an ear for "the speech of the street" and a talent for "clever, lively and colorful language."[35] Contemporary memories back this up. Quintas and journalist Néstor Sánchez's son both describe him as "extraordinarily funny" with a memory for "hundreds of jokes."[36] Dozens of market vendors remember him touring their stalls, bending over with laughter as he exchanged gossip and gags with shoppers and sellers. During the mid-1930s Ramírez started to display these talents by writing a series of scandalous and funny *calavera* poems, which he would hand out around the *zócalo* on the Day of the Dead. His poem to the skirt-chasing head of the local hospital, Dr. Landero, for example, went as follows:

La muerte de este pelón	The death of this baldy
Fue cuestión de pocas horas	Was a question of a few hours
Y al agonizar decía	And in his agony he said
Ahora si quedaron viudas	That now were widows
Todas las enfermeras	All the nurses[37]

At 10¢ a copy, single *calavera* flysheets could sell thousands, and such efforts gained Ramírez a reputation. In 1937, Guillermo Aguilar Varela, the director of the city's new independent newspaper *El Momento*, invited the amateur poet to contribute a regular column. Anticipating what would become his trademark style, the column entitled "What El Chapulín Saw" mixed scurrilous gossip with political satire. It soon became the centerpiece of the publication.[38]

El Momento's other contributors were also nonprofessionals. Aguilar was a print worker by training. He contributed occasional editorials to the newspaper, but focused on the technical and financial aspects of the production. He would eventually leave *El Chapulín* for *El Imparcial* in the early 1950s.[39] The other principal writer was Guillermo Villa Castañeda. Villa was born in 1910, the son of a military officer from Durango and a Oaxaca woman from a well-known local family. Unlike the other members of the gang, Villa received an upper-class education at the local Catholic school and he remained close to the city's elites throughout his life. His uncle, Luis Castañeda Guzmán, would become rector of the university and head of the local branch of the PAN. During the 1930s Villa became a rural teacher in the predominantly Mixtec villages to the northwest of the city around Tlaxiaco. Here he developed a lifelong loathing for the radical grandstanding and petty corruption of the teachers union. In 1941, he first contacted *El Momento* through the letters page to complain about "communist" teachers in the area monopolizing the good positions. Over the next decade, his articles became regular features. During the 1940s he adopted the pen name Bradomín, after the hero of radical Spanish writer Ramón del Valle-Inclán's *Sonata* series. He used his itinerant teaching job to become *El Momento*'s roving reporter, filing pieces on political repression and economic exploitation from around the state. During the 1950s his reporting eventually got him sacked from his teaching job and he returned to the city, where he now wrote a regular editorial entitled "A Finger in the Wound." The pieces were less humorous than Ramírez's work, but they were no less strong. Thoughtful, well-informed, and surprisingly unpartisan, they were often republished in right-wing national newspapers like *La Nación*.[40]

Three other writers made up the rest of *El Momento*'s gang. The first was the railway worker Alfonso Saavedra Cruz. Like Ramírez, Saavedra was a working-class autodidact with a talent for comedic verse. Under his pen name Fray Tijeras [literally Friar Scissors] he would contribute songs, poems, and his annual *calaveras* to the newspaper. The second was Enrique Mijangos Soriano. Mijangos, like Villa, came from a pretty wealthy family, but from outside the capital in the Oaxaca Valley town of Ocotlán. During the 1930s he made his money as an industrialist before moving to the capital city. Once in Oaxaca City, he tried his hand at politics and poetry before becoming news editor of *El Chapulín* in 1948. Finally, there was Augusto García Moguel, a nostalgic Oaxaca customs official stuck out in the Mexico-Guatemala border town of Tapachula. Like Villa, he joined the gang after sending in a series of outraged correspondence to the newspaper.[41]

Though *El Momento*'s writers came from diverse backgrounds, they all shared a similar appreciation of the role of a provincial journalist. Central to this value system was personal honor. This was a legacy of the era of *periódi-*

cos de combate. As Piccato argues, during the nineteenth century a journalist's honor validated his right to represent public opinion and, if necessary, challenge the honor of other men. As such, it became the "social currency" of public debate. Though financial concerns gradually eroded such assessments during the postrevolutionary period, the importance of honor lived on, especially in the underfinanced provincial press. Here honor and business were not antithetical and journalists could still "exploit their reputation as part of their social capital."[42] For *El Momento*'s journalists, a sense of honor drove their work and, in their eyes at least, legitimized their reputation among the reading public. In a 1954 editorial, Ramírez argued that it was not his intellect or his knowledge that made him a popular journalist, but rather his "solvencia moral," or trustworthiness. This allowed him to deal with "anomalies in the conduct of private citizens" not through "compadrazgo, financial exchanges, or in the heat of the moment" but with "a rectitude of judgment." Villa's 1943 poem "The Journalist" played with similar ideas. The work, dedicated to Ramírez, argued that good reporters had a "generous, elevated, and noble" mission, "never got down on their knees . . . nor sold out nor humiliated themselves," "preferred dying at the hands of a hit man than the shame of cowardly silence," and possessed the "same combative and valiant spirit" as a soldier.[43]

Harking back to nineteenth-century values had some worth, especially in Oaxaca's nostalgic literary scene. But what made *El Momento* so interesting, and I would argue so popular and enduring, was the way Ramírez and the other writers mixed traditional conceptions of honor with revolutionary-era ideas about wealth and social standing. Unlike traditional *periódicos de combate* writers, *El Momento*'s journalists linked honor to class, specifically working-class identity. In his mock annual reports, Ramírez always addressed his "fellow proletarians and brother workers." Villa described Ramírez as possessing "the heart of Don Quixote and the pen of a worker."[44] In fact, *El Momento*'s writers claimed it was the conservation of this working-class identity that underpinned the quality of their journalism. In another passage, Villa argued that Ramírez and the director Varela "had not forgotten their class, the class that they have insisted on defending unlike others that having risen up and forgotten that they come from the pueblo." It was also this sharp, often chippy pride in their class identity that prevented them from taking money from politicians or other elites. For Ramírez, poverty was synonymous with honesty: "While other journalists have got rich, we have preferred to stay poor rather than sell our consciences." Such an attitude even shaped Ramírez's public persona. When he wandered the markets and taverns of Oaxaca City, he always wore the same laborers' overalls.[45] As he explained in a rare interview, they both dovetailed with his identity and visibly demonstrated he was not on the take. "I don't need money, look at my workers' outfit; if I needed it I would have dressed like one of those new dandies of the Revolution."[46]

If honor, a working-class identity, and penury defined *El Momento*'s ideas on good journalism, the lack of these values marked what they deemed poor reporting. Bad journalists—a category that *El Momento*'s writers extended to most other Oaxaca writers—were ignoble, ambitious, and exchanged money for "blowing incense on anyone who throws them scraps" and deforming "the truth of things before the eyes of the people."[47] The epitome of these bad journalists was the *lambiscón*. The term was a postrevolutionary neologism, drawn from the verb *lamer*, to lick. No one knows the exact origin of the term. Novo speculated that it was first used to describe the young boys who helped out Mexico City's bus drivers in exchange for paltry tips.[48] But whatever the source, by the 1940s it had shifted to the political sphere and was widely used to describe journalists and political hangers-on, who lauded politicians in exchange for cash. As such, it could be translated as "bootlicker" or the even stronger "arselicker." For *El Momento*'s journalists, the *lambiscón* of the state-backed industrial press embodied all the contrary values to their poorly put-together but independent artisan efforts. As Villa explained, *lambiscones* were a step down even from previous press sell-outs. They, at least, had "some sense of shame, some honor." The *lambiscón* had none: "To make money in the current atmosphere he has to be even more servile."[49] Ramírez's poem "Los Lambiscones" was even more direct, connecting the *lambiscón*'s lack of honor to his lack of manliness. (Even for the most awkward, critical journalists, the public sphere was still a resolutely male space.)

Lastima me causan estas pobres gentes	These poor people cause me hurt
Quienes de los hombres son muy diferentes	They are very different from men
Ni siquiera pueden presumir de honrados	You can't presume they're honorable
Y amoralmente se encuentran castrados	They're amoral and castrated[50]

Ramírez's refusal to accept any form of official payment not only shaped the contents, but also the production and form of the newspaper. The publication's expenses were minimal. As journalism was considered a civic duty rather than a profession, none of the writers took a salary. The sole wages went to the print maker, Varela, and a single young apprentice. Varela owned the printing press, and when he stepped down Ramírez got a cheap rate at local journalist Eduardo Pimentel's workshop. Occasionally paper came from

PIPSA, but often *El Momento*'s writers had to make do with printing on sub-standard paper not designed for newspapers. To cover these limited costs, revenue came from two sources—private publicity and sales. Ads came mostly from local businesses, which were charged between 2 and 25 pesos for adver-tising in the newspaper. During the 1940s the paper held around forty to fifty advertisements per issue. Together they probably brought in around 500 pe-sos per week. As such they made up between a third and half the income. Most were standard, graphic-free commercials, which simply listed the name of the commercial establishment, the type of wares, and the address. But *El Chapulín*'s writers also offered a deluxe publicity service, where they slotted the name of products into humorous verse. Business and satire aligned. The local Corona beer merchant, in particular, was a big fan of these productions. As competition warmed up for the 1950 gubernatorial elections, *El Chapulín* played on the tendency to buy votes by giving out free booze. "To Darío L. Vas-concelos / It has come to mind / That to arrive at the governorship / Corona is the beer / That he should hand round."[51]

The other source of income was sales. These are more difficult to quantify. The price of *El Momento* rose steadily throughout its first fifteen years from a paltry 5¢ in 1937 to 10¢ in 1944, 20¢ in 1948, and 30¢ in 1952. According to Quin-tas, average sales by 1952 were around 2,500 copies once a week or a quarter of Oaxaca City households. But they peaked at 5,000 during the 1952 movement to unseat the governor, when they ran one issue every two days. They also went up to 5,000 for the special *cavalera* issue on November 2 each year. Such sales probably produced a weekly income of 750 pesos by the 1950s. Circula-tion figures, however, only tell us something about the paper's reach. Quintas speculates that as many as ten people read each issue of the newspaper. In the *vecindades*, neighbors read particularly scandalous or funny articles to each other. Many inhabitants went to the university and listened to students dis-claim the latest reports.[52] The food stalls of the markets always had a copy of *El Momento* by the side of the dining area.[53]

The contents of *El Momento* changed over time. The early issues aped most regional newspapers and contained at least a few articles on national news. But by the early 1940s such pretensions had disappeared. The newspaper now embraced an intense insularity. Mentions of the president, for example, were reduced to one fairly offensive poem every *calavera* issue. Beyond a hand-ful of Villa's roving reports, almost all news happened within a thirty-mile ra-dius of the *zócalo*. Even the ads were designed to appeal to a small in-the-know group. They often held no address or assumed the reader already knew the proprietor. ("Seller of fine liquors. Beers of all types. Come and talk to Fortino

Rojas today.")[54] This was editorial *campanilismo*.[55] This was journalism as an expression of the Rousseauian city-state, an imagined but not entirely fictitious version of the state capital where "all the private individuals knew all the citizens" and could "decide as one body on the recommendations of their leaders about the most important public matters."[56]

In the pages of *El Momento*, such journalism took four forms. First, there was basic local gossip. This was published on the front page and took the form of unreconstructed rumors overheard by Ramírez and his team. Much involved the everyday concerns of the city's civil society. Themes included unrepaired potholes, poor sewage, overpriced health care, irregular running water, and noisy cantinas. But other news exposed acts of individual corruption. Targets comprised swindling tax collectors, police connected to the vice trade, monopolistic merchants, and bribe-happy bureaucrats. In these cases, *El Momento*'s journalists used the paper's limited focus to their advantage. To escape charges of slander or *libertinaje* they avoided the direct naming of functionaries. Instead they revealed the officials' identities by inviting readers to partake in a jokey game of *Guess Who?* At times, nicknames sufficed. The 1950s local major, who was a well-known protector of the city's brothels, was called "Burruchurtu," a play on "burro" [donkey] and the name of the Mexico City mayor, Ernesto Uruchurtu. Other times, the hints were more opaque. An overcharging merchant was described as "a man with a citric name." Was this Austreberto Aragón also known by his rhyming nickname "La Paleta Limón" [The lime popsicle]? Together the adverts, the gossip, and the playful games, with their expectations of prior knowledge, not only drew consumers into a community of readers but also provided a kind of print version of an excursion through the city center, replete with tittle-tattle, commerce, and jokes.[57]

Second, *El Momento* also published longer satirical pieces. Like *Presente*'s faux society news, most came in the form of parodies. Sometimes these were of obvious religious forms like the creed or the litany or common political discourses like the annual gubernatorial report. Other times they replicated newfangled press styles like the entertainment column, the popular survey, or the dream analysis. Their subjects could be individuals. Mock movie synopses often placed local elites in the position of characters in thinly veiled versions of well-known films. The Three Singletons (a play on *Los Tres Garcías*) named three Oaxaca womanizers in the main roles; for the horror flick *Demons at the Wheel* he suggested the head of the bus driver union as the main protagonist.[58] But most of the time, Ramírez focused on the hypocrisy of the revolutionary regime. He mocked the space between the revolution's ideals and contemporary reality. His 1944 state of the union address extolled the virtues of judges "who save us money by letting criminals go free," closed-down schools "which allow teachers more time for politics," and high taxes "which allow our bureaucrats to construct magnificent palaces."[59] The "revolutionary corrido," "The Synthetic Zapatistas," compared Zapata's cries of Land and Freedom with the 1950s political pressure organization, the Frente Zapatista. "Without knowing who was Zapata / Many opportunists / Criminals and thieves / Today come together / Calling themselves Zapatistas."[60] But perhaps the clearest example of this kind of critique came as part of his periodic dream conversations with the martyred revolutionary leader Francisco Madero. In these exchanges, Madero asked about the fate of his political ideals.

MADERO: What of democracy? Is it possible a journalist knows nothing of democracy?

RAMÍREZ: I know what the word democracy means, but its essence I don't know, that is to say, I don't know of its existence, like most Mexicans. We are now governed by the PRI, an official party.

MADERO: How is it governed by a party or a faction and not by institutions and the election of the people? I didn't realize that the blood spilt by the Revolution was so useless. I thought one of the aims of the Revolution was to rid us of the cientificos.

RAMÍREZ: Well one difference is that at least some of the cientificos were honest and responsible. The majority of positions are now held by pure sons of . . . the PRI. "Effective suffrage" only exists as a dictum on official documents.[61]

Third, *El Momento* provided a forum for civil society. In fact, such popular interaction formed the basis for the newspaper's claims to represent the public. Some of the paper's methods were quite original. The newspaper ran a survey of readers' political opinions. Many of the questions were written in a sarcastic style, which revealed the writers' opinions on the various subjects. "Which of our governors has revealed himself most revolutionary by becoming a multimillionaire fastest?" But others were more open and illuminating. "Which of our merchants is the most avaricious and tightfisted and most worthy of the title exploiter of the people?" To publicize the results, Ramírez would plaster the summaries over the front doors of the major commercial emporiums the following week. The survey not only provided a snapshot of public opinion, but also played a regulatory role by admonishing the most unpopular elites.[62] But the centerpiece of *El Momento*'s reader interaction was the letters page. The section was entitled "La Tribuna Pública," or public forum. For thirty years it provided space for the demands and complaints official publications refused to publish. Often they came from the most disenfranchised members of society. In November 1949 the newspaper circulated a series of grievances from the city's prisoners. They trashed the state's claims to having cleaned up the jail and accused the prison teacher of shaking down the convicts for cash.[63]

Finally, *El Momento* also formed the mouthpiece for the city's civil associations. Some of these campaigns were semipermanent. Positive coverage of the inner workings of the UEM and CDEM was commonplace. The official letters of both organizations were frequently republished in the "La Tribuna Pública" section. Rarely a week went by without *El Momento*'s journalists criticizing the bane of both groups—the unpopular commercial tax, the *alcabala*.[64] Such relentless coverage not only reflected the paper's popularity among market vendors, but also the source of much of its advertising revenue. The newspaper also published a list of donors and the accounts of the Red Cross on a monthly basis.[65] But other campaigns were more improvised and reflected the sudden coming together of civil society over particular problems. In 1943 and 1944, for example, the newspaper provided a forum for the city's water protestors, the LRUAO. At first, the paper simply covered the formation of the organization and republished its demands. Ramírez played the role of investigative reporter, verifying claims of leaking sewage, unfinished infrastructure, and the unequal distribution of water. But from March 1944 onward *El Momento* threw its weight behind a general payment strike to dispute the introduction of water meters. The publication now came out twice a week and published repeated extras. Here Ramírez republished the protestors' complaints, denied official accusations of Sinarquista backing, and offered up-to-date coverage of the confrontations between strikers and the state police. The campaign, like many of *El Momento*'s confrontations with the state, was successful. In May 1944 the state government scrapped the plan for water meters and lowered the price of water.[66]

El Momento's gossipy exposés, strong language, and firm links to combative social movements generated official disapproval. Attempts to censor the newspaper were frequent. At least four governors offered Ramírez large amounts of cash in exchange for his silence. Governor Pérez Gasga even tried to give him the titles to over a thousand square meters of prime urban real estate. As money failed, officials often turned to coercion. Sometimes these efforts were cloaked in legality. In 1939, Governor Chapital tried to change the state's version of the press law in order to prosecute the journalist. Thirteen years later, Governor Heredia Mayoral accused Ramírez of starting a riot and tried to jail him for sedition. But most endeavors were the usual blend of threats and nonfatal violence. In 1943, 1947, and 1952 officials or their bodyguards tried to beat up Ramírez. On at least four occasions, the journalist was bundled onto a train and told to go to Mexico City and never come back. In 1959, hit men made a failed attempt on Villa's life as he strolled through the city.[67]

El Chapulín versus the Governors

Ramírez's talent for representing the demands of civil society, even in the face of official censorship, was never clearer than during the confrontations with Oaxaca's governors in 1947 and 1952. On both occasions, his newspaper highlighted growing dissatisfaction with the governors, provided a forum for civil society to express its demands, and supported citywide protests. But the conflicts of 1947 and 1952 also underscore another relationship between provincial civil society and the press. During both movements, protestors not only cooperated with journalists like Ramírez to make their voices heard, but also combatted what they saw as unsupportive or progovernment papers. At times of high political tension, strategies moved from passive resistance (like not buying the papers) to active aggression. In 1947 and 1952, crowds used force to close down the progovernor papers. In 1947, they even took over the official press and started their own publication. Together the struggles suggest that mid-century political conflicts not only concerned citizens' political preferences and economic demands, but also the nature of provincial journalism. Or to put it another way, such conflicts not only happened in but were also fought over the shape of the public sphere.

The movements to oust Oaxaca's governors ran from January 6–18, 1947, and from March 20 to June 24, 1952. The first focused on the administration of Edmundo Sánchez Cano; the second on the administration of Manuel Mayoral Heredia. They had much in common. Both were undergirded by long-standing grievances about taxes and services and were sparked by the impositions of new tax laws designed to increase state revenue. They both became more formal challenges to the governors after gunmen shot and murdered demonstrators. The composition of the movements was also extremely similar. The bulk of the protestors came from the civil society networks and associations established during the late 1930s and 1940s. On both occasions they included the market organizations and the water and electricity protestors. These formed the bulk of the protestors, grouped together into the Oaxaca Civic Committee (Comité Cívica Oaxaqueña, CCO). Furthermore, the popular leaders, who played key roles in linking the elites to the urban masses, also came directly from these organizations. In 1947 they included the ACM head Austreberto Aragón and the CDEM leader Dolores "La Diabla" González. Five years later, Aragón was run out of town by government thugs. But new leaders from the same groups took their place. They included Aragón's wife, the grocer María "La China" Sánchez, his son Hermenegildo, and the new CDEM chief, Genoveva Medina.[68]

Ramírez's satirical weekly proved crucial to both movements. In 1947, the newspaper's principal function was to lay the groundwork for the eventual protests. In fact, by January 1947 Sánchez Cano judged the paper so pernicious he ordered thugs to bust up the press, threatened the journalists with execution, and put Ramírez on a train to Mexico City. Though Ramírez waited out the protests by hiding in the capital, when he restarted the newspaper under his pen name *El Chapulín* in March 1947, letters and telegrams of congratulations all acknowledged his role in the successful ousting. As he put it in a rare self-congratulatory editorial, "I started the fight against monopolies, alcabalas, and nepotism, I started the fight for Oaxaca to have a worthy government."[69]

His role in the run-up to the movement was essentially twofold. On the one hand, the newspaper provided space for the city's diverse associations to present their grievances and solidify their links. These alliances would eventually form the basis of the CCO. Between mid-1945 and the end of 1946, the paper published the official letters and committee minutes of the electricity and water protestors and both market organizations. The newspaper highlighted their shared causes and common enemies. In late October 1945 the paper celebrated the coming together of the more elite electricity consumers with the more radical water protestors in a series of payment strikes. Eight months later he also applauded the series of joint statements by the two market unions, which up to this point had been firm rivals. On the other hand, Ramírez's writings provided both the underlying complaints and the narrative framework for the January 1947 movement. Front page exposés highlighted particularly rapacious tax collectors, pinpointed rises in the popular *alcabala* tax, presented small-scale investigations into the poor administration of services, and humiliated members of the Sánchez Cano family and administration as drunks, womanizers, and incompetents. Such tales would provide both the meat of January 1947's complaints and the scurrilous rumors contained in flysheets and corridos.[70]

At the same time, Ramírez's editorials started to bring together these diverse stories into a coherent narrative of administrative failure. Like many Oaxaca citizens, his attitude to Sánchez Cano changed over time. During the first six months of the governor's rule, *El Momento* offered relatively balanced coverage of the administration. But by late 1945 the newspaper turned against the governor. Editorials now started to present Sánchez Cano as nepotistic, ineffectual, and authoritarian. Some of the pieces were satirical. In one paper he asked jokingly whether the local tax collectors had thought of charging the cinema, which was showing a film about animals, for bringing livestock into the city.[71] But others were more serious. On March 30, 1946, Ramírez published a front page simply headlined "S.O.S." It was deliberately aimed to get the attention of the visiting president, Manuel Avila Camacho. In a series of short, sharp paragraphs, Ramírez put forward the full range of public demands for "light and water," "the repression of cacicazgos," "the cutting of alcabalas, which oppress the city's humble merchants," and "an end to monopolies ... which enrich the few at the expense of the hunger of the many." The piece ended with the simple statement that Sánchez Cano was "the worst governor Oaxaca ha[d] ever suffered."[72]

Five years later, Ramírez and his fellow journalists were even more involved. As in 1947, the paper's steady drip-drip of political stories on poor services, illegal taxes, municipal maladministration, and increasingly (and for a change) the protection of the vice industry and judicial corruption, provided the official complaints and the gossipy subtext of the eventual movement. As in 1947, alarmist editorials drew together complaints into a coherent pattern of gubernatorial incompetence.[73] In January 1952 the paper ran a revised version of the S.O.S page, this time addressed to presidential candidate Ruiz Cortines. Mayoral Heredia was a "worse governor than Sánchez Cano" and his collaborators were "some of Mexico's most corrupt men."[74]

But this time *El Chapulín* went even further. In fact, it was Ramírez's relentless coverage of Mayoral Heredia's attempts to impose a new tax code, which eventually sparked the actual protests. The insinuations started early. On December 20, 1951, the newspaper published the government budget for 1952. It totaled 17 million pesos, a rise of 6.5 million pesos over the preceding year. Ramírez demanded to know how the government planned to raise the extra funds. Less than a week later, the local legislature passed a new fiscal code but refused to publish the exact details. The move incensed Ramírez, who claimed that the governor was trying to levy extra taxes on the sly. Over the next three months, he ran a series of articles on the supposed contents of the code. Some pieces were relatively serious and based on leaks, presumably from sympathetic congressmen. But other pieces were heavily satirical and designed to portray the administration as both rapacious and ridiculous. In one editorial he claimed that Mayoral Heredia would now charge the owners of dogs and radios a hundred pesos a year. The mix of fact and alarmist fiction was effective. By the time Mayoral Heredia published the decrees on March 20, most citizens were firmly against the code. They took to the streets and prevented the more pliant elite merchants from negotiating a revised version. As Ramírez rather bluntly put it, the code was "born dead."[75]

El Chapulín's close involvement at the start of the 1952 movement brought the usual reprisals. On March 20 Mayoral Heredia sent a hit man to accost the journalist. He walked up to Ramírez, shoved a gun under his ribs, forced him into a waiting car, and drove him to the state palace where Mayoral Heredia threatened to kill him unless he stopped his unfavorable coverage. Ramírez bluntly refused, returned to the newspaper offices, and revealed the encounter in a hastily compiled extra. According to Ramírez, the issue sold 5,000 copies. Protestors read out its articles during the demonstration the following day. Furthermore, the governor neglected to go through with his threat. Instead, unlike in 1947, *El Chapulín* continued to put out issues, often three a week, throughout the 1952 protests. The coverage played a crucial role in sustaining and directing the protestors.[76]

Together with the new daily *El Imparcial*, the paper offered a narrative of the movement and critiqued the line of the progovernment press. On March 27, for example, the newspaper published a special issue on the massacre of protestors four days earlier. The piece gave a blow-by-blow account of events, made direct accusations against the governor's bodyguards, and denied reports in the national newspapers that the demonstrators were opposition party members or had fired first.[77] The newspaper kept up the pressure on both the federal and state governments. In late March, the Alemán administration had pledged to sort out the problem after the June elections. The strategy was designed to rob the protestors of momentum.

To an extent, it worked. In late March and early April, many elite merchants accepted the sacking of a few officials and derogation of the new tax code as a sufficient compromise. But many lower-class stallholders and artisans remained unsatisfied. They wanted Mayoral Heredia removed.[78] In the weeks leading up to the elections, *El Chapulín* echoed their demands by repeatedly reminding its readers of Alemán's promise, questioning the federal government's integrity ("maybe we live under one law, but it is chomped and spat out like chewing gum by those in power"), and drumming up support for another tax strike.[79] Finally, *El Chapulín*'s writing also fed into the propaganda efforts of the more radical plebeian protestors. The strike committee's bulletins were printed on *El Chapulín*'s press. These bulletins reprinted Ramírez's investigations into covert murders, his rallying cries to stand firm, and even the newspaper's satirical songs. Saavedra's "Corrido of Mayoral Heredia" and the "Corrido of the Strike of Oaxaca" were distributed in both *El Chapulín* and on official CCO paper.[80]

The relationships between the artisan press and the civil society of Mexico's provincial capitals often simply involved highlighting mundane problems or providing readers with a hollow laugh at the expense of tawdry bureaucrats. But during the 1940s and 1950s, the underpowered party machinery also provided space for these relationships to have real political force. Alliances of civic associations and journalists were effective and constructive. At times, they got potholes fixed; at other times, they could take down governors. But the close bond between newspapers and readers in places like Oaxaca City could also have rather more destructive consequences. In 1947 and again in 1952, protestors closed down, smashed up, and even took over progovernment newspapers. Discovering why is somewhat tricky. The protestors left little evidence of their motives beyond condemnations of the publications and broad assertions that they wanted the press to reproduce their demands. Perhaps, one might suggest it reflected the popularization of nineteenth-century ideas of journalistic honor, which now reached beyond individual writers to the civil society they claimed to represent. Just as old journalists defended their honor through duels, so mid-century civic movements defended their honor through impromptu, if also broadly acceptable, acts of violence. Whatever the underlying reasons, what is clear is that the provincial public sphere not only was an open and combative space, but was also up for grabs.

From 1945 to 1947, Governor Sánchez Cano's administration published its own newspaper, *La Voz de Oaxaca*, on the state's printing press. It was replete with good news stories on supposed administrative achievements, published federal and state press bulletins verbatim, and even took a whole week to reprint the governor's state of the union address in full. In early 1947, as protestors started to come together against the governor's new tax regulations, *La Voz de Oaxaca* first played down the changes, arguing that they would lead to a decrease rather than an increase in popular contributions. But as demonstrations coalesced into a planned commercial strike, the newspaper became more aggressive. On January 9, the paper ran a succession of stories designed to undercut the movement's credibility. In particular, they let loose on the leaders, describing them with gloriously rude free-form insults as "a hairy ape, a pedant, a pseudo-wise intellectual, a landlord, a wannabe lawyer, the descendent of a well-known fraudster, and a disgusting popsicle salesman."[81] Four days later, protestors rioted at the governor's refusal to negotiate. The targets were quite specific—the property registry (where the government kept property and most importantly tax records) and the government printing office. Here, they smashed the templates for *La Voz de Oaxaca* and formatted their own newspaper, *La Nueva Vida*. The masthead read "A New Political Life, A New Social Life, No More Hunger, No More Slaves." With Ramírez in hiding in Mexico City, the newspaper soon became the mouthpiece for the movement.[82]

Five years later, protestors leveled a similar strategy at a new target. Unlike most Oaxaca governors, Mayoral Heredia had refused to establish his own newspaper in the state printing press. Instead he relied on a privately owned newspaper, *El Nuevo Diario*. The owner was Juan Abarca Pérez, a Michoacán media entrepreneur and a kind of small-scale García Valseca. Abarca already had a couple of publications in Tuxtla Gutiérrez, Tapachula, and Morelia. In 1950, he arrived in Oaxaca City and established the fourth link in his putative chain. Like García Valseca, Abarca started by poaching the state's best journalists and loudly disclaiming the publication's independence. Like García Valseca's newspapers, *El Nuevo Diario* immediately drew in readers with a *nota roja* scoop. In early 1951 the paper started to examine the death of a prisoner in police custody. The investigation revealed evidence of torture, murder, and a deliberate cover-up. By late April Mayoral Heredia was forced to disband the judicial police. Even the *El Chapulín* journalist Villa was impressed, writing in his private diary that the newspaper "showed real spirit."[83]

Yet such public enthusiasm for the newspaper did not last long. The most cynical journalists (including the *El Chapulín* gang) soon suggested that the whole investigation was a setup, deliberately framed so that Mayoral Heredia could get rid of his predecessor's appointees. By mid-1951 the newspaper had become unrelentingly *oficialista*. When the legislature passed the new fiscal code later in the year, the paper reported that all the members of the Chamber of Commerce had signed up to the new laws.[84] As Villa succinctly stated in his diary, "it is clear that this and all other news on the subject in this newspaper is inexact and tendentious."[85] A flysheet from early 1952 claimed that Abarca was "a blackmailer," who charged the governor 10,000 pesos a month for favorable coverage.[86]

El Nuevo Diario's support for the new fiscal code soon developed into a war of words with the city's other newspapers. While *El Chapulín*, *El Imparcial*, and the PP newspaper *El Pueblo* criticized the legislation and voiced the concerns of the civic associations, the Abarca organ ignored the gradual buildup of public dissatisfaction, repeated the line that merchants supported the new code, and increasingly insulted the protestors and their leaders. On March 13 an anonymous columnist claimed that *El Chapulín* was a gossipy blackmail mag, whose owner was an "evil rumormonger, who went after anyone who refused to pay for his alcoholic benders." Finally, as pressure on the governor increased, on March 19, 1952, the paper ran the headline "Is a Henriquista Plot Being Prepared in Oaxaca." The article spoke conspiratorially of "a secret report," which had fallen into the hands of certain "workers' leaders" and detailed links between the protestors and the opposition presidential candidate.[87] The next day, the newspaper followed up the story, this time leading the front page with the headline "Edmundo Sánchez Cano and Vicente González Fernández Are Directing the Movement." Again, the article relied on rumor and supposition, whispered obliquely of "secret juntas," and hinted at the possibility of a military coup by the two former governors. The piece capped off the fabrication by falsely claiming that the movement's leaders had decided to call off the commercial strike.[88]

The following day, March 21, protestors marched against the new code. As they approached the governor's home, his gunmen opened fire, killing at least two demonstrators and injuring nearly a dozen. According to the Quintas, the street ran with blood. During the night, the protestors rioted. Government agents described the riot as "an orgy of destruction." But again, they had very specific targets. They broke the windows of the governor's home, hurled stones at a couple of unpopular members of the elite, burned the city's tax records, and broke into the offices of *El Nuevo Diario*. Here, they smashed up the press and broke the journalists' typewriters and desks. On the front of the office, protestors wrote "Abarca Lives off Blackmail." The editor was forced to flee to his offices in Chiapas. Few journalists lamented the paper's demise. But in one of Ramírez's editorials he did hint at the reason for the crowd's fury. The paper, he said, had "disgraced the honor of Oaxaca's journalism."[89]

Decentering the Public Sphere

It is easy to focus on the negative aspects of the state's repeated skirmishes with *El Momento* and its band of confrontational journalists. In the last decade of the paper's existence, Villa especially was extremely pessimistic about the power of the provincial press. But looking back over *El Momento*'s letters pages and crusades, especially in the first two decades of its existence, what actually strikes the reader are the relative achievements of these campaigns. Between 1937 and 1955 Ramírez and his fellow writers represented the complaints and demands of civil society in a fairly effective manner. Their links to the Oaxaca City community were strong. For many, Ramírez encapsulated the "voice" and the "humor" of the city and in particular the market. According to Quintas, after the two antigovernor movements he rarely bought a meal in the market, relying instead on the grateful giveaways of stallholders.[90]

Furthermore, despite the confrontations, state administrations seemed to listen to public opinion. This often necessitated the combination of journalistic pressure and popular disturbances. (Riots may not have been strictly rational, but they were part of the rules of the provincial public sphere.) During the 1940s and 1950s an underpowered and undersupported PRI often had to respond. Things got done. Potholes were filled in, markets were rebuilt, and schools were opened. Bureaucrats and policemen were dismissed or at least shunted away from the public eye, unpopular council members were removed, and even governors were sacked. The unscrupulous teacher from the local prison was even fired.

There were, of course, limits. This was not Alexis de Tocqueville's imagined vision of America or Jürgen Habermas's Enlightenment England. Regulatory censorship, including threats and beatings, was frequent. Given the penury of state administrations, unpopular commercial taxes were hard to completely rein in. *El Chapulín* was still bemoaning their existence in the 1960s. Underfunding also made problems with electricity and water tough to sort out. Most important, relations among the state, civil society, and the press changed over time. By the late 1950s the PRI popular sector had expanded sufficiently to ignore many of *El Chapulín's* sniping demands. The Cold War made what had been local conflicts national and even international in scope—to be decided at a much higher level than state or municipal authorities. For example, *El Chapulín's* support for the railway workers of Matías Romero in 1959 fell on deaf ears.[91] But up to this point a functioning public sphere did exist. It may have avoided national policies, focused on local issues, and replicated the "decentered" shape of provincial politics, but it did provide space for debate and a means for civil society to communicate with the state.[92]

CHAPTER EIGHT

The Singer

Civil Society, Radicalism, and Acción in Chihuahua

In late 1959, eight hundred peasants from the mountain town of Ciudad Madera walked to the state capital of Chihuahua as part of a "caravan of hunger." They were protesting the takeover of their lands and the brutal murder of one of their leaders. They met with the part-time dancehall singer and press publicity agent Judith Reyes. They offered her coffee from their scant supplies and begged that she use her position on the paper to write on their behalf. "The press doesn't say the truth. Can you write the things as they are? Perhaps we don't have the money to be in the papers, but look señorita, if you write justly about us, I'm sure God will pay you." According to Reyes's autobiography, the meeting made up her mind. She was not simply going to support the peasants, she was going to help voice their demands. "From this moment on, I converted myself into a reporter." Convinced of her new role, she claimed she left the protestors with an assurance that "I am going to write about your problems. I am not only going to write, I am going to sing. I am going to write songs about all the things I see among you."[1]

Judith Reyes would eventually become one of Mexico's most celebrated protest singers, a member of Latin America's "nueva canción" movement who was often compared to U.S. folk artist Joan Baez. She would compile the first songs about the 1968 student movement and be forced into exile for her outspoken lyrics.[2] But this chapter is not about Reyes's skills as a songwriter. Instead it concerns the first part of her promise to the Ciudad Madera peasants—to become a reporter. She kept her agreement and between 1960 and 1966 became a left-wing journalist. At first, she was forced to reinvent a local newspaper's society pages as a space for her exposés. But by 1962 she had set up her own fortnightly, *Acción*. It was one of the first newspapers designed to spread beyond the press's traditional urban audience. For the next four years, the tabloid linked readers in the state capital to readers in Chihuahua's villages. By doing so, Reyes helped forge a powerful, cross-class alliance. This was eventually overshadowed by the 1965 guerrilla attack on the Ciudad Madera barracks. But for a time it caused the government considerable problems and provided the basis for future alliances in Chihuahua's squatter slums.

On one level, this chapter, like chapter 4, is about radicalization and how Mexico's 1960s journalists started to break the rules of the game. But it also ties into the shifting relationship between the press and civil society. In Chihuahua, Reyes's publication rested on a tradition of interaction between journalists and protestors going back decades. As we saw in chapter 7, in states with limited administrative control and traditions of opposition newspapers, local publications could build strong links to readers. Furthermore, these alliances could successfully press for political change. In Chihuahua, similar conditions existed. Elites were beset by multiple divisions; the state authorities were weak; and the control of popular organizations was fragile. At the same time, the public sphere was combative and conflictive. Here, as in Oaxaca, the cooperation between newspapers and members of civil society sometimes solidified into cogent protests. In 1955, an exposé of high-level impunity generated a social movement, which toppled the state governor. Similar processes undergirded *Acción*'s initial popularity. But Reyes also went further. Rather than simply echoing the complaints of urban readers, she attempted to establish links between them and the radical peasants of the countryside. In doing so, the paper not only tapped into the growing number of literate peasants but also consciously connected the civic movements of the 1950s to the radical protests of the 1960s. Such efforts were not entirely successful, but they culminated in a series of clashes between government forces and this cross-class movement in early 1964.

From Cabaret to Countryside

Judith Reyes was born on March 22, 1924, in the dusty oil town of Villa Cecilia [later called Ciudad Madero] on the Tamaulipas coast. Within a year her family moved to the bustling port city of Tampico. Here her father found work in the oil fields and her mother sold charcoal and milk at the city market. Beyond her immediate family, two institutions marked her upbringing. The first was the Protestant Church. In the early years of the twentieth century, Tampico was a center of Mexican Protestantism. Foreign oil workers brought their churches to the city and a relatively high proportion of Mexicans converted. Reyes's mother was one such convert. She took her family to the local Baptist establishment every Sunday, taught them to read the Bible, and entertained them by singing evangelical songs. At school, Reyes's religion caused considerable teasing. Though Reyes gave up the religion as soon as she became an adult, she thought the experience not only taught her the value of communal singing, but also a certain toughness and independence. The second was the petrol workers union. Reyes was particularly close to her maternal uncle, Jesús Hernández. He was head of the union in the petrol-processing town of Ebano. She often stayed at his house and hung out with her cousins at union meetings. By the time she was fourteen she had joined a troop of variety singers who would tour festivals organized by the petrol workers union as far south as Tuxpan in Veracruz.[3]

By the end of the 1930s, Reyes and her siblings were almost adults. One brother went back to San Luis Potosí to work as an *ejidatario*. Her sister trained as a nurse in Puebla. Meanwhile Reyes and her mother traveled to Mexico City. They accompanied the youngest brother, who had just received a place at the IPN. Soon, Reyes took up music again. At first she worked as a backing singer, performing in the variety shows put on by entertainment entrepreneurs in tents in the poorer neighborhoods. At the age of sixteen, she met and married a fellow singer-songwriter. Within a year, she was pregnant with her first child.[4]

These years were hard, but there were a few high points. She traveled to the United States as part of a touring folk group, completed a short-hand typing course, got a job at the songwriters' union, and wrote a few hits for contemporary singers like Tito Guízar and Jorge Negrete. But her marriage went from bad to worse and eventually she went north to seek counsel from her uncle, the union organizer from Ebano. "Get your freedom back because with that man you will never be happy," he advised. The meeting made up her mind. When she returned to Mexico City, she took her child to her mother's house. She grabbed her guitar and a suitcase of performance costumes and headed back up north. For the next decade, Reyes lived a transient life. She found work in a series of cabarets, nightclubs, and radio stations along the border. She visited Reynosa, Matamoros, Mexicali, and Ciudad Juárez. She even worked in a circus in Torreón.[5]

Finally, in 1959 she moved to Chihuahua City where she found work as a publicity agent for the one of the city's newspapers and met the protestors from Ciudad Madera. Following her promise to write on their behalf, she tried to get a job as a reporter. She moved her family yet again, this time to the mountain town of Parral. She started work for the new local daily, *El Monitor*. For the next two years, Reyes became increasingly involved in the state's peasant movement. Around town, she became known as "the communist." She got close to local peasant leaders like Alvaro Rios and radical teachers like Arturo Gámiz and Pablo Gómez.[6] At first her role in the protests was not on the front line. She used her contacts from *El Monitor*'s society pages to act as a link between the city and the squatter communities. On one occasion, she started a charity trust and collected food, clothing, shoes, and medicine as well as money for the peasants. On another occasion, one peasant leader asked for her help to get credit from local farmers to buy maize and beans. Many locals were reluctant to offer the products, especially to peasants squatting precariously on a fellow landowner's property. But Reyes managed to persuade them, eventually collecting eight tons of seeds for the peasants' fields.[7]

As promised, she also started to give voice to the peasant movement. Most famously, she adapted the revolutionary corrido and compiled at least a dozen songs on the land invasions and peasant movements of the era.[8] But she also adapted her role at Parral's *El Monitor*. When she joined the publication, the paper was in its first year. It was started by a local businessman, Domingo Salayandia, and was still struggling to find a secure readership. Parral was no major metropolis. During the early twentieth century, the town had transformed from a mining center to a trading hub for southern Chihuahua and northern Durango. The population in 1960 was 45,080, or less than a third of that of Chihuahua City. And the town already had a newspaper, the well-established, forty-year-old *El Correo*. The newspaper was critical, right-wing, and often supportive of the opposition PAN; it was also relatively popular. According to stated sales, in 1960 circulation reached 6,000 copies a day. But Parral was also an expanding market. The population was growing at 3.5 percent a year; and, perhaps most important, Parral's inhabitants had a taste for reading the news. The 1967 U.S. survey on regional reading habits claimed that 79 percent of the population read newspapers at least once a week. Nearly half bought a newspaper every day.[9]

Salayandia attempted to reach this market by presenting *El Monitor* as Parral's confrontational, left-wing alternative. During the 1960s, the strategy was extremely popular among small-town editors. It reflected the extension of literacy and purchasing power to an expanding group of poorer urban readers and led to a rise in combative local dailies throughout Mexico's provinces. Pieces on the failure of land reform, the plight of miners, or the corruption of officials were frequent.[10] Salayandia also employed Reyes as the reporter for the newspaper's society pages. In August 1961 she started writing her column, "Ubicua y Yo" [Ubiquitous and I]. The title referred to the society journalist's supposed knowledge of all levels of local life. But it also may have had further significance. Another newspaper connected to the cross-class social movements of the period—Acapulco's *La Verdad*—also ran a society page under the same rubric.[11] Perhaps Reyes simply hijacked the name.

Reyes's job at the newspaper followed traditional gender roles. In local newspapers, like in the nationals, most women were relegated to nonpolitical writing about the social sphere. Traditionally, the society section focused on the social calendar of the provincial elites and middle classes. Topics included baptisms, weddings, *quinceañeras*, and exclusive charity events. The tone was exaggerated flattery. Columns were designed to appease the upper classes and instruct nonelites in the subtle divisions of the social hierarchy. At times, Reyes fulfilled this role. "The radiant Irma Espinosa yesterday attended a hen party put on by her beautiful friends . . . She will marry Efraín Prieto on September 23. We note that those who attended included Yolanda Loya and Rosita Urquidi," or "The arrival of a baby in the house is always good news. The birth of Salustio González will bring happiness and joy. Our congratulations."[12]

But "Ubicua y Yo" was no traditional society column. Between this formulaic society news, Reyes regularly inserted items that revealed her more radical agenda. Some were extremely general. She wrote approvingly of the government's controversial free textbook plan and she applauded Fidel Castro's campaign to eliminate hunger. But others were small-scale exposés of local malpractice. In November 1961 she related the story of José María Labrado, a miner from the nearby town of Santa Barbara. He had worked for the U.S. mining giant ASARCO for a decade. But he had recently been sacked without severance pay or benefits. The local union representative refused to stand up for him, so Reyes used her column to start a collection for his food and medicine. The following month, she related the story of Aurelio Muñoz García, who had been stabbed by two men and was now resting in the hospital. She asked why the local authorities were not investigating the crime and suggested that the attackers were relations of the head of police. She also cast an ironic eye over broader political problems. "At last the PRI loses an election," she titled her take on the loss of the PRI candidate for Ciudad Juárez's carnival queen. "Perhaps we could make him ambassador?" she greeted news that a particularly corrupt governor was seeking asylum in the United States.[13]

By developing such a hybrid society column, Reyes played a double game. On the one hand, she played up to expectations. The short, positive pieces on engagements and piano recitals cemented links to Parral's well-to-do. These links allowed her to fund her own charity work for peasant land invaders. But the space also permitted Reyes to write about more political matters. During the 1960s, female journalists were still prevented from commenting on political news. When Nidia Marín wrote a joint piece with one of her male colleagues on the 1968 student movement, the director removed her name from the byline.[14] Radical magazines may have broken some of the rules of postrevolutionary journalism, but the idea that political journalism was a man's game was still firmly in place. In seven years, *Política* published pieces by only one female journalist, Raquel Tibol. *Por Qué?* published articles by female authors even more sporadically.[15] Consequently, like Reyes, politicized female journalists often sought to put forward their positions in subtle or covert manners. During the student movement Elena Poniatowska used her column in *Novedades*'s cultural section to applaud previous student uprisings, thus subtly subverting condemnatory government rhetoric.[16] Mercedes Padrés used the cover of *Sucesos* human-interest stories to explore the lives of low-income workers, exploited cabaret servers, and women forced into prostitution.[17]

"Ubicua y Yo" lasted less than a year. Gradually, Reyes decided that her campaign of campfire corridos and subversive society pages was not enough. *El Monitor* paid meager wages, her oldest daughter was about to go to the Autonomous University of Chihuahua (Universidad Autónoma de Chihuahua), and Parral's authorities were becoming increasingly intolerant of her exposés. She decided that what the state's peasants needed was not the subversion of orthodox press genres but rather a new journalistic form, a free, populist mass-market tabloid that would link rural farmers to urban supporters. She conceived of the paper as the antithesis of the traditional press. Instead it would act as a "tribune to denounce injustices and a weapon at the exclusive service of those who did not manage to obtain the support of the *gran prensa*."[18] In summer 1962 she moved back to Chihuahua City to set up *Acción*.

Civil Society and the Regional Press

The success of *Acción* built on long-established regional connections between civil society and the press. García Valseca's Chihuahua City and Ciudad Juárez titles led circulation, at least until the early 1960s. As we saw in chapter 6, though they often followed the logic of extortion, they also generated popular followings through crime news and campaign journalism. At the same time, they opened the way (or at least failed to close it) for a series of smaller, critical dailies and weeklies. Together these newspapers covered a broad ideological spectrum, provided ample room for debate, and generated considerable criticism of state officials. They also allowed popular input and developed close links with local civic organizations. Such alliances could acquire considerable force. In 1955, Chihuahua City's *El Norte* not only uncovered the murder of a local taxi driver and exposed the subsequent cover-up, but also provided space for the establishment of a social movement that coalesced around the affair. The movement focused on the fair provision of justice, brought together members from across the social spectrum, including large groups of recently enfranchised women, and culminated in a series of statewide protests. These eventually persuaded the national government to force the governor to step down. With *Acción*, Reyes would attempt to extend the ambit of the state's civic-minded protestors to include the peasants.

The García Valseca chain dominated newspaper sales in Chihuahua. By 1960 the morning *El Fronterizo* and the afternoon *El Mexicano* sold 40,000 copies between them in Ciudad Juárez. In Chihuahua City, sales of *El Heraldo* and *El Heraldo de la Tarde* totaled 30,000. At least initially, they developed strong relations with their readerships, often through the *nota roja*. But by the early 1960s they were also involved in extorting local authorities and swung wildly between adulation and condemnation. Such tactics occasionally generated good journalism, but could also lose readers. (*El Fronterizo*'s circulation actually decreased between 1954 and 1960.) They also allowed the establishment and survival of rival publications, with less financial backing but more consistently critical editorial lines. Despite the chain's heavy involvement in the state, other newspapers thrived. By the 1960s there were six rival dailies spread over the two main cities as well as smaller towns like Parral and Ciudad Delicias. There were also at least twelve weekly or biweekly papers and seventeen monthly magazines. Together they sold over 50,000 copies. When combined with the chain's figures, Chihuahua had one of the highest rates of newspaper readership in Mexico. On average, every urban household in the state bought a paper.[19]

Many of these smaller-scale publications were deeply critical of the local authorities. Some were run by opposition parties. The PAN, in particular, had a strong base of support in the state. During the 1950s, the party gained considerable backing from Ciudad Juárez's business-friendly civil organization, the Civic Association (Asociación Cívica, AC). In 1955 it gained a seat in the federal congress. Over the following years, it engaged in close electoral conflicts in Ciudad Juárez, Chihuahua City, and the state as a whole. In 1958, the national party even put forward an AC member, Luis H. Alvarez, to represent the PAN in the national elections.[20] Though Alvarez lost, the party remained popular, especially on the border. In the early 1960s the government estimated that it still had 15,000 card-carrying members in Ciudad Juárez alone.[21] Such support ensured a regular readership of the party's newspapers, like Parral's *El Correo* and Ciudad Juárez's *La Antorcha*. These papers followed the party line and contained long, dry excerpts on political philosophy and Catholic morality. But like the PAN's national magazine, *La Nación*, they also devoted space to exposing corruption, state violence, and electoral fraud.[22]

Other critical newspapers were linked to particularly difficult journalists, like the old, nineteenth-century *periódicos de combate*. In fact, Ciudad Juárez had two such publications. The first, *El Alacrán*, was established in 1932 by a lawyer's son, Juan Sáenz Avalos.[23] Described on the front as "A Jokey-Serious Biweekly and of Combat," the publication specialized in exposing corruption, revealing the links between the authorities and organized crime, and mocking hapless functionaries. The sparse remaining issues contain stories on officials ripping off electricity users, taking money from brothel owners, stealing funds for national celebrations, practicing electoral fraud, and protecting the infamous heroin dealer Ignacia Jasso, "La Nacha." Like many other border publications, the newspaper specialized in *nota roja* stories and ran a Sunday supplement devoted to true crime. Like many of Mexico's critical, artisanal weeklies, it attempted to develop a gossipy, confessional relationship to its readers. The use of nicknames was frequent ("El Gordo" supplied "La Nacha" with drugs; "El Chinito" was a rival trafficker). So were articles, which demanded readers' involvement. Formal reading intersected with street chatter. In "Do you know him, reader?" Sáenz would depict a particular functionary or businessman by listing his various crimes.[24]

Ciudad Juárez's second critical weekly was *La Jeringa*, which was established by Ernesto Espinosa in 1946. Like *El Alacrán*, it specialized in denouncing corruption and described itself as a "Jokey-Serious Weekly, Independent, and of Combat." The government summed up the newspaper as "critical, insulting, and offensive."[25] Where *La Jeringa* differed from *El Alacrán* was the emphasis on humor. Jokey trumped serious. Stories were written in a heavily ironic tone. (Officers squeezed information out of a suspect using "that most modern and democratic policing method—torture." The policeman who ordered it was "an example of civic beauty, the crème de la crème of service to the community.") Parodies of formal government speeches and celebrations were frequent. Serious articles were larded with quickfire gags. (After market inspectors confiscated fifteen sacks of donkey meat, Espinosa pondered whether slow-witted local politicians were concerned that they might be next for the butcher's slab.) Puns and jokey acronyms were common. Rival journalists formed part of the United Front of Arselickers (Frente Unico de Lambiscones, FUL).[26]

Other newspapers were linked to out-of-favor PRI factions. High politics in the state was extremely divided. By the early 1960s at least five personal cliques of politicians vied for control of the official party. All these groups either established their own newspapers or funded those already in existence. At times (and especially when presidential candidates were visiting), these newspapers played nice, toed the official line, and presented a unified front. But more often than not they were used to attack rival factions. As in Oaxaca and Sonora, interelite squabbling allowed space for journalism to thrive.[27] In

Ciudad Juárez, the local *cacique*, Antonio J. Bermúdez, teamed up with his brother-in-law, René Mascareñas, to create *El Correo*. The aim of the newspaper was to critique the competing PRI group, which now held power in the city. To do so, they poached some of the García Valseca chain's best journalists and set about exposing official sleaze and government links to the vice trade. State spies described the publication as "devoted to yellow journalism, with exaggerated and scandalous articles that exploit the nota roja." The editor's political column, "Ecuanyl," was particularly popular. It played off the tradition of *periódicos de combate* and offered a vicious, humorous, and cynical take on local politics. So was the regular "Esta Justicia" (This Justice). Each week, the column focused on a particular case of police corruption or judicial malpractice.[28]

Once political factions had made the initial investment in these publications, editors and journalists could also wander off message. In 1958, for example, the governor, Teófilo Borunda, helped his young protégé, Guillermo Gallardo, establish the Chihuahua City weekly *Indice*. He cemented this arrangement by appointing Gallardo as head of the state's PIPSA office. Initially, the newspaper was designed as a counterweight to the occasionally critical dailies of the García Valseca chain. Articles were left-wing but generally supportive of the state administration. But soon, alliances changed. Borunda paid off the chain, and its newspapers returned to an editorial line of unquestioning support. He also pulled funding from *Indice*. In response, Gallardo moved the publication further to the left and started to criticize the policies of Borunda's government.[29] At first, attacks focused on his mismanagement of the university, the teachers union, and agrarian reform.[30] The following year, the paper was revealing dodgy land deals, calling for the governor's resignation, and publishing "insulting" cartoons of voters throwing portraits of Borunda into the trash.[31] Opposition suited Gallardo, and he reveled in exposing the corruption of Chihuahua's ruling class. In 1960, he was the only journalist to defend the man accused of murdering the local banking tycoon Eloy S. Vallina, by leaking that Vallina's son had kidnapped and raped the accused's daughter.[32] Such an approach brought Gallardo into contact with Reyes and her fellow agrarian activists. In summer 1962 his help would be crucial to getting *Acción* off the ground.[33]

Together, Chihuahua's mix of schizophrenic chain newspapers and smaller publications formed a relatively open, pluralist, and argumentative public sphere. They also developed strong civic links, through open-ended and conversational styles—as in the cases of *El Alacrán* and *La Jeringa*—and through support for popular campaigns. As in Oaxaca, various crusades forced authorities to sack unpopular ministers, prosecute protected criminals, close down brothels, and improve sanitation. The highest-profile campaign concerned the provision of justice and was instigated by Chihuahua City's *El Norte*. The newspaper was established in August 1954 by the journalist Luis Fuentes Saucedo and his son, civic-minded lawyer Luis Fuentes Molinar.[34] For months, the paper struggled to gain a foothold in the city's crowded newspaper market. But in November that year, the paper's journalists started to investigate the murder of a local man. The investigation revealed connections to the vice industry, nepotism, police incompetence, an official cover-up, and the employment of torture. It also generated a popular mobilization that demanded justice and called for the dismissal of the governor, Oscar Soto Maynez. By August the following year, the combination of mass marches and critical newspaper coverage proved too much. The president forced Soto Maynez to stand down.

On November 27, 1954, a Chihuahua City taxi driver, Juan Cereceres, picked up his hired vehicle and started his regular night shift. The following day, he did not come home. The car was found in the center of the city. There was a bullet hole in the windscreen and the driver's seat was drenched in blood. Rumors started immediately. They pointed the finger at two young members of the state's political elite—Gaspar Maynez Jr. and Gerardo Caraveo. Maynez Jr. was the son of the chief of police and the first cousin once removed of the governor; Caraveo was a rural cop and son of a revolutionary general. They alleged that Maynez and Caraveo had ambushed and shot the driver after he tried to stop them harassing a young woman at one of the city's drinking spots. For two weeks, the capital's newspapers avoided the issue. Then, on December 10, *El Norte* broke the silence. Fuentes Molinar wrote an emotive piece on the state of mourning in the Cereceres household. He emphasized the poverty of the family home, which contained "only four seats, a bed, and a sewing machine." He described the driver's young daughters "crying when they should be laughing" and imagined that they "missed the hand that stroked their hair every morning" and knew that "the man that took them to the cinema every Sunday would never return." The article concluded with the cry of Cereceres's mother, "My son, where is my son?"[35]

For the next two months, *El Norte*'s journalists doubled as detectives and employed modern policing techniques to crack the Cereceres case. The newspaper's inquiry repeatedly showed the flaws in the authorized investigation, and made clear that politicians and policemen were trying to cover for the real authors of the crime. On December 12 *El Norte* organized a reconstruction of events. They traced Cereceres leaving the taxi rank at just past midnight on November 28. They located his last customer, a Ciudad Delicias man named Heriberto Cervantes. They discovered a witness who placed Cereceres at the Huerta Luz, a cheap cabaret club on the banks of the Chuviscar river an hour later. And they gathered together further bystanders who claimed that he left the club with two leather-coated, pistol-carrying men. Finally, they tracked down a newspaper vendor who saw the same two men exiting Cereceres's bloodstained car at 6 A.M. the following morning.[36]

In response, the governor called in investigators from Mexico's secret police, the DFS. After briefly interviewing the witnesses, they released their own report claiming that a Mexican-American drug trafficker, David Gates Guerrero, had killed Cereceres. The motive was revenge. According to the DFS, up to a few years before, Cereceres had been a member of the criminal underworld. To escape a criminal charge, he had reported Gates to the police. To back up the allegations, the DFS presented the statement of an anonymous witness, who claimed that six years earlier Gates had sworn to murder Cereceres while in the Ciudad Juárez jail, and the positive identification of the suspect by an early morning newspaper vendor. Immediately *El Norte*'s journalists interrogated the theory. They asked the name of the anonymous witness; they asked why Gates had left it six years to kill Cereceres; they asked where the body was; they asked why the police had yet to arrest Gates; and they asked whether the DFS had any evidence of Cereceres's shady past. They also tracked down the witnesses mentioned in the report, who claimed that their statements were completely fictitious. The journalists concluded that "most people ha[d] not only refused to take this version seriously, but actually laughed at it." For the next week, the *El Norte* team demolished the remaining pillars of the DFS case. They traced Cereceres's boss during his supposed stint in the Ciudad Juárez underworld. He stated that he had hired the young driver to haul corn and beans from the state capital to the border city. He described Cereceres as a model employee, whom he often trusted with loads worth up to 40,000 pesos. They also used contacts in the U.S. police forces to track down Gates. They found him living peaceably and without a grudge in a small town in Arizona. They even interviewed his mother, who presented reporters with proof of Gates's whereabouts on the night on the murder.[37]

In response, the state officials jettisoned the entire DFS line. Instead they presented a new narrative. On December 24 they accused Arturo Chávez López, the guard at the Huerta Luz nightclub, of committing the crime. Chávez was a rather better patsy. He was a former rural cop with a short fuse. He was wildly reviled and alleged to have shot at least three suspects in the line of duty. Four days later they also pointed the finger at Cervantes, the taxi driver's final passenger. This thesis was rather more problematic. Cervantes was blind and had been since birth. To overcome this, officials claimed that Cervantes had paid Chávez to commit the murder. Again *El Norte*'s journalists investigated the charges. They pointed to the lack of motive, poked holes in the government's timeline, and re-interviewed witnesses from the Huerta Luz club, all of whom denied the official version of events. They also managed to gain access to the supposed "autor intelectual," Cervantes, and the alleged shooter, Chávez. Both claimed that they had been tortured into confessions. Cervantes had been strapped to a metal chair that was then plugged into the mains, and Chávez had been dunked repeatedly underwater. The technique, *El Norte* informed readers, was called "el buzo," or "the diver."[38]

At this point, things got even more embarrassing for the officials. On December 29 a pedestrian found Cereceres's corpse discarded by the side of the road. For a corpse that had remained open to the elements for over a month, the body seemed in surprisingly good shape. There was limited decomposition, no signs of attacks by animals or insects, and Cereceres's clothes were not dirty or dusty. The government doctors explained the state of the corpse by arguing that a combination of dry air, shade, and unseasonably cool temperatures had prevented rapid decay. Again, *El Norte*'s writers countered the claims. They suggested that officials close to the two main suspects had deliberately frozen the corpse. One reporter even suggested that the corpse had remained in the police chief's freezer. Without a body, successful prosecutions were difficult if not impossible to achieve. This gave officials time to put together a case against a handful of scapegoats. As soon as official charges were made, they defrosted and dumped the corpse. They were ready, they hoped, for a successful prosecution. *El Norte*'s headline read "The Government Descends into the Grotesque." The investigation had become a "tragicomic farce."[39]

For the next month, the macabre accusations became the focus of *El Norte*'s stories. *Nota roja* met modern forensics. First, they pushed for the release of the body for Cereceres's family. Then they employed a respected doctor to do his own autopsy on the corpse. He concluded that there were signs of "mummification on the skin of the face, the hands, the arms and the feet" and "marks of ecchymosis" on different parts of the body. For those not au fait with modern medicine, *El Norte* explained that such trauma was inconsistent with prolonged exposure. The doctor also opened the corpse and found all the organs completely intact. He concluded that "they could only have been kept this way through refrigeration." Beyond the autopsy, *El Norte*'s reporters asked a meteorologist to put together a review of weather on the Chihuahua City-Cuauhtémoc Road. He claimed that far from being unseasonably cool, temperatures had soared in December, hitting an average of 30 degrees Celsius a day. They also sent pieces of Cereceres's ears and toes to laboratories over the border in El Paso. Experts concluded that the skin showed signs of frostbite "consistent with refrigeration." Finally they interviewed farmers, who worked around the area the body was found. They all confirmed *El Norte's* thesis that scavengers and insects would devour any animal within a week of its death. "All that would remain is bones."[40]

The newspaper's dogged investigation laid bare the chasm that separated popular and official ideas of justice. By late December, popular outrage at the government's handling of the case reached crisis point. Groups of concerned citizens joined together to form a pressure group, the Committee Projustice and the Rights of Citizens (Comité Pro-Justicia y los Derechos de Ciudadanos, CPJDC). For the next six months, the CPJDC publicly demanded the proper provision of justice or what they termed "a clean justice, a justice without leguleyos [bad lawyers] and a justice without official protection." To make their point, they petitioned the national government, held massive demonstrations, and collected thousands of pesos to pay for the fees of lawyers and forensic scientists.[41]

Like Oaxaca's CCO, the CPJDC was a grassroots civil society organization, unconnected to any political party or union group. The three leaders were the city's chief mason and the owner of a furniture business, Lázaro Villareal, his wife, Dolores D. de Villareal, and Ana María Echave, who worked as a nurse at a local sanatorium. Members came from across the political spectrum. They included anticlerical masons, like Villareal, and supporters of Catholic organizations, official party stalwarts, union members, and PANistas. They also came from every tier of the social hierarchy. Some were taxi drivers like Cereceres; many were miners and railway workers; others still were white-collar workers from Chihuahua City.

But there was one characteristic that did set the CPJDC apart from most public organizations. The majority were women. The group actually started out as the Projustice Committee of Women before changing its name. Women dominated the speeches at the group's rallies and they received the most enthusiastic applause. Women outnumbered men on the board of the committee two to one, and lists of donations indicated that three times as many women gave money to the organization as men. As in the Anchondo case a decade earlier, the story of murder and impunity played to traditional norms. In Mexico's highly gendered public sphere, women's discussion of conventional politics was still frowned upon. But demands for protection and justice were acceptable. At the same time, throughout the 1940s and 1950s, nonaligned social movements like the CPJDC provided acceptable avenues for women to practice politics without getting involved in the messy, violent, and still resolutely masculine world of elections.[42]

The support of *El Norte* was crucial to the growth and maintenance of the CPJDC. By refusing to accept the official version, the newspaper's journalists kept the story in the public eye. They collaborated with CPJDC members to seek out medical specialists and trace witnesses. As civil society and the press intertwined, *El Norte* also provided a vital space for the group to organize and coalesce. On the one hand, the newspaper became a forum for the group's members. The letters section was expanded to a full page and retitled "The Voice of the People." Here, readers declared their solidarity, discussed the case, condemned the government's actions, and broadened the debate to include other examples of injustice.[43] On a more practical level, *El Norte*'s headquarters also doubled as the CPJDC treasury. From December 17 onward, citizens dropped off their contributions at the newspaper's offices in the center of town. The following day, citizens could read about their donations and those of their fellow activists on the back pages of the newspaper. The strategy offered transparency, generated trust, and offered donors the impression they were part of a broader movement. Over the next three weeks, the CPJDC collected 24,563 pesos from over 7,000 sources. Some groups donated collectively. The local branch of the railway workers union gave 257 pesos, and the employees of the El Potosí workshop donated 26 pesos. But most were small-scale individual donations like the 80¢ given by a nurse from Coyame or the peso handed over by an anonymous shoeshine boy.[44]

If the justice movement had its roots in *El Norte*'s newsroom, it soon spread to the streets. On December 31 Cereceres's funeral was held at the Chihuahua City cathedral. The bishop presided over the function. Over 20,000 mourners turned out to pay their respects and packed the square in front of the church.[45] A month later, the CPJDC held its first mass demonstration. By 11 A.M. on January 30, 60,000 people, nearly a third of the city's population, had congregated in the center of the city. For four hours, they heard the speeches by the organization's female leaders, by the father of one of the tortured suspects, and by the head of Cereceres's taxi rank.[46] Two months of revelations had taken the lid off public discourse. The speeches even went beyond what was printed in the critical press. The nurse, Echave, described the governor as possessed by "the vanity of power and a severe inferiority complex." In the concluding speech, the father of the blind suspect described a citizenry "sick of insecurity, anxiety, fear, official brutality, torture, the immorality of judicial functionaries and the professional mafias of lawyers and doctors, the discontent among poorly paid employees, and the despotism with which the governor treats them."[47] Subsequent meetings and marches never reached the numbers of the late January demonstration. But for the next five months, the CPJDC maintained its physical presence in the city. Taxi drivers carrying the group's badge held regular stoppages each week. Groups of between 500 and 2,000 mostly female members met on a regular basis.[48]

Despite the movement's influence, Governor Soto managed to hold on to power for six months. Concessions proved key. In January he sacked his police chief. In February he appointed a panel of two allegedly impartial lawyers to investigate the case, who drew out their inquiry for months. But so did attempts to undercut the movement's legitimacy. Soto's principal weapons were the newspapers from the García Valseca chain. Newspapers could also counter the claims of civil society. A conflict over the provision of justice transformed into a struggle over control of the public sphere. In January 1955 chain journalists denigrated the mass march, claiming it was a "vulgar political protest," arguing that no more than 2,000 attended the event, and assuring readers that the majority were transported in from out of town. For the next three months, they pulled coverage of the CPJDC completely. Instead they promoted stories that portrayed the governor in a positive light. Finally, in early May they published the confessions of a former leader of the organization, who claimed that the furniture tycoon Villareal was linked to a group of dissident Henriquistas and was using pliable members of the CPJDC to plot the assassination of the governor.[49] The charges were, of course, false. But using press revelations of potential violent sedition to undercut the credibility of social movements would become a popular strategy for government press officials and right-wing columnists for the next two decades.[50]

In the end, the attempts were in vain. Tax increases and disastrous local election results pushed the federal government to force Soto to quit.[51] On August 10 he announced his resignation.[52] But the cross-class alliances generated by the Cereceres case did not go away. When Reyes arrived in the city in summer 1962, she would use her newspaper to harness these connections to the state's emerging peasant movement. For the next two years, *Acción* became the cornerstone of a broader and more radical version of civil society.

Acción in Action

Between 1955 and 1962, politics in Chihuahua was still highly fragmented. Elites continued to vie for top office, urban civil society movements continued to resist integration into the party, and by the late 1950s they were joined by groups of radical teachers and discontented peasants. By establishing *Acción*, Reyes tapped into both rural and urban discontent. Only two years of publications remain in the archives. In her autobiography Reyes speculated that CIA agents visited the national newspaper library and ripped out the later issues.[53] But the style, contents, and tone of the newspaper were clear. Journalists included a wide range of nonjournalists involved in the state's various social movements. Funding depended on a Mexican Cold War mix of Cuba, "new left" organizations, and left-leaning or civic-minded merchants. To appeal to as broad an audience as possible, the design was heavily tabloid. Reyes mixed *nota roja* reports with news on teacher and peasant movements. Like national "new left" publications, criticism of both local and national politicians was acute and commonplace. But two aspects differentiated *Acción* from magazines like *Política* and *Por Qué?* First, Reyes exploited gendered journalistic traditions and pushed the society column toward its logical politicized conclusion. Her gossipy, sarcastic style now focused exclusively on stories of official incompetence and political corruption. Second, the letters page started to dominate the publication. Like *El Norte* in 1955, the last two pages of the paper provided a forum for peasants and squatters to state their complaints and demands and build alliances. By early 1964 *Acción* not only had a devoted readership in both the city and the countryside, but also had helped to fuse both rural and urban protest groups into a powerful cross-class movement.

Seven years after Soto's resignation, high politics in the state was still a mess. Individual cliques attached to former governors and regional power-brokers sought to dominate the state administration. The appointment of the relatively neutral governor, Práxedes Giner Durán, was designed to pacify these competing currents. Instead it did the exact opposite. Giner was a hapless negotiator who was unable to placate any of the factions. The official party, understood as both a forum for elite negotiations and a mass, corporatist organization, fell apart. Even in well-organized states, the PRI's corporatist apparatus struggled to extend meaningful influence over peasants, workers, or the urban middle classes.[54] In Chihuahua, the party was virtually nonexistent. The state's political factions refused to cooperate with the governor or allow their followers to work under the umbrella of the PRI. The head of the state branch came from a rival faction that was attempting to undermine the governor by actively destroying the organization's infrastructure from within. The party's usual electoral cannon fodder—the members of the peasant sector— were disorganized, disaffected, or members of opposition unions. Proindependence factions of the railway and miners unions dominated worker politics. The popular sector was "a complete fiction." (In fact, the only listed members of the sector were trainee teachers who wanted to get official CNOP T-shirts so they could infiltrate a PRI rally and barrack the presidential candidate.) The management of elections was equally haphazard. Two months before the 1964 council votes, state agents reported that there were no lists of PRI candidates or registered voters.[55]

Elite factionalism and the governor's confrontational style combined with growing socioeconomic problems to generate three powerful opposition movements. The first comprised the remnants of 1955's civil society movement. In Chihuahua City, they continued to play an important role. In 1962, the former CPJDC leader Lázaro Villareal again drew together citizens from across the social spectrum, this time to oppose a new municipal tax and the rising price of water. As before, the group resisted political affiliation. PRI activists and PAN supporters were turned away from mass meetings. At these events, Villareal stressed that the organization was formed to "defend the common interests of the inhabitants of the city without imparting ideological, religious, or political concepts."[56] The second were the state's trainee teachers and working-class students who were concentrated in three teacher training colleges and the state capital's trade school. During the 1960s such places were hubs of radicalization. Most students came from poor, often peasant, families. The sense of companionship and solidarity was intense, and old revolutionary ideas on socialist education and land reform mixed productively with new ideas on U.S. imperialism and rural insurgency imported from Cuba.[57] Third, there were the state's landless peasants. These were concentrated just south of Ciudad Juárez around Villa Ahumada, southeast of Chihuahua City around the cotton-producing region of Ciudad Delicias, and to the northwest of the capital in the logging zone of Ciudad Madera. During the late 1950s they had left the government-controlled peasant union, joined the more radical General Union of Workers and Peasants of Mexico (Unión General de Obreros y Campesinos de México, UGOCM), and started to employ land invasions in order to push their demands.[58] Together, these groups would form the readers of Reyes's *Acción*.

Reyes released the first issue of *Acción* in September 1962. She wrote a fair proportion of the copy, especially the initial news stories. She also ran her own column. But there were other writers. Like Reyes, most were new to journalism. Together they formed a relatively representative spectrum of Mexico's 1960s radicals. Some came from the state's various social movements and included teachers like the future guerrilla Arturo Gámiz, left-wing students like Carlos Montemayor, and leading members of the state's civic movements, like the lawyer Salustio González Delgado. But some came from within the state's institutions. José Santos Valdés, a Chihuahua school inspector, wrote a series of articles on rural Mexico. So did the dissident DAAC employee Victor Manuel Bueno, who had been an agronomist but broke the rules of bureaucratic practice by repeating peasant grievances in public. Finally, there was a representative of the church's shift toward liberation theology, Father Carlos Aguirre Escápite. (In Chihuahua the movement had considerable support, especially among young, dissident members of the PAN party.)[59]

Funding for the newspaper came from multiple sources. New official sources of left-wing cash proved helpful. The first few issues contained bland two-page spreads on Castro's speeches and indicate that the Cuban embassy was paying for *gacetillas*. By 1964 Mexico's unofficial leftist party, the FEP, provided a printing press and paper for the publication in return for unmarked publicity.[60] But most patronage came from Chihuahua. A handful of the city's journalists helped with the technical features of the job. Gallardo, the editor of *Indice*, offered weekly use of his printing press. He also provided paper through his role as the regional PIPSA agent. (In the provinces even the most dissident newspapers relied one way or another on government subsidies.)[61] Another *Indice* writer, Jesús González Raizola, gave advice and encouragement and wrote the occasional article.[62] Local merchants provided the bulk of the money. Some did so anonymously, donating cash without placing ads in the newspapers. Others were more overt in their support. Villareal placed fortnightly ads for his furniture emporium. Other local businessmen, either from the masons or involved in the protests, purchased publicity for their hotels, restaurants, book emporiums, and electronics shops. Perhaps most surprisingly, some officials also offered their support. On the newspaper's first anniversary the commander of the Ciudad Juárez police department (who was involved in a spat with Giner's brother) and four deputies from an anti-Giner clique ran ads congratulating the publication.[63] Together they reflected the links between the radical left of the early 1960s and both broader civic movements and internal PRI factions.[64]

The style of the newspaper was resolutely populist and designed to appeal to rural peasants and urban squatters on the edge of literacy. The paper was twelve pages long and tabloid size, like the regional *nota roja* papers. At first, the front page contained one or two of the main stories. But in September 1964 Reyes reworked the design. Like the capital's *La Prensa, Acción* now covered the front page with four or five alarmist headlines in large type, designed to flag the contents to readers: "Is General Olachea a Latifundista?," "The Scandalous Takeover of the CCI," "Guanajuato and the Dodgy Finances of [Governor] Torres Landa," "The Guerrillas of Chihuahua Speak."[65] Inside, the writing was short, simple, and to the point. The only articles that indulged in the traditionally long-winded rhetoric of the left were Castro's speeches and the occasional instructive pieces by rural teachers. Especially in Reyes's own column, the use of jokey nicknames and street phrases was commonplace. Finally, pictures were frequent if not action-packed. Reyes had no professional photographer on her staff and she relied on individual reporters to illustrate their stories. At times, they managed to capture arresting images of marching peasants or heavily armed soldiers. One particularly shocking image, designed to demonstrate the link between local government and the vice industry in Ciudad Juárez, showed a row of students entering their school right next to an open brothel.[66] But these were rare. Instead, like *Política*, *Acción* tended to invert the intention of official publicity photographs, using them to accompany stories that apportioned blame for acts of corruption or violence. After a government attack on students in February 1964, Reyes dotted the front page with pictures of the military officials responsible.[67]

Reyes also developed her own distribution scheme. As contributors wrote for free, paper came direct from PIPSA (or later the FEP) supplies, and ads covered the costs of her labor and travel, she circulated the newspaper for free. The strategy covered regions rarely touched by local newspapers, penetrated a group of readers whose illiteracy usually prevented access to the press, and achieved an extremely high ratio of readers to printed issues. To do so, she employed four existing networks. The first were the *ejidos*. Using the free postage, Reyes sent twenty to thirty copies to every group in Chihuahua as well as those who wrote in from further afield. The peasants then either made copies of particularly relevant stories or read the articles aloud at their meetings. Reyes's daughter remembered dozens of peasants in the fields around Parral reading the paper during their breaks.[68] The second were the teachers. Reyes sent out copies to both rural teachers and the teacher training colleges. The recipients then either read the newspaper on their own or organized meetings at which they read it aloud to peasants or pupils.[69] The third were the students of Chihuahua City's higher education establishments. In this case, her daughter, who was a student at the university, probably provided access. Finally, there were the capital's civic groups. Villareal distributed the newspaper at the groups' various meetings.[70] Such networks generated impressive growth. The newspaper started on a small scale, issuing only 1,000 copies. By 1963 this had risen to 5,000, and during 1964 circulation hit 22,000 copies.[71] Given the number of readers, more people were probably reading *Acción* than papers from the García Valseca chain.

Reyes envisaged the publication as reporting the stories the mainstream media refused to print, or as she put it "the information that didn't interest the major presses of the bourgeoisie." To do so, she developed a distinctly organic way of newsgathering, which was free of government control. There were no articles from press agencies or national newspapers. In fact, news from outside Chihuahua was rare. As in Oaxaca, this was localocentric journalism. There were also no reprints, rewrites, or even careful critiques of official press bulletins from inside the state. The type of stories *Acción* printed very rarely overlapped with those of the right-wing *El Heraldo* or even the left-wing *Indice*. Instead Reyes relied on tips and hints from her readers. Then she either got a nearby activist to follow up on the story or traveled to the scene of the article herself. "My permanent sources of information were precisely them, the peasants. I don't think there ever was a newspaper with so many correspondents. This was because we always found space to deal with their problems."[72] Such an approach not only avoided the official framing of the news, but also tightened the bonds between the publication and the readers. Peasants (and also poor urban inhabitants) now had a space that focused on their complaints and demands.

As a result, most of the newspaper's articles dealt with the conflicts between peasants and the state. Unlike orthodox treatments, which tended to avoid apportioning blame and talked vaguely of "conflicts" and "struggles," *Acción*'s pieces highlighted the violence of the state actors. Stories of thugs aggressively dislodging land invaders were commonplace. In July 1963 Reyes described a military lieutenant, surrounded by a group of *pistoleros*, destroying the huts of Ciudad Madera's peasants on behalf of the local ranchers, arresting the leaders, and sticking them in jail on trumped-up charges. Contrary to journalistic convention, criticism of the army was frequent. Soldiers were described as "ferocious thugs," "gorillas," and "unofficial white guards of the landowners." And, again contrary to convention, ranking officers were named.[73] There were also repeated articles on the murder of peasants. In January 1963 she reported that landowners had killed seven peasants in Guadalupe y Calvo.[74] A year later, she wrote that the rural police had beaten to death an *ejidatario* from Ignacio Zaragoza.[75] In recounting such stories, Reyes always did her best to include the voices of the peasants. Quotes from peasant witnesses were common. Telegrams or letters were often tacked on at the end of the relevant pieces to flag veracity. Finally, there were multiple stories on the murky workings of the agrarian bureaucracy for which the help of whistleblower agronomist Bueno was crucial. In 1963 he used his knowledge of the inner workings of the agrarian bureaucracy to write a series of articles on how landowners got around the law, infringed the constitution, and paid off officials. Again, accusations were specific. In January he explained how Hilario

Gabilondo had bribed the head of the state agrarian officials to lie about the extent of his properties. In fact, according to Bueno's study, they totaled double what the latifundista claimed.[76]

Though stories on rural Chihuahua dominated *Acción*'s coverage, there were also articles aimed at the newspaper's other readers—teachers and the urban poor. The newspaper's coverage of education concentrated on the struggle between the state authorities and the teachers union. In late 1963 *Acción* published stories that examined the head of education's attempts to oust the union leadership, throw out teachers involved in the land invasions, reduce wages, and dock salaries for party dues. Stories on urban problems also focused on labor issues. There were articles on low wages and poor working conditions among municipal workers, in the city's private baths, and at various local mines. There were stories that linked into the Chihuahua City social movement on the price of water.[77] And there was also a smattering of stories on the vice industry that contrasted the noble efforts of the state's teachers with the drugs and prostitution rackets run by the state's bigwigs. Such stories generated some of Reyes's most alarmist headlines: "300 Children in Danger"; "Depraved People Smoke Marijuana While Children Try to Learn."[78]

News stories provided the core of *Acción*'s coverage. They made the publication different and provided the link between journalists and readers. But there were also editorials in the inside pages. They were predominantly written by Reyes and sought to bring together the everyday tales of poverty, corruption, and repression into a coherent narrative. Unlike other contemporary left-wing publications like *Política* and even *El Día*, the pieces refrained from using complex language or dotting the text with Marxist phrases. In fact, despite the handful of initial Cuban *gacetillas*, she was keen to play down foreign influence. "We did not import this idea from the Russians who are conquering space; it was born here, in the Chihuahua countryside, where we see the *campesinos* perish before the indifference of our government."[79] Instead the pieces took an intensely personal line, blaming the failure of agrarian reform on a cabal of wealthy, conservative businessmen-politicians. Regional newspapers had a much stronger tradition of direct ad hominem assaults on public figures. But nevertheless, *Acción*'s editorials made for strong reading. Both local governors in particular were roundly attacked. The front page of the second issue called Borunda a "deserter of the Revolution." Inside, the editorial surmised that the outgoing pontiff had "left an economy bankrupt, public works in paralysis, and reactionaries in all the main government positions." Giner received even greater flak and was variously described as a "liar," "a defender of the landlords," "a cowardly and bestial gorilla," and "a dope fiend." The

PRI presidential candidate was treated with equal severity. Reyes described the nominee as "a citizen of undoubted reactionary ideology . . . and the candidate of the Alemanistas, the bankers, the latifundistas, the landowners, and the fanatics." If Mexico elected him, they would "drive back the country to the Porfiriato."[80]

Beyond *Acción*'s standard articles, Reyes included two other more distinctive sections. The first was her political column. In many ways, it was an extension of *El Monitor*'s "Ubicua y Yo." But unlike the previous column, there was no society news. Reyes had left behind the traditional role of the female journalist and moved into the male sphere of the political column. At the time, political columns were not only written exclusively by men, they were also formulated in a style that excluded the average reader. Even at the regional level, their language was deliberately opaque and their subject matter concerned the higher echelons of political power. Reyes's column broke the rules. It was written in an accessible and popular style and dotted with slang and Reyes's favorite sayings, like Pácatelas! [Bang!]. It concerned relations between state representatives and the urban and rural poor. It relied not on top-down rumors from the corridors of power, but bottom-up gossip from the fields and the streets. Rather than masking corruption and ineptitude with euphemisms, it reveled in exposing it to readers. In many ways, the column foreshadowed the more populist, antiestablishment columns of the big nationals during the 1970s. But at the time it was novel and different. Reyes seemed well aware of the fact and called it "Taconazos" [blows from the heel of a high-heeled shoe]. The term encapsulated the contrasting ideas of femininity and violence and in doing so both highlighted the author's gender and signposted the column's critical, condemnatory stance.

Many "Taconazos" comprised offensive stories about Chihuahua's upper classes. They were designed to legitimize rumors and undercut the elite's cultivated aura of respectability. They were, in essence, the obverses of the traditional society snippets. Reyes revealed that local dandy Emilio Pinocelly owned 800,000 hectares of land and was trying to get the government to condemn the land invaders as communist agents. She disclosed that Spanish *hacendado* Macario Pérez possessed 500,000 hectares, was overheard describing Mexicans as a "race of dogs," and personally ordered the imprisonment of a handful of difficult peasants. Others focused on rumors of official corruption, like the head of the local water board skimming off percentages, the chief of the military zone teaming up with a former governor's brother to sell off publicly purchased agricultural hardware, or the son of the state secretary of public education being caught trafficking drugs. Others still brought together the accusations of far-flung peasant communities. She accused Ciudad Madera rancher Florentino Ibarra of murdering a local teacher, and she claimed that a local deputy was deliberately holding up the distribution of lands in the area because his brother had a financial stake in the forestry business. Finally, other pieces were simply pointed jokes. She implied that the head of the government's peasant union was so stupid he had recently suggested crossing chickens with pigs so they could make eggs with bacon. And she floated the idea of prosecuting Díaz Ordaz's parents for high treason for imposing "such an ugly man on Mexico."[81]

Acción also included an important letters page. Over the years, the section grew from one or two letters a week to around ten. By mid-1964 it covered over two pages or nearly a quarter of the paper. On the most basic level, the letters reflected how the publication had managed to extend beyond the provinces' traditional urban readers. At least a third of the correspondents stated that they came from peasant communities. Many simply expressed their gratitude for the publication's focus and its candor. The members of the Colonia Adolfo Ruiz Cortines sent in 10 pesos to thank her for publicizing their case. One writer from the tiny logging hamlet of El Vergel claimed that the entire village "like[d] it when you throw stones at everyone." But increasingly, peasants, students, and teachers used the page to communicate their own news. The back pages became a message board, a bottom-up forum for informing, discussing, and debating the local peasant world. Many letters took the form of traditional letters to the state and simply flagged problems with agrarian reform. Complaints included tardiness, the mismeasuring of lands, and conflicts between federal and state authorities.[82]

But others adopted the shape of *nota roja* articles. As forum met form the line between journalist and reader dissolved. In October 1962 the widow of Alberto Ronquillo wrote in to describe how a professional hit man had murdered her husband, then mutilated the body by cutting off his balls and tongue. She narrated the hit man's previous crimes, which included killing the head of the Casas Grandes *ejido*, a peasant union leader, and a Chihuahua City civic leader, and speculated that he was the elite's go-to assassin. In August 1963 another woman wrote in to denounce the murder of Guadalupe Rios, a "poor cowboy" from Saucillo. She attacked the authorities, who "made out they were Sherlock Holmes de petate [of straw]" but did nothing. She criticized *El Heraldo*, which dismissed the killing as performed by an unknown vagrant. Instead she suggested that the authorities knew the assassin and were deliberately covering up the case. Like the formal crime news, these letters not only dignified the victims' families, but also invited reader participation. In the following weeks, other peasants wrote in offering commiserations, similar stories, and in the first case tales of the hit man's powerful protectors.[83]

To an extent, Reyes's gender probably protected her from the more extreme forms of regional censorship. As a woman, Reyes struggled to enter the public sphere, but once she did so she was afforded a degree of license and given the kind of protection denied her male colleagues. Journalists often came to Reyes's defense; concerned peasant leaders sent their own "bodyguards" to protect her office; and even Giner was perhaps reluctant to order the murder of a female journalist. But she did suffer frequent, if not life-threatening attacks. Officials drew from the usual strategies used to silence local newspapers. She was beaten twice, on both occasions by anonymous gunmen. She was threatened at least once by the chief of the state's judicial police, who told her she practiced "not journalism but agitation" and said he would put her in jail. She was actually arrested and thrown in jail twice, both times without specific charges. On the second occasion, she seemed to cause more problems behind bars than outside. After complaining about her seclusion in solitary confinement, she was released into the general prison population. Here she elicited gossip from the jailed madams on their upscale customers, daubed the walls with political propaganda, and entertained the prisoners with a smuggled guitar and versions of her "Corrido de Díaz Ordaz."[84]

Despite these rather haphazard attempts at state censorship, for the first two years of its existence *Acción* created a public that included both the usual urban consumers of the provincial press and more rural readers. In doing so, it helped generate links of sympathy, common interest, and political alliances not only among isolated, fractious peasant communities but also between these groups and supportive urban allies. Furthermore, these political alliances did not remain relegated to the printed page. In fact, between 1963 and 1964 they translated into powerful and contentious protests in both the countryside and the city. These demonstrations not only reveal the broad cross-class nature of the left-wing coalitions of the early 1960s but also the links between these movements and the prodemocracy civic protests of the late 1940s and 1950s.

The first signs of this alliance were the wave of land invasions that shook Chihuahua during the early 1960s. These started to include teachers, students, and other urban protestors as well as peasants.[85] Gradually, this urban-rural alliance transferred to the capital city. In June 1963 students demonstrated in the Plaza Hidalgo in support of arrested peasants. In early September eighty peasants, mostly from Ciudad Delicias, held a demonstration in front of the capital's agrarian offices, gave out leaflets, and held a march around the city. The move into the city strengthened cross-class links. The civic leader Villareal lent the peasant organizers his offices. On September 14 teachers, students, and left-wing politicians joined peasants and held a mass rally in front of the statehouse. Such efforts also started to achieve results. At the end of the year peasant leaders met the visiting president and put forward their demands. But despite these conciliatory gestures, over the next year conflicts between state forces and the alliance turned increasingly violent. On February 22, 1964, trainee teachers, members of Villareal's civic committee, and peasants again took the state's agrarian offices. This time, riot police reacted with force and ejected the protests. Outside in the Plaza Hidalgo, the confrontation turned into a running battle. Students burned a coffin with Giner's name on it. One of the heads of the civic committee read out a jokey funeral oration. When the police used tear gas, the protestors responded with rocks and stones.[86]

Clashes reached a peak during the PRI presidential nominee's visit on April 6. The Chihuahua leg of the candidate's tour had already started poorly; students in Ciudad Juárez had pelted him with rotten eggs. In the state capital, things got worse. During the speech, trainee teachers and other activists barracked Díaz Ordaz. Then two students got on the stage, grabbed the microphone, and demanded an interview. The intervention precipitated a barrage of shouting and name-calling aimed at the governor and his administration. Then demonstrators hurled sticks, fruit, bottles, and rocks at the stage. The candidate's handlers quickly bundled him back to his hotel. The crowd took over the plaza and set fire to the wooden stage and the PRI banners. As the propaganda burned, flames even scorched the edges of the statehouse. Inevitably the police reacted with force, evicting the demonstrators and then sweeping up suspects in house-to-house arrests.[87]

In the following weeks, the city's activists came together and tried to stop the government prosecuting those deemed responsible for the riot. Villareal formed another civic committee to fight for the rights of imprisoned protestors. He brought masons, miners, journalists, teachers, left-wing politicians, peasants, and even dissident members of the PAN into the group and petitioned the government on behalf of students arrested after the demonstrations of April 6. He paid for their lawyers and provided them with food. He set up regular Monday meetings, distributed propaganda, and held press conferences to publicize the committee's aims. Rather than embracing the left-wing rhetoric of the protestors, the sixty-nine-year-old Villareal relied on the traditional discourse of justice and the law. Whether the jailed students were guilty or not was irrelevant. They had the right to receive a fair trial and not endure torture. Within these limited bounds, the campaign was broadly successful. The governor was forced to sack his attorney general and the students were released.[88]

But summer 1964 was also the beginning of the end for the cross-class movement. The crackdown after the April 6 riot imprisoned many of the leading activists. Some got out, but many were intimidated and others fled. Federal spies now joined state police in monitoring and harassing trainee teachers and students especially. On September 6 Villareal, the man who had provided a link between the old civic movements and the contemporary radical protests, died. Mourners lined the ten-kilometer stretch from his ranch on the edge of the capital to the city's cemetery.

Meanwhile, in the Sierra a handful of teachers and peasants had already renounced what they deemed bourgeois reformism. They formed a guerrilla group and were led by the teacher and ideologue Arturo Gámiz. On July 15, 1964, they committed their most daring attack yet—an assault on the judicial police stationed in Ciudad Madera. The confrontation drove government forces to scour the surrounding area for the guerrillas, who were eventually forced to flee to Mexico City. When they returned the following year, they launch an ill-fated attack on the Ciudad Madera barracks. Thirteen poorly armed guerrillas were confronted by over a hundred well-trained soldiers. The result was a massacre. But the confrontation also had other consequences. After the assault, Chihuahua City's cross-class movement divided over the guerrilla strategy. Some, like Reyes and Gallardo, remained cautiously respectful. Others, especially from Villareal's civic organization, tried to distance their group from those willing to use violence and accepted government concessions.[89]

The Singer and Her Legacy

In the years following the Ciudad Madera attack, Reyes moved to Mexico City, threw herself into the capital's radical movements, left journalism, and returned to song writing. In 1968, she sang at student get-togethers and wrote a series of corridos on the clashes with the Díaz Ordaz government. Eventually, after state agents kidnapped and threatened her, she decided to move to Europe, where she gained a reputation as Mexico's representative of the *nueva canción* movement. Though Reyes eventually gained fame as a singer-songwriter, in many ways it was her journalism that was more pathbreaking. She built on traditional alliances between civil society and provincial newspapers and attempted to extend the public sphere's limited ambit to include increasingly literate peasant readers. The attempt had parallels throughout Mexico. In

Acapulco, de la Hoya used articles in *La Verdad* to connect urban discontent to *cacique* repression in the state's sierra. From 1958 to 1960 the newspaper became the voice of the Guerrero Civic Association (Asociación Cívica Guerrerense).[90] In Atoyac, Guerrero, the autodidact journalist Simón Castro used *La Voz del Ejido* to do the same.[91]

In Chihuahua *Acción* also had an important legacy. In the wake of the Ciudad Madera attack, reformist members of the early 1960s alliance founded the utopian squatter colony Francisco Villa on the edge of Chihuahua City. Here one of *Acción*'s former journalists published a newspaper, *El Martillo*, each week. The publication formed a central strategy of the new population center. Like Reyes's newspaper, it combined unfiltered local news with a large section devoted to readers' own denouncements. Civil society still had a voice.[92] Finally, Reyes's role as journalist also demonstrated both the gendered constraints of the public sphere and the ways in which women started to subvert these limits. During the early 1960s, she converted a traditional newspaper society column into a forum for political opinion and news. As editor of *Acción*, she built on this tradition to produce an open and radical political column. She up-ended the fawning tone of conventional society columns, and gossip and politics converged to form a powerful critique of the state's political and landowning elites.

Conclusion

On July 8, 1976, rival journalists, workers, and paid thugs held an impromptu meeting of the *Excélsior* cooperative and voted to sack Julio Scherer from the editorship. Officially they claimed that Scherer had used his position to illegally take over lands in the south of Mexico City. But both Scherer's supporters and most outside observers concluded that the *Excélsior* "coup" was engineered by the outgoing president, Luis Echeverría, as a punishment for unfavorable coverage. In the months following the coup, Scherer and his supporters refused to give up. Instead they used contacts in the national and international media and (though less was made of it) the provinces to put together a new, critical political magazine, *Proceso*.[1] Over the next decade, other *Excélsior* journalists also went on to found other critical publications like *Vuelta*, *Unomásuno*, and *La Jornada*.

For journalists, media scholars, and political scientists, the *Excélsior* coup was a turning point in relations between the press and the state and between the press and civil society. The coup itself was held to reflect the decades of pervasive control the federal government had asserted over the Mexican media. At the same time, the establishment of *Proceso* heralded a new dawn for the newspaper industry and the beginning of a free, independent media that actually reflected public opinion.[2] There is something to this. The *Excélsior* coup alienated many intellectuals who had been close to Echeverría, and pushed them into opposition.[3] But the importance of the *Excélsior* coup should not be exaggerated. As historians of Mexico's press are starting to discover, *Excélsior* was no beacon of liberal opinion, the pressures on Scherer came from both inside and outside the cooperative, and many of the changes introduced by *Proceso* were already being developed by Mexico City journalists close to the state, like Manuel Buendía.[4]

Furthermore, the real changes to Mexico's postrevolutionary newspaper industry occurred outside the world of the *gran prensa*. Between 1940 and 1976 readership of the press expanded markedly. Until 1940 readers were concentrated among members of the upper and upper middle classes and some of the capital's workers and artisans. In the following decades, rising literacy, urbanization, and road building created new markets for Mexican publications. Low paper prices, cheap printing costs, and rising advertising spending allowed an increasing number of press entrepreneurs to take advantage of these social shifts. There was a rapid upsurge in the sheer number of printed publications. Though the capital's stuffy broadsheets only experienced slow readership growth, tabloids targeted at the urban working classes and regional newspapers aimed at the inhabitants of smaller cities and towns witnessed particular progress. By the 1960s urban Mexicans received their news through the press.

The growing importance of newspapers and the establishment of links between private advertising companies and the government combined to produce more intensive state control of the press. Especially during the 1940s and 1950s, some of this was unnecessary. Editors and journalists not only shared the aims and prejudices of politicians, but also adopted certain codes of conduct, which militated against direct criticism of the government. Nevertheless, throughout the period press offices expanded their roles from running propaganda campaigns aimed at the illiterate masses, through producing press bulletins, to ensuring that these bulletins were printed in the manner and the place officials wanted. Financial inducements also grew from sporadic payments, through loans and subsidies, to substantial regular disbursements. Some major newspapers only survived due to state largesse, and many Mexico City journalists enjoyed luxurious lifestyles on the public purse.

But such changes should not obscure the spaces for dissent that continued to exist throughout the period. In Mexico City, these spaces were concentrated in the satirical magazines of the 1940s and the radical, left-wing publications of the 1960s and 1970s.[5] They also survived in the mainstream national press, in the cartoons of the broadsheets and political magazines, and in the crime sections of the tabloids.[6] But, most of all, they endured in the provinces where independent newspaper owners, editors, and journalists made careers out of criticizing, mocking, and investigating both national and regional politicians. During the 1960s these traditions—imported to Mexico City by regional journalists like Mario Menéndez and Carlos Ortega—did as much to liberalize the Mexican media as changes within the capital's major broadsheets.

Furthermore, the closing of these spaces rarely involved the kind of carefully contrived, covert campaign that was aimed at *Excélsior*.[7] Censorship was never institutionalized as it was in many authoritarian states. Especially outside the capital, silencing journalists relied on an impromptu mix of imprisonment, threats, violent attacks, and ad hominem propaganda campaigns. These were risky undertakings and could be counterproductive. Some campaigns led to the closure of cowed or penniless presses. But others generated broad-based social movements in favor of under-fire publications.

If the state struggled to assert pervasive control over the press, other sectors of society were often more successful. Particularly in the provinces, business leaders shaped local newspapers. They included press entrepreneurs like García Valseca and industrialists like the Monterrey Group. By the 1940s they had started to run their own papers or subsidize other high-selling publications. At times, editorial policy ran in lockstep with government policy. But this was not always the case. Provincial elites regularly fell out with national and regional politicians. Newspapers in the García Valseca chain periodically blackmailed governors for cash and favors. Such "gangster journalism" may have run contrary to the high ideals of many commentators, but it could also produce high-quality investigations and critiques of those in power.[8]

Finally, members of civil society were also able to shape what was written about in the press. As the case studies of *El Momento/Chapulín* and *Acción* highlight, this was particularly the case for small-scale, local newspapers. These were often run by nonelite journalists; had low overheads and minimal staff; relied predominantly on sales and local advertising; and either built on traditions of critical newspapers (as in Oaxaca) or exploited the space between warring elites (as in Chihuahua). As a result, they were able to reflect the concerns and demands of their communities. They did this through farming out newsgathering to readers and neighborhood gossips, cloaking criticisms in a jokey mixture of nicknames and knowing asides (provincial Mexico's version of Aesopian language), and opening up large sections of the newspapers to readers' letters.[9] During the 1940s and 1950s many of these newspapers were broadly right-wing or at least bloody-mindedly contrarian. But by the 1960s many of these newspapers sympathized with more radical causes. Furthermore, Mexican readers could not only influence sympathetic newspapers, but also those deemed to support unpopular functionaries or policies. Sometimes tactics took the form of informal purchase strikes, popular demonstrations, and offensive corridos. But on other occasions they spilled over into violence. The attacks on *oficialista* newspapers in Oaxaca City in 1947 and 1952 were repeated elsewhere. During the electoral conflicts of the late 1950s protestors in Tijuana smashed the windows of *El Reportaje*'s offices, burned piles of pro-PRI newspapers on the street, and stole others and painted over their front pages with the letters PAN.[10]

Such conclusions not only challenge previous appreciations of the press, but also imply a reassessment of more general historical assumptions. They place print culture—rather than celebrations, festivals, mural art, or music—at the center of negotiations between the state and Mexican citizens. Such negotiations were often lopsided. By the 1960s the state invested substantial manpower, resources, and time in manipulating the print media. But they were not entirely unequal, and members of civil society, including editors, writers, and readers, could affect what was printed. They also suggest that by the middle of the twentieth century journalists were beginning to supersede both priests and teachers as the essential intermediaries between the state and civil society.[11] Many were card-carrying members of the PRI; others were cynical opportunists and chancers; others were self-righteous believers in reflecting public opinion and writing what they deemed "the truth." Others—perhaps the majority—changed over time and made pragmatic decisions on what to write based on an immediate blend of financial and professional considerations and personal sympathies.

Such conclusions also cement the findings of ongoing work on the Mexican state. Though a no-holds-barred *lucha libre* is still some way off, over the past decade there has been increasing, if quietly stated (pretenure?), disagreement over the shape, nature, and strategies of the one-party-dominant state. For some scholars, particularly those examining the institutional aspects of rule, power under the PRI was relatively weak and diffuse. Presidents oversold their power over governors; governors overstated their power over mayors; and at the municipal level, voters—as much as party functionaries and local *caciques*—held sway over who was elected.[12] For others, especially those studying the emergence of Cold War counterinsurgencies, the state was not only authoritarian, but also unified, efficient, and violent. Hierarchical chains of command were firmly entrenched, and certain state agencies, including the army and the DFS, used their powers to forcibly repress dissenting groups.[13] As the battle lines have yet to be drawn, the details are hazy. There is still ample debate over the timing of the emergence of this harder, more unforgiving state (late 1940s, post-Cuban Revolution, or mid-1960s?), its primary promoters (the U.S. government, Presidents Alemán, Díaz Ordaz, or Echeverría, the military or the state's security organizations) its primary focus (unions, teachers, peasants, students, or guerrillas?), and its geographical coverage (just radical hotspots like Guerrero, Sinaloa, and Chihuahua, or countrywide?).

Yet looking at the state's relationship with the print media can help us etch the contours of this *dictablanda*. The suppression of satirical publications and street theater indicates that 1948—perhaps as much as 1959 and 1968—was a key turning point in state-society relations at least in the capital. The establishment of well-manned press offices, the distribution of payments, and the running of sophisticated press campaigns suggest that a more cogent, powerful, and authoritarian state was already emerging in Mexico City by the 1950s. Yet the leap in the scale of disbursements and the array of government strategies indicates that this type of state could only operate with any prolonged efficiency by the mid-1960s. Furthermore, even under Presidents Díaz Ordaz and Echeverría there were distinct limits. Censorship was never institutionalized or even strictly planned. (In fact, the sheer number of Ministry of the Interior think pieces on propaganda during the period stand testament not to the absolute control of the media but rather to muddled government thinking over the matter.) Even in Mexico City, during the height of the crackdown on students, regulation of the printed press was enacted by multiple agencies, ad hoc, and not entirely successful. In fact, during the crisis *Por Qué?*'s strident denunciations and bloody visuals outsold all the more cautious newspapers and magazines. Finally, outside the capital city, state power was even more diffuse. Funding was low, key state agencies like the DFS and PIPSA were controlled at the federal level, and socioeconomic elites rarely overlapped exactly with political leaders. As a result, print media often carried dissenting voices.

Such conclusions also suggest that to understand the Mexican state it is important to look beyond formal political organizations and start to examine spaces created and controlled by civil society. Though these associations often explicitly distanced themselves from traditional parties, they continued to play important roles in shaping politics, especially in Mexico's regions. During the 1920s and 1930s the church's charity and social organizations provided crucial networks in resisting the postrevolutionary state's anticlerical policies.[14] Some were brought to heel by the ecclesiastical authorities, but others continued to organize school strikes and fund private institutions well into the 1950s.[15] At the same time, other secular associations—including the Masons, the Lions Club, the Rotary Club, local sports societies, and infrastructure boards—provided spaces for citizens to cement connections, perform what political scientists might term "politics with a small p," and then, if necessary, move into the world of mobilizations, political parties, and elections.[16] In fact, many of the civic committees that challenged top-down rule in states throughout the 1940s and 1950s—like Oaxaca's CCO or Chihuahua's CPJDC—were built on these foundations. Furthermore, these civic committees often formed the bases for the more radical organizations of the 1960s and 1970s.[17]

Finally, these findings also indicate new ways to reconfigure and refine Habermas's model of the public sphere for the study of Mexico.[18] First, they hint that the revolution succeeded in getting rid of class restrictions, which curtailed public writing during the Porfiriato. Upstart businessmen like García Valseca now owned vast media chains, cooperatives took control of major nationals, and taxi drivers, dancehall singers, and peasants wrote in the press.[19] Second, they suggest that though explicit ideas linking honor and public speech declined, gendered ideas of the public sphere still shaped Mexican newspapers. They structured the division of labor in the newsroom and provided a framework for the everyday culture and the value system of Mexican reporters. They also helped curtail political writing, preventing male journalists from exposing corruption by indulging in designated female pursuits of *murmuración,* or *libertinaje.* Sometimes journalists deliberately subverted these conceptions by coopting female spaces—like the society news—to critique official graft. Other times women, like Judith Reyes, used acceptable spaces for female writing in order to write about politics. But in both cases, state authorities cracked down on such infringements, often publicly using these examples in order to restate the rules of the public sphere. Third, they suggest that geography, as much as class or gender, was one of the key factors limiting public debate. In mid-century Mexico, functioning public spheres were extremely localized both in terms of their participants and their subject matter.

Extrapolating contemporary lessons even from recent history is a dangerous game. But it would be remiss to not make some comment on the contemporary situation of the press in Mexico. As I finish this book, Mexico is ranked 149th in Reporters' Without Borders World Press Freedom Index. It ranks lowest in mainland Latin America. The combined effect of state, commercial, and criminal censorship is to leave Mexico below Afghanistan, Burma, Russia, and Zimbabwe in terms of press freedom. The murder of journalists has become commonplace and the country has become the most dangerous location to pursue journalism outside the Middle East. Though the Committee to Protect Journalists estimates that only forty-one journalists were killed between 2006 and 2016, the actual number is far higher.[20] At the most basic level, the current situation demonstrates the dangers of applying democratization theory, with its assumptions linking electoral freedom, press liberalization, and declining violence. Soft authoritarian Mexico was a much safer place for journalists than contemporary democratic Mexico. Though attacks on provincial reporters were frequent, they very rarely extended to murder. Fifty years ago local newspapers were able to expose the links between political authorities and organized crime in a way that they are not able to do now.

But if this history of the press has highlighted the differences between the Mexican press in these two periods, it has also hinted at certain continuities. The cartography of censorship remains broadly consistent with the mid-century. The same states (Veracruz, Oaxaca, Tamaulipas) that topped the tables of attacks on journalists during the period of one-party rule, remain bastions of press suppression today.[21] Strategies of silencing newspapers have retained a distinctly regionalized hue. Gangster journalism also casts a long shadow. As before, this is difficult to prove. And state authorities often muddy the waters by suggesting that the victims of violence were punished for attempted blackmail. But, no doubt, the practice endures. In fact, the perception that most journalists are killed because they have reneged on unwritten financial agreements has become widespread. Opinions of the honesty of print writers have declined precipitously since 2000. In a recent survey, only 22 percent of Mexicans claimed that they trusted the press.[22] If certain negative traditions have molded the nature of Mexico's democratic press, other more positive customs have also challenged this systematic narrowing of the public sphere. The blend of investigative reporting and *nota roja* pioneered by *Por Qué?* still provides an important space for criticizing the state in the provinces.[23] In Mexico City journalists like Anabel Hernández, Diego Osorno, Humberto Padgett, and Jesús Ezquivel continue to produce justifiably alarmist exposés of the links between politicians and organized crime.[24] Though the artisan papers of the mid-century have declined, they have been replaced by online blogs and social media. In highly controlled states like Veracruz and Tamaulipas, sites like *Plumas Libres* and *Valor por Tamaulipas* are the only places to ascertain what is actually going on. Like their forebears, they are run on a tight budget, employ minimal staff, avoid flashy graphics, and often have a very limited regional focus.[25]

Notes

Introduction

1. The clippings are in these folders: AGN/ALM/542.1/249; AGN/ALM/111/2588; AGN/ALM/151.3/209; AGN/ALM/703.4/906; *Por Qué?*, 08/15/1968.

2. *El Chapulín*, 09/02/1958.

3. Rodríguez Castañeda, *Prensa*, 13; Stevens, *Protest*, 34; Cline, *Mexico*, 185–86.

4. Volpi Escalante, *La Imaginación*, 34; Lawson, *Building*, 25.

5. Cosío Villegas, "The Press," 288; De Mora, *Por la Gracia*, 236.

6. Monsiváis quoted in Secanella, *El Periodismo*, 121.

7. Cosío Villegas, *El Sistema*, 76.

8. Monsiváis, *A Ustedes*, 54; Scherer Garcia and Monsiváis, *Tiempo*, 159.

9. Hughes, *Newsrooms*, 50.

10. Cosío Villegas, *El Sistema*, 79.

11. Lomnitz, "Ritual," 35.

12. Some of the most important works include Joseph and Nugent, *Everyday Forms*; Vaughan, *Cultural Politics*; Vaughan and Lewis, *Eagle*; Hayes, *Radio Nation*; Wood, *Agustín Lara*; Rubenstein, *Bad Language*; Beezley, Martin, and French, *Rituals of Rule*; O'Malley, *Myth*; Brunk, *Posthumous*.

13. Saber, NARA/RG306, MX-6901.

14. For the U.S. press, see Herman and Chomsky, *Manufacturing*; Gitlin, *Whole World*; Cook, *Governing*; MacArthur, *Second Front*. For the UK press, see Hall, "Rediscovery"; Page, *Murdoch*.

15. For an introduction see Curran and Park, *De-Westernizing*, and De Burgh, *Making Journalists*.

16. Much of this was self-praise. Leñero, *Los Periodistas*; Scherer, *Los Presidentes*; Scherer Garcia and Monsiváis, *Tiempo*; Rodríguez Castañeda, *Prensa*, 135–77; Hughes, *Newsrooms*, 120–21; Lawson, *Building*, 66–69. For a careful debunking of the mythology surrounding the *Excélsior* coup, see Burkholder, "El Olimpo," and Burkholder, "La Red."

17. Hallin, "Media," 91; Calmon Alves, "Lapdog to Watchdog," 183–84.

18. Darnton, "Early Information Society."

19. Similar findings have been made for the nineteenth century. Piccato, *Tyranny*; Buffington, *Sentimental Education*; García, *El Imparcial*; Díaz, "Satiric Penny Press"; Clark and Speckman Guerra, *La República*; Covo, "La Prensa"; Gantus, *Caricatura*. Initial treatments of the history of the twentieth-century press include Ortiz Garza, *México en Guerra*, "Fighting for the Soul," and *Ideas en Tormenta*; Niblo, *Mexico in the 1940s*, 311–60; Camp, *Intellectuals*, 177–207. Recent historical work on the press includes Musacchio, *Granados Chapa*; Piccato, "Murders"; Piccato, "A History of Infamy"; Serna, "La

Vida" and "Prensa"; González Marín, *Prensa*; Del Castillo Troncoso, *Ensayo* and "Foto-periodismo"; Mraz, *Looking for Mexico* and *Nacho López*; Freije, "Secrets and Revelations"; Burkholder, "La Red" and "Olimpo"; Gamiño Muñoz, *Guerrilla*; García and Solís Hernández, *La Nota Roja*; Rodríguez Munguia, *La Otra*. Also see the essays in Gillingham, Lettieri, and Smith, *Journalism*. Finally, scholars have started to integrate the study of the press into broader histories of Cold War Mexico. See Keller, *Mexico's Cold War*, 47, 48, 50, 58–60; Pensado, *Rebel Mexico*, 152–55, 228–31; Horcasitas, *La Democracía*, 204–6.

20. Darnton, *Forbidden*; Darnton, "What."

21. For a critique see Curran and Park, "Beyond"; Wasserman and De Beer, "Toward."

22. Examples include Scherer Garcia, *Los Presidentes*, and *La Terca Memoria*; Scherer Garcia and Monsiváis, *Tiempo*; Monsiváis, *A Ustedes*; Becerra Acosta, *Dos Poderes*. For an example of overstating state power, see Cosío Villegas, "The Press," 279: "The government is the promoter of every large undertaking, whether economic, social or political. It has the largest resources, the best minds, and also the highest purposes, for it alone can and often does reconcile the opposed interests of groups, classes or factions. Most important of all, it has power, infinite power, because there are no limits to it, and if it should encounter any, it can always get around them."

23. For example, over twenty years ago John Mraz had to rely on Armando Bartra's private collection to investigate the satirical magazine *Presente*. Now there is a full print run in the Hemeroteca de la Nación. Mraz, *Looking*, 284.

24. Del Palacio Montiel, "Introducción," 3.

25. Monsiváis, *A Ustedes*, 60.

26. Cosío Villegas, "The Press," 276. See also Hallin, "Media," 91.

27. See particularly Del Palacio Montiel, *Siete, Rompecabezas de Papel, La Prensa*, and *Violencia*.

28. Thompson, "Eighteenth," 134.

29. Rodríguez Castañeda, *Prensa*; Fernández Christlieb, *Los Medios*; Bohmann, *Medios*, 240–304.

30. Knight, "The Weight"; Knight, "Historical Continuities"; Hernández Rodríguez, *El Centro*; Rubin, *Decentering*; Bertaccini, *El régimen*; Hernández Rodríguez, *Amistades*; Gillingham and Smith, *Dictablanda*.

31. Gauss, *Made*; Loaeza, *Clases*.

32. Esquivel Hernández, *El Norte*, 59–61.

33. See chapters 7 and 8.

34. Keller, "Whose News?"

35. For an introduction to civil society in the Tocquevillian sense as a set of voluntary associations free of state control and in the Habermasian sense as a public sphere of open debate, see Edwards, *Civil Society*.

36. There are many works that implicitly or explicitly play down Mexico's civil society. See Paz, *Labyrinth*; González Casanova, *Democracy*; Almond and Verba, *The Civic*; Castañeda, *Mañana*; Somuano, *Sociedad*; Haber, *Power*. For an interesting challenge to this vision for the nineteenth century, see Forment, *Democracy*. For a contemporary challenge, see Butcher, *Mexican Solidarity*.

37. For a historical look at "civic journalism" see Nord, *Communities*. For civic journalism in Mexico see Hughes, *Newsrooms*, 5–6; Huerta and Pacheco, *Crónica*.

38. Habermas, *Stuctural*. For caveats over applying the concept to Mexico or Latin America, see Piccato, "Notes," "Introducción," and "Public Sphere."

39. Pérez Rayón, "La Prensa"; Cosío Villegas, *La República*; Piccato, *Tyranny*.

40. For the idea of multiple public spheres, see Calhoun, "Introduction."

41. Novo, *La vida en México en el periodo presidencial de Lázaro Cárdenas*, 321.

Chapter One

1. Fuentes, *Where the Air Is Clear*, 5, 123, 202, 294.

2. Alan Riding quoted in Adler, "Media Uses," 83.

3. González Casanova, *Democracy*, 88–89.

4. E.g., Castellanos, *México*, 37–55; Riva Palacio, "Culture of Collusion," 22.

5. Bohmann, *Medios*, 127–32; Merrill, Bryan, and Alisky, *Foreign Press*, 180–81; Rodríguez Castañeda, *Prensa*, 154.

6. Robert Adams to State Department, 11/29/1962, NARA/RG59/1961–1963/22.

7. Buffington, *Sentimental Education*, 9–12; García, *El Imparcial*.

8. González Navarro, *Historia Moderna*, 532–55; Rubenstein, *Bad Language*, 14; González Casanova, *Democracy*, 217.

9. Lewis, *Five Families*, 13

10. Vélez Ibañez, *Rituals*, 46.

11. Wilkie, *The Mexican Revolution*, 164. Literacy is obviously a problematic concept. The figures mentioned here refer to adult literacy. They are principally based on census records, which probably tended to overestimate those who had a working knowledge of reading and writing. Rubenstein, *Bad Language*, 15.

12. Cárdial Reyes, "El Período," 336; González Cosío, "Los Años," 410.

13. Loyo, "La Lectura," 254–56, 259–66, 281–86.

14. Cárdial Reyes, "El Período," 327–59; Torres Septién, "La Lectura," 310–11, 323–29.

15. Henkin, *City Reading*, 3.

16. Ferrer, *Enfoques*, 42; Secretaría de Industria y Comercio, *VII Censo Industrial*.

17. Informe, 06/07/1973, AGN/DGIPS/1659D.

18. García Canclini, Castellanos, and Mantecón, *La Ciudad*, 12, 56, 43.

19. Jiménez, *Picardía*, 9.

20. Vélez Ibañez, *Rituals*, 47.

21. Garza, *La Urbanización*, 41–49.

22. Wilkie, *The Mexican Revolution*, 143; *50 años de Revolución*, 99.

23. Gonzalez, *San José*, 221.

24. Erlandson, "The Press," 137–38.

25. Padgett, *Mexican Political System*, 215.

26. Lewis, *Life in a Mexican Village*, 40–41.

27. Stoppelman, *People of Mexico*, 98.

28. Bortz, *Los salarios*, 194; *Medios Publicitarios Mexicanos* (May–August 1960).

29. The exceptions are Berry, "PIPSA," and Zacarias, "El Papel."

30. *Política*, 08/01/1966.

31. Berry, "PIPSA," 33–34.

32. Pérez Siller et al., *México-Francia*, 107–8; *Excélsior*, 02/19/1938.

33. *Excélsior*, 02/19/1938; Enríquez Simoní, *La Libertad*, 24–28.

34. *El Universal*, 07/13/1932.

35. *Excélsior*, 07/15/1932; *El Universal*, 08/06/1932; *El Universal*, 08/18/1932.

36. *El Universal*, 08/29/1932; *El Universal*, 10/13/1932; *El Universal*, 12/12/1932; *El Universal*, 12/22/1932.

37. *Excélsior*, 03/23/1933.

38. Informe Confidencial, 06/01/1936, AGN/LCR/432.2/92.

39. *El Nacional*, 08/20/1935; *El Universal*, 08/15/1935; Berry, "PIPSA," 12–13.

40. *Excélsior*, 02/19/1938.

41. *Excélsior*, 08/24/1935; Fallaw, *Cárdenas Compromised*, 125–57; Smith, "Public Drug Policy"; Ochoa, *Feeding Mexico*, 39–70.

42. Informe Confidencial, 01/06/1936, AGN/LCR/432.2/92.

43. *El Universal*, 02/16/1938; *El Nacional*, 02/18/1938; *Excélsior*, 02/15/1938; *Excélsior*, 02/18/1938.

44. *Excélsior*, 03/06/1938.

45. Cane, *Fourth Enemy*, 184.

46. E.g., *El Nacional*, 11/27/1943.

47. Maximino Avila Camacho to Manuel Avila Camacho, 02/29/1944, Holmes to Avila Camacho, 01/28/1944, AGN/MAC/513.52/144.

48. Gerente General de Ferrocarriles to Secretario Particular, 02/12/1945, Secretario Particular to Secretaria de Relaciones Exteriores, 11/07/1945, AGN/MAC/513.52/144.

49. *El Nacional*, 07/14/1951; PIPSA to Miguel Alemán Valdés, 06/22/1951, AGN/MAV, 111/5304-A; *Excélsior*, 08/15/1951.

50. *Excélsior*, 06/09/1954.

51. Report on paper mill, 03/16/1955, CUSDCF/Mexico/ IA/1955-9/20.

52. Robert Eisenberg to U.S. Embassy, 07/28/1958, CUSDCF/Mexico/IA/1955-9/20.

53. Report on paper mill, 9/29/1959, CUSDCF/Mexico/IA/1955-9/20; PIPSA to Oscar Sánchez, 06/08/1969; PIPSA meeting, 03/28/1969, AGN/DGIPS/2944.

54. Precios históricos, nd, AGN/DGIPS/2944.

55. Stevens, *Protest*, 39; By 1965 there were PIPSA offices in Chihuahua, Guadalajara, Mazatlán, Monterrey (2), Oaxaca, Puebla, San Luis Potosí, Hermosillo, Tijuana, Toluca, and Veracruz. Clientes y documentos, 02/28/1965, AGN/DGIPS/2944.

56. Mario Moya Palencia to Luis Echeverría, 06/08/1968, AGN/DGIPS/2944.

57. Bunker, *Creating*.

58. *Crónica*, 101.

59. Heitman, "The Press," 98.

60. Moreno, *Yankee*, 152–71; Ortiz Garza, *México*.

61. Ferrer, *Cartas*; Annual Marketing Report 1970, Thomas Sutton Papers, Duke University.

62. *Crónica*, 56; Annual Marketing Report 1970, Thomas Sutton Papers, Duke University; Ferrer, *Cartas*, 143; *Heraldo de México*, 06/08/1973.

63. Bernal Sahagún, *Anatomía*, 85.

64. Carson to Williams, 09/25/1941, NARA/RG229/138 No. 10.

65. Ferrer, *Enfoques*, 45. In this period, the peso underwent two devaluations.

66. Bernal Sahagún, *Anatomía*, 124, 127.

67. Heitman, "The Press," 54; Borrás, *Historia*; News vs. Advertising, 09/1955, CUSDCF/Mexico-IA/1955-59/23.

68. Heitman, "The Press," 61.

69. Corson to Williams, 09/25/1941, NARA/RG229/138 No. 10.

70. Nolan, "Relative Independence," 38–51. In this period, the peso underwent two devaluations.

71. Junco, de la Vega, *Problems*, 23–25.

72. Erlandson, "The Press," 213.

73. Felipe Causey Olmos, 09/28/1966, AHEBC/JCA.

74. Borrego, *Cómo*, 134–38.

75. Informe, 10/15/1941; Luis Novaro to Secretaría de la Economia Nacional, 10/03/1940, AGN/SCFI/DGFC/5.

76. Roberto Blanco Moheno to President Alemán, undated, 1948, AGN/MAV/111/2000.

77. Heitman, "The Press," 43.

78. Lewis, *Five Families*, 13.

79. *Hoy*, 01/15/1938.

80. "A Study of Audience Opinions of 'El Mundo en Marcha,'" 1958, NARA/RG306, IRI-Mex-20.

81. Hidalgo, *Entre*, 75; Annual Marketing Report 1970, Thomas Sutton Papers, Duke University; Bernal Sahagún, *Anatomía*, 124, 127.

82. Bernal Sahagún, *Anatomía*, 124; Paxman, "Cooling," 320.

83. *Directorio de Medios*, 08/67.

84. González de Bustamante, *Muy buenas*, 33.

85. "Effectiveness of Newspaper Supplement, 1967," 1967, vol. 7, NARA/RG306, MX-6702.

86. Erlandson, "The Press," 183–91; Bohmann, *Medios*, 127–28; Trejo Delarbre, "Periódicos"; Riva Palacio, "Culture," 22

87. *Medios Publicitarios Mexicanos*, May–August 1960; *Directorio de Medios*, August 1967; Estadísticas sobre periódicos, Jul–August 1966, AGN/DGIPS/2951.

88. Lepidus, "History," 67; See data on sharing in "A Study of Opinions about International Affairs," 1958, NARA/RG306, IRI-Mex-19; Report on Newspapers in Jalisco and Colima, TJ Hohenthal, 06/26/1950, CUSDCF/Mexico/IA/1950-54/43; *Directorio de Medios*, August 1967.

89. It is unclear quite why this happened. The López Mateos administration may have pulled funding from a lot of newspapers established under the previous administration. Or the Postal Service may have wiped a selection of defunct publications from its statistics.

90. *Anuario Estadístico Compendiado* (1942–74).

91. Cole, "The Mass," 96.

92. Ibarra de Anda, *El Periodismo*, 89; Heitman, "The Press," 77; Erlandson, "The Press," 188–89, 231; Cole and Hester, *Mass Communication*, 15; Report on El Popular, 02/11/1947, CUSDCF/Mexico/IA/1945-49/32; Orden de Tiro de El Nacional, 12/24/1965, AGN/DGIPS/2930.

93. Zolov, "Jorge Carreño," 20; *Directorio de Medios*, August 1967.

94. Joint State-USIA Report on Non Communist Press, 04/07/1954, CUSDCF/Mexico/IA/1950-54/42.

95. "Effectiveness of Newspaper Supplement, 1967," 1967, NARA/RG306, MX-6702.

96. Moncada, *30 Años*, 124.

97. Carson to Hadley, 03/14/1941, NARA/RG229/138 No. 13.

98. Joint State-USIA Report on Non Communist Press, 04/07/1954, CUSDCF/Mexico/IA/1950-54/42.

99. Jiménez de Ottalengo, "Un Periódico."

100. "Effectiveness of Newspaper Supplement, 1967," 1967, NARA/RG306, MX-6702.

101. Joint State-USIA Report on Non Communist Press, 04/07/1954, CUSDCF/Mexico/IA/1950-54/42.

102. Roberto Blanco Moheno to President Alemán, undated, 1948, AGN/MAV/111/2000.

103. Mraz, *Looking for Mexico*, 155.

104. Estadísticas sobre periódicos, July–August 1966, AGN/DGIPS/2951.

105. *Excélsior*, 11/30/1918.

106. Roberto Blanco Moheno to President Alemán, undated, 1948, AGN/MAV/111/2000.

107. Merrill, "U.S. as Seen from Mexico." In comparison, a late 1960s study of fifteen U.S. newspapers from the U.S.-Mexican border discovered that barely 1 percent of coverage focused on Mexico. Price, *Tijuana*, 17.

108. *Por Qué?*, 10/10/1970.

109. Ibargüengoitia, *Instrucciones*, 91–92, 101–2.

110. Adler, "Media," 200–206.

111. *Novedades*, 08/01/1948; *Novedades*, 07/27/1948.

112. Monsiváis, *A Ustedes*, 52.

113. Mario Moya Palacia to Luis Echeverría, 10/10/1968; Mario Moya Palencia to Luis Echeverría, 11/05/1968, AGN/DGIPS/2944A.

114. *Medios Publicitarios Mexicanos*, May–August 1960; Piccato, "History of Infamy"; *Directorio de Medios* (August 1967).

115. Martínez, S., *La Vieja*, 266; *Medios Publicitarios Mexicanos* (May–August 1960).

116. "Tirajes diarios de periódicos principales," 03/17/1969, AGN/DGIPS/2951; *Medios Publicitarios Mexicanos* (May–August 1960); *Directorio de Medios* (August 1967).

117. Piccato, "History of Infamy"; *Directorio de Medios* (August 1967).

118. Piccato, "History of Infamy."

119. Carson to Hadley, 05/14/1941, NARA/RG229/138.

120. Joint State-USIA Report on Non Communist Press, 04/07/1954, CUSDCF/Mexico/IA/1950-54/42.

121. AGN/ALM/542.1/249; AGN/ALM/111/2588; AGN/ALM/151.3/209; AGN/ALM/703.4/906.

122. Lewis, *Five Families*, 102, 271–72.

123. Nolasco Armas, *Cuatro*, 227.

124. *Nosotros los Pobres*.

125. García Canclini, Castellanos, and Rosas Mantecón, *La Ciudad*, 13, 78, 56; *Siempre!*, 09/1953.

126. Piccato, "History of Infamy."

127. In the same survey 29 percent favored the sports news, 27 percent the society news, and only 6 percent the editorials. "A Study of Newspaper Readership in Aguascalientes," 1958, NARA/RG306, IRI-Mex-17.

128. Piccato, "Murders," 195.

129. Robles, *Retrato*, 210.

130. Sánchez García, *El Plumaje*, 165–66.

131. Guerrero Chiprés, "Zapatos," 23.

132. *Anuario Estadístico Compendiado* (1942–43), and *Anuario Estadístico Compendiado* (1975), AGN/DFS; Comparison of table in Garza, *La Urbanización*, Cuadro A-2; Cole and Hester, *Mass Communication*, 45.

133. Jiménez de Ottalengo, "Un Periódico," 776.

134. Borrego, *Cómo*; Russell B. Jeraza to U.S. Embassy, 01/03/1954, CUSDCF/Mexico/IA/1950-5/20,

135. For an excellent definition of industrial newspapers see Nerone, *Media and Public Life*, 5.

136. *Directorio de Medios*, August 1967.

137. Erlandson, "The Press," 366–67.

138. Ibid., 341.

139. Hernández, "Narcomundo," 127–31; *Anuario Estadístico Compendiado* (1954).

140. The figures on households and circulations come from a table in *Directorio de Medios*, Aug. 1967.

141. "A Study of Newspaper Readership in Aguascalientes," 1958, NARA/RG306, IRI-Mex-17.

142. Effectiveness of Newspaper Supplement, 1967, Vols I–VI, NARA/RG/306 MX-6702.

143. Erlandson, "The Press," 317.

144. Nolan, "Relative," 32–37.

145. *Medios Publicitarios Mexicanos*, May–August 1960.

146. Paul B. Carr to U.S. Embassy, 04/14/1950, CUSDCF/Mexico/IA/1950-54/20.

147. Alisky, "Growth," 75.

148. Robles, *Retrato*, 101.

149. Gutiérrez de Alba, *Tric Trac*, 17

150. Fromm and Maccoby, *Social Character*, 46.

151. Martínez de Verburg and Verberg Moore, "San Miguel," 67.

152. *Novedades,* 10/31/1952; Gutiérrez de Alba, *Tric Trac,* 74–75.

153. *Don Roque* 03/03/1946; *Don Roque* 03/10/1946; *Don Roque* 03/17/1946; *Don Roque* 03/24/1946.

154. *Verbo,* 10/28/1958.

155. *Epoca Nueva,* 10/07/1964; *La Voz del Istmo,* 10/13/1964.

156. Lewis, *Life in a Mexican Village,* 201.

157. Aguilar Domingo, *Zacatepec,* 18.

158. Tannenbaum, *Peace,* 301. Also see Pérez, *Diary,* 17.

Chapter Two

1. Scott, *Domination,* 2; This appreciation for freedom of the press went back to the early liberal period. Castaño, *El Régimen,* 23–27.

2. Castaño, *El Régimen,* 40.

3. Rodríguez Castañeda, *Prensa,* 15–32.

4. Gardner, *Inter-American Press,* 36, 44, 79–80, 143, 167–68.

5. Cosío Villegas, "The Press," 277.

6. *Espejo* (November–December 1964).

7. Serna, "La Vida," 133.

8. Coleman, *Public,* 46.

9. The CCPRI brought only seven publishers to court between 1944 and 1953, of whom only four paid any fines. It was, however, later used to shut down critical magazines in 1969, 1974, and 1986. Rubenstein, *Bad Language,* 109–32, Loret de Mola, *Denuncia,* 140–50; State Department Telegram, Kissinger Cables, Wikileaks, 09/06/1974, https://wikileaks.org/plusd/cables/1974MEXICO07626_b.html 03/21/2017; "Revistas picardías mexicanas," 06/03/1969, AGN/DGIPS/2959A.

10. *El Nacional,* 08/11/1944.

11. Darnton, *Censors,* 84.

12. Monsiváis, *A Ustedes,* 54.

13. Granados Chapa, "Aproximación," 49–50.

14. Muller, "Censorship," 1–32.

15. Bourdieu, *Language,* 37.

16. The reasons for this shift are dealt with in chapter 4.

17. For the best introduction to these policies see Torres Ramírez, *Hacía*; Martínez, *El Despegue.* For press anticommunism, see Servín, "Propaganda."

18. Confidential personal reports, 04/06/1959, NA/FO/371/126251. González de Bustamante, *Muy Buenas,* 1–4, 33–35.

19. Joint USIS/Embassy Field Message, 08/13/1969, NARA/RG59-1967-1969/389, PPB Mex 1-1-67; Cole and Hester, *Mass Communication*; 1959 American Press Institute Project, 01/29/1959, CUSDCF/Mexico/IA/1955–1959/24; Erlandson, "The Press," 243–44.

20. Erlandson, "The Press," 255.

21. Castillo Nájera, *Renato*, 301; Santos, *Memorias*, 903.

22. Confidential personal reports, 04/06/1959, NA/FO/371/126251; http://www .proceso.com.mx/173197/pleitos-de-familia-no-1037 09/14/2016.

23. Burkholder, "La Red."

24. Scherer García and Monsiváis, *Tiempo*, 19–20.

25. Consejos de Administración y Vigilancia 11/13/1950, AGN/SCFI/DGFC/4, Legajo 5.

26. Frente Reinvindicador to Carlos Torres, 09/19/1972, AGN/SCFI/DGFC/4, Legajo 8.

27. Lawson, *Building*, 28.

28. E.g., Día de la Libertad de la Prensa, 06/071963, AGN/DFS/VP, Rómulo O'Farrill.

29. Montgomery, "Mexican," 34, 41.

30. Francisco Lanz Duret to Luis Echeverría, 06/30/1968, AGN/DGIPS/1472, Exp. 2.

31. Enríquez Simoní, *La Libertad*, 31–32; Scherer García and Monsiváis, *Tiempo*, 152–55; García and Solís Hernández, *La Nota*, 89.

32. Martínez S., *La Vieja*.

33. Scherer García and Monsiváis, *Tiempo*, 21; Becerra Acosta, *Dos Poderes*, 67; Mejido, *Con la Máquina*, 10.

34. *Anuario Estadístico Compendiado* (1964–1965, 1970–1971).

35. Spicer Nichols, "Coyotes," 112.

36. Mahieux, *Cube*.

37. The exception was Magdalena Mondragón. Martínez, S., *La Vieja*, 231–34.

38. Hidalgo, *Entre*, 57–73.

39. Sindicato Nacional de Redactores de la Prensa (SNRP) to President Ruiz Cortines, 12/05/1957, AGN/ARC/432/220; Padrés, *El Diario*, 6.

40. Mraz, *Looking*, 154; Report by Fornay A. Rankin, 07/24/1952, CUSDCF/Mexico/ IA/1950–1954/42; Ortiz Garza, *México*, 42; Urías Horcasitas, "Una Pasión," 599–628.

41. Borrego, *Derrota*.

42. Burkholder, "Construyendo," 98.

43. Urías Horcositas, "Una pasión," 599–628. Pensado, *Rebel Mexico*, 228–30.

44. Informe, 11/09/1964, AGN/DFS/VP Rómulo O'Farrill.

45. "Periodistas Comunistas," 09/06/1970, AGN/DFS/VP Mario Menéndez.

46. Hughes, *Newsrooms*, 52.

47. Zolov, "Jorge Carreño's" 13–38; Del Río, *Rius*, 131.

48. President Ruiz Cortines speech, undated, AGN/ARC/135.2/83.

49. President Díaz Ordaz to Becerra Acosta, 06/03/1966, AGN/GDO/726.

50. Condés Lara, *Represión*, 1: 45.

51. Egan, "Entrevistas," 275–94.

52. Scherer García, *La Terca*, 87.

53. Gillingham, "How Much."

54. Lomnitz, "Ritual," 21–51.

55. *Siempre!*, 01/15/1959.

56. *La República*, 02/16/1950, AGN/MAV/161.1/41.

57. Rodríguez Castañeda, *Prensa*, 37–38.

58. *El Universal*, 06/08/1966.

59. Borrego, *Periodismo*, 130–55, 181–90.

60. *Espejo* (November–December 1964).

61. Castaño, *El Régimen*, 64–65.

62. *El Universal*, 07/07/1944; *Excélsior*, 03/13/1944.

63. *Siempre!*, January 1959.

64. Report on Freedom of Press, 06/09/1961, NARA/RG59/1961–1963/22.

65. *El Sol de México*, 06/06/1966; *La Prensa*, 05/12/1968.

66. President Ruiz Cortines Speech, undated, AGN/ARC/135.2/83.

67. Cole and Hester, *Mass Communication*, 19

68. *Excélsior*, 03/08/1967.

69. Novo, *New Mexican*, 39.

70. Alba, *Sísifo*, 47; Hidalgo, *Entre*, 101–15; Cuevas Paralizábal, *Entre*, 89.

71. Castillo Nájera, *Renato*, 258.

72. Mejido, *Con la Máquina*, 63.

73. Blanco Moheno, *La Noticia*, 147.

74. Castillo Nájera, *Renato*, 302

75. Scherer García, *La Terca*, 88.

76. Las Extrañas enfermedades del Lic. Bernardo Ponce, AGN/SCFI/DGFC/8.

77. Moncada, *30 años*, 134.

78. Suárez, *Puente*, 10.

79. Hidalgo, *Entre*, 84.

80. Suárez, *Puente*, 76.

81. Tapped telephone call, 07/24/1962, AGN/DGIPS/2894A.

82. Camp, *Political Recruitment*, 14, 18, 121, 234, 237; Camp, "Camarillas."

83. Spicer Nichols, "Coyotes," 258.

84. Blanco Moheno, *Memorias*, 69.

85. Hidalgo, *Entre*, 83–84.

86. Scherer García, *La Terca*, 88.

87. Mejido, *Con la Maquina*, 56; Burkholder, "La Red," 78–85.

88. Blanco Moheno, *Memorias*, 69.

89. Rodríguez Castañeda, *Prensa*, 26–29.

90. Erlandson, "The Press," 246–47; Interview with Ramón Beteta by Hildyard, 06/18/1960, NA/FO/371/6781.

91. Guerrero Chiprés, "Zapatos," 32; Del Río, *Rius*, 84–87.

92. Pilatowsky Goñi, "Reconstruyendo," 71–76.

93. Novo, *La vida en México en el Período Presidencial de Lázaro Cárdenas*, 482.

94. Pilatowsky Goñi, "Reconstruyendo," 71.

95. Ibid., 186–293.

96. José Altamirano to President Avila Camacho, 05/25/1942, AGN/ARC/545.2/99; Empleados de la Dirección, AGN/DGI/11, Exp. 50.

97. José Altamirano to President Avila Camacho, 05/2/5/1942, AGN/ARC/545.2/99.

98. Conrado Velazquez, Proyecto de Plan de Trabajo, 08/18/1949, AGN/DGIPS/119, Exp. 38.

99. See also Monsiváis, *A Ustedes*, 53.

100. Hoy-Manuel Avila Camacho Controversy, 22/05/1941, CUSDCF/Mexico/IA/1940–1944/65.

101. Ibid.

102. The timing and nature of the shift ties in with Rodríguez Kuri's analysis of the Ruiz Cortines presidency. Rodríguez Kuri, "Los Años."

103. Report, 03/23/1953, CUSDCF/Mexico/IA/1950–1954/43; *Excélsior*, 03/12/1953.

104. AGN/DGI/11, Exp. 44; "Datos . . . que corresponden a actividades desarrolladas," AGN/DGI/20, Exp. 5.

105. Castellanos, *México*, 42.

106. Study of Journalist Opinions of USIS, 1958, NARA/RG306.

107. Hidalgo, *Entre*, 84.

108. Garmabella, *Renato*, 150.

109. Monsiváis, *A Ustedes*, 54.

110. *Espejo* (Nov.–Dec. 1964).

111. Leduc, "La Corrupción," 69.

112. "Algunas preguntas . . ." 03/04/1955, AGN/ARC/704/876.

113. Pensado, *Rebel Mexico*, 125.

114. "Lineas Esenciales . . . ," undated, AGN/ARC/577/163–68.

115. Ibid. Toluca was a large city to the west of the capital. Police often drove prisoners along the road to the city, faked their attempted escape, and then shot them in the back. This was termed the *ley fuga*. See Piccato, "Pistoleros." Publicists from other countries call the *caja china* strategy by other names. In the U.K., the Conservative Party spin doctor, Lynton Crosby, dubbed it the "dead cat" maneuver. The idea is to leak a story so outrageous that it distracts the public from the story the publicist wants buried. He likened it to ending an argument at a dinner party by hurling a dead cat onto the table, see http://www.telegraph.co.uk/news/worldnews/europe/eu/9906445/This-cap-on-bankers-bonuses-is-like-a-dead-cat-pure-distraction.html 03/09/2017.

116. *Excélsior*, 09/24/1954; *La Prensa*, 09/25/1954.

117. There were some protests in Mexico City. But the most vociferous demonstrations were in Tampico, where taxi drivers and workers blocked off the port for nearly a week. *La Prensa*, 09/2/7/1954; *El Mundo*, 09/2/9/1954; *El Mundo*, 10/07/1954.

118. *Excélsior*, 10/08/1954; *La Prensa*, 09/28/1954; Various clippings, AGN/ARC/577/163–68; *La Prensa*, 10/08/1954.

119. Richardson, *Between Worlds*, 34.

120. *La Prensa*, 09/27/1954.

121. *La Prensa*, 10/04/1954; *La Prensa*, 10/07/1954; *La Prensa*, 10/15/1954.

122. *La Prensa*, 09/17/1954; *La Prensa*, 09/18/1954; *La Prensa*, 09/19/1954.

123. The *amparo* is a guarantee of protection of an individual's constitutional rights. Reich, "Recent."

124. *La Prensa*, 09/22/1954; *La Prensa*, 09/27/1954; *La Prensa*, 10/03/1954; *La Prensa*, 10/07/1954; *La Prensa*, 10/14/1954.

125. Velasquez, *El Caso*, 88–103.

126. For the links between the U.S. government and private advertisers developed during World War II, see Laurie, *Propaganda Warriors*; Fox, *Madison*.

127. *Excélsior*, 11/26/1959.

128. *Por Qué?*, 08/05/1971.

129. Ruiz Ocampo, *El Consejo*, 67–121, 83–84.

130. Antonio Menéndez to President Díaz Ordaz, 01/17/1963, AGN/DGIPS/2894A.

131. Menéndez, *Movilización*.

132. Alicio Rafael Ordoño, "La Información . . . ," 09/25/1965, AGN/GDO/302.

133. Plantamientos de Política Interior, undated, AGN/DGIPS/2959A.

134. "La tiranía invisible," undated, AGN/DGIPS/2998A.

135. Rodríguez Munguía, "La Tiranía Invisible."

136. *Política*, 09/15/1966.

137. Erlandson, "The Press," 146.

138. E.g., AGN/DGI/95, Exp. 1.

139. Instruments of Press Control by James Johnston, 12/08/1961, NARA/RG59/1961–1963/22.

140. Scherer, *Los Presidentes*, 20.

141. Informac, 05/16/1966, AGN/DGIPS/2917A; Metrolineaje, Nov. 1969, AGN/DGIPS/1413A.

142. Rodríguez Munguia, *La Otra*, 81–178, 197–234.

143. A discussion of the newspaper situation in Mexico, 08/13/1969, NARA/RG59/1967–1969/389, PPB Mex 01/01/1967.

144. Rodríguez Munguía, *La Otra*, 340–42.

145. Ibid., 364–68.

146. *La Política en México, Información Quincenal*, 12/15/1968. Aguayo, *De Tlatelolco*, 20; Rodríguez Munguía, *La Otra*, 159–71.

147. *Política*, 05/01/1963.

148. Cordona, "El Ultimo Dinosaurio."

149. Scherer, *La Terca*, 81–82; Becerra Acosta, *Dos Poderes*, 44–46.

150. E.g., José G. Morales to Díaz Ordaz, 10/08/1965, AGN/GDO/253.

151. *Carta Política Confidencial*, 10/23/1967.

152. Operación de Prensa para Michoacán, 09/30/1966, AGN/GDO/301.

153. Octavio A. Hernández, "Sugestiones . . . ," 01/20/1969, AGN/DGIPS/1460, Exp. 30.

154. See staff increases in *La Prensa* and *Excélsior*, AGN/SCFI/DGFC/5, Legajo 5; Miembros de la Cooperativa, 02/26/ 1965, AGN/SCFI/DGFC/8.

155. Cia Periodística Nacional, Egresos 1964, AGN/DGIPS/2851B.

156. Deudas El Popular, 11/05/1954, AGN/ARC/704/90.

157. Alfredo Kawage to President Ruiz Cortines, 02/17/1953, AGN/ARC/111/512.

158. *Política*, 10/15/1961.

159. Erlandson, "The Press," 256.

160. Cia Periodística Nacional, Egresos 1964, AGN/DGIPS/2851B; Juan Francisco Ealy Ortiz, 02/14/1966, AGN/DGIPS/2851; Informe sobre El Universal, 04/23/1969, AGN/DGIPS/2946A.

161. Rodríguez Munguía, *La Otra*, 181–90.

162. Blair, "Nacional."

163. President Ruiz Cortines to Kawage, undated, AGN/ARC/111/512; *Política*, 06/15/1961; *Por Qué?*, 11/13/1969.

164. *Política*, 10/15/1961; Fernández Christlieb, *Los Medios*, 61–63.

165. A discussion of the newspaper situation in Mexico, 08/13/1969, NARA/RG59/1967–1969/389, PPB Mex, 1-1-67.

166. Operadora de Teatros, 10/05/1968, AGN/DGIPS/2947A.

167. Various documents, AHEBC/SG/217.

168. Cole and Hester, *Mass Communication*, 20; Erlandson, "The Press," 145.

169. Lista de Deudas, 1944, AGN/SCFI/DGFC/5.

170. Metrolineaje, 1969, AGN/DGIPS/1413A.

171. Keenan, "How Advertising."

172. Cole, "Mass Media," 109.

173. Mraz, *Nacho*, 47

174. Moncada, *30 Años*, 134.

175. Scherer García, *La Terca*, 92.

176. Report on El Popular 02/11/1947, CUSDCF/Mexico/IA/1945–1949/32.

177. Report of Fornay Rankin, 02/04/1953, CUSDCF/Mexico/IA/1950–1954/43.

178. Lista de Subsidios, 1955, AGN/ARC/565.4/1804.

179. Rodríguez Munguía, *La Otra*, 348–49.

180. Underwood, "Survey of Contemporary Newspapers," 352.

181. Working Arrangement, 04/20/1954, CUSDCF/Mexico/IA/1950–54/42.

182. Informe, undated, AGN/ARC/111/512.

183. "El Popular Expires," 01/22/1962, NARA/RG59/1961–1963/22.

184. *Política*, 10/15/1960.

185. Report of Fornay Rankin, 02/04/1953, CUSDCF/Mexico/IA/1950–1954/43.

186. Rodríguez Munguía, *La Otra*, 114–22.

187. Conferencia de Rubén Salazar Mallén, 01/09/1954, AGN/ARC/120/2050.

188. *Indice*, 06/01/1961.

189. Mraz, *Looking*, 69.

190. For the regularization of the *iguala*, see "Lineas Esenciales . . . ," undated, AGN/ARC/577/163–68.

191. Taped conversation of Mario Santaella and Manuel Buendía, 10/26/1961, AGN/DGIPS/2894A.

192. "Relación de los periodistas . . . CNC," undated, AGN/DGIPS/1461B, Exp. 29.

193. Sercan Vallimarescu, 12/16/1960, NARA/RG59/1961–1963/22.

194. Lista de subsidios, undated, AGN/DGIPS/2953B.

195. Cole, "The Mexican," 65–81.

196. *Por Qué?*, 12/28/1972; Leduc, "La Corrupción," 82.

197. http://eleconomista.com.mx/columnas/columna-especial-politica/2013/10/07/chayote-origen-paternidad, 04/03/2017.

198. Spicer Nichols, "Coyotes," 113.

199. Leduc, "La Corrupción," 79.

200. *Índice*, 07/01/1961.

201. Castellanos, *México*, 50.

202. Moncada, *30 Años*, 142.

203. Underwood, "Survey of Contemporary Newspapers," 129–30.

204. SNRP to President Ruiz Cortines, 01/02/1953; Reynaldo Hijar to President Ruiz Cortines, 05/06/1956, AGN/ARC/111/169.

205. Arturo Sotomayor to President Ruiz Cortines, 08/05/1954, AGN/ARC/111/169.

206. Arturo Sotomayor to President Ruiz Cortines, 06/15/1958, AGN/ARC/143/1.

207. Rentería Arróyave, *Mi vida*, 60.

208. Acuerdo Presidencial, 02/23/1948, AGN/DGI/11, Exp. 50.

209. "Memorandum sobre el conflicto . . . ," 02/20/1973, AGN/DGIPS/1659C, Exp. 9.

210. Asociación Agricola Local to President Ruiz Cortines, 06/14/1956, AGN/ARC/111/2663; Bernardino González to President Ruiz Cortines, 03/06/1957, AGN/ARC/503.11/413.

211. Working Arrangement, 04/20/1950, CUSDCF/Mexico/IA/1950–54/42.

212. Becerra Acosta, *Dos Poderes*, 88.

213. Moncada, *30 Años*, 190.

214. Guerrero Chiprés, "Zapatos," 44.

215. Aguayo, *1968*, 54.

216. Scherer, *Los Presidentes*, 20.

217. Condés Lara, *Represión*, 1:48.

218. Sercan Vallimarescu, 12/15/1960, NARA/RG59/1961–1963/22.

219. Berry, "PIPSA," 7.

220. Smith, *Forced Agreement*; Cane, *Fourth Enemy*; Kenez, *Birth of the Propaganda State*.

221. Hall, "Rediscovery of Ideology," 86; Gitlin, *Whole World*; Herman and Chomsky, *Manufacturing*.

222. For lack of direct criticism of the president, see Montgomery, "Criticism," 673–79; Stevens, *Protest*, 36; Leñero, *Periodistas*, 293. For lack of coverage of guerrillas, see Gamiño Muñoz, *Guerrilla*. For lack of coverage of military massacres, see cover-up over La Trinitaria. Informe, 08/26/1955, AGN/DGIPS/2014B, Exp. 31.

223. Wikileaks, Kissinger Cable, Conversation with Fausto Zapata, 07/31/1976, https://wikileaks.org/plusd/cables/1976MEXICO09834_b.html 03/17/2017.

224. Piccato, "A History"; Camp, "Cartoons"; Zolov, "Jorge Carreño."

225. See the issues of the weekly newspaper survey Informac, which often recounted attacks on cabinet ministers during the Díaz Ordaz *sexenio*. AGN/DGIPS/2917A.

226. Smith, "Who Governed?"; Lista de editores, 1969, AGN/DGIPS/2971. For a parallel in the United States see critique of Chomsky by Hallin, *We Keep America*, 13. For criticism of cabinet ministers see Montgomery, "Criticism." Informac, 16 May 1966, AGN/DGIPS/2917A.

Chapter Three

1. *Presente*, 03/17/1949.

2. Report, 08/29/1950, NA/FO/AM1015/2.

3. Informe, 08/04/1948, AGN/DGIPS/112, Exp. 1.

4. Monsiváis, "La crónica," 25.

5. For "temporalities," see Sewell, *Logics of History*.

6. Asociación Mexicana de Periodistas to President Alemán, 10/12/1948, AGN/MAV/542.1/700.

7. Greer Johnson, *Satire*.

8. Luzuriaga, "Teatro y Revolución," 12–16; Ortiz Bullé Goyri, "Orígines."

9. *El País*; De María y Campos, *El Teatro*, 133.

10. Novo, *La vida en México en el Período Presidencial de Lázaro Cárdenas*, 178.

11. Luzuriaga, "Teatro y Revolución," 13.

12. De María y Campos, *El Teatro*, 363.

13. De María y Campos, *El Teatro*, 394–96, 399, 420; Roberto Soto to President Alemán, 02/06/1947, AGN/MAV/523.3/5.

14. Pilcher, *Cantinflas*, 18.

15. Daniels, *Shirt-Sleeve*, 447–50.

16. De María y Campos, *El Teatro*, 437–38.

17. Pilcher, *Cantinflas*, 18, 49–51.

18. Agustín, *Tragicomedia*, 56.

19. Gantus, *Caricatura*; Barajas, *El País de "El Ahuizote"*; Barajas, *El País de "El Llorón de Icamole"*; Buffington, *Sentimental Education*.

20. Wright Rios, *Searching*, 134–67.

21. Mraz, *Looking*, 61–69.

22. Rubenstein, *Bad Language*, 185–86; Martínez, S., *La Vieja*, 234.

23. Museo Nacional de Culturas Populares, *El País*, 9.

24. Wright Rios, *Searching*, 140.

25. Pilcher, *Cantinflas*, 43.

26. *Don Timorato*, 07/14/1944; Museo Nacional de Culturas Populares, *El País*, 9.

27. Ramos Camacho, "Este era Palillo," 157.

28. Beardsell, *Theatre for Cannibals*, 56–65.

29. De María y Campos, *El Teatro*, 406, 403.

30. E.g., *Don Timorato*, 06/30/1944; *Don Timorato*, 07/07/1944.

31. Gil Mendieta, Schmidt, and Ruiz León, *Estudios*; Alexander, "Fortunate Sons"; Camp, "Education."

32. Niblo, *Mexico*, 216.

33. Agundis, *El Verdadero*.

34. Report to Commissioner of Customs, 08/17/1947, NARA/RG170/160.

35. León Ossorio, *El Pantano*, 14–15.

36. Agundis, *El verdadero*, 153–58; Maríano Narro to Secretario Particular, 11/24/1949, AGN/MAV/568.1/5.

37. *La Nación*, 05/15/1948; *Presente*, 09/14/1948; *Heraldo de San Luis*, 01/12/1955.

38. Report to Commissioner of Customs, 08/17/1947, NARA/RG170/160.

39. Flores, "La lógica," 152–53.

40. Carlos Serrano file, NARA/RG170/160; Astorga, *Drogas*, 74–75, Niblo, *Mexico*, 259–61.

41. Report of Maurice Holden, 07/16/1947, NARA/RG59/22.

42. Carlos Serrano file, NARA/RG170/160; Aguayo, *La Charola*, 61–76.

43. Quintana, *Maximino Avila*, 112.

44. Gómez Estrada, *Gobierno*.

45. Agundis, *El Verdadero*, 65–69; Rodman, *Mexican Journal*, 48.

46. Niblo, *Mexico*, 258.

47. León Ossorio, *El Pantano*, 38, 41–42.

48. Report, 06/03/1946, CUSDCF/Mexico/IA/1945–9/32.

49. *La Prensa*, 08/21/1948; *Novedades*, 03/03/1948.

50. Cosío Villegas, "La Crisis"; Niblo, *Mexico*, 103.

51. Rath, "Paratroopers"; Piccato, "Pistoleros," 329–34; *Novedades*, 03/10/1948.

52. Rath, *Myths*, 94–101.

53. Smith, *Pistoleros*, 289.

54. Niblo, *Mexico*, 176–79; Informe, 07/23/1948, AGN/DGIPS/112, Exp. 1.

55. Middlebrook, *The Paradox*, 107–58.

56. *La Nación*, 04/24/1948; *La Nación*, 05/01/1948; *La Nación*, 05/15/1948.

57. Torres Ramírez, *Hacia*, 119–31.

58. Bortz, *Los Salarios*, 40–51.

59. Informe 07/25/1948; Informe 07/28/1948; Informe, 08/08/19481948, AGN/DGIPS/111, Exp. 2 (Carestia).

60. Similar discontent was also recorded by eavesdropping secret service officials in 1973 in times of similar economic pressure. Walker, "Spying."

61. Internal report on DGIPS, AGN/DGIPS/1980B, Exp. 2.

62. Informe, 08/02/1948, AGN/DGIPS/111, Exp. 2.

63. Informe, 08/10/1948, AGN/DGIPS/111, Exp. 2.

64. Informe, Lamberto Ortega Peregrina. 07/24/1948, AGN/DGIPS/111, Exp. 2.

65. Memorandum, 07/28/1948, AGN/DGIPS/111, Exp. 2.

66. Memorandum, Jesus González Valencia, 07/22/1948, AGN/DGIPS/111, Exp. 2.

67. Informe, Lamberto Ortega Peregrina. 07/24/1948, AGN/DGIPS/111, Exp. 2.

68. Memorandum, Inspector, SF 54, 07/23/1948, AGN/DGIPS/111, Exp. 2.

69. Informe, Lamberto Ortega Peregrina. 07/24/1948, AGN/DGIPS/111, Exp. 2.

70. Cadena de Libertad, AGN/DGIPS/111, Exp. 2.

71. Memorandum, 07/23/1948, AGN/DGIPS/111, Exp. 2.

72. Memorandum, Inspector 15 RJD, 07/16/1948, AGN/DGIPS/111, Exp. 2.

73. White, "Telling More."

74. Informe, 08/12/1948, AGN/DGIPS/111, Exp. 2.

75. Memorandum, 08/13/1948, AGN/DGIPS/111, Exp. 2.

76. Memorandum, 08/31/1948, AGN/DGIPS/24, Exp. 3.

77. John R. Speaks to ambassador, 08/03/1948, NARA/RG59.

78. Fernando Fagoaga, Informe, 07/22/1948, AGN/DGIPS/111, Exp. 2.

79. Informe, 07/23/1948, AGN/DGIPS/111, Exp. 2.

80. On popular satirical songs, see Darnton, *Forbidden*, 159.

81. Mondragón, *Los Presidentes*, 134.

82. Memorandum, 08/12/1948; Cadena de liberación, AGN/DGIPS/111, Exp. 2.

83. *La Prensa*, 08/19/1948.

84. Darnton, *Forbidden*, 158.

85. Martínez, S., *La Vieja*, 89–106; Orozco and Stephenson, *José Clemente*, 114.

86. Martínez, S., *La Vieja*, 89–106.

87. Novo, *La vida en México, en el Período Presidencial de Miguel Alemán*, 226; Novo, *La vida en México en el Período Presidencial de Manuel Avila Camacho*, 152–53.

88. Blanco Moheno, *Memorias*, 97.

89. *Novedades*, 02/04/1948; *Novedades*, 03/06/1948.

90. E.g., Piño Sandoval to Rogerio de la Selva, 04/21/1948, AGN/MAV/549.3/19A.

91. *Novedades*, 05/23/1948; *Novedades*, 05/24/1948.

92. *Novedades*, 05/26/1948; *Presente*, 07/14/1948.

93. Garmabella, *Renato*, 293–99.

94. Holden, "The Creative Writing."

95. *Presente*, 07/14/1948.

96. Ibid.; *Presente*, 07/21/1948.

97. *Presente*, 07/28/1948; *Presente*, 09/04/1948.

98. E.g., *La Prensa*, 07/24/1948.

99. *Presente*, 08/18/1948.

100. *Presente*, 07/28/1948.

101. For rise in society pages, see Agustín, *La Tragicomedia*, 71. *Presente*, 07/28/1948.

102. *Presente*, 08/04/1948.

103. *Presente*, 08/26/1948.

104. *Presente*, 08/18/1948.

105. Ibid.

106. *Presente*, 07/28/1948.

107. *Presente*, 08/18/1948.

108. *Presente*, 08/04/1948.

109. *Presente*, 08/11/1948.

110. Ibid.

111. Ibid.

112. Report on *Presente*, 09/10/1948, CUSDCF/Mexico/IA/1945–49/32; *Presente*, 03/17/1949.

113. Heitman, "The Press," 202.

114. Juan García Bernal to Lamberto Ortega Peregrina, 07/30/1948, AGN/DGIPS/111, Exp. 2.

115. Cadena de Liberación, AGN/DGIPS/111, Exp. 2.

116. *Presente*, 08/26/1948.

117. *Presente*, 03/17/1949.

118. *Presente*, 08/11/1948.

119. *Presente*, 09/14/1948.

120. *Presente*, 08/04/1948; *Presente*, 10/12/1948.

121. Piño had tried this to some success a year earlier. *Novedades*, 09/05/1947.

122. *Presente*, 08/26/1948.

123. *Presente*, 09/01/1948.

124. Blanco Moheno, *Memorias*, 294; Blanco Moheno, *La Corrupción*, 284–85; De María y Campos, *El Teatro*, 423.

125. Mondragón, *Los Presidentes*, 134–48; *Presente*, 09/14/1948.

126. *La Prensa*, 08/23/1948; PS 16 Informe, 08/03/1948, AGN/DGIPS/111, Exp. 2.

127. *La Prensa*, 08/14/1948.

128. *La Prensa*, 08/22/1948; *La Prensa*, 08/22/1948.

129. Informe, 08/11/1948; Informe, 08/14/1948, AGN/DGIPS/111, Exp. 2.

130. *Novedades*, 08/30/1948.

131. *Presente*, 03/17/1949.

132. *Excélsior*, 08/13/1948.

133. *Presente*, 08/18/1948.

134. *Novedades*, 08/20/1948.

135. *Excélsior*, 08/19/1948.

136. *Presente*, 08/18/1948.

137. "Ay Miguelito"; "Coronel de Generales"; "Enemigos Emboscados," AGN/DGIPS/111, Exp. 2.

138. *Excélsior*, 08/28/1948.

139. *La Prensa*, 08/13/1948.

140. Cadena de Libertad; Informe, 07/28/1948, AGN/DGIPS/111, Exp. 2.

141. Underwood, "A Survey of Contemporary Newspapers," 129–30.

142. Such propaganda fed off the anticommunist rhetoric Servín noticed increasing in force and regularity the previous year. Servín, "Propaganda."

143. *La Prensa*, 08/10/1948.

144. *La Prensa*, 08/21/1948.

145. *La Prensa*, 08/22/1948. See also *Excélsior*, 08/22/1948.

146. *La Prensa*, 08/14/1948; *La Prensa*, 08/12/1948; "El Murmurador," AGN/DGIPS/111, Exp. 2; *Excélsior*, 08/13/1948.

147. *La Prensa*, 08/30/1948.

148. *La Prensa*, 08/12/1948.

149. *Presente*, 07/14/1948.

150. Garmabella, *Renato*, 152–53.

151. *El Universal*, 08/28/1948.

152. *Presente,* 08/26/1948; *La Prensa,* 08/23/1948; *Excélsior,* 08/24/1948.

153. *La Prensa,* 08/19/1948; *Novedades,* 08/20/1948.

154. Agundis, *El Verdadero,* 45–50.

155. *Novedades,* 08/20/1948.

156. *Presente,* 08/26/1948.

157. *La Prensa,* 08/27/1948.

158. *La Prensa,* 08/30/1948.

159. *La Prensa,* 08/27/1948.

160. *El Universal,* 08/27/1948; Monsiváis, *Los Mil,* 27; *Presente,* 09/07/1948. Email correspondence with Paul Gillingham.

161. Blanco Moheno, *Memorias,* 292–93; Blanco Moheno, *La Corrupción,* 246–48.

162. See Aguayo, *La Charola,* 83–87.

163. *Presente,* 08/26/1948.

164. *La Prensa,* 08/30/1948.

165. *Presente,* 08/11/1948.

166. *Excélsior,* 08/31/1948.

167. *Excélsior,* 09/11/1948.

168. President Alemán to Alfonso Anaya, 10/27/1948, AGN/MAV/542.1/700.

169. Novo, *La vida en México en el Período Presidencial de Miguel Alemán,* 346.

170. *Presente,* 10/12/1948.

171. *Presente,* 03/17/1949.

172. Martínez, S., *La Vieja,* 92.

173. See the accounts in *Guerra al Crimen,* Mar. 1949; *El Popular,* 12/1/1949, 11/26/1948; *Presente,* 11/19/1948. Moncada, *Del México,* 81–84.

174. De María y Campos, *El Teatro,* 424–25; Blanco Moheno, *Memorias,* 295–98; Blanco Moheno, *La Corrupción,* 285–87.

175. Martínez, S., *La Vieja,* 234.

176. Asociación Mexicana de Periodistas to President Alemán, 10/12/1948, AGN/MAV/542.1/700; *Presente,* 09/14/1948.

177. Mraz, *Looking for Mexico,* 256; *El Apretado,* 06/02/1951; *El Apretado,* 01/19/1952.

178. *Rototemas,* 01/17/1959; Various documents, AGN/ALM/704/211.

179. De María y Campos, *El Teatro,* 433–99.

180. Lista de subsidios, undated, AGN/DGIPS/2953B; Manuel Alvarez to Jorge Piño Sandoval, 07/07/1950, AGN/MAV/272.2/272.

181. Asociación Agricola Local to President Ruiz Cortines, 06/14/1956, AGN/ARC/111/2663; Bernardino González to President Ruiz Cortines, 03/06/1957, AGN/ARC/503.11/413; Martínez, S., *La Vieja,* 235–36.

182. Monsivais, *A Ustedes,* 75–77.

183. Pilcher, *Cantinflas,* 147.

184. AGN/ARC/704/259; *Correo Privado,* 01/07/1954.

185. Camp, "Cartoons"; Zolov, "Jorge Carreño."

186. Scherer García and Monsiváis, *Tiempo,* 150–51.

187. For common frameworks that govern humor, see Hutchinson, *Theory of Parody*; Hutchinson, *Irony's Edge*; Critchley, *On Humour*; Bergson, *Laughter*.

188. The original *carta secreta* was the *Buro de Investigación Política* which was established in 1948. Others included *Correo Privado* and *Temas*. For coding of political columns see *Por Qué?*, 10/10/1970.

189. Schmidt, *Seriously Funny*, 11; Schmidt, "Elitelore." There was a resurgence of popular political satire in 1969/1970. Again, it was tied to shifts in the newspaper industry. On one level, satirical writers like Jorge Ibargüengoitia started to write about politics in mainstream newspapers like *Excélsior* (Ibargüengoitia, *Autopsias*). On another level journalists again worked as satirical entrepreneurs, bringing covert rumors of official malfeasance into the public sphere. Journalist Manuel Buendía was even allegedly employed by the Monterrey industrial group to write jokes about Luis Echeverría (Walker, "Spying").

190. Jiménez, *Picardía*, 119.

191. Pilcher, *Cantinflas*, 67.

192. Portillo, *Fenomenología*, 81, 93–95.

193. Bartra, *Cage of Melancholy*, 129, 140–42.

Chapter Four

1. Wikileaks, Secretary of State Telegram 09/13/1974, https://wikileaks.org/plusd/cables/1974MEXICO07855_b.html 03/16/2016; Informe 09/10/1974; Informe, 10/05/1974, AGN/DFS/VP, Roger Menéndez.

2. E.g., *Excélsior*, 10/09/1974.

3. Trejo Dalarbre, *La Prensa*, 115–16.

4. De la Grange and Rico, *Marcos*, 132.

5. Casteñeda, *La Herencia*, 89; Castañeda, *Utopia*, 97, 357.

6. *Por Qué?*, 05/21/1970.

7. Interview with Jorge Felix-Baez, Mar. 2016.

8. See the various trajectories of the Excélsior journalists: Leñero, *Los Periodistas*; Burkholder, "El Olimpo Fracturado"; Becerra, *Dos Poderes*; Mejido, *Con la Máquina*.

9. Keller, "Whose News?"; Cull, *Cold War*; Stonor Saunders, *Cultural Cold War*.

10. *Excélsior*, 02/09/1965; *Excélsior*, 02/10/1965.

11. For this radical early career see *Por Qué?*, 12/09/1971; Wells and Joseph, *Summers*, 233; Carey, *Mexican Revolution*, 12–13, 137, 190; Montalvo Ortega and Vallado Fajardo, *Yucatán*, 120.

12. Fallaw, "Politics of Press"; Castaño, *El Régimen*, 215–25.

13. Fallaw, *Cárdenas Compromised*; Report on Diario de Yucatán, 02/26/1942, CUSDCF/Mexico/IA/1940–1944/64.

14. Blanco Moheno, *La Noticia*, 158.

15. E.g., Augusto Miquis, *Por Qué?*, 10/30/1968.

16. *El Tiempo*, 03/22/1967; Berry, "PIPSA," 90; *The Nation*, 07/06/1970.

17. http://narconews.com/Issue64/article4047.html, 03/16/2017.

18. Erlandson, "The Press," 383; *Medios Publicitarios Mexicanos* (May–August 1960).

19. Menéndez, *Yucatán o el Genocidio*, 128; Informe, undated, 1970, AGN/DFS/VP, Mario Menéndez; Merida Consulate to Embassy, 12/03/1964, NARA/RG59/PPV, Ex 1-1-64/442.

20. Fallaw, *Cárdenas Comprimised*, 125–68.

21. Memorandum on Yucatán, 09/24/1965, AGN/DFS/VP, Carlos Loret de Mola.

22. Memorandum, 04/17/1963, AGN/DFS/VP, Mario Menéndez.

23. Menéndez, *Yucatán o el Genocidio*, 5.

24. Ibid., 37, 82, 7–132.

25. Ibid., 123, 71, 143–304.

26. Ibid., 5, 128–29, 230–31, 59–60, 170.

27. Ibid., 169, 174.

28. Paul Dwyer to Embassy, 12/03/1964, NARA-RG 59-PPV, Ex 1-1-64/442.

29. AGN/DFS/VP, Mario Menéndez, Memorandum, 10/29/1964; Paul Dwyer to Embassy, 02/10/1965, NARA/RG59/PPV, Ex 1-1-64/442.

30. For the new left in general see Gosse, *Where the Boys Are*. For the new left in Mexico see Zolov, "Expanding"; Pensado, *Rebel Mexico*, 152–57; Keller, *Mexico's Cold War*, 51–60, 105–17, 149–56; Carr, *Marxism*, 225–56. For the CCI see Sanderson, *Land Reform*. For the FEP see Reyes del Campillo, "El Frente."

31. For the role of United States and other noncommunist news agencies, see Trejo Delarbre, *Las agencias*; Jiménez de Ottalengo, "Un Periódico"; Bohmann, *Medios*, 215–39.

32. For an introduction, see Keller, "Whose News?"

33. Sercan Vallimarescu, 12/16/1960, NARA/RG59/1961–1963/22.

34. Underwood, "Survey," 163–68; *Excélsior*, 10/16/1963.

35. Memorandum, 02/27/1965, AGN/DFS/VP, José Pagés Llergo.

36. By 1974 there were a total of seven communist news agencies in Mexico. USIA, Communist Information . . . 1973, NARA/RG306, R-10-74; Memorandum on Prensa Latina, 01/12/1967, AGN/DFS/VP, José Pagés Llergo.

37. Cruz Vázquez, *1968–2000*, 45.

38. Zolov, "Jorge Carreño."

39. Burkholder, "La Red."

40. Keller, "Testing"; Sánchez Sierra, "Crisis Mistica." For evidence of Ernesto Uruchurtu's support for the magazine, see *Política*, 09/15/1966. For evidence of Cuban backing, see Informe Confidencial, 08/21/1963, AGN/DFS/VP, Manuel Marcué Pardiñas.

41. Memorandum, 02/22/1966, AGN/DFS/VP, Manuel Marcué Pardiñas.

42. *Política*, 05/01/1963; *Política*, 11/01/1963.

43. Del Río, *Rius*, 148.

44. *Medios Publicitarios Mexicanos* (May–August 1960); Mora, *Mexican Cinema*, 107.

45. E.g., *Sucesos Para Todos* (shortened hereafter to *Sucesos*), 10/01/1965.

46. Salgado, *Una Vida*, 23.

47. Rodriguez Munguía, *La Otra*, 227; Aguayo, *1968*, 53.

48. Padrés, *El Diario*, 105–6; see *Sucesos*, 05/27/1977; *Sucesos*, 05/14/1977.

49. Salgado, *Una Vida*, 21–23; Del Río, *Rius*, 167–70.

50. Salgado, *Una Vida*, 25.

51. See *Sucesos*, 10/01/1965.

52. *Sucesos*, 10/08/1965; *Sucesos*, 10/15/1965; *Sucesos*, 11/05/1965; *Sucesos*, 05/20/1966; *Sucesos*, 01/01/1967.

53. Morley, *Our Man*, 261–62.

54. For the predominantly negative coverage of the doctors' strike, see Horcasitas, *La Democracía*, 204–6.

55. *Sucesos*, 11/05/1965; *Sucesos*, 01/01/1967; Memorandum, 06/14/1966, AGN/DFS/VP Mario Menéndez.

56. *Sucesos*, 01/01/1967.

57. *Sucesos*, 01/15/1967; Del Río, *Rius*, 166–70, 96; Cruz Vázquez, *1968–2000*, 55–56.

58. Morales Flores, "La Guerrilla."

59. Morales Flores, "La Guerrilla"; *Sucesos*, 02/19/1966; *Sucesos*, 02/26/1966; *Sucesos*, 04/09/1966.

60. *Sucesos*, 09/10/1966; *Sucesos*, 12/24/1966.

61. Keller, "Whose News?"

62. Memorandum, 06/14/1966, AGN/DFS/VP, Mario Menéndez.

63. *Sucesos*, 02/19/1966; *Sucesos*, 09/10/1966; *Sucesos*, 07/081967.

64. For "new journalism," see Mills, *New Journalism*.

65. Exposure to USIS Communications, 1968, NARA/RG306, MX-6801 Part I.

66. Ulloa Bornemann and Schmidt, *Surviving*, 99.

67. E.g., *Sucesos*, 01/28/1967; *Sucesos*, 10/15/1965.

68. Memorandum, 06/14/1966, AGN/DFS/VP, Mario Menéndez; taped telephone conversation, 10/18/1965, AGN/DFS/VP, Manuel Marcué Pardiñas.

69. E.g., *Sucesos*, 01/21/1967.

70. Salgado, *Una Vida*, 25–57; "Desaparición del Periodista," 03/17/1967, AGN/DFS/VP, Mario Menéndez; *El Tiempo*, 03/27/1967.

71. *Sucesos*, 07/01/1967; *Sucesos*, 07/08/1967; *Sucesos*, 07/15/1967; Cedillo Cedillo, "El Fuego," 193; De la Pedraja, *Wars*, 191.

72. *El Tiempo*, 03/19/1967; *El Tiempo*, 03/21/1967.

73. *El Tiempo*, 05/29/1969; *La Nacion*, 06/22/1967; Undated biography, AGN/DFS/VP, Mario Menéndez; PPB Mex 1-1-67; Report from Freeman, 07/23/1967, NARA/RG59/1967–1969/389.

74. There is a copy in AGN/DFS/VP Mario Menéndez.

75. Cedillo Cedillo, "El Fuego," 193; Salgado, *Una Vida*, 59–60.

76. Memorandum, Editorial Reportaje S.A. undated, AGN/DFS/VP, Mario Menéndez.

77. Memorandum, Editorial Reportaje S.A. undated; Grant Advertising Memorandum, 03/17/1969, AGN/DFS/VP, Mario Menéndez; *Por Qué?*, 02/28/1968; *Por Qué?*, 03/13/1968; *Por Qué?*, 03/27/1968.

78. *Por Qué?*, 02/28/1968; *Por Qué?*, 03/13/1968; 07/17/1968; AGN/DGIPS/2964 Memorandum from Echeverría, undated.

79. See the files in AGN/DFS/VP, Manuel de la Isla Paulín; González Ruiz, *Muro*, 288–93.

80. Emergence of Magazine *Por Qué?*, 03/01/1968, NARA/RG59/1967–1969/389 PPB Mex 1-1-67.

81. *Por Qué?*, 02/28/1968.

82. *Por Qué?*, 02/28/1968; *Por Qué?*, 03/13/1968; *Por Qué?*, 04/10/1968; *Por Qué?*, 05/22/1968; *Por Qué?*, 07/21/1968.

83. For an overview, see Aguayo, *1968*, 111–89, 205–16.

84. Monsiváis, *A Ustedes*, 89.

85. See Del Castillo Troncoso, *Ensayo*; Aguayo, *1968*; Serna, "La Vida"; Brewster, "The Student Movement of 1968."

86. For spaces of dissent see Hesse, "Mexican Newspapers"; Del Castillo Troncoso, "Fotoperiodismo."

87. Sánchez Rivera, Cano Andaluz, and Martínez Nateras, "Los Libros."

88. Aguayo, *1968*, 268–69; Pensado, *Rebel Mexico*, 145–67; Rodríguez Kuri, "El Lado."

89. *Por Qué?*, Extra, September 1968. *Por Qué/Cuartel de Caballeros*, 08/15/1968.

90. *Por Qué?*, Extra, September 1968; *Por Qué?*, 08/28/1968.

91. Ortega G., *Democracía*; Ortega G., *Tijuana*; *Por Qué?*, 03/25/1970; *La Nación*, 10/15/1968.

92. The point is made by Picatto, "A History."

93. *Por Qué?*, Extra, September 1968; *Por Qué?*, 10/04/1968.

94. Glanville, *Football*, 89.

95. *Por Qué?*, Extra, October 1968; *Por Qué?*, Extra, September 1968.

96. *Por Qué?*, 10/11/1968; *Por Qué?*, 11/04/1968; *Por Qué?*, 10/30/1968.

97. Revista *Por Qué?*, n.d.; Informe, 10/10/1968, AGN/DFS/VP, Mario Menéndez.

98. *Ramparts*, 10/26/1968; *The Nation*, 07/06/1969.

99. Report from Freeman, 10/10/1968, NARA/RG59/1967–1969/389, PPB Mex 1-1-67.

100. Alvarez Garín, *Los Procesos*, 31; Del Castillo Troncoso, *Ensayo*, 78.

101. Memorandum, 08/28/1968, AGN/DFS/VP, Mario Menéndez.

102. Trejo Delarbre, *La Prensa*, 115.

103. Memorandum by Fernando Gutiérrez Barrios, undated, AGN/DFS/VP Mario Menéndez.

104. *Por Qué?*, 12/13/1968.

105. Berry, "PIPSA," 28–30.

106. Moya Palencia to Echeverría, 04/08/1969, AGN/DGIPS/2944A.

107. *Por Qué?*, 12/13/1968; Editorial Reportaje SA, undated, AGN/DFS/VP Mario Menéndez.

108. *Ramparts*, 10/26/1968.

109. *Por Qué?*, 10/30/1968.

110. Keller, "Testing."

111. "Cómo se Compra Una Conciencia," "Alerta Estudiantes," AGN/DFS/VP, Mario Menéndez; Excélsior, 06/03/1969.

112. *Por Qué?*, 01/15/1969.

113. Report from Dearborn, 03/03/1969, NARA/RG59/1967–1969/389, PPB Mex 1-1-67.

114. Salgado, *Una Vida*, 73–118; Interview with Jorge Felix-Baez, October 2016; *Por Qué?*, 11/30/1972; *Por Qué?*, 03/23/1972.

115. *Por Qué?*, 04/02/1970; *Por Qué?*, 04/30/1970; *Por Qué?*, 03/19/1970.

116. *Por Qué?*, 12/18/1969; *Por Qué?*, 12/25/1969.

117. *Por Qué?*, 08/07/1969; *Por Qué?*, 08/14/1969; *Por Qué?*, 08/28/1969; *Por Qué?*, 09/04/1969.

118. See the follow-up over La Quina, *Por Qué?*, 07/11/1970.

119. Walker, *Waking*, 23–43; Johnson, *Mexican Democracy*, 38–89; Gamiño Muñoz, *Guerrilla*.

120. The phrase is often attributed to Carlos Fuentes (*Proceso*, 05/20/2012), but Benítez actually popularized the saying. *Por Qué?*, 05/04/1972.

121. For a summary of this stance see De Mora, *Por la Gracia*.

122. For a critique of this revisionist historiography, see Knight, "The Mexican Revolution"; for the popularization of these ideas about the Revolution, see Sheppard, *Persistant Revolution*.

123. *Por Qué?*, 01/06/1972; *Por Qué?*, 03/30/1973.

124. *Por Qué?*, 08/07/1969; *Por Qué?*, 08/14/1969; *Por Qué?*, 09/25/1969; *Por Qué?*, 10/02/1969.

125. *Por Qué?*, 09/25/1969; *Por Qué?*, 11/23/1969; *Por Qué?*, 10/04/1969; *Por Qué?*, 10/16/1969; *Por Qué?*, 08/07/1969.

126. *Por Qué?*, 10/23/1969. See also Keller, *Mexico's Cold War*, 194–95; Buendía, *La CIA*, 211–12.

127. Morley, *Our Man*, 94, 106, 147, 210, 256, 258–59, 289–90, 308. Doyle and Morley, "Litiempo." Philip Agee, the former CIA spy, made these allegations in the Spanish-language version of his book as early as 1979 (http://www.proceso.com.mx/126000/Echeverría-era-litempo-14 03/29/2017).

128. *Por Qué?*, 12/10/1970.

129. *Por Qué?*, 05/30/1973; *Por Qué?*, 09/14/1972, 11/23/1972; *Por Qué?*, 10/12/1972; *Por Qué?*, 04/20/1972; *Por Qué?*, 11/02/1972; *Por Qué?*, 09/12/1972; *Por Qué?*, 10/26/1972.

130. *Por Qué?*, 08/07/1969; *Por Qué?*, 07/15/1971; *Por Qué?*, 07/22/1971; *Por Qué?*, 07/29/1971.

131. F. Avila to M. Menéndez, 06/09/1969, AGN/DFS/VP, Mario Menéndez; Rodríguez Munguía, *La Otra*, 217; *Por Qué?*, 10/30/1969; *Por Qué?*, 07/24/1969.

132. *Por Qué?*, 08/14/1969.

133. Salgado, *Una Vida*, 9–15, 153–61.

134. AGN/DFS/VP, Manuel de la Isla Paulín; Cedillo Cedillo, "El Fuego," 201; Rodríguez Munguía, *La Otra*, 293–302.

135. *Por Qué?*, 10/02/1969.

136. Scherer García and Monsiváis, *Parte*, 79.

137. Salgado, *Una Vida*, 26.

138. Cedillo Cedillo, "El Fuego," 205, 189.

139. Ibid., 206–19; Interview with Raymundo López del Carpio, 02/11/1970; Interview with Ignacio González, 02/11/1970; Informe at Tenosique, 02/24/1970, AGN/DFS/VP, Mario Menéndez.

140. "Investigación relativa a actos terroristas," 02/21/1970; Interview with Raúl Enrique Pérez Gasque, 04/09/1974; Interview with Raúl Sergio Morales Villarreal, 02/17/1974, AGN/DFS/VP, Mario Menéndez.

141. Interview with Andres García Lavín, 07/28/1969; "Investigación relativa a actos terroristas," 02/21/1970, AGN/DFS/VP, Mario Menéndez; *Por Qué?*, 02/26/1970.

142. See, for example, the trial of Filemeno Mata in 1961. Mata Alatorre, *La Verdad*.

143. *Por Qué?*, 04/30/1970; *Por Qué?*, 03/25/1970; *Por Qué?*, 03/12/1970; "Fieles a las 'enseñanzas,'" AGN/DFS/VP, Mario Menéndez.

144. Aviña, *Specters*, 131.

145. *Por Qué?*, 03/25/1970; *Por Qué?*, 04/30/1970.

146. Informe by Miguel Nazar Haro, 05/03/1981, AGN/DFS/VP, Mario Menéndez; http://www.proceso.com.mx/156447/con-el-apoyo-de-manzanilla-schaffer-mario -Menéndez-convierte-en-diario-por-esto-rdquo 03/29/2017.

147. Musacchio, *Granados Chapa*; Del Río, *Rius*; Padrés, *El Diario*.

148. Nelson, *British Counter-Culture*; Forde, *Challenging the News*, 22–56; Streitmatter, *Voices of Revolution*.

149. Freije, "Secrets."

Chapter Five

1. For a good overview see Knight, "Cárdenas and Echeverría"; Informe, Dia de la Libertad de Prensa 06/07/1976, AGN/DGIPS/1028; *El Sol de Mexico*, 06/08/1976; *El Universal*, 06/08/1976.

2. Fregoso Peralta and Sánchez Ruiz, *Prensa*, 17–18, 34–37.

3. Informe on El Porvenir, 05/02/1969, AGN/DGIPS/1326; Nolan, "Relative," 16–28.

4. Esquivel Hernández, *El Norte*, 59–61.

5. *El Día*, 06/11/1976.

6. Report on El Mundo, 08/06/1942, CUSDCF/Mexico/IA/1940–1944/64.

7. Robles, *Retrato*, 244–45.

8. Marín Rodríguez, *Tiempo*, 176.

9. Blancornelas, *Conversaciones*, 46–59.

10. Marín Rodríguez, *Tiempo*, 79–83.

11. Report of agent E.A.C., 01/25/1949, AGN/DGIPS/810.

12. Elecciones Municipales, Cuernavaca, AGN/DGIPS/1280.

13. Castillo, *La Otra*, 12–19; Ortega, *Democracía*, 26.

14. Millán Peraza, *A Tijuana!*, 7.

15. Marín Rodríguez, *Tiempo*, 54.

16. Moncada, *30 Años*, 56.

17. Yañiz, *Oaxaca*, 115.

18. Marín Rodríguez, *Tiempo*, 176.

19. Rios Martínez to Arroyo Ch., 01/03/1938; García Ramos to Arroyo Ch., 12/12/1938; González to Rivera, 04/24/1938, AGN/DGI/95, Exp. 1.

20. Sánchez García, *El Plumaje*, 197; Moncada, *30 Años*, 59–60.

21. Sánchez García, *El Plumaje*, 198–201; Moncada, *30 años*, 59–60; José Morales to Noriega, 12/091959, AHEBC/SG/217.

22. Nolan, "Relative," 56–59.

23. Gustavo Angeles to Ernesto Pérez 07/18/1966, AHEBC/SG/21, Exp. 29.

24. Sánchez García, *El Plumaje*, 210, 213; Report to Milton Castellanos Everardo, 12/30/1971, AHEBC/SG/112, Exp. 66.

25. Erlandson, "The Press," 384–85; Peniche Vallado, *Sombras*, 55–60.

26. Blancornelas, *Conversaciones*, 65.

27. Deudas a PIPSA, 12/31/1968, AGN/DGIPS/2944.

28. Report on Diario de Durango, 02/26/1942, CUSDCF/Mexico/IA/1940–1944/64.

29. Moncada, *30 Años*, 45.

30. Memorandum, "Relación de periódicos . . . ," 06/11/1960, AGN/DGIPS/1279.

31. Noriega to Treasurer, 03/10/1960, AHEBC/SG/ 217.

32. Robles, *Retrato*, 99–100.

33. Editora de Baja California, AHEBC/JCA.

34. *ABC de la Costa* to treasurer, 03/03/1961; Miguel Maldonado to treasurer, 12/10/1959; Noriega to Treasurer, 03/10/1960, AHEBC/SG/217.

35. Robles, *Retrato*, 89.

36. Tomasini to Noriega, 02/04/1961; Delgado to Noriega, 05/13/1960, AHEBC/SG/217.

37. Nolan, "Relative Independence," 40.

38. Moncada, *30 Años*, 82.

39. SNRP to secretario particular, 07/26/1944; José Luis Navarro to President Avila Camacho, 03/24/1946; Pedro Villar Esperanza to President Avila Camacho, 05/16/1944, AGN/MAC/418.2/12; Francisco Ruvalcaba Villaseñor to secretario particular, 08/03/1953, AGN/ARC/503.11/213.

40. Manuel Lechuga to President Ruiz Cortines, 10/05/1955, AGN/ARC/418.2/85.

41. Elecciones Municipales, Cuernavaca, AGN/DGIPS/1280.

42. Biografía de Raúl Albertos Betancourt, Jul. 1965, AGN/DGIPS/1023.

43. Ibid.

44. Quintanilla, *Aprendiz*, 11.

45. Peniche Vallado, *Sombras*, 8.

46. Junco de la Vega, *Problems*, 14.

47. Rodríguez Lozano, *Cierre*, 78.

48. Cobb, "Provincial Journalism," 57.

49. Procurador General to Esteban Cibrían, 11/12/1945, AGN/MAC/542.1/900.

50. Marín Rodríguez, *Tiempo*, 1.

51. Sánchez García, *Plumaje*, 96–101.

52. Esquivel Hernández, *El Norte*, 17; Nieto de Leyva, *Por qué?*, 10.

53. Sánchez Hernández, *Un Mexicano*, 2–4.

54. Rodríguez Lozano, *Cierre*, 8–10.

55. Martínez Mora, *Gente*, 11–14.

56. Castro, *De Albañil*, 22.

57. Gutiérrez de Alba, *Tric Trac*, 161–65.

58. Del Campo Venegas, *Del Niño*, 34–36.

59. Martínez Mora, *Gente*.

60. Rangel, *Forjando*, 53.

61. Castro, *De Albañil*, 56–57.

62. Demetrio Vallejo to President Avila Camacho, 08/01/1944, AGN/MAC/542.1/1009.

63. See chapter 7.

64. Aboites Aguilar, *Excepciones*; Smith, "Building."

65. Keller, "Testing."

66. Tomo 1, "Varios problemas ocurridos . . . ," 10/01/1964, AGN/DGIPS/1560A.

67. "Informe sobre los comisionistas de PIPSA," 08/16/1969, AGN/DGIPS/2943.

68. AGN/DFS/Medios, volume 2.

69. Interview with Claudio Sánchez, Oaxaca, July 2012.

70. Case ID 7524, Faustino Alatorre Vidal, 1938, Casa de la Cultura Jurídica, Ciudad Juárez.

71. Erlandson, "The Press," 380, 383.

72. Gutiérrez y Falcón, *Periodista*, 9.

73. Erlandson, "The Press," 341–42.

74. Ibid., 347.

75. Interview with Claudio Sánchez, July 2012.

76. Moncada, *30 Años*, 33.

77. Smith, "Who Governed?"; Bertaccini, *El régimen*; Hernández Rodríguez, *Amistades*; Knight, "Historical Continuities"; Gillingham, "Mexican Elections"; Pansters, "Tropical Passion."

78. E.g., Esquivel Hernández, *El Norte*, 59–61.

79. Informe, 01/18/1967, AGN/DGIPS/2949B. Moncada, *Diez*, 135–40, 151–54.

80. Most incidents are recorded in the AGN/Presidentes files for MAC, MAV, and ARC. Most can be found under the files 542.1 Atropellos. I have extended the date range to 1960 due to the list of attacks included in the article "Libertad de Prensa o Demagogia," *El Chapulín*, 01/10/1960, and the much sparser AGN/Presidentes files for ALM.

81. *Oaxaca en México*, May 1965.

82. Ortega, *Democracía*.

83. Santiago Rivas to President Ruiz Cortiens, 01/30/1956, AGN/ARC/703.4/1002.

84. Hernández Rodríguez, "Strongmen"; Hernández Rodríguez, *Presidencialismo*.

85. For comparative readership rates see Jiménez de Ottalengo, "Un Periódico," and Effectiveness of Newspaper Supplement, 1967, NARA/RG306, MX-6702. For opposition party in Baja California see Shirk, *Mexico's*, 66–69.

86. Memorandum on Poza Rica, 07/06/1961, AGN/DGIPS/6038; Arguelles Navarro, "Análisis," 18.

87. AGN/DFS/VP, Alberto Altamirano. *El Universal*, 02/29/1957; Antonio Garza to President Ruiz Cortines, 05/15/1957, AGN/ARC/542.1/1371; *El Sol de Tampico*, 02/06/1958; Raúl Gibb Quintero to President Ruiz Cortines, 06/13/1958, AGN/ARC/542.1/1371.

88. These were the murders of Vicente Villasana (1947) and Manuel Acosta Meza (1956). Blancornelas, *En Estado*, 117–20; AGN/DGIPS/794, Exp. 9.

89. Ignacio Carbajal to President Avila Camacho, 11/22/1942, AGN/MAC/544.1/18-4.

90. *El Momento*, 12/07/1945.

91. SNRP to President Ruiz Cortines, 12/13/1956, AGN/ARC/556.63/159.

92. Solomon, "Measure," 123.

93. *El Chapulín*, 01/10/1960.

94. Alberto del Valle to President Avila Camacho, 09/27/1943, AGN/MAC/542.1/835.

95. Gonzalo N. Santos to Rodríguez Cano, 01/07/1955, AGN/ARC/542.1/202.

96. Wiretapped phone call between Francisco Hernández y Hernández and partner, 12/29/1961, AGN/DGIPS/2894A.

97. Piccato, *Tyranny*.

98. Paz, *Other Mexico*, 150.

99. Hugo Pedro González to "Chueco," 01/03/1947, AGN/MAV/412/91.

100. Between 1946 and 2000, 70 of the 252 governors were removed from power. Hernández Rodríguez, *El Centro*, 80. Marín Rodríguez, *Tiempo*, 13.

101. Castaño, *El Régimen*, 60–94.

102. Raúl Escobedo Loya to President Ruiz Cortines, 12/19/1953, AGN/ARC/542.2/195.

103. Procurador General to Esteban Cibrían, 11/12/1945, AGN/MAC/542.1/900.

104. Periodistas de Baja California to Governor Juan Felipe Rico, 08/02/1944, AGN/MAC/542.1/835; *Detective Internacional*, Aug. 1944.

105. Eustaquio Sánchez to President Ruiz Cortines, 06/06/1956, AGN/ARC/542.1/1024. See also Jesús Castellanos to President Ruiz Cortines, 05/12/1959, AGN/ARC/542.1/235; Antonio Garza to President Ruiz Cortines, 09/06/1956, AGN/ARC/542.1/125; Jesús Castellanos to President Ruiz Cortines, 07/01/1960, AGN/ARC/542.1/235.

106. Robles, *Retrato*, 145–46.

107. Daniel De los Reyes Ocampo, 07/14/1965, AGN/DGIPS/1461B, Exp. 9.

108. Blas Corras to President Avila Camacho, 02/16/1945, AGN/MAC/542.1/1192.

109. Raúl Aceves to President Alemán, 01/28/1947, AGN/MAV/542.1/67.

110. *Novedades*, 06/09/1946; *Don Roque*, 06/10/1946.

111. Luis Constantino Hernández to President Ruiz Cortines, 01/19/1953, AGN/ARC/542.2/26.

112. SNRP to President Ruiz Cortines, 05/03/1954, AGN/ARC/542.1/679.

113. Guillermo Trejo Oviedo to President Ruiz Cortines, 07/25/1956, AGN/ARC/111/721.

114. Alberto Ahuja to President Ruiz Cortines, 06/25/1955, AGN/ARC/542.1/249. Erlandson, "The Press," 333–38.

115. Marín Rodríguez, *Tiempo*, 12–14; *Oaxaca en México*, April 1964.

116. Prensa Asociada de Baja California to President Alemán, 02/23/1957, AGN/ARC/542.1/1251.

117. *La Prensa*, 06/30/1953; *La Prensa*, 07/14/1953.

118. *El Chapulín*, 01/10/1960.

119. Luis Rico to President Avila Camacho, 05/21/1946; A. Garza Ruiz to President Avila Camacho, 07/03/1945, AGN/ARC/542.1/1228.

120. Juan Vivalde to President Ruiz Cortines, 05/25/1955, AGN/ARC/704/270.

121. Sánchez García, *El Plumaje*, 170–79.

122. Rogelio Elizondo to President Ruiz Cortines, 02/02/1955; Gustavo Cerrillo to President Ruiz Cortines, 04/20/1954, AGN/ARC/432/243.

123. *Don Roque*, 08/25/1946; *Don Roque*, 08/11/1946; *Don Roque*, 08/04/1946; *Don Roque*, 05/12/1946; *La Prensa*, 02/07/1947; Aurelio D. Hernández to President Alemán, 02/07/1947, AGN/MAV/542.1/112.

124. Natalia G. de Joch to President Ruiz Cortines, 02/05/1955; Natalia G. de Joch to President Ruiz Cortines, 10/10/1954; Natalia G. de Joch to President Ruiz Cortines, 07/27/1953, AGN/ARC/444.1/191.

125. For the inference of links between drug trafficking and left-wing activists (in these cases Oaxaca communist Graciano Benítez and Morelos radical Ruben Jaramillo), see *Política*, 11/15/1961; *Política*, 06/01/1962.

126. Erlandson, "The Press," 341. Luis García Larrañaga to Gobernador Territorio, 10/04/1949, AGN/MAC/422.1.

127. Moncada, *Del México*, 63–120.

128. Ibid., 74–81; *El Mundo*, 03/12/1947; *El Mundo*, 03/21/1947. See documents in AGN/MAV/162/4 and AGN/DGIPS/794, Exp. 9.

129. Moncada, *Del México*, 74–81; AGN/MAV/162/4; AGN/DGIPS/794 exp 9.

130. Moncada, *Del México*, 87. Joining the dots between Moncada's investigation and my discovery of the following book, the Sinaloa journalist was probably killed for writing and publishing *La Vida Accidentada y Novelesca de Rodolfo Valdéz el Gitano*.

131. Moncada, *Del México*, 90–95; *El Detective Internacional*, Jan. 1945; *San Diego Union*, 08/03/1956; Ortega, *Tijuana*; Blancornelas, *En Estado*, 17–43.

132. Moncada, *Del México*, 90–95, 103–14; Ortega, *Tijuana*, 12–32; *The Tijuana Story*; Blancornelas, *En Estado de Alerta*, 17–43; *San Diego Union*, 11/24/1956; *San Diego Union*, 01/05/1957; *San Diego Union*, 02/22/1957; *San Diego Union*, 11/15/1957; *San Diego Union*, 10/07/1956; *San Diego Union*, 04/23/1957; *San Diego Union*, 07/31/1957.

133. Moncada, *Del México*, 102–13; *San Diego Union*, 09/04/1956.

134. *El Chapulín*, 01/10/1960; Various documents, AGN/DFS/VP Alberto Altamirano.

135. Moncada, *Del México*, 107–20; *Epoca Nueva*, 10/27/1964.

136. De la Hoya to President Ruiz Cortines, 08/20/1956; De la Hoya to President Ruiz Cortines, 01/20/1958; De la Hoya to President Ruiz Cortines, 03/21/1958, AGN/ARC/542.1/1214. De la Hoya to President López Mateos, 01/16/1959, AGN/ALM/542.1/15.

137. Pablo Rosete to President López Mateos, 05/03/1962; Sergio Bribiesco to President López Mateos, 02/06/1962; Francisco Rodríguez to President López Mateos, 02/29/1960, AGN/ALM/542.1/15; Informe, 10/04/1961, AGN/DGIPS/1475A, Exp. 19.

138. *Por Qué?*, 10/30/1969; Archivo Histórico de la Suprema Corte de Justicia, Amparos, Ignacio de la Hoya Pineda, Leg. 85, Exp. 511.

139. Montgomery, "Stress."

140. Gillingham, "How Much."

141. AGN/DFS/Medios, volume 2. Of 483 papers listed, 326 were described as progovernment. The rest were described as yellow journalism, opportunist, liberal, clerical, or antigovernment.

142. Miguel Flores Villar to President Avila Camacho, 07/20/1946; *El Norte* cutting, AGN/MAC/544.1/18-4.

143. *La Jeringa*, 10/18/1948.

144. *El Chapulín*, 11/02/1950.

145. Informe 08/26/1955, AGN/DGIPS/2014B, Exp. 31.

146. *El Sol de San Luis*, 11/31/1958.

147. Alegre, *Railroad Radicals*, 188, 222.

148. Erlandson, "The Press," 383; Cole and Hester, *Mass Communication*, 41.

149. Cline, *Mexico*, 183.

Chapter Six

1. *Newsweek*, 12/04/1950.

2. Borrego, *Cómo*; Cordero y Torres, "Nacimiento."

3. *Buro de Investigación Política*, 08/02/1954; *Indice*, 02/27/1960; *Indice*, 04/04/1961.

4. Report on Sol de Guadalajara, 01/22/1948, CUSDCF/Mexico/IA/1945–1949/32.

5. Erlandson, "The Press," 428–29.

6. Sánchez Pontón, *El Olor*, 118.

7. Cadena Z., *El Verdadero*, 6.

8. Cadena Z., *Por el Ojo*.

9. Monsiváis, *A Ustedes*, 62–65.

10. Bohmann, *Medios*, 16–17; Pensado, *Rebel*, 178.

11. Fuentes, *Death*, 6, 69, 88.

12. Borrego, *Cómo*, 12–27.

13. Sánchez Pontón, *El Olor*, 140.

14. Cordero y Torres, "Nacimiento," 288–95.

15. Sánchez Pontón, *El Olor*, 82–83.

16. Borrego, *Cómo*, 27–39; Cordero y Torres, "Nacimiento," 302–7.

17. Cadena Z., *El Verdadero*, 8.

18. *La Opinion*, 03/16/1947.

19. Borrego, *Cómo*, 40; Cordero y Torres, "Nacimiento," 307–9; Rubenstein, *Bad Language*, 93–94.

20. Carrillo Reveles, "Nacionalismo"; González Landeros, "Estrellas"; Sánchez Pontón, *El Olor*, 139.

21. Gillingham, "Maximino's Bulls"; *Presente*, 08/04/1948.

22. Cordero y Torres, "Nacimiento," 287; Borrego, *Cómo*, 54–55. For Hearst's continuing interest in Mexico see "Mexico End of an Empire," *Time*, 09/07/1953.

23. *Periódico Oficial del Estado de Puebla*, 07/12/1940.

24. Quintana, *Maximino*, 73–102; Valencia Castrejón, *Poder*.

25. Paxman, "Changing."

26. Niblo, *Mexico*, 90–94.

27. Quintana, *Maximino*, 124–29.

28. Ortiz Garza, "El Eslabón."

29. E.g., *Esto*, 12/01/1942; *Esto*, 12/12/1943.

30. Ortiz Garza, "El Eslabón."

31. Report of David Thomasson, 07/19/1945, CUSDCF/Mexico/IA/1945–1949/32.

32. Cadena Z., *El Verdadero*, 11–12; Sánchez Pontón, *El Olor*, 35–39.

33. Borrego, *Cómo*, 60–61; Sánchez Pontón, *El Olor*, 54–55.

34. Paxman, "Jenkins."

35. Borrego, *Cómo*, 70–76; Cordero y Torres, "Nacimiento," 338–52; Lazere, *American Media*, 55.

36. García Valseca and Ebner, *We Have*, 134–36.

37. *Novedades*, 11/03/1946.

38. Gutiérrez de Alba, *Tric Trac*, 85–86.

39. Secretario Particular to President Alemán, 06/30/1952, AGN/MAV/111/5304-A; Rodríguez Castañeda, *Prensa*, 15–32.

40. Scherer García and Monsiváis, *Tiempo*, 163.

41. Cole and Hester, *Mass Communication*, 16.

42. Sánchez Pontón, *El Olor*, 96–117; Blanco Moheno, *Memorias*, 127.

43. Memorandum de los Periódicos Unidos de los Estados, 06/18/1945, AGN/MAC/704/41.

44. *Política*, 10/01/1961; Erlandson, "The Press," 428–29.

45. Wikileaks, Kissinger Cables, Secretary of State Telegram, 08/02/1974, https://wikileaks.org/plusd/cables/1974MEXICO06547_b.html 03/04/2017.

46. Donato Miranda to Manuel Tello, 04/09/1962, AGN/ALM/121.3/1.

47. E.g., Bloque Periodístico to José Altamirano, 12/29/1946, AGN/MAV/705.2/11.

48. Sánchez Pontón, *El Olor*, 77–82; Accionistas de PIPSA, undated, AGN/DGIPS/2944 A,.

49. Berry, "PIPSA," 21–22.

50. Borrego, *Cómo*, 101–2.

51. Deudas a PIPSA, 12/31/1968, AGN/DGIPS/2944. It must be noted that when divided by the number of newspapers in the chain, the debts were not that extensive—less than a million pesos per paper.

52. Blanco Moheno, *Memorias*, 136.

53. Marín, *Tiempo*, 30–39; Gonzalo Santos to Rodríguez Cano, 12/30/1954, AGN/ARC/542.1/202; Santos, *Memorias*, 887.

54. Luévano Díaz, "1945," 257–69; Cordero y Torres, "Nacimiento," 322–23.

55. Gutiérrez de Alba, *Tric Trac*, 53.

56. Cadena, *El Verdadero*, 10.

57. Various letters and telegrams, AGN/MAV/432.2/5; *La Opinión de Puebla*, 12/06/1946; *La Opinión de Puebla*, 02/25/47; *La Opinión de Puebla*, 03/10/1947; *La Opinión de Puebla*, 06/11/1947.

58. A. García Estrada to President Ruiz Cortines, 10/07/1953, AGN/ARC/704/212.

59. Rincón Rodríguez, *"Amanecer,"* 70–73.

60. Gutiérrez de Alba, *Tric Trac*, 90.

61. Report on Newspapers in Jalisco and Colima from T. J. Hohenthal, 06/26/1950, CUSDCF/Mexico/IA/1950–1954/43.

62. *El Informador*, 01/03/1948; Gutiérrez de Alba, *Tric Trac*, 41–43; Borrego, *Como*, 89; Borrás, *Historia*, 81.

63. Blas Rojo to President Alemán, 04/02/1948, AGN/MAV/705.2/11.

64. Gutiérrez de Alba, *Tric Trac*, 62–63; *Indice*, 07/07/1959.

65. Report on Newspapers in Jalisco and Colima from T. J. Hohenthal, 06/26/1950, CUSDCF/Mexico/IA/1950–1954/43; Report on Sol de Guadalajara, 01/22/1948; Henderson to Embassy, 04/30/1948, CUSDCF/Mexico/IA/1945–1949/32.

66. Astorga, *Mitología*, 95.

67. Report from Kennedy Crockett, 01/03/1954, CUSDCF/Mexico/IA/1950–1954/43.

68. Report on Newspapers in Jalisco and Colima from T. J. Hohenthal, 06/26/1950, CUSDCF/Mexico/IA/1950–1954/4; Gutiérrez de Alba, *Tric Trac*, 63; Borrego, *Cómo*, 62; Torres y Cordero, "Nacimiento," 341–47; Erlandson, "The Press," 430.

69. Sánchez García, *El Plumaje*, 170.

70. Blanco Moheno, *Memorias*, 125.

71. Petley, *Censorship*, 124.

72. Garmabella, *Renato*, 139–48.

73. Erlandson, "The Press," 430–31.

74. Borrego, *Derrota*.

75. Borrego, *Como*.

76. *Indice*, 07/07/1959; *Indice*, 02/28/1961.

77. E.g., José García Valseca to President Avila Camacho, 07/11/1946, AGN/MAC/704/699.

78. A Study of the Awareness of the Vietnam War, 1967, NARA/RG306, MX-6701.

79. *El Heraldo*, 02/27/1961; *El Heraldo*, 03/07/1961; *El Heraldo*, 04/30/1960; *Indice*, 05/06/1960.

80. "Algunas preguntas . . . ," 03/04/1955, AGN/ARC/704/876.

81. Sánchez Pontón, *El Olor*, 45–47.

82. Gillingham and Smith, "Introduction"; Report on Newspapers in Jalisco and Colima from T. J. Hohenthal, 06/26/1950, CUSDCF/Mexico/IA/1950–1954/43.

83. Report on Newspapers in Jalisco and Colima from T. J. Hohenthal, 06/26/1950, CUSDCF/Mexico/IA/1950–1954/43.

84. *Septimo Censo; Sexto Censo.*

85. Gutiérrez de Alba, *Tric Trac*, 19.

86. *El Fronterizo*, 12/23/1944; *El Fronterizo*, 12/24/1944; *El Fronterizo*, 12/28/1945.

87. *El Fronterizo*, 12/22/1944; *El Fronterizo*, 12/25/1944.

88. *El Fronterizo*, 12/22/1944; *El Fronterizo*, 12/23/1944.

89. *El Fronterizo*, 02/01/1945; *El Fronterizo*, 12/26/1944; *El Fronterizo*, 12/28/1944.

90. *El Fronterizo*, 12/24/1944; *El Fronterizo*, 12/26/1944; *El Fronterizo*, 12/28/ 1944; *El Fronterizo*, 01/06/1945.

91. For a similar process in the United States, see Nord, *Communities.*

92. Gutiérrez de Alba, *Tric Trac*, 28; *El Fronterizo*, 12/24/1944; CUSDCF/Mexico/IA/1950–1954/43, Report on newspapers in Ciudad Juárez consular district, 01/05/1954.

93. Monsiváis, *A Ustedes*, 65.

94. Sánchez Pontón, *El Olor*, 42–43.

95. E.g., Martínez, *Prensa Negra.*

96. E.g., Alberto del Valle to President Avila Camacho, 09/04/1944, AGN/MAC/542.1/835.

97. Marín González, *Tiempo*, 54–55.

98. Ramírez, *Gangsters*, 101.

99. Ibid., 98.

100. AGN/MAV/703.4/58, Sánchez Pontón to President Alemán, 06/25/1947; Marín González, *Tiempo*, 54–55.

101. Hernández, "Strongmen."

102. Rangel, *Forjando*, 134–58; Borjas Benavente, "El Tratamiento."

103. Rincón Rodríguez, *"Amanecer,"* 107–17.

104. *Indice*, 12/12/1960.

105. Francisco García to Ruiz Cortines, 09/25/1958, AGN/ARC/704/719.

106. Informe on Queretaro, 09/01/1960, AGN/DFS/100-20-1; Rincón Rodríguez, "Amanecer," 115.

107. Informe, Chihuahua, 09/04/1964; Información sobre el Estado de Chihuahua, 06/25/1963, Informe sobre Chihuahua 05/16/1964, AGN/DFS/VP Práxedis Giner Durán; *Indice*, 03/11/1963; *Indice*, 03/11/1963; *Acción*, Jan. 1963.

108. Informe by Colonel DEM, 03/05/1963, AGN/DFS/VP, Práxedis Giner Durán.

109. Informe, 05/14/1964, AGN/DGIPS/1560A.

110. *El Heraldo*, 01/15/1963.

111. *Indice*, 03/04/1963; *Indice*, 11/06/1963; *El Heraldo*, 03/02/1963.

112. E.g., *El Heraldo*, 01/10/1964; *El Heraldo*, 01/12/1964; *El Heraldo*, 01/14/1964.

113. *Acción*, July 1964; *Indice*, 06/16/1964.

114. Monsiváis, *A Ustedes*, 62.

115. *Directorio de Medios* (August 1967).

116. A Study of Newspaper Readership in Aguascalientes, 1958, NARA/RG306, IRI-Mex-17; Effectiveness of Newspaper Supplement, 1967, NARA/RG306, MX-6702.

117. *El Heraldo*, 04/14/1961.

118. Informe, 05/13/1966, AGN/GDO/726.

119. E.g., *El Sol de San Luis*, 07/19/1958; *El Sol de San Luis*, 12/07/1958; *El Sol de San Luis*, 12/08/1958; *El Sol de San Luis*, 01/04/1959.

120. Borjas Benavente, "El Tratamiento," 133.

121. *El Sol San Luis*, 03/27/1961; *El Sol de San Luis*, 04/22/1961; *El Sol de San Luis*, 07/24/1961; *La Tribuna*, 07/13/1961.

122. *La Tribuna*, 07/26/1961.

123. Estrada M., *La Grieta*, 130, 187.

124. Aguayo, *La Charola*, 52.

125. For an introduction to ideas about the deep state, see Söyler, *Turkish Deep State*.

126. Borrego, *Cómo*, 188–96.

127. José García Valseca contract with NF, 06/13/1967, AGN/DGIPS/2944A.

128. "Lo usó para apoderarse de la Cadena, dice," *Proceso*, 02/22/1986.

129. Report by George Rylance, 07/18/1969, NARA/RG 59/1967-1969/389, PPB Mex 1-1-67.

130. Borrego, *Cómo*, 201–4.

131. Sánchez Pontón, *El Olor*, 147.

132. Borrego, *Cómo*, 206–9.

133. Garmabella, *Renato*, 147–49.

134. García Valseca and Ebner, *We Have*, 139.

135. Informe, 11/29/1971, AGN/DFS/VP, José García Valseca.

136. See Saragoza, *The Monterrey Elite*.

137. Esquivel Hernández, *El Norte*, 59–61, 67–68.

138. Antonio Sáenz de Miera to President Ruiz Cortines, 07/24/1953, AGN/ARC/542.1/290.

139. Esquivel Hernández, *El Norte*, 71–72.

140. Adler Hellman, *Mexico*, 152–68; Walker, *Waking*, 45–72.

141. Report by George Rylance, 07/18/1969, NARA/RG 59/1967-1969/389, PPB Mex 1-1-67.

142. Borrego, *Cómo*, 213.

143. Borrego, *Cómo*, 217–18.

144. Fernández Menéndez, *Nadie*, 34–38, 116–21; López Olivares, *Cartel del Globo*, 49, 70.

145. Bartley and Bartley, *Eclipse*, 195–97, 224.

146. Fernández Menéndez, *Nadie*, 116, 118–23, 142; On Ventura see *Proceso*, 09/26/1988; Aldrete, *Me dicen*; Mills, *Underground Empire*, 535; Shannon, *Desperados*, 207–8, 347.

147. *El Informador*, 09/19/1988; García Cabrera, *1920–2000*; *El Pastel*, 2:30–32.

148. Fernández Menéndez, *Nadie*, 116–21; *Excélsior*, 09/20/1988; *Excélsior*, 09/21/1988; For Salinas's father's and uncle's links to Gulf cartel founder Juan Nepomuceno Guerra, see Hernández, *Los Señores*, 36; Flores, *Historias*, 176.

149. For Bartlett's alleged links to the drug trade see Esquivel, *La CIA*, 47–49, 87–89, and *Proceso*, 01/05/2014. Adela Cedillo has suggested, plausibly I believe, that the

Ventura killings rather than the Garza Sada hit were more likely the work of what we might term Mexico's "deep state." Private conversation with Adela Cedillo, 03/03/2017.

150. http://www.proceso.com.mx/143055/lo-uso-para-apoderarse-de-la-cadena-dice 03/20/2017; Wikileaks, Kissinger Cables, Department of State Telegram, 08/17/1976, https://wikileaks.org/plusd/cables/1976MEXICO10575_b.html 03/20/2017.

151. AGN/DFS/Medios, volume 2; *Ultimas Noticias*, 06/04/1974; Informe on Asociación Nacional de Periodistas, 06/20/1972, AGN/DGIPS/1659C, Exp. 9.

152. Sánchez García, *El Plumaje*, 177.

Chapter Seven

1. *El Momento*, 02/16/1943; *El Momento*, 03/03/1943.

2. The quote comes from Heitman, "The Press," 9. But ignoring or playing down the importance of the local press is common throughout most studies of the Mexican media. See Monsiváis, *A Ustedes*, 71–73; Lawson, *Building*; Scherer García and Monsiváis, *Tiempo*; González Marín, *Prensa*.

3. Knight, "Weight of the State"; Smith, *Pistoleros*, 3; Attorney General of Oaxaca to President Alemán, 01/14/1947 AGN/DGG/7Bis2-314-1(17)-1.

4. *Antequera*, 01/25/1943; *La Voz de Oaxaca*, 03/25/1948; Informe on CNOP, 03/04/1954, AGPEO/Gobierno.

5. The masons still had a branch named after Porfirio Díaz in 1926. Archivo de la Gran Logia "Benito Juárez" de Oaxaca, Libro 48, 1926. For the attempt to repatriate Porfirio Díaz see *La Voz de Oaxaca*, 10/01/1948; *La Voz de Oaxaca*, 04/02/1949.

6. For early versions of the Guelaguetza see *El Oaxaqueño*, 12/02/1935; *Oaxaca Nuevo*, 09/19/1941; *Oaxaca Nuevo*, 11/26/1941; Governor González Fernández to President Avila Camacho, 08/26/1941, AGN/MAC/505.1/27. For critiques of Gualaguetza see *El Chapulín*, 08/03/1956; *El Chapulín*, 11/03/1960.

7. Smith, *Pistoleros*, 269–71.

8. *Sexto Censo*; *Septimo Censo*.

9. Beals, "Oaxaca Market," 29; Diskin, "Structure," 65; Smith, *Pistoleros*, 271–74.

10. *Buro de Investigación Política*, 03/31/1952.

11. Wright-Rios, *Revolutions*, 98–140.

12. Junta Diocesana de Oaxaca, José Reyes to ACM, nd 1938, Albino López, nd 1938; Austreberto Aragón to ACM, September 1943, AACM, 2.10; Interview with María Teresa Valera Flores, January 2004; Hayner, *New Patterns*, 164–65.

13. Smith, *Pistoleros*, 278–82.

14. Interview with Austreberto Aragón, 06/08/1966; Interview with Rafael Ojeda, 06/20/1966, Statutes of UEM; Interview with Gregorio Pérez, 08/17/1965, Box 58; Geneology of Inocencia Enríquez, Box 60, Ralph L. Beals Collection, NAA.

15. *Momento*, 07/18/1945.

16. *El Globo*, 02/17/1948; Smith, *Pistoleros*, 342.

17. Overmyer-Velazquez, *Visions*, 35; Ruiz Cervantes and Sánchez Silva, "Prensa."

18. Chassen de López, *From Liberal*, 424–27; Overmyer-Velazquez, *Visions*, 35–39.

19. Abramo, *El estadio*, 146; Overmyer-Velazquez, *Visions*, 37; Ruiz Cervantes and Sánchez Silva, "La Imprenta," 25–37; *El Huarache*, 11/01/1881. For the history of the Mexico City satirical press see Buffington, *Sentimental Education*; Díaz, "Satiric Penny Press."

20. *Annuario Estadístico*, 1955; *Directorio de Medios* (Aug. 1967); Memorandum, "Relación de periódicos . . . ," 06/11/1960, AGN/DGIPS/1279.

21. Erlandson, "The Press," 388–91; *Nuevo Diario*, 09/17/1951; e.g., *Oaxaca Gráfico*, 09/17/1954.

22. Smith, *Pistoleros*, 346.

23. "Maria de los Angeles," 267–78.

24. E.g., *El Imparcial*, 12/11/1953; *El Imparcial*, 06/28/1953; *El Imparcial*, 09/02/1958.

25. Memorandum, 06/11/1960, AGN/DGIPS/1279; *Medios Publicitarios Mexicanos* (May–Aug. 1960); Erlandson, "The Press," 389–90.

26. Ruiz Cervantes and Sánchez Silva, "Prensa," and *Los Oaxaqueños*.

27. Lomnitz, *Death*, 375–78; *Carteles del Sur*, 07/09/1965. For examples of these *calaveras*, see *Pancho Pasqual*, 11/01/1884; *Calaveras de Oaxaca* by Lucia Pereya Mejia, undated, Brioso y Candiani Collection, Biblioteca Francisco de Burgoa.

28. Ruiz Cervantes and Sánchez Silva, "Prensa."

29. *Zancudo*, 01/30/1922; *Zancudo*, 02/30/1922; *Zancudo*, 07/01/1922. For Judas burnings see Beezley, *Judas*, 89–124.

30. This is down to the editor of *Carteles del Sur* and founder of the local newspaper library, Néstor Sánchez Hernández, who collected an almost complete print run of the newspaper.

31. Data from https://familysearch.org; Tamayo, *Oaxaca*, 19.

32. *Carteles del Sur*, 10/04/1966.

33. *Calaveras del Momento*, 11/01/1937.

34. Interview with Gabriel Quintas, July 2012.

35. *Carteles del Sur*, 10/04/1966; *Oaxaca en México*, May 1965; *El Momento*, 12/01/1944.

36. Interview with Gabriel Quintas, July 2012; Interview with Claudio Sánchez, July 2012.

37. Ibid.

38. *El Momento*, 07/13/1938; *El Momento*, 07/20/1938.

39. *El Momento*, 07/02/1942.

40. Yañiz, *Oaxaca*, 73; Interview with Guillermo Villa, Jul. 2012; *El Momento*, 06/18/1941; Interview with Eloy David Morales Jiménez, Aug. 2012.

41. Quintas Castellano, "El Movimiento," 42–43; *Momento*, 05/07/194; Interview with Claudio Sánchez, July 2012; Saavedra Cruz, *Vámonos!*

42. Piccato, "Notes."

43. *El Chapulín*, 09/26/1954; *El Momento*, 05/04/1943.

44. *El Chapulín*, 09/23/1953.

45. *El Chapulín*, 12/18/1952; *El Momento*, 11/02/1943.

46. *Oaxaca en México*, Apr. 1965.

47. *El Momento,* 07/02/1942.

48. Novo, *New Mexican,* 25. For a psychological reading of the *lambiscón,* see Luquín, *Análisis.*

49. *El Momento,* 04/03/1943.

50. *El Chapulín,* 03/05/1947.

51. Information on the finances came from an interview with Gabriel Quintas, Jul. 2012; *El Chapulín,* 10/26/1950.

52. Interview with Gabriel Quintas, Jul. 2012.

53. Interview with Eloy David Morales Jiménez, August 2012.

54. *El Chapulín,* 04/01/1954.

55. Van Young, "In the Gloomy," 49.

56. Quoted in Piccato, "Introducción," 23.

57. *Carteles del Sur,* 10/04/1966; *El Chapulín,* 02/22/1956.

58. *El Chapulín,* 10/23/1953.

59. *El Momento,* 10/20/1944.

60. *El Chapulín,* 04/01/1954.

61. *El Chapulín,* 12/05/1954.

62. *El Momento,* 11/26/1938; *El Chapulín,* 04/05/1951.

63. *El Chapulín,* 11/03/1949.

64. *El Chapulín,* 07/21/1948.

65. *El Chapulín,* 01/03/1950.

66. *El Momento,* 12/13/1943; *El Momento,* 01/25/1944; *El Momento,* 05/20/1944; *El Momento,* 05/27/1944.

67. *Carteles del Sur,* 10/04/1966; Moncada, *Del México,* 11; *El Momento,* 12/16/1943; *El Chapulín,* 01/10/1952; Interview with Guillermo Villa, July 2012.

68. Smith, *Pistoleros,* 289–328, 362–401.

69. *El Chapulín,* 03/05/1947; *Carteles del Sur,* 10/04/1966.

70. E.g., *El Momento,* 10/25/1945; *El Momento,* 12/26/1944; *El Momento,* 02/02/1945; *El Momento,* 04/12/1945; *El Momento,* 07/04/1945; *El Momento,* 01/02/1946.

71. *El Momento,* 01/16/1946.

72. *El Momento,* 03/30/1946.

73. E.g., *El Chapulín,* 12/28/1950; *El Chapulín,* 10/25/1951; *El Chapulín,* 09/20/1951; *El Chapulín,* 11/24/1951.

74. *El Chapulín,* 01/28/1952.

75. *El Chapulín,* 12/20/1951; *El Chapulín,* 12/27/1951; *El Chapulín,* 01/10/1952; *El Chapulín,* 01/17/1952.

76. *El Chapulín,* 01/10/1952.

77. *El Chapulín,* 03/27/1952.

78. *El Chapulín,* 03/22/1952; *El Chapulín,* 04/03/1952; *El Chapulín,* 04/17/1952; *El Chapulín,* 05/01/1952.

79. *El Chapulín,* 05/08/1952.

80. "Corrido de Mayoral Heredia"; "Corrido de la Huelga," Hemeroteca Pública de la Ciudad de Oaxaca, Collección Mayoral Heredia.

81. *La Voz de Oaxaca*, 01/10/1947; *La Voz de Oaxaca*, 01/09/1947, AGN/DGG /2/314/1 (17)1.

82. *Nueva Vida*, 01/13/1947; *Nueva Vida*, 01/14/1947, AGN/DGG/2/314/1 (17)1.

83. Private Archive of Guillermo Villa, José María Bradomin, *Efemérides del Siglo, 1950–1959* (manuscript); *El Nuevo Diario*, 02/09/1951; *El Nuevo Diario*, 03/13/1951; *El Nuevo Diario*, 04/06/1951.

84. E.g., *El Nuevo Diario*, 09/06/1951; *El Nuevo Diario*, 09/16/1951; *El Nuevo Diario*, 09/17/1951; *El Nuevo Diari/o*, 02/11/1952; *El Nuevo Diario*, 03/13/1952.

85. Private Archive of Guillermo Villa, José María Bradomin, *Efemérides del Siglo, 1950–1959* (manuscript).

86. "El Chantajista Vividor," Hemeroteca Pública de la Ciudad de Oaxaca, Colección Mayoral Heredia.

87. *El Nuevo Diario*, 03/19/1952.

88. *El Nuevo Diario*, 03/20/1952; *El Nuevo Diario*, 03/21/1952.

89. Quintas Castellanos, "El Movimiento," 47. Private Archive of Guillermo Villa, José María Bradomin, *Efemerides del Siglo, 1950–1959* (manuscript); *Diario del Sur*, 05/05/1952; *El Chapulín*, 04/17/1952; *El Chapulín*, 03/22/1952.

90. Interview with Gabriel Quintas, July 2012.

91. *El Chapulín*, 03/30/1959.

92. For the best introduction, see Rubin, *Decentering*.

Chapter Eight

1. Reyes, *La Otra*, 101.

2. See the documents in AGN/DFS/VP, Judith Reyes Hernández; Marsh, "Writing"; García Sánchez, *Judith*, 92–106.

3. Reyes, *La Otra*, 3–23; García Sánchez, *Judith*, 31–36.

4. Reyes, *La Otra*, 24–43; García Sánchez, *Judith*, 39–44.

5. Reyes, *La Otra*, 55–69; García Sánchez, *Judith*, 47–32.

6. Reyes, *La Otra*, 80–92; García Sánchez, *Judith*, 55–62.

7. Reyes, *La Otra*, 93–103; García Sánchez, *Judith*, 60–61.

8. There were fifteen songs collected in her 1965 record *La Otra Cara de la Patria*, vol. 1.

9. *Medios Publicitarios Mexicanos* (May–August 1960); Effectiveness of Newspaper Supplement, 1967, NARA/RG306, MX-6702.

10. E.g., *El Monitor del Parral*, 07/08/1961; *El Monitor del Parral*, 07/10/1961; *El Monitor del Parral*, 07/11/1961.

11. *La Verdad*, 10/02/1959.

12. On society pages, see Agustín, *La Tragicomedia*, 71; *El Monitor del Parral*, 10/01/1961.

13. *El Monitor del Parral*, 10/01/1961; *El Monitor del Parral*, 10/08/1961; *El Monitor del Parral*, 11/06/1961; *El Monitor del Parral*, 12/08/1961; *El Monitor del Parral*, 12/15/1961.

14. Cruz Vázquez, *1968–2000*, 78–79.

15. Sánchez Sierra, "Periodismo."

16. Brewster, *Responding*, 87.

17. Padrés, *El Diario*, 163.

18. Reyes, *La Otra*, 103.

19. *Medios Publicitarios Mexicanos* (May–August 1960); Report on newspapers in Ciudad Juárez consular district, 01/05/1954 CUSDCF/Mexico/IA/1950–1954/43; *Anuario Estadístico*, 1958. In 1960, 474,568 inhabitants of Chihuahua lived in urban areas. They comprised around 120,000 households or around the same number of newspapers produced daily.

20. For the PAN in Chihuahua see D'Antonio and Form, *Influentials*, 37–39, 168–80; Shirk, *Mexico's*, 72–74; *El Norte*, 07/04/1955; *El Norte*, 07/05/1955.

21. Memorandum, Situación Política en Chihuahua, 11/19/1960, AGN/DFS/VP, Práxedis Giner Durán, Legajo 1.

22. *La Antorcha*, February 1964; *La Antorcha*, May 1964; Memorandum, 07/08/1953, AGN/DFS/VP, Oscar Maynez Soto.

23. Gutiérrez de Alba, *Tric Trac*, 23–24.

24. *El Alacrán*, 11/13/1941; *El Alacrán*, 03/29/1942; *El Alacrán*, 10/29/1942; *El Alacrán*, 09/29/1942; *El Alacrán*, 07/13/1947.

25. "Varios problemas ocurridos," 10/01/1964, AGN/DGIPS/1560A, Exp 1.

26. *Jeringa*, 11/23/1946; *Jeringa*, 12/31/1946; *Jeringa*, 02/01/1947; *Jeringa*, 04/26/1947; *Jeringa*, 01/10/1948; *Jeringa*, 03/20/1948; *Jeringa*, 01/30/1966.

27. For divisions in the elite, see "Varios problemas ocurridos," 10/01/1964, AGN/DGIPS/1560A, Exp. 1; D'Antonio and Form, *Influentials*, 41–42, 172–73.

28. Gutiérrez de Alba, *Tric Trac*, 105–9; Chris Petrew to Embassy, 09/16/1959, CUSDCF/Mexico/IA/1955–1959/24; University of Texas, El Paso, Digital Commons, Interview no. 234, René Mascarenas Miranda, 02/02/1976, http://digitalcommons.utep.edu/interviews/234/ 04/12/2017.

29. "Varios problemas ocurridos," 10/01/1964, AGN/DGIPS/1560A, Exp. 1; *Indice*, 09/01/1958; *Indice*, 10/25/1958; *Indice*, 11/14/1958.

30. *Indice*, 09/20/1959.

31. *Indice*, 03/19/1960; *Indice*, 04/03/1960; *Indice*, 01/23/1961.

32. For the Vallina case, see *Indice*, 02/27/1960; Ceniceros Rios, *Comentarios*.

33. García Sánchez, *Judith*, 62.

34. "Varios problemas ocurridos," 10/01/1964, AGN/DGIPS/1560A, Exp. 1.

35. *El Norte*, 12/09/1954; *El Norte*, 12/10/1954.

36. *El Norte*, 12/13/1954; *El Norte*, 12/14/1954; *El Norte*, 12/15/1954; *El Norte*, 12/17/1954; *El Norte*, 12/18/1954.

37. *El Norte*, 12/09/1954; *El Norte*, 12/17/1954; *El Norte*, 12/20/1954. There is an excellent summary of events in *La Nación*, 01/09/1955.

38. *El Norte*, 12/13/1954; *El Norte*, 12/24/1954; *El Norte*, 12/28/1954; *El Norte*, 01/13/1955; *El Norte*, 01/16/1955.

39. *El Norte*, 12/30/1954; *El Norte*, 12/31/1954; *El Norte*, 12/31/1954 EXTRA; *El Norte*, 01/03/1955; *El Norte*, 01/06/1955; *El Norte*, 01/09/1954.

40. *El Norte*, 01/03/1955; *El Norte*, 01/04/1955; *El Norte*, 01/09/1954.

41. For the emergence of the CPJDC see *El Norte*, 12/21/1954.

42. For Villareal's background see Lázaro Villareal to President López Mateos, 05/12/1959, AGN/DGG/2/311M (6)/47; Memorandum, 02/20/1955, 01/05/1955, AGN/ARC/541/477; Lázaro Villareal to President Ruiz Cortines, 08/20/1955, AGN/ARC/549.44/841; Mendoza Medrano, "A La Breve Historia," http://alphasigloxxi.org/historia_gran_logia.html 03/20/2017. For the predominantly female makeup of the organization see *El Norte*, 12/21/1954.

43. E.g., *El Norte*, 01/05/1954; *El Norte*, 01/08/1955; *El Norte*, 01/21/1955.

44. *El Norte*, 12/17/1954; *El Norte*, 01/04/1954.

45. *El Norte*, 01/03/1955.

46. *El Norte*, 01/31/1955.

47. Ing Ricardo Muñoz Aguero to President Ruiz Cortines, 02/02/1955, AGN/ARC/541/477.

48. Memorandum, 02/20/1955, Villareal to Ruiz Cortines, 01/31/1955, AGN/ARC/541/477; Memoranda from Fausto Morales, 03/28/1955, 05/12/1955, 05/18/1955, 05/25/1955, AGN/DFS/VP, Oscar Maynez Soto.

49. *El Heraldo de Chihuahua*, 01/07/1955; *El Heraldo de Chihuahua*, 01/29/1955; *El Heraldo de Chihuahua*, 01/31/1955; *El Heraldo de Chihuahua*, 05/13/1955; *El Heraldo de Chihuahua*, 05/27/1955.

50. E.g., in San Luis Potosí. *El Sol de San Luis*, 03/27/1961; *El Sol de San Luis*, 04/22/1961; *El Sol de San Luis*, 07/24/1961; *La Tribuna*, 07/13/1961.

51. *El Norte*, 07/04/1955; *El Norte*, 07/05/1955; *El Norte*, 08/10/1955.

52. *El Norte*, 08/11/1955; *El Heraldo de Chihuahua*, 08/10/1955.

53. The issue that was ripped out was the September 1964 issue, which contained an interview with guerrilla Arturo Gámiz.

54. For the weakness of PRI, see Smith, "Who Governed"; Bertaccini, *El régimen*.

55. For Chihuahua's PRI see Informe, Chihuahua, 08/21/1964; Memorandum, 03/13/1964; Situación Política en Chihuahua, 11/19/1960, AGN/DFS/VP, Praxedis Giner Duran; Memorandum, 01/23/1962, AGN/DFS/100-5-1-62; Memorandum sobre tendencias políticas, 11/30/1963; Memorandum, 03/13/1964, AGN/DFS/VP, Oscar Soto Maynez; Informe sobre Chihuahua, 10/13/1963, AGN/DGIPS/2964E; Blanco Moheno, *La Noticia*, 99.

56. Memoranda, 01/11/1962, 01/14/1962, 06/03/1962, 06/24/1962, AGN/DFS/VP, Práxedis Giner Durán.

57. Memorandum, 11/24/1963, AGN/DFS/VP, Judith Reyes Hernández; Padilla, "Rural Education."

58. Henson, "Madera 1965"; Problemas en el Municipio de Madera, 07/28/1964; Memorandum Informativo, 02/25/1960; Informe, 08/21/1964, AGN/DGIPS/1560A, Exp. 1.

59. *Acción*, 10/04/1962; *Acción*, January 1963. With regard to dissident members of the PAN, see Memorandum, 06/01/1962, AGN/DFS/100-5-1-62.

60. *Acción*, 10/04/1962; Memorandum, 02/16/1964, AGN/DFS/VP, Judith Reyes Hernández.

61. Memorandum, 02/16/1964, AGN/DFS/VP, Judith Reyes Hernández.

62. García Sánchez, *Judith*, 62; *Indice*, 12/12/1960.

63. *Acción*, 10/03/1963; *Acción*, Dec. 1962.

64. Aviña, *Specters*, 40–89.

65. *Acción*, September 1964.

66. *Acción*, June 1963.

67. *Acción*, February 1964.

68. Reyes, *La Otra*, 150.

69. *Acción*, May 1963; *Acción*, June 1963.

70. Memorandum, 02/16/1964, AGN/DFS/VP, Judith Reyes Hernández.

71. García Sánchez, *Judith*, 64.

72. Reyes, *La Otra*, 150.

73. *Acción*, July 1963.

74. *Acción*, January 1963.

75. *Acción*, 02/07/1964.

76. *Acción*, January 1963; *Acción*, May 1963.

77. *Acción*, April 1963; *Acción*, May 1963; *Acción*, February 1963; *Acción*, 03/10/1963.

78. *Acción*, June 1963.

79. Ibid.

80. *Acción*, November 1962; *Acción*, 09/18/1963; *Acción*, November 1963; Memorandum by DEM, 11/19/1963, AGN/DFS/VP, Judith Reyes Hernández.

81. *Acción*, 10/04/1962; *Acción*, 12/23/1963; *Acción*, January 1963; *Acción*, 02/07/1964; *Acción*, 01/25/1964.

82. *Acción*, 10/04/1962; *Acción*, 02/25/1964; *Acción*, 08/18/1963; *Acción*, July 1963.

83. *Acción*, 10/04/1962; *Acción*, 08/18/1963; *Acción*, 09/03/1963, *Acción* 09/18/1963.

84. García Sánchez, *Judith*, 66–69; Reyes, *La Otra*, 135–42; *Indice*, 06/16/1964; *Acción*, 02/25/1964.

85. Henson, "Madera 1965," 112–14; Informe sobre Chihuahua, 08/21/1964, AGN/DGIPS/1027.

86. Henson, "Madera 1965," 127–28, 144–45; *Acción*, 10/03/1963; 02/25/1964; *Indice*, 03/07/1964; Informe, 02/23/1964, AGN/DGIPS/1305.

87. Henson, "Madera 1965," 152–54; *Acción*, 04/30/1964; Reyes, *La Otra*, 129–32; *Indice*, 04/07/1964; Entrevista con José Franco Almaraz, AGN/DGIPS/1560A, Exp 1.

88. Informe, 04/28/1964; Informe, 05/01/1964; Informe, 05/17/1964; Informe, 06/14/1964, AGN/DGIPS/1560A, Exp 1.

89. *Indice*, 09/12/1964; Henson, "Ciudad Madera 1965."

90. Paul Gillingham, "How Much News."

91. Castro, *De Albañil*.

92. Trejo Dalarbre, *La Prensa*, 120–22; *Por Qué?*, 04/30/1970; *Por Qué?*, 09/20/1972; Orozco, "Las luchas," 49–66.

Conclusion

1. Contacts in the international media included Alan Riding, the *New York Times* journalist, who turned the coup into an international scandal. Freije, "Censorship." Contacts in the national media included Pagés Llergo, who lent Scherer *Siempre!*'s printing press. Johnson, *Mexican*, 53. What was much less well known was that Jesús Alvarez del Castillo, the owner of Guadalajara's *El Informador*, actually gave Scherer the start-up money for the magazine. *Proceso*, Special Edition no. 9, November 2001.

2. Hughes, *Newsrooms*, 86, 120–21; Lawson, *Building*, 39–69; Calmon Alvez, "From Lapdog," 185; Hallin, "Media," 91; Rodríguez Castañeda, *Prensa*, 168–77; Caletti-Kaplan, "Comunication"; Johnson, *Mexican*, 53–54; Krauze, *Mexico*, 750–51; Riding, *Distant*, 104–9; Camp, *Intellectuals*, 195–96.

3. The exception was Carlos Fuentes, who maintained his support for Echeverría even after the coup. Brewster, *Responding*, 91.

4. Burkholder, "La red"; Burkholder, "El Olimpo"; Gamiño Muñoz, *Guerrilla*, 80–111; Brewster, *Responding*; Freije, "Secrets"; Bartley and Bartley, *Eclipse*, 15–41.

5. As Ben Fallaw argues, these spaces were probably preceded during the 1930s by Mexico City's aggressive right-wing tabloids like *Omega* and *Hombre Libre*. Fallaw, *Religion*, 8, 29. Also see the interview with the editor of *Hombre Libre* in Borrás, *Historia*, 148–56.

6. Camp, "The Cartoons"; Zolov, "Jorge Carreño's"; Del Río, *Rius*; Piccato, "Murders." Though there is still research to be done, Paul Gillingham asserts that the sports pages of the tabloids and nationals also provided space for relatively free criticism and debate. Gillingham, "Maximino's Bulls."

7. Burkholder, "Prensa."

8. For a condemnation of such practices, see Martínez, *Prensa Negra*.

9. Loseff, *On the Beneficence*.

10. Ortega, *Democracía*, 13, 67, 189.

11. Taylor, *Magistrates*, 180–206; Rockwell, "Schools," 202; Vaughan, *Cultural*, 180.

12. Knight, "The Weight"; Knight, 'Historical Continuities"; Hernández Rodríguez, *El Centro*; Rubin, *Decentering*; Bertaccini, *El régimen*; Hernández Rodríguez, *Amistades*; Smith, "Who Governed?"; Gillingham, "Mexican Elections"; Pansters, "Tropical Passion"; Hernández Rodríguez, *Presidencialismo*; Hernández Rodríguez, "Strongmen"; Henson, "Ciudad Madera, 1965"; Freije, "Secrets."

13. Navarro, *Political*; Padilla, *Rural Resistance*; McCormick, *The Logic*; Pensado, *Rebel*; Bortz and Aguila, "The Rise"; Herrera Calderón and Cedillo Cedillo, *Challenging*; Condés Lara, *Represión*; Aviña, *Specters*.

14. Fallaw, *Religion*.

15. Smith, *Roots*, 246–93; Torres Septién, "Guanajuato."

16. Smith, "Who Governed?" David Tamayo, a graduate student at Berkeley, is currently working on a thesis on these civil associations in the 1940s and 1950s. Personal communication with David Tamayo.

17. Aviña, *Specters*; Henson, "Ciudad Madera 1965."

18. The literature refining Habermas's ideas on the public sphere is enormous. For a good introduction, see Calhoun, "Introduction"; Fraser, "Rethinking"; Landes, *Women*.

19. The point is made in Piccato, "A History"; Serna, "Prensa."

20. https://rsf.org/en/ranking#; https://cpj.org/killed/americas/mexico 03/29/2017; http://www.jornada.unam.mx/ultimas/2016/06/07/de-2000-a-la-fecha-han-asesinado -a-144-periodistas-en-mexico-cndh 03/29/2017.

21. Rios, "Quien Mata."

22. http://www.sinembargo.mx/02-09-2016/3087706 03/29/2017.

23. See Hernández and Rodelo, "Dilemas," and the essays in Del Palacio Montiel, (ed.) *Violencia*.

24. Hernández, *Señores*; Esquivel, *La CIA*; Osorno, *La Guerra*; Padgett, *Tamaulipas*.

25. Eiss, "Front Lines"; Eiss, "Narcomedia."

Bibliography

Archives

UNITED STATES

Durham, North Carolina
    Thomas Sutton Papers, Duke University

Washington, DC
National Anthropological Archives (NAA)
    Ralph L. Beals Collection
National Archives and Records Administration (NARA)
    Record Group 59 (RG59)
    Record Group 170 (RG170)
    Record Group 229 (RG229)
    Record Group 306 (RG306)

MEXICO

Ciudad Juárez
Casa de la Cultura Júridica

Mexicali
Archivo Histórico del Estado de Baja California (AHEBC)
    Junta de Conciliación y Arbitraje (JCA)
    Secretaría de Gobierno (SG)

Mexico City
Archivo General de la Nación (AGN)
    Presidentes Lázaro Cárdenas del Río (LCR)
    Presidentes Manuel Avila Camacho (MAC)
    Presidentes Miguel Alemán Valdés (MAV)
    Presidentes Adolfo Ruiz Cortines (ARC)
    Presidentes Adolfo López Mateos (ALM)
    Presidentes Gustavo Diaz Ordaz (GDO)
    Dirección General de Investigaciones Políticas y Sociales (DGIPS)
    Dirección Federal de Seguridad, Versión Pública (DFS/VP)
    Dirección General de Gobierno (DGG)
    Secretaría de Comercio y Fomento Industrial, Dirección General de Fomento
        Cooperativo (SCFI/DGFC)

Dirección General de Información (DGI)
Archivo Histórico de la Suprema Corte de Justicia
Biblioteca Miguel Lerdo de Tejada
Colegio de México
  Biblioteca Daniel Cosío Villegas
Hemeroteca Nacional
Universidad Iberoamericana
  Archivo de Acción Católica Mexicana (AACM)

Oaxaca de Juárez
Archivo General Público del Estado de Oaxaca (AGPEO)
Archivo de la Gran Logia "Benito Juarez" de Oaxaca
Biblioteca Francisco de Burgoa
  Brioso y Candiani Collection
Guillermo Villa Private Archive
Hemeroteca Pública de la Ciudad de Oaxaca
  Colección Mayoral Heredia

UNITED KINGDOM
London
London School of Economics Library
  Confidential U.S. State Department Central Files, Mexico, Internal Affairs,
    1940–1959 (CUSDCF/Mexico/IA)
National Archives (NA)
  Foreign Office (FO)

Dissertations, Theses, and Unpublished Manuscripts

Adler, Ilya. "Media Uses and Effects in Large Bureaucracies: A Case Study in Mexico."
  PhD diss., University of Wisconsin–Madison, 1986.
Alexander, Ryan M. "Fortunate Sons of the Mexican Revolution: Miguel Alemán and
  His Generation, 1920–1952." PhD diss., University of Arizona, 2011.
Argüelles Navarro, Victor Manuel. "Análisis del Proceso Electoral de 1985 en Poza
  Rica, Veracruz y su región." BA diss., Universidad Autónoma Metropolitana, 1990.
Berry, Timothy John. "PIPSA and the Mexican Press." MA diss., University of Oregon,
  1974.
Borjas Benavente, Leticia. "El Tratamiento Periodístico de la Información del
  Movimiento Político Denominado Navismo, 1958–1963." BA diss., Universidad
  Iberoamericana, 1992.
Burkholder de la Rosa, Arno Vicente. "La Red de los Espejos. Una Historia del Diario
  Excélsior (1916–1976)." PhD diss., Instituto Mora, 2007.
Cedillo Cedillo, Adela. "El Fuego y el Silencio: Historia de las Fuerzas de Liberación
  Nacional Mexicanas (1969–1974)." BA diss., Universidad Nacional Autónoma de
  México, 2008.

Cobb, Phillip Eugene. "Provincial Journalism and National Development in Mexico, with Special Consideration of Monterrey, Guadalajara and Mexico." MA diss., University of Texas–Austin, 1971.

Cole, Richard. "The Mass Media of Mexico: Ownership and Control." PhD diss., University of Minnesota, 1972.

Eiss, Paul. "Front Lines and Back Channels: The Fractal Publics of El Blog del Narco." Unpublished manuscript, 2016.

Erlandson, E. H. "The Press of Mexico with Special Consideration of Economic Factors." PhD diss., Northwestern University, 1963.

Fallaw, Ben. "The Politics of Press Freedom during the Maximato: The Case of the *Diario de Yucatán*." Unpublished manuscript, 2016.

Freije, Vanessa. "Censorship in the Headlines: National News and the Contradictions of Mexico City's Press Opening in the Long 1970s." Unpublished manuscript, 2016.

Gillingham, Paul. "How Much News Was Fit to Print? The Regional Press Boom, 1940–1960." Unpublished manuscript, 2016.

González Landeros, Alejandro. "Estrellas, Medios, y Relatos de Fútbol en México (1941–2002)." PhD diss., Michigan State University, 2016.

Heitman, John Russell. "The Press of Mexico: Its History, Characteristics, and Content." PhD diss., Northwestern University, 1948.

Henson, Elizabeth. "Ciudad Madera, 1965: Obsessive Simplicity, the Agrarian Dream, and Che." PhD diss., University of Arizona, 2015.

Hernández, Carlos Armando. "Narcomundo, How Narcotraficantes Gained Control of Northern Mexico and Beyond, 1945–1985." PhD diss., UCLA, 2015.

Hesse, Mark. "Mexican Newspapers and the Night of Sadness." MSc diss., University of Kansas, 1971.

Holden, Paul Howard. "The Creative Writing of Jorge Ferretis, Ideology and Style." PhD diss., University of South Carolina, 1966.

Keller, Renata. "Testing the Limits of Censorship? Política Magazine and Mexico's Perfect Dictatorship." Unpublished manuscript, 2016.

———. "Whose News? Cuba's Prensa Latina and the Cold War Contest over Information." Unpublished manuscript, 2016.

Martínez de Verburg, Graciela, and John A. Verberg Moore. "San Miguel Coatlinchán, Estudio Sobre un ejido marginal en el estado de México." BA thesis, Universidad Autónoma Nacional de México, 1964.

Montgomery, Louise F. "Mexican Newspaper Elites' View of the Masses: Maintaining the Status Quo." MA diss., University of Texas, 1979.

———. "Stress on Government and Mexican Newspapers' Commentary on Government Officials: 1951–1980." PhD diss., University of Texas, 1983.

Nolan, Sidney David. "Relative Independence of Two Mexican Dailies: A Case Study of El Norte and El Porvenir of Monterrey." MA thesis, University of Texas–Austin, 1965.

Ortiz Garza, José Luis. "El Eslabón más Debil: García Valseca no Fundó la Cadena de Periódicos que lleva su Nombre." Unpublished manuscript, 2016.

Paxman, Andrew. "Changing Opinions in *La Opinión*: Maximino Ávila Camacho and the Puebla Press, 1936–1941." Unpublished manuscript, 2016.

———. "Jenkins of Mexico: How a Southern Farm Boy Became a Mexican Magnate." Unpublished manuscript, 2015.

Piccato, Pablo. "A History of Infamy: Crime, Truth, and Justice in Mexico." Unpublished manuscript, 2015.

———. "Notes for a History of the Press in Mexico." Unpublished manuscript, 2016.

Pilatowsky Goñi, Priscila. "Reconstruyendo el Nacionalismo: Impresos, Radio, Publicidad y Propaganda en México (1934–1942)." PhD diss., Universidad Autónoma Nacional de México, 2013.

Rath, Thomas. "Paratroopers under the Volcano: Animal Disease, Sovereignty, and Scandal in Cold War Mexico." Unpublished manuscript, 2015.

Rincón Rodríguez, Irma. "*Amanecer* y el Poder Político en Queretaro: Una Relación Compleja, 1951–1962." MA diss., Universidad de Queretaro, 2012.

Rodríguez Munguía, Jacinto. "La Tiranía Invisible o el Origen de la Dictadura Perfecta." Unpublished manuscript, 2016.

Spicer Nichols, John. "Coyotes of the Press: Professionalization of Mexican Journalists." PhD diss., University of Minnesota, 1979.

Underwood, Robert Bruce. "A Survey of Contemporary Newspapers of Mexico." PhD diss., University of Missouri, 1965.

Published Works

50 años de Revolución Mexicana en cifras. Mexico City: Nacional Financiera, 1963.

Aboites Aguilar, Luis. *Excepciones y Privilegios: Modernización Tributaria y Centralización en México, 1922–1972*. Mexico City: Colegio de México, 2003.

Abramo Lauff, Marcelo. *El estadio: la prensa en México (1870–1879)*. Mexico City: Instituto Nacional de Antropología e Historia, 1998.

Adler Hellman, Judith. *Mexico in Crisis*. London: Homes & Meier, 1978.

Aguayo, Sergio. *1968: Los Archivos de la Violencia*. Mexico City: Grijalbo, 1998.

———. *De Tlatelolco a Ayotzinapa: Las Violencias del Estado*. Mexico City: Proceso, 2015.

———. *La Charola: Una Historia de los Servicios de Inteligencia en México*. Mexico City: Grijalbo, 2001.

Aguilar Domingo, Martin. *Zacatepec, Mixe*. Oaxaca: Casa de la Cultura, 1992.

Agundis, Teódulo Manuel. *El Verdadero Jorge Pasquel, Ensayo Biográfico sobre un Carácter*. Mexico City: Atenea, 1956.

Agustín, José. *Tragicomedia Mexicana*. Mexico City: Planeta, 1990.

Alba, Victor. *Sísifo y su tiempo: memorias de un cabreado, 1916–1996*. Barcelona: Laertes, 1996.

Aldrete, Sara. *Me dicen la Narcosatánica*. Mexico City: DeBolsillo, 2008.

Alegre, Robert F. *Railroad Radicals: Gender, Class and Memory in Cold War Mexico*. Lincoln: University of Nebraska Press, 2013.

Alisky, Marvin. "Growth of Newspapers in Mexico's Provinces." *Journalism & Mass Communication Quarterly* 37, no. 1 (1960): 75–82.

Almond, Gabriel, and Sidney Verba. *The Civic Culture: Political Attitudes and Democracy in Five Nations.* New York: Sage, 1963.

Alvarez Garín, Raúl. *Los Procesos de México 68: Acusaciones y Defensa.* Mexico City: Estudiantes, 1970.

Anonymous. *La Vida Accidentada y Novelesca de Rodolfo Valdéz el Gitano.* Mazatlán: El Correo de la Tarde, 1949.

Anuario Estadístico Compendiado de los Estados Unidos Mexicanos. Mexico City: Talleres Gráficos de la Nación, 1942–1974.

Astorga, Luis. *Drogas sin fronteras. Los Expedientes de una Guerra Permanente.* Mexico City: Grijalbo, 2003.

———. *Mitologia del "Narcotraficante" en México.* Mexico City: Plaza y Valdés, 1995.

Aviña, Alexander. *Specters of Revolution: Peasant Guerrillas in the Cold War Mexican Countryside.* New York: Oxford University Press, 2014.

Barajas Durán, Rafael. *El País de "El Ahuizote": La Caricatura Mexicana de Oposición durante el Gobierno de Sebastián Lerdo de Tejada (1872–1876).* Mexico City: Fondo de Cultura Económica, 2005.

———. *El País de "El Llorón de Icamole": Caricatura Mexicana de Combate y Libertad de Imprenta durante los Gobiernos de Porfirio Díaz y Manuel González (1877–1884).* Mexico City: Fondo de Cultura Económica, 2007.

Bartley, Russell H., and Sylvia E. Bartley. *Eclipse of the Assassins: The CIA, Imperial Politics, and the Slaying of Mexican Journalist Manuel Buendía.* Madison: University of Wisconsin Press, 2015.

Bartra, Roger. *The Cage of Melancholy, Identity and Metamorphosis in the Mexican Character.* Translated by Christopher J. Hall. New Brunswick: Rutgers University Press, 1992.

Beals, Ralph L. "The Oaxaca Market Project." In *Markets in Oaxaca,* edited by Scott Cook and Martín Diskin, 27–44. Austin: University of Texas Press, 1976.

Beardsell, Peter. *A Theatre for Cannibals, Rodolfo Usigli and the Mexican Stage.* Rutherford, NJ: Associated University Presses, 1992.

Becerra Acosta, Manuel. *Dos Poderes.* Mexico City: Grijalbo, 1985.

Beezley, William H. *Judas at the Jockey Club and Other Episodes of Porfirian Mexico.* Lincoln: University of Nebraska Press, 2004.

Beezley, William, Cheryl Ann Martin, and William French, eds. *Rituals of Rule, Rituals of Resistance: Public Celebrations and Popular Culture in Mexico.* Wilmington, DE: Scholarly Resources, 1994.

Bergson, Henri. *Laughter: An Essay on the Meaning of the Comic.* Mansfield Centre: Martino, 2014.

Bernal Sahagún, Victor M. *Anatomía de la Publicidad en México: Monopolios, Enajenación y Desperdicios.* Mexico City: Nuestro Tiempo, 1974.

Bertaccini, Tiziana. *El régimen priísta frente a las clases medias, 1943–1964.* Mexico City: Conaculta, 2009.

Blair, Calvin P. "Nacional Financiera: Entrepreneurship in a Mixed Economy." In *Public Policy and Private Enterprise in Mexico*, edited by Raymond Vernon, 191–240. Cambridge, MA: Harvard University Press: 1964.

Blanco Moheno, Roberto. *La Corrupción en México*. Mexico City: Bruguera Mexicana de Ediciones, 1979.

———. *La Noticia Detrás de la Noticia*. Mexico City: Siglos, 1975.

———. *Memorias de un Reportero*. Mexico City: Siglos, 1979.

Blancornelas, Jesús. *Conversaciones Privadas*. Mexico City: Graficas Monte Alban, 2001.

———. *En Estado de Alerta, Periodistas y Gobierno Frente al Narcotráfico*. Mexico City: Random House, 2005.

Bohmann, Karin. *Medios de Comunicación y sistemas informativos en México*. Mexico City: Conaculta, 1989.

Borrás, Leopoldo. *Historia de Periodismo Mexicano, del Ocaso Porfirista al Derecho a la Información*. Mexico City: Universidad Nacional Autónoma de México, 1983.

Borrego E., Salvador. *Cómo García Valseca fundó y perdió 37 Periódicos y cómo Eugenio Garza Sada Trató de Rescatarlos y Perdió la Vida*. Mexico City: Editorial Tradición, 1984.

———. *Derrota Mundial*. Mexico City: n.p., 1979.

———. *Periodismo Transcendente*. Mexico City: Editorial Jus, 1961.

Bortz, Jeffrey Lawrence. *Los Salarios Industriales en la Ciudad de México, 1939–1975*. Mexico City: Fondo de Cultura Económica, 1984.

Bortz, Jeffrey Lawrence, and Marcos Aguila. "The Rise of Gangsterism and Charrismo: Labor Violence and the Postrevolutionary State." In *Violence, Coercion, and State-Making in Twentieth-Century Mexico: The Other Side of the Centaur*, edited by Wil Pansters, 185–211. Stanford: Stanford University Press, 2012.

Bourdieu, Pierre. *Language and Symbolic Power*. Cambridge, UK: Polity, 1992.

Brewster, Claire. *Responding to Crisis in Contemporary Mexico: The Political Writings of Paz, Fuentes, Monsiváis and Poniatowska*. Tucson: University of Arizona Press, 2005.

———. "The Student Movement of 1968 and the Mexican Press: The Cases of 'Excélsior' and 'Siempre!'" *Bulletin of Latin American Research* 21, no. 2 (2002): 171–90.

Brunk, Samuel. *The Posthumous Career of Emiliano Zapata: Myth, Memory, and Mexico's Twentieth Century*. Austin: University of Texas Press, 2008.

Buendía, Manuel. *La CIA en México*. Mexico City: Oceano, 1996.

Buffington, Robert. *A Sentimental Education for the Working Man: The Mexico City Penny Press, 1900–1910*. Durham, NC: Duke University Press, 2015.

Bunker, Steven B. *Creating Mexican Consumer Culture in the Age of Porfirio Díaz*. Albuquerque: University of New Mexico Press, 2012.

Burkholder de la Rosa, Arno Vicente. "Construyendo una nueva Relación con el Estado: El Crecimiento y Consolidación del Diario *Excélsior* (1932–1968)." *Secuencia* 73 (2009): 84–107.

———. "El Olimpo Fracturado. La Dirección de Julio Scherer García en *Excélsior* (1968–1976)." *Historia Mexicana* 59, no. 4 (2010): 1339–99.

Butcher, Jacqueline. *Mexican Solidarity: Citizen Participation and Volunteering*. New York: Springer, 2010.

Cadena Z., Daniel. *El Verdadero García Valseca: Una Amnesia Extraordinaria o los Millones de Maximino.* Mexico City: n.p., 1961.

———. *Por el Ojo de la Aguja: Novela.* Mexico City: n.p., 1961.

Caletti-Kaplan, R. "Communication Policies in Mexico: The Historical Paradox of Words and Actions." In *Media and Politics in Latin America: The Struggle for Democracy*, edited by E. Fox, 67–81. London: Sage, 1988.

Calhoun, Craig. "Introduction: Habermas and the Public Sphere." In *Habermas and the Public Sphere*, edited by Craig Calhoun, 1–48. Cambridge, MA: MIT Press, 1992.

Calmon Alves, Rosental. "From Lapdog to Watchdog: The Role of the Press in Latin America's Democratization." In *Making Journalists: Diverse Models, Global Issues*, edited by Hugh de Burgh, 183–202. London: Routledge, 2005.

Camp, Roderic Ai. "Camarillas in Mexican Politics, the Case of the Salinas Cabinet." *Mexican Studies/Estudios Mexicanos* 6 (Winter 1990): 85–108.

———. "The Cartoons of Abel Quezada." *Studies in Latin American Popular Culture* 4 (1985): 125–38.

———. "Education and Political Recruitment in Mexico: The Aleman Generation," *Journal of Interamerican Studies and World Affairs* 18, no. 3 (Aug. 1976): 295–321.

———. *Intellectuals and the State in Twentieth-Century Mexico.* Austin: University of Texas Press, 1985.

———. *Political Recruitment across Two Centuries, Mexico, 1884–1991.* Austin: University of Texas Press, 1995.

Cane, James. *The Fourth Enemy: Journalism and Power in the Making of Peronist Argentina, 1930–1955.* University Park: Pennsylvania State University Press, 2011.

Cárdial Reyes, Raúl. "El Periodo de Conciliación y Consolidación, 1946–1958." In *História de la Educación Pública en México*, edited by Fernando Solana, II, 327–59. Mexico City: SEP, 1982.

Carey, James C. *The Mexican Revolution in Yucatán, 1915–1924.* Boulder, CO: Westview Press, 1984.

Carr, Barry. *Marxism and Communism in Twentieth-Century Mexico.* Lincoln: University of Nebraska Press, 1992.

Carrillo Reveles, Veremundo. "Nacionalismo y Xenophobia en México: Debates en la Prensa sobre los Jugadores Extranjeros y Naturalizados, 1943–1945." *Desacatos* 51 (2016): 50–69.

Castañeda, Jorge G. *La Herencia: Arqueología de la Sucesión Presidencial en México.* Mexico City: Aguilar, 1999.

———. *Mañana Forever: Mexico and the Mexicans.* Mexico City: Knopf, 2011.

———. *Utopia Unarmed: The Latin American Left after the Cold War.* New York: Knopf, 1993.

Castaño, Luis. *El Régimen Legal de la Prensa en México.* Mexico City: Arpe, 1958.

Castellanos, José J. *México Engañado: Por Qué la Prensa No Informa.* Mexico City: n.p., 1983.

Castillo, E. *La Otra Mafia.* Tijuana: n.p., n.d.

Castillo Nájera, Oralba. *Renato Leduc y sus amigos.* Mexico City: Editorial Domés, 1987.

Castro, Simón Hipolito. *De Albañil a Preso Político*. Mexico City: Editorial Posada, 1978.

Ceniceros Ríos, Eduardo. *Comentarios sobre dos Juicios*. Mexico City: n.p., 1961.

Chassen de López, Francie. *From Liberal to Revolutionary Oaxaca: The View from the South: Mexico, 1867–1911*. University Park: Pennsylvania State University Press, 2004.

Clark de Lara, Belem, and Elisa Speckman Guerra, eds. *La República de las Letras: Asomos a la Cultura Escrita del México Decimonónico*. Mexico City: Universidad Nacional Autónoma de México, 2005.

Cline, Howard F. *Mexico: Revolution to Evolution, 1940–1960*. Oxford: Oxford University Press, 1962.

Cole, Richard. "The Mexican Press System: Aspects of Growth, Control and Ownership." *International Communication Gazette* 21, no. 2 (1975): 65–81.

Cole, Richard, and Albert Hester. *Mass Communication in Mexico, Proceedings of the March 11–15 1974 Seminar in Mexico City*. Mexico City: International Communication Division, 1975.

Coleman, Kenneth M. *Public Opinion in Mexico City about the Electoral System*. Chapel Hill: University of North Carolina Press, 1972.

Condés Lara, Enríque. *Represión y Rebelión en México (1959–1985)*. 2 vols. Mexico City: Porrúa, 2007.

Cook, Timothy. *Governing with the News: The News Media as a Political Institution*. Chicago: University of Chicago Press, 1998.

Cordero y Torres, Enrique. "Nacimiento de la Cadena García Valseca (1943–1968)." In *El Periodismo en México, 450 años de historia*, edited by María del Carmen Ruiz Castañeda, Luis Reed Torres, and Enrique Cordero y Torres, 285–377. Mexico City: Editorial Tradición, 1974.

Cordona, Rafael. "El Ultimo Dinosaurio." *Crónica* (Sept. 2011): 12.

Cosío Villegas, Daniel. *El Sistema Político Mexicano: Las Posibilidades de Cambio, Ensayo*. Austin: University of Texas, Institute of Latin American Studies, 1972.

———. "La Crisis en México." *Cuadernos Americanos* 32 (1947): 29–51.

———. *La República Restaurada: La vida política*. Mexico City: Hermes, 1955.

———. "The Press and Responsible Freedom in Mexico." In *Responsible Freedom in the Americas*, edited by Angel del Río, 272–80. Garden City, NY: Doubleday & Company, 1955.

Covo, Jacqueline. "La Prensa en la Historiografía Mexicana: Problemas y Posibilidades." *Historia Mexicana* 42, no. 3 (1993): 689–710.

Critchley, Simon. *On Humour*. London: Routledge, 2010.

Crónica de la Publicidad en Mexico. Mexico City: Editorial Clio, 2002.

Cruz Vázquez, Eduardo. *1968–2000, Los Silencios de la Democracía*. Mexico City: Planeta, 2008.

Cuevas Paralizábal, Roberto. *Entre los Hijos de la Revolución: Andanzas de un Reportero*. Mexico City: n.p., 2003.

Cull, Nicholas J. *The Cold War and the United States Information Agency: American Propaganda and Public Diplomacy, 1945–1989*. Cambridge: Cambridge University Press, 2008.

Curran, James, and Myung-Jin Park. "Beyond Globalization Theory." In *De-Westernizing Media Studies*, edited by James Curran and Myung-Jin Park, 3–8. London: Routledge, 2000.

———, eds. *De-Westernizing Media Studies*. London: Routledge, 2000.

Daniels, Josephus. *Shirt-Sleeve Diplomat*. Chapel Hill: University of North Carolina Press, 1947.

D'Antonio, William V., and William H. Form. *Influentials in Two Border Cities: A Study in Community Decision-Making*. Notre Dame: University of Notre Dame Press, 1965.

Darnton, Robert. *Censors at Work: How States Shaped Literature*. New York: W. W. Norton, 2014.

———. "An Early Information Society: News and Media in Eighteenth Century Paris." *American Historical Association* 105, no. 1 (2000): 1–35.

———. *The Forbidden Best-Sellers of Pre-Revolutionary France*. New York: Harper Collins, 1996.

———. "What Is the History of Books?" *Daedalus* 111, no. 3 (1982): 65–83.

De Burgh, Hugh, ed. *Making Journalists: Diverse Models, Global Issues*. London: Routledge, 2005.

De la Grange, Bertrand, and Maite Rico. *Marcos, la Genial Impostura*. Mexico City: Nuevo Siglo, 1995.

De la Pedraja Tomán, René. *Wars of Latin America, 1948–1982: The Rise of the Guerrillas*. Jefferson, NC: McFarland & Company, 2013.

Del Campo Venegas, Oscar. *Del Niño de la Calle . . . a Periodista*. Tijuana: Talleres Color Gráphico, 1997.

Del Castillo Troncoso, Alberto. *Ensayo sobre el Movimiento Estudiantil de 1968: La Fotografía y la Construcción de un Imaginario*. Mexico City: Instituto Mora, 2012.

———. "Fotoperiodismo y Representaciones del Movimiento Estudiantil de 1968. El Caso de *El Heraldo de México*." *Secuencia* 60 (2004): 137–72.

Del Palacio Montiel, Celia. "Introducción." In *Siete Regiones de la Prensa en México, 1792–1950*, edited by Celia del Palacio Montiel, 1–42. Guadalajara: CONACYT, 2006.

———, ed. *Rompecabezas de Papel: La Prensa y el Periodismo desde las Regiones de México, Siglos XIX y XX*. Guadalajara: Porrua, 2006.

———, ed. *Siete Regiones de la Prensa en México, 1792–1950*. Guadalajara: CONACYT, 2006.

———, ed. *Violencia y Periodismo Regional en México*. Mexico City: Juan Pablos Editor, 2015.

Del Río, Eduardo. *Rius para Principiantes*. Mexico City: Grijalbo, 2008.

De María y Campos, Armando. *El Teatro de Género Chico en La Revolución Mexicana*. Mexico City: Instituto Nacional de Estudios Históricos de la Revolución Mexicana, 1956.

De Mora, Juan Miguel. *Por la Gracia del Señor Presidente, México la Gran Mentira*. Mexico City: Editores Asociados, 1975.

Díaz, María Elena. "The Satiric Penny Press for Workers in Mexico, 1900–1910: A Case Study in the Politicization of Popular Culture." *Journal of Latin American Studies* 22, no. 3 (1990): 497–526.

Diskin, Martin. "The Structure of a Peasant Market System in Oaxaca." In *Markets in Oaxaca*, edited by Scott Cook and Martin Diskin, 49–66. Austin: University of Texas Press, 1977.

Doyle, Kate, and Jeff Morley. "Litiempo: The CIA's Eyes on Tlatelolco: CIA Spy Operations in Mexico." http://nsarchive.gwu.edu/NSAEBB/NSAEBB204/#6 03/29/2017.

Edwards, Michael. *Civil Society*. Malden, MA: Polity Press, 2004.

Egan, Linda. "Entrevistas con Periodistas Mujeres sobre la Prensa Mexicana." *Mexican Studies/Estudios Mexicanos* 9, no. 2 (1993): 275–94.

Eiss, Paul. "The Narcomedia: A Reader's Guide." *Latin American Perspectives* 41, no. 2 (2014): 78–88.

Enríquez Simoní, Guillermo. *La Libertad de Prensa en México: Una Mentira Rosa*. Mexico City: Costa-Amic, 1967.

Esquivel, Jesús. *La CIA, Camarena y Caro Quintero: La Historia Secreta*. Mexico City: Grijalbo, 2014.

Esquivel Hernández, José Luis. *El Norte, Lider sin Competencia*. Monterrey: Cerda, 2003.

Estrada M., Antonio. *La Grieta en el Yugo*. Mexico City: Jus, 1961.

Fallaw, Ben. *Cárdenas Compromised: The Failure of Reform in Postrevolutionary Yucatán*. Durham, NC: Duke University Press, 2001.

———. *Religion and State Formation in Postrevolutionary Mexico*. Durham, NC: Duke University Press, 2013.

Fernández Christlieb, Fátima. *Los Medios de Difusión Masiva en México*. Mexico City: Juan Pablos, 1982.

Fernández Menéndez, Jorge. *Nadie Supo Nada, La Verdadera Historia del Asesinato de Eugenio Garza Sada*. Mexico City: Grijalbo, 2006.

Ferrer, Eulalio Sr. *Cartas de un Publicista*. Mexico City: Editorial Diana, 1966.

———. *Enfoques sobre Publicidad (un Tema de Nuestro Tiempo)*. Mexico City: Editorial Diana, 1965.

Flores Pérez, Carlos. *Historias de Polvo y Sangre: Génesis y Evolución del Tráfico de Drogas en el Estado de Tamaulipas*. Mexico City: CIESAS, 2013.

———. "La lógica del bótin. Reconfiguración Cooptada del Estado y su Efecto en el Proceso de falla." In *Margens da Violência. Subsídios ao Estudo do Problema da Violência nos Contextos Mexicano e Brasileiro*, edited by Antonio Carlos de Souza Lima and Virginia García-Acosta, 129–170. Mexico City: CIESAS, 2014.

Forde, Susan. *Challenging the News: The Journalism of Alternative and Community Media*. Basingstoke, UK: Palgrave, 2011.

Forment, Carlos. *Democracy in Latin America, 1760–1900*. Chicago: University of Chicago Press, 2003.

Fox, Frank. *Madison Avenue Goes to War: The Strange Military Career of American Advertising, 1941–45*. Provo, UT: Brigham Young University Press, 1975.

Fraser, Nancy. "Rethinking the Public Sphere: A Contribution to the Critique of Actually Existing Democracy." *Social Text* 25/26 (1990): 56–80.

Fregoso Peralta, Gilberto, and Enrique Sánchez Ruiz. *Prensa y Poder en Guadalajara.* Guadalajara: Universidad de Guadalajara, 1993.

Freije, Vanessa. "Secrets and Revelations: Manuel Buendía, *Columnismo,* and the Unraveling of One-Party Rule in Mexico, 1965–1984." *The Americas* 72, no. 3 (2015): 377–409.

Fromm, Erich, and Michael Maccoby. *Social Character in a Mexican Village: A Sociopsychoanalytical Study.* London: Prentice Hall, 1970.

Fuentes, Carlos. *The Death of Artemio Cruz.* New York: Farrar, Strauss and Giroux, 1964.

———. *Where the Air Is Clear.* New York: Farrar, Strauss and Giroux, 1980.

Gamiño Muñoz, Rodolfo. *Guerrilla, Represión, y Prensa en la Década de los Setenta en México. Invisibilidad y Olvido.* Mexico City: Instituto Mora, 2011.

Gantus, Fausta. *Caricatura y Poder Político: Crítica, Censura y Represión en la Ciudad de México, 1876–1888.* Mexico City: Colegio de México, 2009.

García, Clara Guadalupe. *El Imparcial: Primer Periódico Moderno de México.* Mexico City: Centro de Estudios Históricos del Porfiriato, 2003.

García, Clara Guadalupe, and Silvia Solís Hernández. *La Nota Roja en México (1934–1985), Selección Antológica.* Mexico City: Centro de Estudios Históricos del Porfiriato, 1999.

García Cabrera, José Luis. *1920–2000 El Pastel!* 2 vols. Bloomington, IN: Palibro, 2012.

García Canclini, Néstor, Alejandro Castellanos, and Ana Rosas Mantecón. *La Ciudad de los Viajeros: Travesías e Imaginarios Urbanos, México, 1940–2000.* Mexico City: Grijalbo, 1996.

García Sánchez, Liliana. *Judith Reyes: Una Mujer de Canto Revolucionario.* Mexico City: Clandestino, 2007.

García Valseca, Jayne, and Mark Ebner. *We Have Your Husband: One Woman's Terrifying Story of a Kidnapping in Mexico.* New York: Berkley, 2011.

Gardner, Mary A. *The Inter-American Press Association: Its Fight for Freedom of the Press, 1926–1960.* Austin: University of Texas Press, 1967.

Garmabella, José Ramón. *Renato por Leduc: Apuntes de una Biografía Singular.* Mexico City: Oceano, 1985.

Garza, Gustavo. *La Urbanización de México en el Siglo XX.* Mexico City: Colegio de México, 2003.

Gauss, Susan. *Made in Mexico: Regions, Nation, and the State in the Rise of Mexican Industrialism, 1920s–1940s.* University Park: Pennsylvania State University Press, 2011.

Gil Mendieta, Jorge, Samuel Schmidt, and Alejandro Arnulfo Ruiz León. *Estudios sobre la Red Política de México.* Mexico City: UNAM, 2005.

Gillingham, Paul. "Maximino's Bulls: Popular Protest after the Mexican Revolution, 1940–1952." *Past & Present* 206, no. 1 (2010): 175–211.

———. "Mexican Elections, 1910–1994: Voters, Violence and Veto Power." In *The Oxford Handbook of Mexican Politics,* edited by Roderic Ai Camp, 53–76. Oxford: Oxford University Press, 2012.

Gillingham, Paul, Michael Lettieri, Benjamin T. Smith, eds. *Journalism, Satire and Censorship in Mexico*. Albuquerque: University of New Mexico Press, 2018.

Gillingham, Paul, and Benjamin T. Smith. "Introduction: The Paradoxes of Revolution." In *Dictablanda: Politics, Work and Culture in Mexico, 1938–1968*, edited by Paul Gillingham and Benjamin T. Smith, 1–44. Durham, NC: Duke University Press, 2014.

Gillingham, Paul, and Benjamin T. Smith, eds. *Dictablanda: Politics, Work and Culture in Mexico, 1938–1968*. Durham, NC: Duke University Press, 2014.

Gitlin, Todd. *The Whole World Is Watching: Mass Media in the Making and Unmaking of the New Left*. Berkeley: University of California Press, 1980.

Glanville, Brian. *Football Memories: 50 Years of the Beautiful Game*. London: Robson, 2004.

Gómez Estrada, José. *Gobierno y Casinos: El origen de la riqueza de Abelardo L. Rodríguez*. Mexicali: UABC, 2007.

González, Luis. *San José de Gracia, Mexican Village in Transition*. Translated by John Upton. Austin: University of Texas Press, 1974.

González Casanova, Pablo. *Democracy in Mexico*. Translated by Danielle Salti. Oxford: Oxford University Press, 1970.

González Cosío, Arturo. "Los Años Recientes. 1964–1976." In *Historía de la Educación Pública en México*, edited by Fernando Solana, II, 403–25. Mexico City: SEP, 1982.

González de Bustamante, Celeste. *Muy Buenas Noches, Mexico, Television, and the Cold War*. Lincoln: University of Nebraska Press, 2012.

González Marín, Silvia. *Prensa y Poder Político: La Elección Presidencial de 1940 en la Prensa Mexicana*. Mexico City: Universidad Autónoma Nacional de México, 2006.

González Navarro, Moises. *Historia Moderna de México: El Porfiriato, vida social*. Mexico City: Hermes, 1957.

González Ruiz, Edgar. *Muro: Memorias y Testimonios, 1961–2002*. Puebla: Gobierno del Estado de Puebla, 2004.

Gosse, Van. *Where the Boys Are: Cuba, Cold War America and the Making of a New Left*. New York: Verso, 1993.

Granados Chapa, Miguel. "Aproximación a la Prensa Mexicana." *Revista Mexicana de Ciencia Política* 69 (1972): 49–50.

Greer Johnson, Julie. *Satire in Colonial Spanish America: Turning the New World Upside Down*. Austin: University of Texas Press, 1993.

Guerrero Chiprés, Salvador. "Zapatos de Reportero." In *Manuel Buendía en la Trinchera Periodística*, edited by Omar Raúl Martínez. Mexico City: Fundación Manuel Buendía, 2013.

Gutiérrez de Alba, Emilio. *Tric Trac, Vieja Guardia*. Ciudad Juarez: AUCC, 2009.

Gutiérrez y Falcón, Alfredo. *Periodista al Desnudo o un Bribón Cualquiera*. Mexico City: n.p., 1967.

Haber, Paul L. *Power from Experience: Urban Popular Movements in Late Twentieth-Century Mexico*. University Park: Penn State University Press, 2006.

Habermas, Jürgen. *The Structural Transformation of the Public Sphere: An Inquiry into a Category of Bourgeois Society*. Cambridge, MA: MIT Press, 1991.

Hall, Stuart. "The Rediscovery of Ideology: Return of the Prepressed in Media Studies." In *Culture, Society and the Media*, edited by Michael Gurevitch, 56–90. London: Methuen, 1982.

Hallin, Daniel. "Media, Political Power, and Democratization in Mexico." In *De-Westernizing Media Studies*, edited by James Curran and Myung-Jin Park James. London: Routledge, 2000.

———. *We Keep America on Top of the World: Television Journalism and the Public Sphere*. London: Routledge, 1994.

Hayes, Joy Elizabeth. *Radio Nation: Communication, Popular Culture, and Nationalism in Mexico, 1920–1950*. Tucson: University of Arizona Press, 2000.

Hayner, Norman S. *New Patterns in Old Mexico: A Study of Town and Metropolis*. New Haven, CT: Yale University Press, 1966.

Henkin, Daniel M. *City Reading: Written Words and Public Space in Antebellum New York*. New York: Columbia University Press, 1998.

Herman, Edward, and Noam Chomsky. *Manufacturing Consent: The Political Economy of the Mass Media*. New York: Pantheon, 1988.

Hernández, Anabel. *Los Señores del Narco*. Mexico City: Random House, 2011.

Hernández, M. E., and F. V. Rodelo. "Dilemas del Periodismo Mexicano en la Cobertura de 'la Guerra contra el Narcotráfico': ¿Periodismo de Guerra o de Nota Roja?" In *Entretejidos Comunicacionales. Aproximaciones a Objetos y Campos de la Comunicación*, edited by Z. Rodríguez, 193–227. Guadalajara: Universidad de Guadalajara, 2010.

Hernández Rodríguez, Rogelio. *Amistades, Compromisos y Lealtades: Lideres y grupos políticos en el Estado de Mexico, 1942–1993*. Mexico City: Colegio de México, 1998.

———. *El Centro Dividido, La Nueva Autonomía de los Gobernadores*. Mexico City: El Colegio de Mexico, 2008.

———. *Presidencialismo y Hombres Fuertes en México: La Sucesión Presidencial de 1958*. Mexico City: Colegio de México, 2015.

———. "Strongmen and State Weakness." In *Dictablanda: Politics, Work and Culture in Mexico, 1938–1968*, edited by Paul Gillingham and Benjamin T. Smith, 108–25. Durham, NC: Duke University Press, 2014.

Herrera Calderón, Fernando, and Adela Cedillo Cedillo, eds. *Challenging Authoritarianism in Mexico: Revolutionary Struggles and the Dirty War, 1964–1982*. New York: Routledge, 2012.

Hidalgo, Berta. *Entre Periodistas: Anécdotas, Sucedidos Notables y Hechos Graciosos de una Profesión Apasionante*. Mexico City: EDAMEX, 1995.

Horcasitas, Ricardo Pozas. *La Democracía en Blanco: El Movimiento Médico en México, 1964–1965*. Mexico City: Siglo XXI, 1993.

Huerta, Francisco, and Ricardo Pacheco. *Crónica del Periodismo Civil: La Voz del Ciudadano*. Mexico City: Grijalbo, 1997.

Hughes, Sallie. *Newsrooms in Conflict, Journalism, and the Democratization of Mexico*. Pittsburgh, PA: University of Pittsburgh Press, 2006.

Hutchinson, Linda. *Autopsias Rápidas*. Mexico City: Vuelta, 1988.

———. *Irony's Edge: The Theory and Politics of Irony*. New York: Routledge, 1995.

Ibargüengoitia, José. *Autopsias rapidas*. Mexico City: Vuelta, 1993.

———. *Instrucciones para Vivir en México*. Mexico City: Joaquín Mortiz, 1990.

———. *A Theory of Parody: The Teachings of Twentieth-Century Art Forms*. Urbana: University of Illinois Press, 2000.

Ibarra de Anda, Fortina. *El periodismo en México: lo que es y lo que debe ser: un estudio del periódista y del periodista mexicanos y de las posibilidades de ambos para el futuro*. Mexico City: Mundial, 1937.

Jiménez, A. *Picardía Mexicana*. Mexico City: Costa-Amic, 1958.

Jiménez de Ottalengo, Regina. "Un Periódico Mexicano, su Situación Social y sus Fuentes de Informacion (Una Ilustración de la Teoría de la Dependencia en el Ambito de la Comunicación)." *Revista Mexicana de Sociología* 36, no. 4 (1974): 767–806.

Johnson, Kenneth F. *Mexican Democracy: A Critical View*. New York: Praeger Press, 1978.

Joseph, Gilbert, and Daniel Nugent, eds. *Everyday Forms of State Formation: Revolution and the Negotiation of Rule in Modern Mexico*. Durham, NC: Duke University Press, 1994.

Junco de la Vega, Rodolfo. *The Problems of a Mexican Provincial Editor*. Austin, TX: School of Journalism Development Program, 1964.

Keenan, Joe. "How Advertising Masquerades as News." In *A Culture of Collusion: An Inside Look at the Mexican Press*, edited by William Orme, 41–49. Miami: North-South Center Press, 1997.

Keller, Renata. *Mexico's Cold War: Cuba, the United States, and the Legacy of the Mexican Revolution*. Cambridge: Cambridge University Press, 2015.

Kenez, Peter. *The Birth of the Propaganda State: Soviet Methods of Mass Mobilization*. Cambridge: Cambridge University Press, 1985.

Knight, Alan. "Cárdenas and Echeverría: Two 'Populist' Presidents Compared." In *Populism in 20th Century Mexico: The Presidencies of Lázaro Cárdenas and Luis Echeverria*, edited by Amelia M. Kiddle and María L. O. Muñoz, 15–37. Tucson: University of Arizona Press, 2010.

———. "Historical Continuities in Social Movements." In *Popular Movements and Political Change in Mexico*, edited by Joe Foweraker and Ann Craig, 78–102. Boulder, CO: L. Rienner Publishers, 1990.

———. "The Mexican Revolution: Bourgeois? Nationalist? Or Just a 'Great Rebellion'?" *Bulletin of Latin American Research* 4, no. 2 (1985): 1–37.

———. "The Rise and Fall of Cardenismo, 1930–1946." In *Mexico since Independence*, edited by Leslie Bethell, 241–320. Cambridge: Cambridge University Press, 1991.

———. "The Weight of the State in Modern Mexico." In *Studies in the Formation of the Nation-State in Latin America*, edited by James Dunkerley, 212–53. London: Institute of Latin American Studies, 2002.

Krauze, Enrique. *Mexico: A Biography of Power*. New York: Harper, 1998.

La Dictadura Perfecta. Directed by Luis Estrada. Bandidos Films. 2014.

Landes, Joan. *Women and the Public Sphere in the Age of the French Revolution*. Ithaca, NY: Cornell University Press, 1988.

Laurie, Clayton. *The Propaganda Warriors: America's Crusade against Nazi Germany*. Lawrence: University of Kansas Press, 1996.

Lawson, Chappell. *Building the Fourth Estate: Democratization and the Rise of a Free Press in Mexico*. Berkeley: University of California Press, 2002.

Lazere, Donald, ed. *American Media and Mass Culture: Left Perspectives*. Berkeley: University of California Press, 1987.

Leduc, Renato. "La Corrupción en la Prensa." In *La Corrupción*, edited by Rosario Castellanos et al., 62–82. Mexico City: Editorial Nuestro Tiempo, 1969.

Leñero, Vicente. *Los Periodistas*. Mexico City: Mortiz, 1978.

León Ossorio, Adolfo. *El Pantano (Apuntes para la historia), Un Libro Acusador*. Mexico City: n.p., 1954.

Lepidus, Henry. "History of Mexican Journalism." *University of Missouri Bulletin* 29, no. 4 (1928): 1–87.

Lewis, Oscar. *The Children of Sánchez: Autobiography of a Mexican Family*. London: Secker and Warburg, 1961.

———. *Five Families: Mexican Case Studies in the Culture of Poverty*. New York: Science Edition, 1962.

———. *Life in a Mexican Village: Tepoztlán Restudied*. Urbana: University of Illinois Press, 1951.

Loaeza, Soledad. *Clases Medias y Política en Mexico: La Querella Escolar, 1959–1963*. Mexico City: Colegio de México, 1998.

Lomnitz, Claudio. *Death and the Idea of Mexico*. New York: Zone Books, 2005.

———. "Ritual, Rumor y Corrupción en la Formación del Espacio Nacional en México." *Revista Mexicana de Sociologia* 58, no. 2 (1996): 21–51.

López Olivares, Oscar. *Cartel del Globo: Genesis del Cartel del Golfo*. np, nd.

Loret de Mola, Rafael. *Denuncia: Presidente sin Palabra*. Mexico City: Grijalbo, 2008.

Loseff, Lev. *On the Beneficence of Censorship: Aesopian Language in Modern Russian Literature*. Munich: O. Sagner in Kommission, 1984.

Loyo, Engracia. "La Lectura en México, 1920–1940." In *Historia de la Lectura en México*, edited by Josefina Zoraida Vazquez, 243–94. Mexico City: Colegio de México, 1988.

Luévano Díaz, Alain. "1945. El Sol del Centro y el Inicio del Periodismo industrial en Aguascalientes." In *Rompecabezas de Papel. La Prensa y el Periodismo desde las Regiones de México. Siglos XIX y XX*, edited by Celia del Palacio Montiel. Mexico City: Porrúa, 2006.

Luquín, Eduardo. *Análisis Espectral del Mexicano*. Mexico City: Costa-Amic, 1961.

Luzuriaga, Gerardo. "Teatro y Revolución: Apuntes sobre la Revista Política en México." *Mester* 21, no. 1 (1992): 11–22.

MacArthur, John R. *Second Front: Censorship and Propaganda in the 1991 Gulf War*. Berkeley: University of California Press, 2004.

Mahieux, Viviane. *Cube Bonifant, Una Pequeña Marquesa de Sade: Crónicas Selectas, 1921–1948*. Mexico City: Universidad Nacional Autónoma de México, 2009.

"Maria de los Angeles Pichardo García, 1910–1965." In *Oaxaqueñas que dejaron huella: Antología*, edited by Dulce María Méndez García et al. Oaxaca: Mujeres en el Tiempo, 2010.

Marín Rodríguez, Gregorio. *Tiempo de Hablar, Otra Cara de Periodismo*. Mexico City: n.p., 1988.

Marsh, Hazel. " 'Writing Our History in Songs': Judith Reyes, Popular Music and the Student Movement of 1968." In *Reflections on Mexico '68*, edited by K. Brewster, 144–59. Chichester: Wiley, 2010.

Martínez, Antonia. *El Despegue Constructivo de la Revolución: Sociedad y Política en el Alemanismo*. Mexico City: Porrúa, 2002.

Martínez, José. *Prensa Negra: Entre la Etica y la Impunidad. Los Limites de la Libertad*. Mexico City: Fundación René Avilés Fábila, 2007.

Martínez, S., José Luis. *La Vieja Guardia, Protagonistas del Periodismo Mexicano*. Mexico City: Plaza Janes, 2005.

Martínez Mora, Eliezer. *Gente del Pueblo*. Puebla: BUAP, 1970.

Mata Alatorre, Luis. *La Verdad en el Proceso y Sentencia de Mata y Siqueiros*. Mexico City: n.p., 1962.

McCormick, Gladys. *The Logic of Compromise in Mexico: How the Countryside Was Key to the Emergence of Authoritarianism*. Chapel Hill: University of North Carolina Press, 2016.

Mejido, Manuel. *Con la Máquina al Hombro*. Mexico City: Siglo XXI, 2011.

Menéndez, Antonio. *Movilización Social*. Mexico City: Bolsa Mexicana del Libro, 1963.

Menéndez, Mario. *Yucatán o el Genocidio*. Mexico City: Fondo de Cultura Popular, 1964.

Merrill, John C. "The U.S. as Seen from Mexico." *Journal of Inter-American Studies* 5, no. 1 (1963): 53–66.

Merrill, John C., Carter R. Bryan, and Marvin Alisky. *The Foreign Press: A Survey of the World's Journalism*. Baton Rouge: Louisiana State University Press, 1970.

Middlebrook, Kevin J. *The Paradox of Revolution, Labor, the State and Authoritarianism in Mexico*. Baltimore, MD: Johns Hopkins University, 1995.

Millán Peraza, Miguel Angel. *A Tijuana! Nosotros Las Gringas*. Tijuana: Talleres Gráficos de California, 1992.

Mills, James. *The Underground Empire: Where Crime and Governments Embrace*. London: Sidgwick & Jackson, 1987.

Mills, Nicolaus. *The New Journalism: A Historical Anthology*. New York: Macmillan, 1974.

Moncada, Carlos. *30 Años en esto: Autobiografía periodística*. Hermosillo: Gobierno del Estado de Sonora, 1984.

———. *Del México Violento, Periodistas Asesinados*. Mexico City: Edamex, 1991.

———. *Diez en el Poder (1943–1997): La Política en Sonora vista a través de sus Ultimos Diez Gobernadores*. Mexico City: Edamex, 1997.

Mondragón, Magdalena. *Los Presidentes Dan Risa*. Mexico City: n.p., 1948.

Monsiváis, Carlos. *A Ustedes les Consta: Antologia de la Crónica en México*. Mexico City: Ediciones Era, 1980.

―――. "La Crónica y el Reportaje cómo Géneros Periodístícos." In *Periodismo: Una Visión desde Nuevo León*. Monterrey: UNL, 1989.

―――. *Los Mil y Un Velorios: Crónica de la Nota Roja*. Mexico City: Conaculta, 1994.

Montalvo Ortega, Enrique, and Iván Vallado Fajardo. *Yucatán: Sociedad, Economía, Política y Cultura*. Mexico City: Universidad Nacional Autónoma de México, 1997.

Montgomery, Louise. "Criticism of Government Officials in the Mexican Press, 1951–1980." *Journalism & Mass Communication Quarterly* 62 (1985): 673–79.

Mora, Carl. *Mexican Cinema: Reflections of a Society*. Berkeley: University of California Press, 1982.

Morales Flores, Monica. "La Guerrilla Guatemalteca en Imagines. Un Acercamiento a la Construcción de una Investigación Histórica (Entrevistas al Comandante César Montes)." *Centro de Documentación de los Movimientos Armados*, 2009.

Moreno, Julio. *Yankee Don't Go Home, Mexican Nationalism, American Business Culture and the Shaping of Modern Mexico, 1920–1950*. Chapel Hill: University of North Carolina Press, 2003.

Morley, Jefferson. *Our Man in Mexico: Winston Scott and the Hidden History of the CIA*. Lawrence: University Press of Kansas, 2008.

Mraz, John. *Looking for Mexico: Modern Visual Culture and National Identity*. Durham, NC: Duke University Press, 2009.

―――. *Nacho López, Mexican Photographer*. Minneapolis: University of Minnesota Press, 2003.

Muller, Beate. "Censorship and Cultural Regulation: Mapping the Territory." In *Censorship and Cultural Regulation in the Modern Age*, edited by Beate Muller, 1–32. Amsterdam: Rodopi, 2004.

Musacchio, Humberto. *Granados Chapa, Un Periodista en Contexto*. Mexico City: Planeta, 2010.

Museo Nacional de Culturas Populares. *El País de las Tandas, Teatro de Revista, 1900–1940*. Mexico City: Museo Nacional de Culturas Populares, 1984.

Navarro, Aaron. *Political Intelligence and the Creation of Modern Mexico, 1938–1954*. University Park: Pennsylvania State University Press, 2010.

Nelson, Elizabeth. *The British Counter-Culture: 1966–73: A Study of the Underground Press*. New York: St. Martin's Press, 1989.

Nerone, John. *The Media and Public Life: A History*. Cambridge, MA: Polity, 2015.

Niblo, Stephen R. *Mexico in the 1940s, Modernity, Politics and Corruption*. Wilmington, DE: Scholarly Resources, 1999.

Nieto de Leyva, Dalia. *Por qué me hice Periodista*. Mexicali: n.p., 1994.

Nolasco Armas, Margarita. *Cuatro Ciudades, El Proceso de Urbanización Dependiente*. Mexico City: INAH, 1981.

Nord, David Paul. *Communities of Journalism: A History of American Newspapers and Their Readers*. Urbana: University of Illinois Press, 2001.

Nosotros los Pobres. Dir. Ismael Rodríguez. Cinema International Media, 2013.

Novo, Salvador. *La vida en México en el Período Presidencial de Adolfo Ruiz Cortines.* Mexico City: Conaculta, 1997.

———. *La vida en México en el Período Presidencial de Lázaro Cárdenas.* Mexico City: Empresas, 1964.

———. *La vida en México en el Período Presidencial de Manuel Avila Camacho.* Mexico City: Consejo Nacional para la Cultura y las Artes, 1994.

———. *La vida en México en el Período Presidencial de Miguel Alemán.* Mexico City: Conaculta, 1994.

———. *New Mexican Grandeur.* Mexico City: Petróleos Mexicanos, 1967.

Ochoa, Enrique. *Feeding Mexico: The Political Uses of Food since 1910.* Wilmington, DE: Scholarly Resources, 2000.

O'Malley, Ilene. *The Myth of Revolution: Hero Cults and the Institutionalization of the Mexican State, 1920–1940.* New York: Greenwood, 1986.

Orozco, José Clemente, and Robert C. Stephenson. *José Clemente Orozco: An Autobiography.* Garden City, NY: Dover, 2001.

Orozco, Victor. "Las Luchas Populares en Chihuahua." *Cuadernos Políticos* (1976): 49–66.

Ortega, G. Carlos. *Democracía Dirigida con Ametralladoras, Baja California, 1958–1960.* El Paso: La Prensa, 1961.

———. *Tijuana, La Ciudad Maldita.* Mexico City: n.p., 1956.

Ortiz Bullé Goyri, Alejandro. "Origines y Desarrollo del Teatro de Revista en México (1869–1953)." In *Un siglo de Teatro en México,* edited by David Olguín, 40–53. Mexico City: FCE, 2011.

Ortiz Garza, José Luis. "Fighting for the Soul of the Mexican Press: Axis and Allied Activities during the Second World War." In *Americas Unidas! Nelson A. Rockefeller Officer of Inter-American Affairs (1940–1946),* edited by Gisela Cramer and Ursula Prutsch, 181–222. Paris: Iberoamericana Vervuert, 2012.

———. *Ideas en Tormenta. La Opinión Pública en Mexico y la Segunda Guerra Mundial.* Mexico City: Ediciones Ruz, 2007.

———. *México en Guerra: La Historia Secreta de los Negocios entre Empresarios Mexicanos de la Comunicación, los Nazis, y EUA.* Mexico City: Planeta, 1989.

Osorno, Diego. *La Guerra de los Zetas: Viaje por la Frontera de la Necropolítica.* Mexico City: Grijalbo, 2012.

Overmyer-Velazquez, Mark. *Visions of the Emerald City: Modernity, Tradition, and the Formation of Porfirian Oaxaca, Mexico.* Durham, NC: Duke University Press, 2006.

Padgett, Humberto. *Tamaulipas: La Casta de los Narcogobernadores.* Barcelona: Ediciones Urano, 2016.

Padgett, Vincent. *The Mexican Political System.* Boston: Houghton Mifflin, 1966.

Padilla, Tanalís. "Rural Education, Political Radicalism, and *Normalista* Identity in Mexico after 1940." In *Dictablanda: Politics, Work and Culture in Mexico, 1938–1968,* edited by Paul Gillingham and Benjamin T. Smith, 341–59. Durham, NC: Duke University Press, 2014.

———. *Rural Resistance in the Land of Zapata: The Jaramillista Movement and the Pax Priísta, 1940–1962.* Durham, NC: Duke University Press, 2008.

Padrés, Mercedes. *El Diario de Una Periodista: La Luz de Bengala.* Mexico City: La Idea, 1998.

Page, Bruce. *The Murdoch Archipelago.* London: Simon & Schuster, 2003.

Pansters, Wil. "Tropical Passion in the Desert: Gonzalo N. Santos and Local Elections in San Luis Potosí, 1943–1958." In *Dictablanda: Politics, Work and Culture in Mexico, 1938–1968,* edited by Paul Gillingham and Benjamin T. Smith, 126–48. Durham, NC: Duke University Press, 2014.

Paxman, Andrew. "Cooling to Cinema and Warming to Television: State Mass Media Policy, 1940–1964." In *Dictablanda: Politics, Work and Culture in Mexico, 1938–1968,* edited by Paul Gillingham and Benjamin T. Smith, 299–320. Durham, NC: Duke University Press, 2014.

Paz, Octavio. *The Labyrinth of Solitude.* London: Penguin, 1990.

———. *The Other Mexico: Critique of the Pyramid.* New York: Grove Press, 1978.

Peniche Vallado, Leopoldo. *Sombras y Palabras: Memorias y Antimemorias.* Merida: Consejo y Editorial de Yucatán, 1987.

Pensado, Jaime M. *Rebel Mexico: Student Unrest and Authoritarian Political Culture during the Long Sixties.* Redwood City, CA: Stanford University Press, 2013.

Pérez, Ramón. *Diary of a Guerrilla.* Houston, TX: Arté Público Press, 1999.

Pérez Rayón, Nora. "La Prensa Liberal en la Segunda Mitad del Siglo XIX." In *La república de las letras,* Vol. 2, *Publicaciones periódicas y otros impresos,* edited by Belem Clark de Lara and Elisa Speckman Guerra, 175–270. Mexico City: Universidad Nacional Autónoma de México, 2005.

Pérez Siller, Javier, David Skerritt Gardner, and Rosalina Estrada Urroz, eds. *México-Francia: Memoria de una Sensibilidad Común: Siglos XIX–XX.* Puebla: BUAP, 1998.

Petley, Julian. *Censorship: A Beginner's Guide.* Oxford: Oneworld, 2009.

Piccato, Pablo. "Introducción. Modelo para armar? Hacia un Acercamiento Critico a la Teoría de la Esfera Pública." In *Actores, Espacios y Debates en la Historia de la Esfera Pública en la Ciudad de México,* edited by Cristina Sacristán and Pablo Piccato, 9–41. Mexico City: Universidad Nacional Autónoma de México, 2005.

———. "Murders of Nota Roja: Truth and Justice in Mexican Crime News." *Past & Present* 223, no. 1 (2014): 195–231.

———. "Pistoleros, Ley Fuga, and Uncertainty in Public Debates about Murder in Twentieth-Century Mexico." In *Dictablanda: Politics, Work and Culture in Mexico, 1938–1968,* edited by Paul Gillingham and Benjamin T. Smith, 321–41. Durham, NC: Duke University Press, 2014.

———. "The Public Sphere in Latin America: A Map of the Historiography." *Social History* 35, no. 2 (2010): 165–92.

———. *The Tyranny of Opinion: Honor in the Construction of the Mexican Public Sphere.* Durham, NC: Duke University Press, 2010.

Pilcher, Jeffrey. *Cantinflas and the Chaos of Mexican Modernity.* Wilmington, DE: Scholarly Resources, 2001.

Poniatowska, Elena. "Adios Manuel." In *Los Dias de Manuel Buendía,* 120–34. Mexico City: Oceano, 1984.

Portillo, Jorge. *Fenomenología del Relajo y Otros Ensayos*. Mexico City: Crea, 1984.

Price, John A. *Tijuana Urbanization in a Border Culture*. London: University of Notre Dame, 1973.

Quintana, Alejandro. *Maximino Avila Camacho and the One-Party State: The Taming of Caudillismo and Caciquismo in Postrevolutionary Mexico*. Plymouth, UK: Lexington Books, 2010.

Quintanilla, Pedro. *Aprendiz de Periodista*. Monterrey: Ayuntamiento de Monterrey, 1984.

Quintas Castellano, Gabriel. "El Movimiento del 52: Crónica de cómo cayó el Gobernador Mayoral Heredia." In *Oaxaca 2010, Voces de la Transición*, edited by Augusto García Moguel Isidoro Yescas y Claudio Sánchez, 42–50. Oaxaca: Carteles, 2010.

Ramírez, Guillermo H. *Los Gangsters del Periodismo*. Durango: Zerimar, 1944.

Ramos Camacho, Gilberto. "Este era Palillo." In *Leyendas, Tradiciones y Personajes de Guadalajara*, edited by Helia García Pérez, 150–61. Guadalajara: Ayuntamiento de Guadalajara, 1996.

Rangel, Salomon H. *Forjando mi Destino (Apuntes de mi vida)*. Mexico City: EPESSA, 1989.

Rath, Thom. *Myths of Demilitarization in Postrevolutionary Mexico, 1920–1960*. Chapel Hill: University of North Carolina Press, 2013.

Reich, Peter L. "Recent Research on the Legal History of Modern Mexico." *Mexican Studies/Estudios Mexicanos* 23 (Winter 2007): 181–93.

Rentería Arróyave, Teodoro. *Mi vida son mis Amigos: Una Historia de los Noticiarios en México*. Puebla: BUAP, 2009.

Reyes, Judith. *La Otra Cara de la Patria*. Mexico City: n.p., 1974.

Reyes del Campillo, Juan. "El Frente Electoral del Pueblo y el Partido Comunista Mexicano (1963–1964)." *Revista Mexicana de Sociología* 50, no. 3 (1988): 217–28.

Richardson, Bill. *Between Worlds: The Making of an American Life*. New York: Putnam, 2014.

Riding, Alan. *Distant Neighbors: A Portrait of the Mexicans*. New York: Vintage, 1989.

Rios, Vidirana. "Quien Mata a los periodistas?" *Nexos* (August 2013).

Riva Palacio, Raymundo. "A Culture of Collusion: The Ties That Bind the Press and the PRI." In *A Culture of Collusion: An Inside Look at the Mexican Press*, edited by William Orme, 21–32. Miami: North South Center Press, 1997.

Robles, Emilio. *Retrato Hablado, De los que hacen Periodismo en Sonora*. Mexico City: Garabatos, 1999.

Rockwell, Elsie. "Schools of the Revolution: Enacting and Contesting State Forms in Tlaxcala, 1910–1930." In *Everyday Forms of State Formation: Revolution and the Negotiation of Rule in Modern Mexico*, edited by Gilbert Joseph and Daniel Nugent, 170–208. Durham, NC: Duke University Press, 1994.

Rodman, Selden. *Mexican Journal: The Conquerors Conquered*. London: Feffer and Simons Inc., 1958.

Rodríguez Castañeda, Rafael. *Prensa Vendida: Los Periodistas y los Presidentes, 40 Años de Relaciones*. Mexico City: Grijalvo, 1993.

Rodríguez Kuri, Ariel. "El Lado Oscuro de la Luna: El Momento Conservador en 1968." In *Conservadurismo y derechas en la historia de México*, edited by Erika Pani, 512–59. Mexico City: Fondo de Cultura Económica, 2009.

———. "Los Años Maravillosos. Adolfo Ruiz Cortines." In *Gobernantes Mexicanos*, edited by Will Fowler, II, 263–321. Mexico City: CFE, 2008.

Rodríguez Lozano, Roberto Jorge. *Cierre de edición: Hablan los Periodistas de la Vieja Guardia*. Monterrey: Fondo Estatal para la Cultura y las Artes, 2006.

Rodríguez Munguia, Jacinto. *La Otra Guerra Secreta: Los Archivos Prohibidos de la Prensa y el Poder*. Mexico City: Debate, 2007.

Rubenstein, Anne. *Bad Language, Naked Ladies, and Other Threats to the Nation: A Political History of Comic Books in Mexico*. Durham, NC: Duke University Press, 1998.

Rubin, Jeffrey. *Decentering the Regime: Ethnicity, Radicalism and Democracy in Juchitán, Mexico*. Durham, NC: Duke University Press, 1997.

Ruiz Cervantes, Francisco José, and Carlos Sánchez Silva. "La Imprenta y la Prensa en Oaxaca, Siglo XIX y XX." *Historia de la Prensa en Iberoamerica*, edited by Celia del Palacio Montiel, 25–37. Guadalajara: Altexto, 2000.

———. *Los Oaxaqueños Pintados por sí Mismos, en el Periódico El Ciclón, 1927–1929*. Oaxaca: Carteles, 2004.

———. "Prensa, Política y Vida Social en Oaxaca, Siglos XIX–XX." In *Siete Regiones de la Prensa en México, 1792–1950*, edited by Celia del Palacio Montiel. Guadalajara: Porrúa, 2006.

Ruiz Ocampo, Alejandro. *El Consejo Nacional de la Publicidad: Origen, Estructura y Trayectoria*. Mexico City: Plaza y Valdés, 1999.

Saavedra Cruz, Alfonso. *Vámonos! Crónicas Ferrocarrileras Oaxaqueñas*. Oaxaca: Carteles, 1990.

Salgado, Armando Lenin. *Una Vida en Guerra*. Mexico City: Planeta, 1990.

Sánchez García, Alfonso. *El Plumaje del Mosco (Páginas Autobiográficas)*. Toluca: Universidad Autónoma del Estado de México, 2001.

Sánchez Hernández, Néstor. *Un Mexicano en la Guerra Civil Española y Otros Recuerdos*. Oaxaca: Carteles, 1997.

Sánchez Pontón, Manuel. *El Olor a Tinta*. Mexico City: Edamex, 1985.

Sánchez Rivera, Roberto, Aurora Cano Andaluz, and Arturo Martínez Nateras. "Los Libros y La Prensa." In *Diálogos sobre el 68*, edited by Silvia González Marín, 115–46. Mexico City: Universidad Nacional Autónoma de México, 2003.

Sánchez Sierra, Juan Carlos. "Crisis Mística, Educación y Juventud: La Formación del Perfil Moral del Periodismo en la Revista Política, 1960–1967." *Estudios de Historia Moderna y Contemporanea de México* 45 (2013): 97–144.

———. "Periodismo Heroico, Moral y Virilidad Revolucionaria: La Juventud y la Mujer en la Revista *Por Qué?* 1968–1974." *Secuencia* 94 (ene.–abr. 2016): 240–72.

Sanderson, Susan R. Walsh. *Land Reform in Mexico, 1910–1980*. Orlando: Academic Publisher, 1984.

Santos, Gonzalo N. *Memorias*. Mexico City: Grijalvo, 1984.

Saragoza, Alex. *The Monterrey Elite and the Mexican State, 1880–1940*. Austin: University of Texas Press, 1988.

Scherer Garcia, Julio. *La Terca Memoria*. Mexico City: Grijalbo, 2007.

———. *Los Presidentes*. Mexico City: Grijalbo, 1986.

Scherer Garcia, Julio, and Carlos Monsiváis. *Parte de Guerra II: Los Rostros de 68*. Mexico City: Nuevo Siglo, 2002.

———. *Tiempo de Saber, Prensa y Poder en México*. Mexico City: Aguilar, 2003.

Schmidt, Samuel. "Elitelore in Politics: Humor versus Mexico's Presidents." *Journal of Latin American Lore* 16, no. 1 (1990): 91–108.

———. *Seriously Funny: Mexican Political Jokes as Social Resistance*. Tucson: University of Arizona Press, 2014.

Scott, James. *Domination and the Arts of Resistance: Hidden Transcripts*. New Haven, CT: Yale University Press, 2009.

Secanella, Petra María. *El Periodismo Político en México*. Barcelona: Editorial Miltre, 1983.

Secretaría de Industria y Comercio, Dirección General de Estadística. *VII Censo Industrial. 1961. Datos de 1960, Imprenta y Litografía Comercial Clase 2813*. Mexico City: Secretaría de Industria y Comercio, 1965.

Séptimo Censo General de Población, 6 de junio de 1950. Resumen general. Mexico City: Dirección General de Estadística, 1953.

Serna, Ana Maria. "La Vida Periodística Mexicana y el Movimiento Estudiantil de 1968." *Signos Históricos* 31 (2014): 116–59.

———. "Prensa y Sociedad en las Décadas Revolucionarias (1910–1940)." *Secuencia* 86 (ene.–abr. 2014): 111–49.

Servín, Elisa. "Propaganda y Guerra Fría: La Campaña Anticomunista en la Prensa Mexicana del Medio siglo." *Signos Históricos* 11 (ene.–jun. 2004), 9–39.

Sewell, William H. *Logics of History: Social Theory and Social Transformation*. Chicago: University of Chicago Press, 2005.

Sexto censo general de población: 1940. Mexico City: Dirección General de Estadística, 1943–48.

Shannon, Elaine. *Desperados: Latin Drug Lords, U.S. Lawmen and the War America Can't Win*. New York: Penguin, 1989.

Sheppard, Randall. *A Persistent Revolution: History, Nationalism and Politics in Mexico since 1968*. Albuquerque: University of New Mexico Press, 2016.

Shirk, David A. *Mexico's New Politics: The PAN and Democratic Change*. Boulder, CO: Lynne Rienner Publishers, 2005.

Smith, Anne-Marie. *A Forced Agreement, Press Acquiescence to Censorship in Brazil*. Pittsburgh, PA: University of Pittsburgh Press, 1997.

Smith, Benjamin T. "Building a State on the Cheap: Taxation, Social Movements, and Politics." In *Dictablanda: Politics, Work and Culture in Mexico, 1938–1968*, edited by Paul Gillingham and Benjamin T. Smith, 255–76. Durham, NC: Duke University Press, 2014.

————. *Pistoleros and Popular Movements: The Politics of State Formation in Postrevolutionary Oaxaca.* Lincoln: University of Nebraska Press, 2009.

————. "Public Drug Policy and Grey Zone Pacts in Mexico." In *Drug Policies and the Politics of Drugs in Latin America*, edited by Beatriz C. Labate, Clancy Cavnar, and Thiago Rodrigues, 33–53. Cham, Switzerland: Springer International Publishing, 2016.

————. *The Roots of Conservatism in Mexico: Catholicism, Society and Politics in the Mixteca Baja, 1750–1962.* Albuquerque: University of New Mexico Press, 2012.

————. "Who Governed? Grassroots Politics in Mexico under the PRI (1958–1970)." *Past & Present* 225 (Nov. 2014): 227–71.

Solomon, Joel. "The Measure of Violence: Problems of Documentation." In *A Culture of Collusion: An Inside Look at the Mexican Press*, edited by William Orme, 121–30. Miami: North-South Center Press, 1997.

Somuano, María Fernanda. *Sociedad Civil Organizada y Democracía en México.* Mexico City: Colegio de México, 2011.

Söyler, Mehtap. *The Turkish Deep State: State Consolidation, Civil-Military Relations and Democracy.* London: Routledge, 2015.

Stevens, Evelyn P. *Protest and Response in Mexico.* Cambridge, MA: MIT Press, 1974.

Stonor Saunders, Frances. *The Cultural Cold War: The CIA and the World of Arts and Communication.* New York: New York University Press, 2000.

Stoppelman, J. W. F. *People of Mexico.* London: Phoenix House, 1964.

Streitmatter, Rodger. *Voices of Revolution: The Dissident Press in America.* New York: Columbia University Press, 2009.

Suárez, Luis. *Puente Sin Fin: Testigo activo de la Historia.* Mexico City: Editorial de Ciencias Sociales de Habana, 2002.

Tamayo, Jorge L. *Oaxaca en el Siglo XX: Apuntes Históricos y Análisis Políticos.* Mexico City: n.p., 1956.

Tannenbaum, Frank. *Peace by Revolution: An Interpretation of Mexico.* Freeport, NY: Books for Libraries Press, 1971.

Taylor, William. *Magistrates of the Sacred: Priests and Parishioners in Eighteenth Century Mexico.* Redwood City, CA: Stanford University Press, 1996.

Thompson, E. P. "Eighteenth Century English Society: Class Struggle without Class?" *Social History* 3, no. 2 (1978): 133–65.

The Tijuana Story. Dir. by Leslie Kardos. California, 1957.

Torres Ramírez, Blanca. *Hacia la Utopía Industrial.* Mexico City: Colegio de México, 1984.

Torres Septién, Valentina. "Guanajuato y la Resistencia Católica en el siglo XX." In *Integrados y Marginados en el México Posrevolucinario. Los Juegos de Poder Local y sus Nexus con la Política Nacional*, edited by Nicolás Cárdenas García and Enríque Guerra Manzo, 83–119. Mexico City: Universidad Autónoma Metropolitana, 2009.

————. "La Lectura 1940–1960." In *Historia de la Lectura en México*, edited by Josefina Zoraida Vazquez, 295–337. Mexico City: Colegio de México, 1988.

Trejo Delarbre, Raúl. *La Prensa Marginal*. Mexico City: El Caballito, 1975.

———. *Las Agencias de Información en México*. Mexico City: Trillas, 1989.

———. "Periódicos: ¿Quién tira la Primera Cifra?" *Nexos*, June 7, 1990.

Ulloa Bornemann, Alberto, and Arthur Schmidt. *Surviving Mexico's Dirty War: A Political Prisoner's Memoir*. Philadelphia: Temple University Press, 2007.

Urías Horcasitas, Beatriz. "Una Pasión Antirevolucionaria: El Conservadurismo Hispanófilo Mexicano (1920–1960)." *Revista Mexicana de Sociología* 72, no. 4 (2010): 599–628.

Valencia Castrejón, Sergio. *Poder Regional y Política Nacional en México: El Gobierno de Maximino Avila Camacho en Puebla (1937–1941)*. Mexico City: INERHM, 1996.

Van Young, Eric. "In the Gloomy Caverns of Paganism: Popular Culture, Insurgency and Nation-Building in Mexico, 1800–1821." In *The Birth of Modern Mexico, 1780–1824*, edited by Christon Archer, 41–66. Lanham, MD: Rowman and Littlefield, 2003.

Vaughan, Mary Kay. *Cultural Politics in Revolution: Teachers, Peasants, and Schools in Mexico, 1930–1940*. Tucson: University of Arizona Press, 1997.

Vaughan, Mary K., and Stephen E. Lewis, eds. *Eagle and the Virgin: Nation and Cultural Revolution in Mexico, 1920–1940*. Durham, N.C.: Duke University Press, 2006.

Velasquez, Victor. *El Caso Alarcón*. Mexico City: n.p., 1955.

Vélez Ibañez, Carlos. *Rituals of Marginality: Politics, Process, and Culture Change in Urban Central Mexico, 1969–1974*. Berkeley: University of California Press, 1983.

Volpi Escalante, Jorge. *La Imaginación y el Poder: Una Historia Intelectual de 1968*. Mexico City: Ediciones Era, 1998.

Walker, Louise. "Spying at the Drycleaners: Anonymous Gossip in 1973 Mexico City." *Journal of Iberian and Latin American Research* 19, no. 1 (2013): 52–61.

———. *Waking from the Dream: Mexico's Middle Classes after 1968*. Redwood City, CA: Stanford University Press, 2013.

Wasserman, Herman, and Arnold S. De Beer. "Toward De-Westernizing Journalism Studies." In *The Handbook of Journalism Studies*, edited by Karin Wahl-Jorgensen and Thomas Hanitzsch, 428–38. London: Routledge, 2009.

Wells, Allen, and Gilbert Joseph. *Summers of Discontent, Seasons of Upheaval, Elite Politics and Rural Insurgency in Yucatán, 1876–1915*. Redwood City, CA: Stanford University Press, 1996.

White, Luise. "Telling More: Lies, Secrets, and History." *History and Theory* 39 (2000): 11–22.

Wilkie, James W. *The Mexican Revolution: Federal Expenditure and Social Change Since 1910*. Berkeley: University of California Press, 1967.

Wood, Andrew Grant. *Agustín Lara: A Cultural Biography*. New York: Oxford University Press, 2014.

Wright-Rios, Edward. *Revolutions in Mexican Catholicism, Reform and Revelation in Oaxaca, 1887–1934*. Durham, NC: Duke University Press, 2009.

———. *Searching for Madre Matiana: Prophecy and Popular Culture in Modern Mexico*. Albuquerque: University of New Mexico Press, 2014.

Yañiz, Arcelia. *Oaxaca de mis Amores, Cosas, Casos y Personajes*. Oaxaca City: Carteles Editorial, 2012.

Zacarias, Armando. "El Papel del Papel de PIPSA en los Medios Mexicanos de Comunicación." *Comunicación y Sociedad*, 25–26 (1995–1996): 73–88.

Zolov, Eric. "Expanding Our Conceptual Horizons: The Shift from an Old to a New Left in Latin America." *A Contra Corriente* 5, no. 2 (2008): 47–73.

———. "Jorge Carreño's Graphic Satire and the Politics of 'Presidentialism' in Mexico during the 1960s." *E.I.A.L.* 17, no. 1 (2006): 13–38.

Index